On the Edge
of the Banda Zone

On the Edge
of the Banda Zone

Past and Present
in the Social Organization
of a Moluccan Trading Network

Roy Ellen

University of Hawai'i Press
Honolulu

Library of Congress Cataloging-in-Publication Data
Ellen, R. F.
On the edge of the Banda Zone: past and present in the
social organization of a Moluccan trading network / Roy Ellen.
p. cm.
Includes bibliographical references and index.
ISBN 0-8248-2676-0 (alk. paper)
1. Moluccans—Commerce—Indonesia—Ceram Island.
2. Moluccans—Fishing—Indonesia—Ceram Island.
3. Moluccans—Indonesia—Ceram Island—Social life and customs.
4. Nutmeg industry—Indonesia—Ceram Island—History.
5. Spice trade—Indonesia—Ceram Island—History.
6. Ceram Island (Indonesia)—Politics and government.
7. Ceram Island (Indonesia)—Social life and customs.
I. Title.
DS632.M65 E45 2003
380.1'41383'095985—dc21
2003001100

Designed by Kaelin Chappell
Printed by The Maple-Vail Book Manufacturing Group

Contents

Preface

In this monograph I seek to show how exchange in a small archipelago in eastern Indonesia must be understood against the backdrop of regional trade and participation in a global system of commerce that goes back more than two thousand years. The focus is on the population of a group of coral reef and volcanic islands off the easternmost tip of Seram—the Seram Laut and Gorom Archipelagoes—plus the adjacent mainland of that larger island. Although the main concern is with the articulation of trading relations as they existed between 1970 and 1990, their wider importance arises because for over five hundred years (and probably much longer) they have served as a corridor between Eurasia and the world of Melanesia and played a vital role in the production and distribution of nutmeg and other high-value commodities that have for centuries had an impact on the global economy. And yet, the islands themselves are minute and fragile ecosystems, economically ultimately dependent on the local networks of which they are part and the long-distance trade that has bound them with mainland Asia and beyond. This book demonstrates the enduring continuities in the local system as it connects with the encompassing changing world; it illuminates how barter, an ecological and social division of labor, the systems properties of patterns of exchange, and the unique arrangement by which the people of Southeast Seram organized trade with the New Guinea coast help us to understand long-term cycles and trends. Methodologically, it treats with that gray area between history and anthropology that both historians and anthropologists enter warily for fear of being judged harshly by the scholastic puritans of the other discipline, but where clearly no progress in our understanding can be gained without running some risks.

The study explores the special ecological and social characteristics of these vulnerable yet manifestly humanly constructed archipelagic micro-environments that, despite their fragility, have nevertheless become important central places. It shows how the evidence we have for this helps us understand changes that took place after the arrival of Europeans in the sixteenth century. The traces and transformations of this early period are illustrated through the analysis of contemporary trading networks. The study draws upon not only a wide variety of historical and physical evidence, but on the ethnography of boat use and navigation, and the cultural particularities of trading organization. Such a deliberately eclectic methodology sheds light not only on the history of the spice trade, by providing the basis for a "production-end account," and on the ethnography of this culturally distinctive part of of Indonesia, but forces us to rethink the relationship between island Southeast Asia and the Pacific, conventional approaches to the study of trade, and the relationship between past and present understood in systems terms.

What is written here is based on fieldwork I undertook in 1981 and 1986 and on archival and library work conducted mainly in the Netherlands in 1984. It develops ideas first explored in a widely cited 1979 essay and extended in a number of articles published since then (Ellen 1984, 1986b, 1987, 1993, 1996, and 1997). The fieldwork has not only been conducted in many places in Southeast Seram (though based on longer periods in Geser and Kataloka) but also has involved work in the Banda Islands, Kei, and Ambon-Lease. It is, therefore, genuinely multisited, in the jargon of modern anthropology, through space and time. Only a small part of the data generated by these field visits has been used directly here, but all of it informs the interpretation that is offered.

Finally, one of the persistent difficulties I have had in writing about this part of Indonesia is how to refer to the protagonists. For a people who speak a common language (and there is little agreement as to what name we might use to describe this), share a common culture, pursue comparable economic lives, and are linked through various traditional political and kinship ties, it might seem strange that they do not identify with a particular ethnonym and stranger still not to have been accorded one by outsiders. True, Dutch writers since the early seventeenth century have referred to "Serammers" and "Gorammers" and "Keffingers," but it is not always clear from the context whether such terms are being used in a narrow sense (say, Serammers as the people of Seram Laut, or Serammers as all the peoples of Southeast Seram). This fuzziness in part stems from the fact that although there is historically a wide area of cultural sharing, the political entities that claim geographic sovereignty have always tended to be small domains; but it is also linked to the way in which the word "Seram," which originally was used to refer only to the area at the southeast tip of mainland Seram (Seram Rei and Seram Laut), has since the seventeenth century come to refer to the entire island. For Ambonese to the west, Seram has always been Nusa Ina, and today the people of Geser speak of Seram as Tanah Besar or Seram Besar. For reasons such as these, I have elected to use East Seram to refer to the area as a whole (which is, after all, the name of the modern administrative subdistrict, Seram Timur) and to use archipelagic Southeast Seram or Geser-Gorom to refer to the focal geographic area, as context requires.

A Note on Spelling

Many of the place-names mentioned in the text are spelled differently depending on historical or contemporary sources (e.g., Seram, Ceram, Seran; Gorom, Goran, Gorong; Manawoka, Manuwoko). Where there is any doubt about the location mentioned, or where variant spellings might be in other ways significant, I have provided the exact spelling found in the text referred to and discussed that doubt. Otherwise I have rendered the place-name in its most common contemporary form (where possible, a reliable written form) using standard Indonesian orthography with regard to local pronunciation.

Words in the language of Southeast Seram are in *italics*. Indonesian words, unless they have a special meaning in the context of this study, are in plain text. On the whole, I have adopted a practice here with respect to spelling similar to that adopted for toponyms. There is wide variation in spelling in the historical sources referred to and also lexical differences between local variants of Indonesian, as between, say, Ambonese Malay and standard Indonesian. Unless these words appear in contexts that might make it misleading, I have, wherever possible, adopted the standard Indonesian spelling as available in the third edition of Echols and Shadily (1989).

Acknowledgments

The fieldwork component of this project was conducted under the auspices of the Indonesian Academy of Sciences (Lembaga Ilmu Pengetahuan Indonesia) in Jakarta. I am especially grateful to Dr. Mochtar Buchori of the Social and Human Sciences Division (Bidang Ilmu Pengetahuan Sosial dan Kemanusiaan) and Dr. E. K. Masinambouw of the Lembaga Kebudayaan Nasional (LEKNAS-LIPI) in this regard. Local sponsorship in Maluku was in the hands of Pattimura University, and in this connection I would like to thank the then rector Dr. Ir. J. Ch. Lawalata, Drs. Mus Huliselan, and Dr. H. Z. Assagaff, dean of the social sciences faculty.

For financial support in 1981 I am indebted to the British Academy and the Sir Ernest Cassell Foundation (for Dr. N. J. Goward). In 1984 I was granted a visiting fellowship at the Netherlands Institute for Advanced Study (NIAS) in Wassenaar, which enabled me to undertake archival and specialist library searches. The Nuffield Foundation generously provided a one-year social science fellowship for 1985–1986, which covered the main fieldwork phase and allowed the University of Kent the privilege of employing Dr. Henrietta Moore for one year. I am also grateful for supplementary support over the longer term from the University of Kent at Canterbury, especially the Centre for Social Anthropology and Computing (CSAC). The 1986 fieldwork represented my first (and first successful) experiment with direct-entry field computing run from solar batteries. Thanks are due in this connection to Michael Fischer and to Epsom for providing the machine.

More people than I can sensibly list individually here have facilitated my work in the field by providing hospitality and research support; for a more complete list the inquisitive reader should consult Ellen (1986a) and Ellen and Goward (1981). There are, however, a few necessary major exceptions. In Ambon I am grateful for the assistance of the now-retired bishop, Monsignor Andrew Sol, and the fraternity of the Uskupan Katolik, and the former raja of Geser, Ryadi Kelian. In Banda Neira, Welki Ruipassa and his family have always been welcoming and helpful. In Geser, the research depended on, much more than his office required, the goodwill of Camat Drs. J. Patty and his family and household. Yusuf Anudato and his family in Geser, the late Raja A. A. R. Wattimena and his wife in Kataloka, and Raja Mohammed Yusuf Keliobas in Amarsekaru all provided faultless and generous hospitality, and extended many kindnesses, as on a lesser scale have community leaders and traders from Warus-warus on the northeastern coast of Seram to Elat, far south in the Kei Islands.

For more specific scholarly services I thank the late Dr. Z. Manusama of the Moluccas History Project in Jakarta. In Leiden, the late Jan Avé provided access to material and photographs, and Gerrit Knaap historical advice and guidance with respect to the *Landbeschrijving* of Rumphius. For access to unpublished manuscripts, I am grateful to Jouke Wigboldus for willingly sharing with me his work on crop history in eastern Indonesia, to Chrijs van Fraassen for permission to use his own unpublished work on the economic history of the northern Moluccas, to Drs. Sollewijn Gelpke for advice on the Rodrigues map, and to Heather Sutherland for allowing me to refer to her work on seventeenth- and eighteenth-century Makassar harbormaster records. Dini Marks has assisted with some translation from old Dutch, Hermien Soselisa has allowed me to use data on Garogos collected during her own fieldwork there, Frank Rowe (formerly of the Natural History Museum in London) assisted me in the determination of trepang specimens, Mark Nesbitt has made available to me the resources of the Centre for Economic Botany at the Royal Botanic Gardens Kew, Jan Christie of the University of Hull and David Bulbeck of the Australian National University have helped me interpret prehistoric material, and Jane Pugh of the London School of Economics Department of Geography has drawn or redrawn most of the maps and illustrations. I am grateful for the assistance rendered by the staff of the Koninklijk Instituut voor Taal-, Land- en Volkenkunde in Leiden, the Rijksarchief in The Hague, and the Map Department of the Koninklijk Instituut voor de Tropen in Amsterdam, and by Lynn Osborne of the Maps Department of the British Library. A visiting fellowship at the Australian National University Research School of Pacific Studies in 1981 provided an opportunity for useful discussions with Tony Milner, Adrian Horridge, George Miller, and Campbell MacKnight. At the University of Kent I thank Philip Green and Simon Platten for assistance in preparing databases from Syahbandar registers, Amy Warren for general support, and Michael Johnson for his patient editing of early drafts of nautical nonsense.

Finally, this monograph incorporates sections of two previously published papers. The first, "Environmental perturbation, inter-island trade and the re-location of production along the Banda arc; or, why central places remain central," appeared in *Human ecology of health and survival in Asia and the South Pacific,* ed. Tsuguyoshi Suzuki and Ryutaro Ohtsuka (Tokyo: University of Tokyo Press, 1987). The second, "Arab traders and land settlers in the Geser-Gorom Archipelago," appeared in *Indonesia Circle* 70:238–252, in 1996. I would like to thank the editors and publishers of both of these works for permission to reproduce copyrighted material.

1
Introduction

> The disappearance of seascapes in the way Westerners view Southeast
> Asia is more than a curiosity of maps. It is symptomatic of the general
> invisibility and underestimation of the region's maritime side.
>
> D. K. EMMERSON

1.1. On Writing of the Spice Trade

The impact of the trade in Indonesian spices between 1450 and 1700 on
global and, more particularly, European history is universally acknowledged. Its importance is reflected in the amount of scholarly attention paid
to the details and consequences of European involvement (e.g., Glamann
1958; Tiele 1877–1887). But until the work of Van Leur (1955), despite the
substantial literature (especially in Dutch) and the many carefully produced and annotated editions of the voyages of early European travelers,
little attention had been given to the role of the Asians in all of this, or to
the indigenous worlds that were the context for the rise of the Dutch East
India Company as a power in the region (Van Leur 1955:153). Archives were
read as documents for the study of European history, systematically either
eliminating references that shed light on local social arrangements or mentioning them only when relevant to understanding the consequences of
events in which Europeans were involved. Thus, as Warren (1979:224),
pointed out, speaking of the Sulu region, the "expansion of external trade
and the growing incidence of slave-raiding have claimed the attention of
most historians *only* when those social forces collided with or were affected
by European policy" (italics added).

But Van Leur's eloquent attack on orthodox colonial historiography
altered the course of studies of the spice trade and shifted European historical scholarship of Asia from colonial and orientalist preoccupations to a
postcolonial, sociological, and altogether more detached view. This sea-
change in vision instigated by Van Leur was followed by a series of major
studies, the most important of which were those of Meilink-Roelofsz (1962)
and Resink (1968). For Meilink-Roelofsz (1962:8), Asian trade was not predominantly small-scale peddling, as had been suggested by Van Leur, but a
mixture. It involved local rulers, aristocracy, native commercial groups,

officials, and foreign merchants, as well as hawkers or itinerant traders, who depended on the "financiers" or "harbor princes." It involved bulk goods such as rice, dried fish, and salt in addition to valuables; it was systematic and flexible rather than anarchic.[1] Nowadays, we recognize its complex and multifaceted character.

By comparison, Resink's contribution was, in an impressive series of papers published in the 1950s and early 1960s (1968), to observe that the character of political relations between the Netherlands and the Indies led to a regiocentric ("regiocentrische") view of Indonesian history, one focused on those dominant polities with which the Dutch had dealings, and one that fostered the independent power of most of the outer islands until well into the colonial period. In many cases, the Dutch East India Company (Vereenigde Oost-Indische Compagnie, hereafter abbreviated to VOC), and after 1800, the government of the Dutch East Indies, was dealing with foreign relations rather than internal administration until about 1910: a world in which there was no Netherlands Indies, but only Dutch Java, Dutch Amboina, and so on, and alongside that a whole autonomous island world of "undiminished vigour" (Smail 1961:87). Now, this view has much to commend it, and I shall be returning to some of its implications later in this book. It is, of course, a polemical assertion to redress a hopeless balance and from an economic and social viewpoint is incorrect. In places, the VOC completely transformed existing social structures; elsewhere it simply dictated the terms of trade. The great merit of Resink's reinterpretation is simply that it forced historians to break through the barrier of the prevailing preoccupation with the colonial relationship (ibid., 91).

All of this was the happy precursor to a new Indonesian national historiography and to a small number of key monographical studies. But although Van Leur and his successors (such as Warren [1979, 1981]) certainly accorded the peoples of the Indies and their indigenous trading zones center stage in the scholarship of the spice trade, they had still to come to terms with the study of the Moluccan islands in particular, as parts of local systems of production, exchange, and consumption. The emphasis remained on long-distance trade, and on the role of intrusive (albeit Asiatic) traders; native Moluccans largely appear simply as suppliers of spices, despite the fact that they provided the ultimate conditions for both the trade and the scholarly edifice that historians have subsequently erected. There is more concern with understanding the economy and society of Malacca or Majapahit—even Srivijaya—than in reconstructing and understanding the social and economic organization of those Moluccans actually engaged in the production and exchange of cloves and nutmeg. Van Leur, then, had left his task incomplete. He had managed to shift from a Eurocentric focus to an Asiacentric one, but had no apparent interest in a production-end account. Though the international spice trade was, ultimately, dependent on complex local trading networks, these were, to a large extent, treated as a black box in the writing of a hegemonic history.

This study seeks, at least in part, to redress the balance, to provide what Resink might have called a "Moluccocentric view." However, I do not claim to offer a full examination of the historical material for particular periods or polities, nor a systematic analysis of original documents in the VOC archive for Amboina and Banda. Indeed, the use of, mainly, nineteenth-century colonial archives simply supplements the existing literature. Nor do I attempt to engage with the worldview of early Moluccans. All these things are best left to the historians (see, e.g., Abdurachman 1981, Andaya 1993, Manusama 1977, Villiers 1990), though there is much left to be done. My aim is to focus an anthropological lens on the dynamics of trade in just one area, as the facts are available to us from the main published sources and through the direct and circumstantial data of ethnography. My earlier work (e.g., Ellen 1979) had already indicated that the growing, harvesting, and trade of spices for export was intricately related to the dynamics of local trading areas. These trading areas linked food-deficient political centers of clove or nutmeg production with vast mainland and insular peripheries providing staple carbohydrates and forest products. Thus, the localized occurrence of a single aromatic plant, valued in international trade, drastically changed the economic and social life of the indigenous people. In many areas subsistence economies based on swidden cultivation of root crops and the extraction of sago were transformed by the sixteenth and seventeenth centuries into plantation economies producing for distant markets. By the early seventeenth century there were three major trading trading systems focused on each of Ternate/Tidore, Ambon, and Banda. In the chapters that follow I provide the detailed evidence for the existence of one of these, the Banda zone, and its localized component networks; outline its major transformations since 1500; and attempt to explain what I regard as an intriguing persistence over at least a period of five hundred years.

A large part of my argument rests, however, not on the ability to detect general patterns and tendencies so much as on the focused investigation of one traditional zone: a zone I shall call here Geser-Gorom or (archipelagic) Southeast Seram. This zone encompasses the small group of islands off the extreme southeastern tip of the island of Seram. If geopolitical events had conspired differently, these islands might have been a center of the first order, along with, say, Ternate. Although circumstances did not so conspire, these same islands nevertheless became a vital secondary link in that system focused on Banda. Unlike Ternate, Tidore, Ambon, and Banda, Geser-Gorom never became a major pin in a constructed colonial economy, and although the trade in spices depended on its existence, it rarely receives a mention in major historical accounts. But for this same reason, its indigenous trading history is more accessible. By explicating the social organization of trade in these islands, I hope to shed light on the general organization of indigenous trade and its relation to the ecology of production and political process, and to understand something of the transformation of local subsistence economies into a key component in a global system of exchange.

1.2. The Early History of Nutmeg and Clove Production

The ancient history of the spice trade has been rehearsed many times, though it is only in recent years that we have been able to place it in a more encompassing archaeological and anthropological context. It is now accepted that by the beginning of the third millennium B.C. substantial improvements had been made in maritime technology, which permitted the emergence of not only interconnecting localized exchange networks in Indonesia of some complexity (appropriately modeled on Melanesian reciprocal exchange cycles), but also regular long-distance trade in outrigger canoes and plank-built boats. On the basis of current evidence it is reasonable to link this to the expansion of pottery use, agriculture, and the distribution of Austronesian-speaking peoples throughout island Southeast Asia between 4500 and 3500 B.P. (Bellwood 1985: chap. 7; Ellen and Glover 1979; Glover 1989:2, 12). It is, in addition, fair to assume that by 3000–1800 B.P., a period that saw the development of iron use, the development of wet rice cultivation, and increased social ranking in western Indonesia, there had also been an accompanying expansion of a complex and powerful mercantile system into the eastern part of the archipelago (Glover 1979:180–181). There is evidence of a movement of crop distribution westward from New Guinea: sugarcane *(Saccharum officinarum),* for example, had probably been domesticated in New Guinea by 5000 B.P. Obsidian dated to 3000–2000 B.P., originating from western New Britain, has been found as far west as Sabah (Swadling 1996:52–53); and before 2000 B.P. metal, glass, and, bronze artifacts provide evidence of eastward trade along the lesser Sundas. We can probably also assume that bird of paradise plumes were being traded out of New Guinea via the Onin coast of New Guinea from the same period, along with the aromatic bark of massoi, *Cryptocarya massoy,* (ibid., 136, Spriggs 1998b: 934–935).

At what point spices became a catalyst in this configuration is not so clear, though by A.D. 300 cloves, nutmeg, and sandalwood seem to have replaced whatever commodity previously dominated westward trade between what Swadling (1996:53, 59) described as "outer Southeast Asia" and mainland Asia. Whether the main commodity replaced was feathers (as Swadling suggested) is almost impossible to confirm. We have uncertain archaeological evidence of cloves *(Syzygium aromatica)* from Terqua in Mesopotamia dated to around 1700 B.C. (Spriggs 1998a:58–60) and literary evidence from Rome and China for its medicinal uses (Andaya 1993:1–2). It has also been long suggested that nutmeg (the seed) and mace (the seed aril) of *Myristica fragrans* had reached the Mediterranean basin from the second millennium B.C. (Warburg 1897:1–2; see also Miller 1969:60), though the evidence here is also controversial. We can be more certain that there had been Chinese contact with the Moluccas from at least the first millennium B.C. (Rockhill 1915). Indeed, the word for nutmeg in most Indonesian languages is a cognate of pala, from Sanskrit "*phala*" (fruit), via Malay. This is a common pattern of lexical replacement, where local products become important trade goods and synonynous with wealth (Chlenov 1980:433, 437). The Moluccas are mentioned also in Tang dynasty sources (A.D. 618–906) (Groenevelt 1960:117), and Chau Ju-Kua of 1225 recorded that the area that later became known to Westerners as the "spice islands" produced cloves, nutmeg, laka wood, and tortoiseshell, which were traded via Java and Sumatra to China. In exchange, the producers—or at least their local middlemen—received such commodities as porcelain, silk, fermented liquor, and coarse salt (Rockhill 1915; Wheatley 1959). By the twelfth century, when spices of Southeast Asian origin (particularly pepper) had become important commodities in Europe, the Chinese were already importing them in considerable quantities. From that time we know that the redistribution of cloves and nutmeg from the Moluccas was controlled by the rulers of eastern Java, which in turn allowed them to foster the pepper trade. By the fourteenth century this control was so complete that even the indomitable Chinese were compelled (through Javanese competition) to buy spices indirectly in Javanese ports (Schrieke 1955:25), rather than using the cross-route mentioned first in the Shun Feng Hsiang Sung nautical compendium of 1430, which led from Mindanao to "Mei-lu-chû," the Moluccas (Mills 1970:182). By the fifteenth century, according to Pires (1515; see Cortasão 1944), cloves and nutmeg were definitely being planted in the Moluccas and not just harvested.

What is significant about these scraps of evidence is not so much that they show how Moluccan spices were seeping out to great civilizations many thousands of miles distant and from a very early time. It is rather that they indicate social relations of trade consistent with the view that the global system began long before the conventional 1500 threshold often used to define the beginning of the modern world, even if the features of capital accumulation found in archaic systems differed from what followed (Gills and Frank 1993:4–5). I do not here want to test the hypothesis of "ceaseless capital accumulation" as it might apply before 1500. If we follow Gills and Frank (ibid., 7), capital accumulation in spice production was evident from infrastructural investment in establishing spice groves, shipbuilding, and social institutions promoting trade (including local trade). But it is curious that even though these authors noted the neglect of Southeast Asia in studies of the emerging world system, they did not really pay much attention to it themselves (ibid., cf. 17, 178).

No doubt the earliest form of clove and nutmeg trade from the places of their original production was simply in terms of slow movement from island to island, between local trading zone and local trading zone. For the

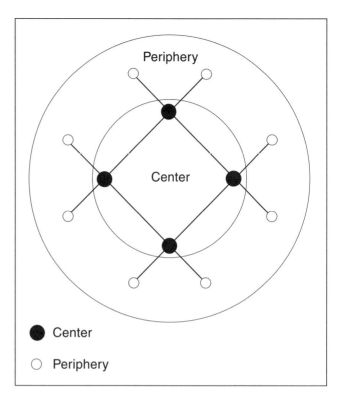

Figure 1.1. The shifting center model of core-periphery trading systems. Reproduced, with permission, from Ekholm and Friedman (1993:64).

most part, intrusive outsiders only come into an area once demand has risen sufficiently (for whatever reason) to merit the undertaking, with all its attendant risks. So, in other words, although we may agree with Polanyi (1975:154) that, "throughout, the external origin of trade is conspicuous" and that "internal trade is largely a derivation of earlier external trade," long-distance trade always presupposes the prior existence of already complex local trading networks; there is always some preexisting system. Looked at this way, we have to reexamine notions of "embeddedness" of economies and our view of trade in such societies as directed only at prestige, conspicuous consumption, and the maintenance of alliances, and be more prepared to dispense with conventional distinctions between market and nonmarket economies (Ekholm and Friedman 1993:59). What local patterns develop depends much upon the regional dimension of the larger system. The center of such systems need not be a single political unit and more often tends to consist of a number of competing/exchanging political units, one of which may exercise hegemony within the center (see Figure 1.1). For Ekholm and Friedman (ibid., 63), "Center periphery structures are unstable because of (the) vulnerability of centers in the external (supply/market) realm which is so difficult to control," and the "development of total systems is not equivalent to the development of individual societies." "Dense trade networks," they argued, "correspond to competition centers...sparse networks correspond to hierarchical territorial structures" (ibid., 69). What evidence we have for coastal New Guinea (see section 1.3) suggests that fragmentation of larger political structures accompanies increasing density of trade. In the Moluccan context it is instructive to compare the more hierarchical structure of the Tidore zone of political influence and trade with the more devolved structure of Geser-Gorom and the historical tension set up between the two. As I shall demonstrate in subsequent chapters, this model is strikingly appropriate to the situation that we find over several hundred years for the trading polities of the Moluccas in general and to the Geser-Gorom Archipelago in particular.

1.3. Moluccan Trade in the World System

Kenneth Hall (1985), employing the ideas of Immanuel Wallerstein (1979), has summarized the changes that took place in the Euroasiatic trading sphere between the fourteenth and early sixteenth centuries, when a new pattern of world trade emerged linking Asia and Europe. Two political developments provided the conditions for this. First, the establishment of the Mameluke dynasty in Egypt (1345) stabilized the Red Sea maritime passage to the Mediterranean; second, the beginning of the Ming dynasty in China (1368) launched an upswing in demand for new Southeast Asian products (such as pepper, tin, and spices) and led to the emergence of new entrepôts on the North Sumatra coast and in the Moluccas as the source of these commodities. In Hall's (1985:222–223) view, no longer was there a dominant "center," but instead "each zone along with the interconnected sea-route from China to western Europe became important to the whole system." With serial coinvolvement of Chinese, Javanese, Indian, and eventually Italian traders, the "long voyages...[to] faraway markets" were transformed into consecutive smaller voyages. In other words, the relationship between distance and the organization of trade underwent a significant alteration: the single voyage across the entire breadth of the Indian Ocean, with its considerable transaction costs, gave way to shorter, "segmented," voyages between a number of large port cities situated at the "circumference of the maximum navigational circle" (Chaudhuri 1985:37–39), the so-called "triple segmentation" with its loci at Malacca, Cambay, and Aden (ibid., 40). These places Chaudhuri described as "emporia," by which he seems to mean more than Polanyi's "port of trade" (ibid., 224). In this world we find many zones of trade dominated by a few seafaring people who sought profit from the transport of goods in each zone, forming complex "trading diasporas" (Cohen 1971:267), not simply merchants but cross-cultural brokers (Curtin 1984). "The dominant ports in each trade zone," argued Hall (1985:223), "become the chief distributors of foreign goods in their region as well as the source of local products for traders from another zone." In this manner the people in the hinterlands, at least in the maritime realm of Southeast Asia, "were brought into contact with the outside world via such dominant ports, and they entered into the mainstream of regional history . . . after being left on the periphery through most of the premodern age." The Indian subcontinent emerged from all this as a core production area of cotton textiles in the world economy, and it was Indian textiles, handled exclusively by Indian and Arab merchants until the arrival in the sixteenth century of the Europeans, that formed the staple commodity of trade with Southeast Asia (Sen 1962:93).

Hall (1985:223–225) identified at least six zones of trade through which goods from China passed on their way to northeastern Europe, focused on southern China, island Southeast Asia, coastal India and Sri Lanka, Alexandria and the Near East, and a zone covering the western Mediterranean and northern Europe, controlled by Italian traders. For a variation on this theme see the eight "circuits" of the thirteenth-century world system in Gills and Frank (1993: fig. 9.4; see also Meilink-Roelofsz 1962; Wallerstein 1979) or the "triple segmentation" of the Indian Ocean described by Chauduri (1985:104), and mentioned earlier in this section. Although we may not agree with Hall (1985:228) that this pattern of trade completely replaced "loose federations of port towns" with states having a single dominant port in the western part of archipelagic Southeast Asia, such states certainly arose.

In the Moluccas, by comparison, "loose federations" seem to have persisted, without the growth of large centralized polities, encouraged by the absence of vast forested interiors where access could be denied by controlling the mouths of the large rivers that were their arteries, where "centers" were smaller and power more diffuse, though trade was every bit as significant in articulating the social system as it had become along the Strait of Malacca. In the central Moluccas trade was not organized through centers of the kind described by Hall. The Banda Islands were certainly an important—indeed the most important—central place, over many hundreds of years, articulating trade over a vast area; but Banda was was not a state, and neither were its composite polities. Moreover, it never claimed territory or exercised conventional political control over people and resources beyond Banda itself. By contrast, there must have been many "nodal" points of trade—more a plurality of shifting centers. To the north, Ternate and Tidore claimed territory and allegiance at the time of European contact, but by then they had adopted a Muslim western Indonesian conception of statecraft, and it is difficult to reconstruct now what preceded it. Moreover, before the sixteenth century, there were no towns, markets, or trading centers as we would normally understand them in the Moluccas. As Polanyi long ago demonstrated, trade does not necessarily require marketplaces for its conduct, even when marketing occurs on a significant scale. For pre-Muslim models we must turn rather to Melanesia, or even Africa. Thus,

Northrup (1978:4–5), writing as a historian but taking his critical cue from a generation of anthropologists writing on acephalous and weakly centralized political systems in Africa, noted that there has been a prejudice against accepting that small-scale nonstate societies might be "quite capable of participating in cultural and economic systems much larger than their political units," observing that "there is then no necessary correlation between large-scale trade and large-scale political institutions."

It is, however, with Melanesia that some of the parallels become really compelling. The extensive sea trade in sago, the role of small offshore islands (often atolls) as crucial nodes in wider trading networks, arguably chosen for defensive purposes (because manpower must have been short in the absence of traders), central places as manufacturing sites, and trading zones as specialized divisions of labor are all discussed for Melanesian localities, in ways that fit well with the Moluccan evidence. Some key studies in this literature focus on Motupore (Allen 1977a, b); Mailu (Irwin 1974, 1978a, b); the Torres Strait islands (Harris 1979); the Trobriands, the Amphletts, and other islands in the Kula area (Malinowski 1922; Irwin 1983; Lauer 1970); Manus and the Admiralty Archipelago (Kennedy 1981; Schwartz 1963); and Siassi in the Vitiaz Strait (Harding 1967:241); some of the general features are discussed by Brookfield and Hart (1971:314–334) and Sahlins (1972). All indicate parallels with Moluccan networks, and provide tempting models for reconstructing Moluccan systems as they existed before incorporation into dominant global relations. The systems of which these small islands are part integrate ecologically and culturally separate communities in the distinctive absence of any political institutions of comparable extent. Almost incidentally, such parallels between the Moluccan and the Melanesian situation illustrate how scholarly anthropological traditions embedded in particular political histories, the Melanesianist facing east toward the Pacific and the Indonesianist facing west toward mainland Asia, have prevented such obvious similarities from being recognized and addressed hitherto (Urry 1981).

None of this, of course, detracts in any way from the more general observation made by Hall (1981:37), that the development of trade of a particular kind in the Indonesian Archipelago in the pre-European age is contrary to the claims of late nineteenth- and early twentieth-century historians, namely that there were no elements of Western capitalism in Southeast Asia before the sixteenth century. Hall was able to show a widespread preoccupation with trade and commerce linked to an emergent cosmopolitan and urban sector, noting that early European records of their experiences in Southeast Asia are on the whole perceptive of local culture and society, attempting to understand it on its own terms; by the nineteenth century historiography was more concerned with molding Southeast Asia's history to fit a preconceived image of what Europeans thought it should be, expecting to prove, as it were, that Southeast Asians had accomplished nothing over time except when foreigners had imposed themselves and provided direction to otherwise hapless native populations (cf. Alatas 1977). In this ethnocentric vision, Indians and Chinese helped Southeast Asians to become civilized in earliest times, but from the sixteenth century onward it was Europe's turn by introducing the capitalist economic and social order. We now know that "from a Southeast Asian perspective the coming of the Europeans contributed to the demise of a developing Southeast Asian commercial class, but this demise was not due entirely to European initiatives" (Hall 1981:37–38). Later, of course, Europeans actively destroyed, directly or through emasculation, industrial and commercial infrastructures (see Reid 1993, especially 267–330).

1.4. The Moluccan Trading Zones and Their Creation

I have, in a series of earlier publications (Ellen 1979, 1984, 1987), presented evidence for the existence of three reasonably distinct trading nexuses located in the present-day Indonesian province of Maluku (the Moluccas) and adjacent areas of the New Guinea coast (Figure 1.2), as these existed in the sixteenth and seventeenth centuries. They have persisted, in a modified form, up to and including the present day and display certain properties that allow us theoretically to specify them as "systems." Each "zone" (in Warren's sense [1998:16] a "borderless world") is focused on a densely populated spice-producing center, dependent upon an extensive sago-producing periphery.[2] This periphery also provided the center with a wide range of forest and marine products, which (together with the sago) were exchanged for imported calico, valuables, and rice. The most northerly zone was focused on Ternate and Tidore, drawing on the resources of Halmahera and elsewhere; a central zone was focused on Ambon-Lease, drawing for resources on Seram and Buru; and a southerly zone was focused on Banda, drawing on resources from a wide arc, including Southeast Seram, the Kei Islands, Aru, and parts of New Guinea. These trading nexuses did not all emerge at the same time, and the conditions of their emergence were in each case significantly different. However, by the early part of the seventeenth century their simultaneous existence is quite well documented, and the consequences of the interaction of external factors with their internal dynamics are evident over the subsequent three-hundred-year period.

Over the course of several hundred years, relatively independent local populations were absorbed into more extensive and complex modes of production and exchange, through local polities, petty states, European

Figure 1.2. (Opposite) Schematic outline of nesting Moluccan trading spheres. The legend takes the form of the accompanying hypothetical taxonomy. Reproduced, with modification, from Ellen (1987).

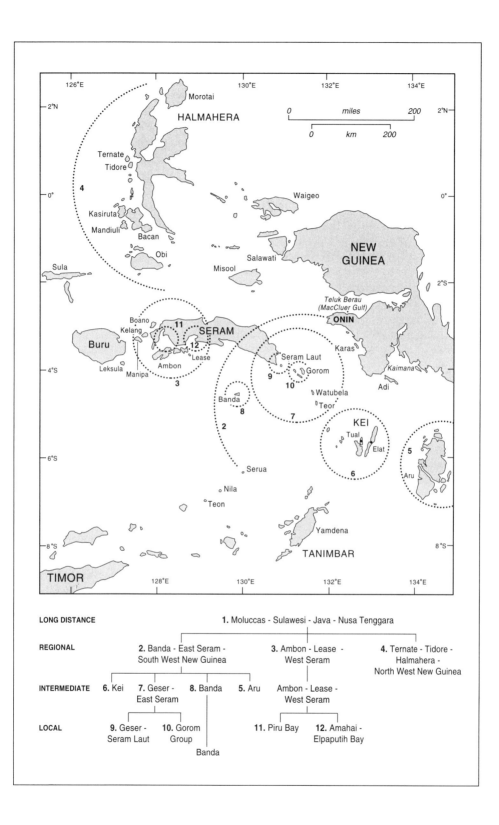

LONG DISTANCE   **1.** Moluccas - Sulawesi - Java - Nusa Tenggara

REGIONAL   **2.** Banda - East Seram - South West New Guinea   **3.** Ambon - Lease - West Seram   **4.** Ternate - Tidore - Halmahera - North West New Guinea

INTERMEDIATE   **6.** Kei   **7.** Geser - East Seram   **8.** Banda   **5.** Aru   Ambon - Lease - West Seram

LOCAL   **9.** Geser - Seram Laut   **10.** Gorom Group   **11.** Piru Bay   **12.** Amahai - Elpaputih Bay

Banda

hegemony, and finally total colonial control. Historically, this process began in the northern Moluccas and Banda, and later spread to the central Moluccas. Sago subsistence both permitted the rapid growth of spice production and prevented the immediate negative economic consequences that are usually associated with a rapid expansion of agricultural production for exchange of crops with no local subsistence value. The communities were able to tolerate the wide and erratic fluctuations in spice production and sales. Paradoxically, it was precisely sago dependence, plus external pressures, that maintained and increased the rate of expansion of spice production in some localities so that an initially adaptive pattern finally proved inadequate. On the small islands heavily involved in spice production, the system adjusted to the depletion of traditional subsistence resources by importing food, particularly sago, from other islands that were less involved directly in the spice trade. However, this made the communities even more dependent on spice production, although they were partly cushioned against total dependence through the possibility of paying for food in locally produced commodities rather than imported items. In this way, specialized local systems were incorporated into a much more specialized regional system with a geographical as well as a social division of labor. Contemporary patterns of local trade and production cannot be understood except in relation to this progressive ecological and economic change.

The islands off Southeast Seram were, for most of the period of European influence and control in Asia, at the far reaches of empire and yet paradoxically, as I try to show in this book, were crucial parts of the colonial system. The Banda group, for example, could not have become a significant center without the trading linkages it maintained to the east and northeast, to Geser-Gorom. It is true that this area was subject to periodic VOC punitive expeditions, first because of the threat the islanders posed to the Dutch monopoly and later because of alleged piracy, but they continued to act independently in most economic and political matters for almost five hundred years after the arrival of the first Europeans. Although the Dutch maintained the fiction that they were part of the Indies, they were not effectively incorporated within it until the late nineteenth century, with the establishment of a small garrison at Geser. Even the increasingly frequent visits by administrators in the first half of the nineteenth century were, for the protagonists, more like official contacts between friendly states. Of course, the domains of Southeast Seram had to operate within a system that had been transformed by a Dutch presence and by the vicissitudes of the world system; but even in the nineteenth century there was no attempt to control their means of production. When political control finally came, warfare decreased and many of the rulers became impotent, but trading went on much as before. There were thus shifts in the levels of control, between the political and the economic, and although not independent in any ultimate sense, the levels had a remarkable degree of autonomy. Thus, many Southeast Seram boats sailed under the Dutch flag during much of the nineteenth century, but for many this was no more than a flag of convenience, which enabled them to call on Dutch help if they got into trouble. The political control that the Dutch exercised in Southeast Seram was not capitalistic in the sense of operating through the control of market forces, labor, or goods. Certainly the dynamic of the VOC had been capitalistic, but in the context of the Indies the VOC operated like any other of the Asian potentates it sought to displace, exacting tribute and punishing those who declined to pay it. The VOC differed from those potentates in its technical mastery and in its control of the means of production of particular products that it saw as vital to its interests.

1.5. Persistence and Emergent Change

The systemic properties of trading zones and networks in the Moluccas have arisen from a combination of environmental, technological, economic, and political forces. Technological changes in transport have meant that trading routes are no longer constrained by the necessity to use sailing vessels. The economic forces that have destroyed or concealed obvious systemic properties are in terms of both imports and exports. On the import side, the accessibility of a wide range of cheap manufactured goods through improved long-distance trade has killed off much local trade and local productive specialization. Radial routes are now emphasized at the expense of lateral ones, lessening the overall connectedness of the networks on the periphery. The availability of imported rice in the center has led to a decline in the local trade of other starch staples, and local pottery is being replaced by plastic and metal alternatives. Even cheap vegetables and roots brought in from Java and Sulawesi are undermining local trade. In short, the economy is showing all the classic symptoms of a familiar form of underdevelopment. Increasing economic centralization has been accompanied by political centralization. Administrative pressures have encouraged the use of particular trade routes. Remote populations on the periphery (Nila, Teun, Serua) have been forced to move nearer the centers and inland mountain villages to the coasts of the larger islands.

The export trade in spices is also changing. The Moluccas as a whole are less important for the production of nutmeg and cloves than they used to be. Although by the 1980s cloves were being planted more widely in the Moluccas, on the periphery as well as at the centers, cloves and nutmeg were also increasingly being grown in other parts of Indonesia. Clove trees, however, were being planted at the expense of nutmeg, because the prices obtainable per kilogram were higher. Thus, although nutmeg used to be the exclusive cash crop in Gorom, after 1950 clove production gradually outstripped the production of nutmeg. By the late 1980s, however, overproduction of cloves had led to a slump in the price and real problems for producers.

The exchange of sago, slaves, and forest products that maintained

Banda at the center of its own trading nexus had virtually disappeared by the 1980s, and the traditional links in the system had been severed. The production of nutmeg and its relative market price had declined. The colonial perkenier system ended with World War II, and the estates declined further under Indonesian nationalization. Butonese replaced Buginese ship handlers. Today, Banda has become more of a trading base than a major center of production, occupying an increasingly more marginal position, ironically more a center for a peddling trade than it has been for five hundred years, with landless peasants relying on selling small quantities of nutmeg to monopolistic government corporations, or trading dried fish, *Trochus* shell, cloves, cinnamon, and kenari nuts *(Canarium commune)* to private merchants, mostly destined for the Ambon market. Despite improvements in communications, Banda has remained poorly placed to supply the Ambon market with its most abundant resource, fresh fish. But even with these changes it is still possible to discern systemic properties in the Banda zone. This is partly because Banda is so deficient in many products that it needs (timber, thatch, coconut), which can still be obtained most easily from Southeast Seram and other points east. It is also partly because Banda still maintains its role as a base and pivot in the long-distance sailing trade. It lies in an advantageous geographical position and provides excellent harbor facilities.

But if the wider Banda system shows signs of disappearing, the local zones of which it is composed maintain a higher degree of systemness: the Kei Islands (focused on Tual and Elat), Aru (focused on Dobo), and, most strikingly, archipelagic Southeast Seram (focused on Geser). Here the classic features of the fish–sago–export product nexus remain intact and provide an excellent opportunity for the investigation of trading patterns that were once found more widely. Some of the features observable today are remarkably similar to those described by Van Leur for early Asian trade up to the seventeenth century. The maritime peddlers receive their capital from rich villagers, government officials, or from their families. The proceeds are distributed according to fixed proportions, and the trading party dissolves when an expedition is over. Relations with trading partners, however, are long-lasting, and enduring networks are maintained. The persistence of trading networks over long periods of time, in fact through several "world systems," speaks, however, for their relative autonomy, with the forms and customs of the peddling trade remaining stable over long periods of time (Evers 1988:91, 99).

1.6. The Structure of an Argument

Before proceeding further it is necessary to clarify some abstract concepts that are used in the course of the discussion that follows. Unfortunately, even the most basic of terms are not transparent, and there is still some confusion in the literature about how the term "trading network" should be employed. Trading networks, as Evers (ibid., 92) put it, can be defined as "social processes of exchange . . . [where] interaction takes place for the primary purpose of exchanging goods over more or less greater geographical distances." This seems to me to be a reasonable start, but Evers (ibid., 93) then went on to list as intermediate trading systems in Southeast Asia the northern Strait of Malacca (Aceh), Riau-Singapore, the Buginese network, the Butonese network, Minangkabau petty trade, the Sulu network, networks of the Java Sea, and the Trengganu-Kelantan-Thai network. It is difficult to know what to make of this hodgepodge, because the examples given are not commensurate: some are defined in terms of ethnicity (corresponding presumably to Cohen's [1971] "trading diaspora" [see also Fallers 1967 and Yambert 1981]), some in terms of objective measurable patterns of interaction, and others apparently more in terms of social relationships that exist in the ideal virtual world of the traders themselves. Of those defined geographically, most are very impressionistic. All in all, the list is reminiscent of Borges' fictitious Chinese encyclopedia in which it is impossible to discern the logic on which its organization is predicated. Of course, in the end what a trading network is, how it is bounded, depends (as with an ecosystem or a society) on the problem at hand (Ellen 1984).

Another part of Evers' definition concerns the purpose of trade: the exchange of goods. In the literal, interactionist, sense this is, of course, palpably true. But the statement requires unpacking and qualification. We know from a noble lineage of anthropological theory going back to Marcel Mauss and Bronislaw Malinowski that mundane exchange of material things may underwrite, disguise, or embellish complex forms of social integration; that it is "not absolutely necessary" for local productive forces but may be socially necessary to maintain group relations. This is evident when prestige goods needed for local transactions (bride-price and other services) and for defining individual social status are imported objects (Ekholm and Friedman 1993:61; Friedberg 1977). However, for the Moluccas, we need to modify such a generalization. Certainly, in large parts of the area (and well into the interior of New Guinea) exchange is not necessary to maintain productive forces but historically has become essential to the maintenance of ritual cycles and systems of inequality (Ellen 1988). The dependence on trade goods for sustaining ritual cycles in both the Moluccas and the westernmost part of New Guinea is richly documented by ethnography from the late nineteenth century onward (the role of imported porcelain, Indian and other textiles, elephant tusks, bronze gongs), and we can only assume that the pattern is one that goes back many centuries, if not millennia. In Tung Hsi Yang K'au book IV (Groenevelt 1960:117–118), for example, a source of 1618 noted that when a (Moluccan) girl marries they buy large quantities of Chinese cups, which they paint outside; rich people purchase many to show their wealth. But in Banda and archipelagic Southeast Seram trade became a crucial part of maintaining the productive forces, especially important in an area with specialized modes of extraction and environmental constraints. It is about this that much of this book is concerned.

I discuss in chapter 7 some of the empirical difficulties in delineating networks and return to the general conceptual issue in chapter 10. My own use of the term "network," as with the unqualified use of terms such as "center" and "periphery," implies the existence of some concrete linkage between individuals or places measured in terms of flows of goods or voyages. The model outlined in section 4 of this chapter illustrates this well. I distinguish between the scale of trading networks (emphasizing connections) and zone (emphasizing areas), and their organization into structured local or regional systems. Scale is about distances, numbers and linkages, size of population, quantities of goods handled, and technological infrastructures, such as types of boats. Using these criteria, we can distinguish (a) local zones that are essentially coastal or within small island groups, (b) intermediate zones (those connecting local zones), (c) regional zones (as in the three zones focused on Ternate/Tidore, Ambon, and Banda, and (d) long-distance zones (as between the Moluccan centers and Java). These distinctions imply no particular kind of organization, and the boundaries between different zones at each level are empirically based, though the point of transition from one to the other must be arbitrary and defined in terms of the objectives of the analysis. Such a schematization does not rule out locally significant trading relations across the boundaries between spheres and is concerned rather with structural and statistical tendencies.

In the Moluccas local trading networks tend to be confined to single islands, small island groups, and stretches of coast and hinterland. In Figure 1.2, the Gorom (10), Banda (8), and Geser (9) networks clearly illustrate this level of organization. In each case, local imbalances in the production of various subsistence crops are usually evened out within the area circumscribed, with different villages often providing certain specialized services, such as pottery manufacture, iron working, or sago production. The degree to which these zones overlap varies and influences their systemic character. The Banda group maintains a high degree of closure in terms of local trade (mainly because of physical isolation), the Gorom group considerably less so. Zones that include stretches of coastline, because of continuous linear habitation, tend to overlap much more. Indeed, some settlements may best be portrayed as simultaneously belonging to two or more local networks with different foci.

At a more inclusive level, the central and southern Moluccan area can be seen as being composed of relatively discrete intermediate networks, at the hub of each of which is a small island (or number of small islands) serving as a redistributive center and point of articulation with the outside world. Thus, in Figure 1.2 West Seram (3) is focused on Ambon and the Lease Islands, Aru (5) on Dobo, Southeast Seram (7) on Geser, and so on.

The trading centers, or foci, show various degrees of dependency on their peripheries and are generally very small islands that appear to owe their importance to their geographical centrality in the local trading area and because they provide intrusive traders or refugees with good harbors and safe havens in otherwise hostile territory. Occasionally the reasons may have been environmental. For example, local inhabitants of Seram Rei claim that it was first inhabited to avoid the mangrove swamps along the southeastern coastline of Seram. But in this case one might ask why not settle at that point on the mainland where the mangroves end. The real reason is more complicated and is probably largely political and economic in character: that an island among banks and shoals provided ready access to desirable sea products, that land elsewhere was politically inaccessible, that anchorages were convenient and safe, and that Seram Rei lay in the immediate vicinity of what was already an important trading center (the Seram Laut archipelago). The reasons for settling on such small islands must have been strong because the disadvantages were often severe. Small islands such as Geser, Kiltai, and Seram Rei are flat, tiny, and exposed coral islets, subject to frequent flooding, vulnerable to tsunamis, with virtually no possibilities for cultivation and with only brackish drinking water. There is oral and written evidence, as well as that of contemporary administrative boundaries, that in the past local political domains rivaled for control of these small strategic islands (Kolff 1927 [1840]:287–288). Islands with so little natural wealth, with the possible exception of sea produce, must be contrasted with powerful political domains such as Kataloka on Gorom, which also exported locally grown spices and had opportunities for subsistence cultivation.

This play-off between precarious environmental conditions and supreme economic advantage does not apply only to minute islands whose entire livelihood depends on the transshipment, rather than production, of commodities. We have already mentioned that access to exotic sea produce may have been an important locational feature for some of the centers, at least since the eighteenth century (Urry 1980). The same is true for certain settlements on the periphery, either populated reefs vulnerable to storms (Garogos) or islands subject to seismic disturbances. Banda, for example, has had a continuous and violent history of volcanism (Hanna 1978), and much the same may be true of Ternate and Tidore. But in these cases, we are not only dealing with ideal centers for transshipment but also with primary locations for the production of nutmeg (Banda) and cloves (Ternate/Tidore).

Very small islands with no possibilities for cultivation are entirely dependent on the import of basic foods and materials: rice and manufactured goods from outside the Moluccas and other starch staples (largely sago), vegetables, fruit, and constructional and craft materials from other islands in the immediate vicinity. Such needs in a hypothetically pristine world might initially have been met through highly local trade, such as between Geser and Seram Laut. Geser, Kiltai, and Seram Rei are still very dependent on the vegetable produce of nearby Seram Laut, and the economic significance of this island is reflected politically in the division between the polity of Kelu on Seram Rei and Kiltai. But long-term requirements for trade objects to exchange for rice and manufactured goods and the increasing scale of such trade and home consumption have led to the growth of a much larger periphery. In the case of Geser, Kiltai, and Seram Rei, it meant the incorporation of the eastern part of mainland Seram and parts of Teluk Berau and the Onin Peninsula of New Guinea.

More encompassing still than the intermediate networks are the regional systems. The three regional systems in the model were identified in section 1.4 (Ambon–West Seram, Ternate/Tidore–Halmahera, and Banda–East Seram). I confine myself here to the Banda system. This can be seen as comprising at least four separate and identifiable intermediate networks plus some less clearly attached networks. The four major intermediate-level components are the Banda, Kei, and Aru groups and the network connecting the Geser-Teor chain with the mainland of East Seram. The attachments are the New Guinea (Papuan) coast from Teluk Berau southeastward to Mimika and the extreme southeastern islands focused on Tanimbar. The systemic properties of the Banda regional nexus derive almost entirely from intrusive long-distance trade. The incorporation of various intermediate networks has depended on the importance of their products outside the Moluccas and, to a lesser extent, demand elsewhere in the system. With the drop in external demand for their products, some intermediate (and local) networks regain something of their earlier autonomy. Thus, strong local subsystemic properties have continually threatened the integrity of the system as a whole.

Connected with this important structural difference between the Ambon and Banda systems is the question of distance and the most appropriate boat technology in each case. In the past the Ambon system could reproduce itself internally by relying on small coastal craft, but the Banda system involved major sea crossings. Historically, this has often meant the employment of much larger vessels, often (though not exclusively) those belonging to intrusive trading groups such as the Buginese and Butonese. This set of issues is examined further in chapter 6.

It would be a mistake, however, to see the emergence and transformation of trading patterns in the Moluccas as simply the working out of some game-theoretic or market rationality under ideal Von Thünen and Christaller-Lösch conditions. Trade relations within any network were always constrained as well as facilitated by other social relations, such as *pela* (intervillage) alliances in the Ambon–West Seram zone or their functional equivalents in Southeast Seram (the *tutu* and *seri-tahun* confederations), marital alliances, and ties of political subordination and control. Although it is difficult at this stage to do much more than speculate regarding the political organization of trade before the European period, the larger systems clearly brought together political entities of very different kinds: semidependent tribal groups (such as the Nuaulu), slave-based domains with chiefs or rajas (such as Kataloka), the sultanates of Ternate and Tidore, and the local "republics" of Banda. From the seventeenth century onward, the number of different kinds of political entity and modes of production increased to include estates run by the Dutch East India Company (Banda) and mercantilist control of peasant producers (Ambon group). It is quite clear that the Dutch period resulted not simply in changes in traditional trading patterns, but in some cases in their consolidation and the accentuation of some of their more distinctive properties. Thus, the geographical division of resources in the Banda Archipelago after 1621 was administratively redefined: firewood could only be taken from the volcanic island of Gunung Api, and it was mandatory that vegetable gardens and nutmeg groves be located in different places. Clove cultivation was prohibited in large parts of Seram (e.g., the Hoamoal Peninsula) to maintain the Dutch monopoly, encouraging these localities to develop other trading specialities. But although Banda under the Dutch East India Company represented an entirely unique kind of social and cultural formation, the expansion and concentration of spice production not only connected Moluccan centers more closely with the world system but, paradoxically, made them more dependent on local trading links as well. The growth and specialization of centers of spice production and trade as the result of colonial policy had the effect of producing a more distinct and complex local division of labor and network of exchange relations. As land under spices and population increased, so also did the local trade in sago, root crops, vegetables, and other products necessary to supply deficient spice-producing areas. When centers already important for trade were adopted as convenient administrative centers by the Dutch, bringing an increasing number of retail enterprises to cater to a growing number of wage earners and bureaucrats, trade routes became increasingly centralized, radiating to and from the administrative center.

Let me recapitulate the main points made in elucidating the model of Moluccan interisland trade discussed in this chapter. Moluccan trading patterns may be conveniently represented as a series of nesting (and sometimes overlapping) zones of various degrees of "systemness." Each local population may participate in up to four levels of trading organization: local, intermediate, regional, and long-distance. Participation is defined minimally in terms of the destination of a population's exports and the origins of its imports. However, the structural significance of participation at any one level depends also on the types, proportions, range, value, and volume of goods traded. For example, it may be important to know the scale of trade in food products or the local significance of trade in "valuables." Collectively, such factors determine the degree and kind of reproductive independence a local social formation maintains and that it maintains at different levels of systemic inclusiveness. Depending on the objective of the analysis and the populations specified, we may decide to emphasize boundaries at the local, intermediate, or regional level; but in all cases we must remember that boundaries are necessarily graded and determined by the structural foci of the systems they encompass (Ellen 1984).

All networks have some systemic properties, but the degree of "systemness" varies. A trading system is composed of one or more zones and is characterized by a network of linkages that theoretically permit its reproduction over time through both a geographical and a social division of economic labor. Each system has a center and a periphery, connected by radial links. A center classically exhibits control over the periphery, although the extent of this control tends to diminish as we move farther from the center. The center connects the system as a whole with the outside world, yet is dependent itself on the resources of the periphery. Settlements on the periphery that are points of production, rather than simply nodes in a trading network, are described here as termini. Nodes that link two or more termini are described as secondary centers, and those that link two or more secondary centers are described as primary centers. In addition to the radial links described, termini and secondary centers may also be connected by lateral linkages that do not pass through primary centers. The extent to which more inclusive systems absorb less inclusive ones depends on the degree and character of external intrusion, and membership of a more inclusive system may in turn redefine the structure and dynamics of local networks. Returning, therefore, to the point at which we began, processes of trade, though they are based on a rationality of individual and group action, can only be understood in the context of interisland organization (cf. Alkire 1965:4), which is simultaneously a context of interacting objective parts that generates its own dynamic and a web of social relationships that, in turn, serve as a conceptual framework for action. This, therefore, in the way it reproduces itself, realizes what we now recognize as Giddens' (e.g., 1986) framework of structuration.

2

Archipelagic Southeast Seram

> On the second day we passed the eastern extremity of Ceram, formed
> of a group of hummocky limestone hills; and, sailing by the islands of
> Kwammer and Keffing, both thickly inhabited, came in sight of the
> little town of Kilwaru, which appears to rise out of the sea like a rustic
> Venice. This place has really a most extraordinary appearance, as not a
> particle of land or vegetation can be seen, but a long way out at sea a
> large village seems to float upon the water. There is of course a small
> island of several acres in extent; but the houses are built so closely all
> round it upon piles in the water, that it is completely hidden. It is a
> place of great traffic, being the emporium for much of the produce of
> these Eastern seas, and is the residence of many Bugis and Ceramese
> traders, and appears to have been chosen on account of it being close
> to the only deep channel between the extensive shoals of Ceram-laut
> and those bordering the east end of Ceram.
>
> A. R. WALLACE, *The Malay Archipelago*

2.1. The Southeast Seram Littoral

This study focuses on that area of mainland and archipelagic Southeast
Seram united by what I shall treat here as a single language. Jim Collins
(1986:125) called this tongue Geser ("the far-flung language of traders,
slavers, sailors and fishermen"), but Loski and Loski (1989) prefer Geser-
Gorom. I shall call it Southeast Seram Littoral (SSL), not only because this
more accurately describes its distribution, but because to call it Geser,
Gorom, or Geser-Gorom is to confuse it with some very specific places that
may or may not be its center of radiation. The SSL area is almost entirely
encompassed by the present-day kecamatan (subdistrict) of Seram Timur
(East Seram), though it excludes the islands of Kesui, Watubela, and Teor in
the southernmost part of the administrative district. It includes mainland
Seram from the Masiwang River in the north[1] southward along the coast,
and from Kilmuri in the south eastward along the coast, as well as the
Seram Laut and Gorom Archipelagoes. It will become clear during the
course of this account that the boundaries of both the subdistrict and the
language area are the outcome of the zone being an important focus of

trade with regional and global dimensions. It reflects, therefore, a socially and culturally coherent space with an identifiable internal structure.[2]

To understand the history of the littoral of Southeast Seram, and its social and economic character, it is therefore necessary to place it within a wider sphere of interaction that extends to part of the coast of New Guinea (Irian Jaya) and, to a lesser extent, the Kei and Aru Archipelagoes. This larger whole was historically articulated with global trade westward through Banda. To begin with, though, I concentrate on the physical geography and ecology of the specific study area, for there are features of the topographic setting alone that have encouraged and molded the development of a system of interisland social ties. These include restricted land area; a limited range of starch staples; endemic environmental hazards, such as volcanism and other seismic activity and the destructive effects of tropical storms; and the uncertainties of marine extraction. With such a pattern of risk in terms of natural disasters and food availability, an interisland economy and social system that allows for flexibility and breadth of resource accessibility, and of human settlement and refuge, is almost a precondition for long-term sustainability.

2.2. **Landforms and Biotopes**

The Southeast Seram littoral has a complex weather pattern, arising from its geographical position. On Geser, rain reaches its peak of 250 millimeters in June and minimum of 54 millimeters in October, but there are really no clear rainy and dry seasons. There is, for example, another low rainfall trough in April. The east monsoon is April–September, bringing much rain, rough seas, and high tides; the west monsoon occurs during November–March, which brings dry weather, calm seas, clear water, and low tides, but with cyclones between December and February. The highest tides are between March and April, between the east and the west monsoons. Between July and September cyclones are not able to enter the area.

Rainwater floods are virtually unknown, though high tides *(tonu)* are a seasonal hazard. Even the standard high tide in Geser lagoon is 1.5 meters, which, without raising the land level, is sufficient to regularly flood paths and the edges of settled land. In 1976 Geser suffered severe flooding, but only in the areas called Lomin and Kilwaru. The ability of spring tides to flood all of Kilwaru (on the island of Kiltai rather than Kilwaru on Geser) was reported by Van der Crab (1864:541), who added that at such times people temporarily moved to Seram Laut. The drinking water from wells in the domain of Kiltai, as on Seram Rei and Geser, is brackish and its potability is reduced even further in times of floods. At such times it is permitted to collect it from Kilwaru (on Kiltai Island), where Wallace had noted in 1860 that the water was of good quality. Quite apart from sea water flooding, the absence of creeks on small islands means that in the dry months sources of water dry up altogether, as on Seram Laut (also known as Maar).

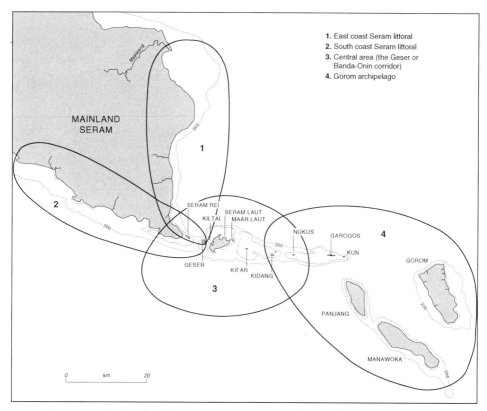

Figure 2.1. Archipelagic Southeast Seram represented as a series of overlapping zones focused on a central area of resource depletion but high trading activity: the Banda-Onin corridor.

The collection of rainwater runoff helps to reduce this risk. *Ruma loi-loi* (houses on stilts) were in the past one obvious solution to the problem of high-tide flooding, though not to that of water supply. However, few of these now remain on the low islands of the Seram Laut Archipelago. Another solution was to raise the level of the land, a matter to which I turn in section 2.3. But although high tides pose a periodic hazard, low tides make it possible in places to walk between islands: between Kiltai and Seram Laut, and between Seram Rei and mainland Seram. This situation is not recent, and indeed the rise of sea levels over the last few decades may have made it more difficult. Rosenberg (1867:132) reported in the 1860s, as Bik (1928 [1824]:16) had noted before him, that it was very easy to walk from Keffing (on Seram Rei) to Kwaos (on the east coast of the mainland).

The area subject to this weather and tidal regime can be divided into four basic geographic zones: (1) the east coast littoral, (2) the south coast littoral, (3) a central area encompassing the Seram Laut Archipelago and the adjacent mainland, and (4) the Gorom Archipelago (Figure 2.1).

Ecologically, we can distinguish seven major biotopes that are distributed unevenly across these zones: tropical rain forest, the coastal cline, a coastal zone of cultivation, coastal mangroves, extensive reefs, small coral atolls and banks, and open sea.

Rain forest is restricted to mainland Seram, overlying sedimentary rocks at higher altitudes and neogenous coralline deposits along the coast. Mature forest, or what is sometimes described as "tanah ewang" on other islands (such as Manawoka), has been extensively modified, with characteristically high densities of useful trees, most prominently *Canarium*. It also included 814 square kilometers of sago *(Metroxylon sagu)* swamp forest in 1977 (Indonesian government, subdistrict Seram Timur Statistik Tahunan 1977–1978). The remaining biotopes are widely distributed throughout the mainland and the Seram Laut and Gorom Archipelagoes, though the central area around Geser is characterized by severe terrestrial resource depletion with little cultivated land. This environmental patterning is crucial to an understanding of the functioning of the area as a social system (Figure 2.2), and in particular the character of the coastal cline, mangroves, and coral reefs.

The coastal cline has a roughly banded structure with a *Canavalia* formation along the herbaceous vegetation edge of the sandy coast. *Canavalia* is a common pantropical beach plant. *Nypa fruticans* is found in places along the edge of the nearest dry land. Behind sandy coast is a formation dominated by *Barringtonia racemosa;* behind rocky coast is a mixture of forest savanna bush, *Macaranga* secondary forest, and *Melaleuca* bush. Finally there is sea grass, *Enchahulus acoroides* (Warburg 1893). Apart from along stretches of the mainland, this structure is only evident on Seram Laut, a hilly limestone island rising to about 90 meters, and on the larger islands of the Gorom and Watubela groups. These latter islands have a similar geology, being largely composed of alluvium, coral reefs, and outcrops of earlier neogenous sedimentary rocks. Gorom itself has a range of low limestone hills reaching 310 meters, and unwooded or cultivated areas there are covered with patches of *Imperata cylindrica.*

The main area of mangroves (*akat*) forms an extensive block at the eastern tip of mainland Seram (Figure 2.3). This area is in many ways crucial to understanding the history of Southeast Seram and local conceptions of the world. A sketch map made in 1986 is given in Figure 2.4, and Figure 2.5 provides us with some indication of its extent and shape perhaps as much as three hundred years earlier. What is instructive in comparing these two maps are the changes in the distribution of the mangrove are over a period of several centuries and the location of human settlements, a matter to which I shall return in chapter 4. There are also mangroves along parts of the Geser lagoon, Seram Laut, and parts of Seram Rei. Several kinds of mangroves are recognized, distributed in a characteristic zonation: *Avicennia* and *Sonneratia* species along the narrow seaward edge, *Rhizophora* in the interior, and *Bruguiera* on the landward side. Mangroves have typical avifauna,

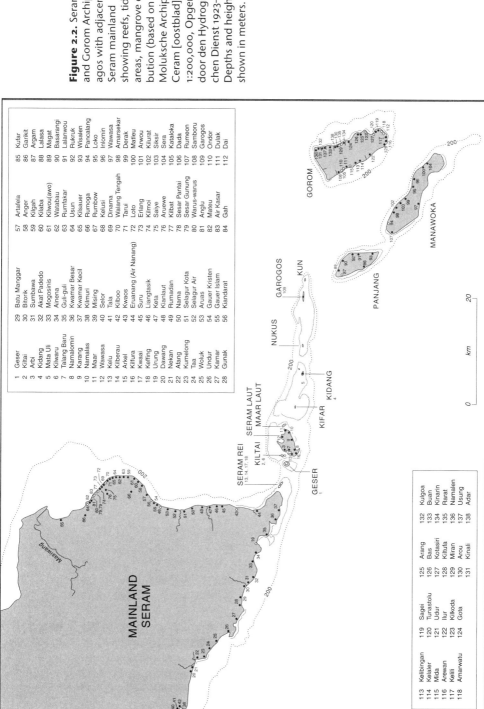

Figure 2.2. Seram Laut and Gorom Archipelagos with adjacent Seram mainland showing reefs, tidal areas, mangrove distribution (based on Moluksche Archipel Ceram [oostblad] 1:200,000, Opgenomen door den Hydrographischen Dienst 1923–1928). Depths and heights shown in meters.

Figure 2.3.
Mangrove fringe on
island of Seram Rei,
domain of Keffing,
10 April 1986.

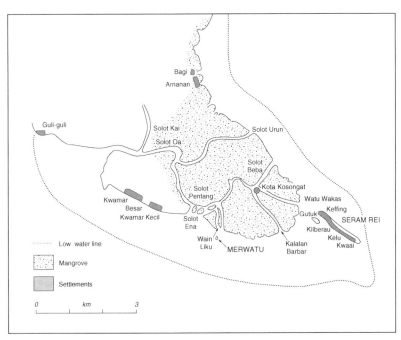

Bagi
Arnanan

Guli-guli

Solot Kai
Solot Oa
Solot Urun

Solot
Beba

Kota Kosongat

Solot
Pentang
Watu Wakas

Kwamar
Besar
Kwamar Kecil
Solot
Ena
Gutuk
Keffing
SERAM REI

Kilberau
Kelu

Wain
Liku
MERWATU
Kalalan
Barbar
Kwaai

.... Low water line

Mangrove

Settlements

0   km   3

Figure 2.4. The Southeast Seram mangrove area as it was in 1986. A sketch map
based on Topographische Inrichting 1919, *Schetskaart van Ceram* (scale 1:100,000).
Modified on the basis of data collected during fieldwork in 1986.

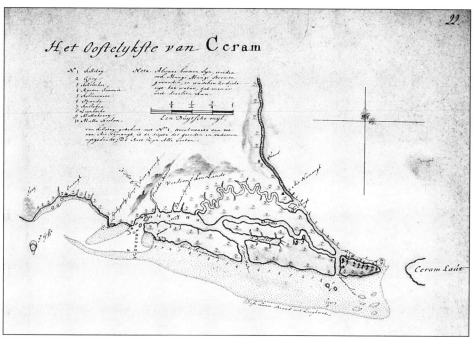

Figure 2.5. Detailed chart of southeastern corner of Seram showing inland waters through the mangroves after 1668. Settlements are indicated as follows using original orthography (but with probable modern equivalents in parentheses): Quans (Kwaos), Air Nanangh (Air Nanang), Oerongh (Urung), Gouly-Gouly (Guli-guli), Quamar (Kwamar); and numbered toponyms: 1, Killetay; 2, Quay; 3, Killeloehoe; 4, Roema Samesit; 5, Killewaroe; 6, Banda; 7, Kullebia; 8, Sumbacko; 9, Mattahenny; 10, Matta Boelan. The significance of this map is explored further in chapter 4. (Source: Rijksarchief VEL 483 Kaart van het Oostelykste gedeelte van Ceram, seventeenth century.)

including large flocks of black sea ducks, gulls, and pelicans that congregate on the cays, or *bas* (see next paragraph), before migrating south to Australia (cf. Monk, de Fretes, and Reksodiharjo-Lilley 1997).

Coral, despite its practical significance in the lives of Serammers, is not recognized as a single lexically defined domain. Coral forming the underlying base of islands is known as *watu lian* (lit. "spikey stone") and contrasts with other types of stone: *watu metan* ("black stone," a quartz-bearing shale found on Seram Laut) and *watu mas* ("gold stone," a conglomerate containing mica found on Maar Laut). Most other hard corals are known as *lodar,* translated into Ambonese Malay as "karang," though some are neither *watu* nor *lodar,* such as *sisifi.* Some islands, for example, Seram Laut, have coral walls dropping into the sea that may reach 50 meters in height, and most islands are surrounded with steep fringing reefs known as *sakaru.* Quite different again are the black, fine, soft corals. Cays or banks of broken

Figure 2.6. Typical cay (tanusang) morphology, to the west of Geser, 30 April 1986.

dead coral thrown up from the reefs (*bas,* or "tanusang" in Ambonese Malay) are a prominent feature of the central zone (Figure 2.6).

2.3. Demography and Patterns of Settlement

Limited land, heavy reliance on trade to supplement subsistence, and concentration of settlement on some decidedly precarious sites have resulted in local human modification of the environment, often in unusual ways. In a very literal sense we can talk about the cultural construction of the environment. First of all, there is heavy local resource depletion: forest removal, depletion of mangroves, overfishing of the commercially valuable alga agar-agar, for example. Second, there is the deliberate use of coral for sea defenses, settlement extension, and maritime-related technology. Mangrove depletion and deliberate landform reconstruction, in particular, have changed local topography over the years, in ways that are historically significant. The island of Kiltai, between Geser and Seram Laut, is a low, flat islet of coral and sand entirely covered in dwellings, the surface (and especially the edges) of which has been reinforced by coral. Coral is broken off from underneath the water level, loaded into canoes, and taken to where it is needed for house building or some other purpose. Coral is also economically important as a source of burnt lime, for building and betel chewing. The atoll of Geser, which is only a few meters above sea level, is composed mostly of loose sand and coral and once contained an island (marked on colonial maps) in the lagoon (Figures 2.7 and 4.1). However, over the years this has been eroded by people taking coral and sand to extend the edge of the village into the lagoon (or *lomin,* literally "inside" or "full") to increase the continuous land area for habitation. Indeed, a common sight in the Geser area is the collection of rocklike reef coral (brain coral) in dugout canoes (*lepa-lepa*) to strengthen the seawall (Figure 2.8). Harbors and piers (*kotar,* or los [Indonesian]), for example on Kiltai, and, most strikingly, *lutur*

Figure 2.7. Flooded Geser lagoon looking toward the settlement of Kilwaru Baru, 5 April 1986. Note lagoon edge reinforcements at bottom right and remnant mangroves. The poles and stones to the left are part of a fish trap.

Figure 2.8. Coastal defenses of coral barrier and wooden groins along sea edge of Kampung Baru, Geser, 1 May 1986.

or stone fish traps (see section 2.6) have been built of coral in various places in the Southeast Seram area.

Coral has been used historically for other structures as well. Coral walls were erected around the enclosures of rulers. Forts (benteng) were built from it by warring domains and later by the Dutch. We know that there were indigenous forts at Ondor and Kataloka in the late eighteenth century made of coral (Bik 1928 [1824]:22–23).[3] Doren (1857:314) reported that in 1659 the inhabitants of Guli-guli had built a fort east of the settlement called "Solothay" (probably Solot Kai, see Figure 2.4), and local inhabitants in the Geser area today identify human-built structures within the mangrove area as the remains of this and similar forts. The fort in the mangroves near Seram Rei is widely said to belong to Rumakat (lit. "house of the mangrove," now the main descent group in Kwamar) and dates from the time of the war with Tidore, which, though Tidore continued to control the coast in the *tutu tolu* alliance area (see section 2.4), Keffing (on Seram Rei) effectively won. The place is called Kota Kosongat and today consists of no more than two piles of coral and some rocks that show some evidence of human modification (Kota Baran and Kota Mala [*baran* and *mala* are two kinds of trees of the mangrove area]). The use of coral continued well into the colonial period. The Dutch built a "karang" road from Air Nanang to Kwaos across the mangrove area before World War I, thus bridging a channel that previously could be negotiated all-year-round only by boat.

The topography of coral reef and lagoon is so culturally dominant in Southeast Seram that it features in myths of origin. The lagoon of the atoll of Geser is said to have been created by removal of a fragment of land that now forms the island of Seram Rei. A myth from Kataloka speaks of Basara coming from Java before the island of Gorom existed and marrying Lomina, a woman from below the sea. Thus *bas* and *lomin,* reef and lagoon, are culturally complementary, in much the same way as mountain and sea, and heaven and earth, are in more generic environments.

What is crucial to patterns of settlement and economic formations, and to the unique character of trade that historically developed here, is hydrography as much as topography. More will be said about this when we come to consider boat handling, but it is worth noting here some limitations on anchorages for larger vessels because these have had some influence on the development of central places. There is a crucial protected anchorage for large vessels that the Dutch had identified early midchannel between Geser and Kilwaru, though "tidal streams are strong, holding poor, and the south going ebb stream meeting southerly winds raises a heavy sea."[4] By contrast, there is no anchorage around Pulau Panjang, which is fringed with steep reefs, and this must account in part for the presence of only a few historically important domains on the island. Manawoka fares a little better, with no good anchorage but several reasonable ones on the south side. There is little protection in the Amar roads and it is liable to heavy seas or swell at the height of the monsoons, especially northwest (when landing is difficult). Shore reef fringes most of the island, steeply in places. However, Manawoka boasts at least one domain that historically has been influential: Amarsekaru. On Gorom, there is an anchorage off Ondor sheltered by drying reefs and shoals, but there are historical references to the particular problems of approaching and finding anchorages at Ondor and Kataloka during the east monsoon. There is no anchorage at Rarat, nor at Amarwatu, nor at Namalen, or Ainikke, though there are east monsoon anchorages at Mida and Dai.[5] There is an inner anchorage suitable for a vessel of from 85 to more than 100 meters. Off Kailakat at the southeastern corner of Gorom, a small vessel of 290 tons can anchor 500 meters offshore and larger vessels in deeper water farther out. The anchorage is sheltered in the northwest monsoon season, but open in the southeast season (ibid., 18).

2.4. Traditional Realms in Contemporary Maluku

At the current time the subdistrict of East Seram is divided into some 37 desa (administrative) units (Appendix 1), with the district administration centered on the tiny atoll of Geser. The total population in 1982 was 44,549, having steadily increased throughout the period for which we have reliable demographic records. However, in particular places that once were of political significance (Geser, Keffing, Kilmuri, Kataloka, Amarsekaru) population is actually declining. Each desa has a government administration (pemerintah negeri) in the form of a raja (*matlaen* in SSL), and each is subdivided into a number of soa (or dusun) depending on their size and geographical and social characteristics. For example, Geser today is divided into Kampung Cina, Kampung Baru, and Kilwaru. Each soa (a term of North Moluccan origin [see Van Fraassen 1987]) has a kepala soa and each desa a sekretaris. Many of the soa recognized for the purpose of Indonesian state administration at the current time are listed in Appendix 1 as "kampung," although these former may not always be the same as those used in practice for the purposes of traditional governance within a domain. Thus, the four soa recognized in Kataloka, for Indonesian purposes, become at least twelve for internal purposes. Traditionally Waruswarus encompassed Sesar and Air Kasar, with one kepala soa for Waruswarus and one for the rest. Part of the apparent confusion here is that the term "soa" is used both as an administrative unit based on locality and (as described in section 2.5) as a descent group.

Since 1974 desa administration has allowed for election as leader someone other than the raja. At the current time rajas are officially elected and the position is open to both sexes. However, most rajas still come from the clans that traditionally have provided them. For the most part, raja titles are inherited. Although the term "raja" is used to describe all desa heads at the current time, local rulers are highly conscious of the fact that historically they were not of comparable status. During the colonial period local rulers were granted titles, such as mayor (Keffing), pattih, orang kaya, and kapitan (Kiltai), all regarded by the Dutch as ranks below raja (Ellen 1986a). Many of those persons styled raja are neither obviously rich nor powerful, though the raja of Kataloka is personally very wealthy and has real power. On the whole, the stronger the traditional raja and the more continuous his historical power, the longer the royal genealogy and the greater the lengths taken to preserve them on paper (as, for example, in Kataloka, Amarsekaru, and Kwaos).

The domains historically have been highly variable in size and political strength, a reality reflected in the Dutch allocation of differential titles. The raja of Kwaos on the Seram mainland had, for example, claims and influence over Mela. Farther north there were autonomous orang kayas in Dinama, Kilmoi, and Kilbat; westward were the orang kaya of Urung and the raja of Kilmuri; in the central zone were the rajas of Kilwaru and Kelu, and the mayor of Keffing, and on Gorom the rajas of Amar, Kataloka, and Ondor. However, it is in Kataloka that the political economy of rajadom comes closest to a form that might be said to resemble precolonial structures. Here the raja does not work his land; rather villagers work for him in rotation, under the direction of the kepala soa. He receives food (sago) in exchange for the use of land, with different kampung or soa taking turns to supply him. Other rajas may, however, be personally wealthy, and their land may not always lie within the boundaries of their domain defined in terms of contemporary desa. The raja of Amarsekaru, for example, has seven nutmeg estates. Broersma (1934:341) reported for the early 1930s that these comprised some 30,000 trees, not only in Amarsekaru itself, but also in Ubas (36,000 hectares) and Mida; and a coconut plantation on Kesui; and jointly with his cousin the raja of Ondor has coconut plantations on Watubela (Efor), Kesui (Leka-leka), and Pulau Panjang, and a nutmeg estate on Teor. In addition the raja of Ondor is heir to the raja of Amarsekaru's estate at Effa on Kesui, an estate that in 1986 had been mortgaged for five years to a trader in Makassar (Ujung Pandang). The raja of Kataloka personally owns most of the land in his domain, including that on which the shops of all traders stand, which has provided him with a significant income and political leverage. In Ondor, by contrast, the raja insists on selling land to traders, even having sold land to pay for his children's education.

The position of raja represents the point of articulation with the precolonial social system, because each desa is for the most part coterminous with the boundaries of a traditional domain. Indeed, the complex territorial and political history of these units is reflected in presentday desa boundaries. This history has meant that in the area around Geser, for example, desa boundaries cut across small islands and include parts of different islands in a way quite confusing to the outsider (Figure 2.9). The historical significance of this will emerge later. But it is clear that, as elsewhere, "interisland modes of interaction are of the same social structure as that which organize activities of the residents of a single island" (Alkire 1965:1); just because people are separated by water does not make the quality of their

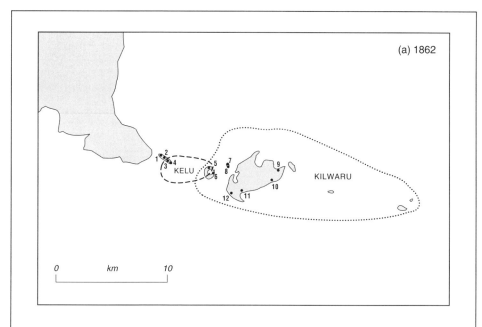

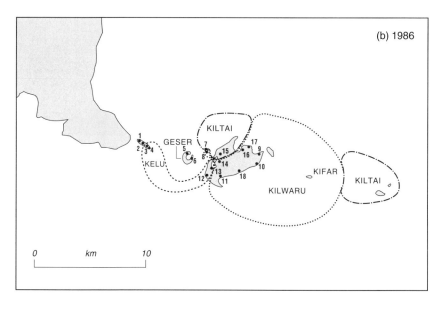

Figure 2.9. Domain (desa) boundaries in the vicinity of Geser: *a* in 1862; and *b* in 1986. Key to settlements: 1, Keffing; 2, Kilberau; 3, Kelu; 4, Kwaai; 5, Geser: Lomin; 6, Geser: Kilwaru; 7, Kiltai; 8, Kilwaru; 9, Maar; 10, Namalas; 11, Namalomin; 12, Kilfura; and the following Butonese settlements: 13, Arkel; 14, Talang Baru; 15, Arbi; 16, Wawasa; 17, Bokan; 18, Karang.

social relations different. At the same time, domains have altered in political significance and in their geographic spread. For example, Kwaai was once an independent domain with its own *matlaen* (during the Dutch period an orang kaya); now it is part of Kelu and looks to the raja of that domain for authority. However, the raja of Kelu has, since the 1940s, lived on Geser. Southeast Seram is notorious for the complicated and changing boundaries of domains and for disputes between them. This was well-known to nineteenth-century Dutch observers, such as Van der Crab (1862:62). In the midnineteenth century, Urung and Guli-guli were linked domains with an orang kaya and a pattih, respectively, Geser with a mayor, and Kiltai with a kapitan, all under the raja of Kilwaru. Indeed, Kilwaru had authority over the entire Seram Laut group, including the islands of Maar Laut and Kidang. In 1883, according to Kniphorst (1883:310), Kampung Baru on Geser, originally from Keffing, was under the authority of the raja of Geser (soa Keffing). At the same time Amarsekaru boasted a raja, Ainikke an orang kaya, and Wisalen both an orang kaya and a pattih. Similarly, at some point in the history of the domain of Amar the raja and his court moved from Amarwatu (on Gorom) to Amarsekaru on Manawoka. The island of Geser used to belong wholly to Kilwaru; the current Kilwaru settlement on Geser, described as a *tewo*, or fragment, is the oldest and came originally from Kilwaru on Kiltai.

Though there has never been any stable or centralized overarching political organization above the domain level in archipelagic Southeast Seram, marital alliance and the presence of loose interdomain confederal arrangements, cemented by a common set of ritual traditions, have served as a basis for cooperation and recruitment, as and when it became necessary. Valeri (1989:121) and others have noted how such confederal orders —articulated through a complex symbolic geography—are found in areas most involved in trade, representing "an embryonic process of political 'centering,'" rather than "centralization," and often on the periphery of centralized systems (ibid., 137). At the level of representation they were the outcome of "the application of pervasive dualistic principle to the regional alliances and conflicts induced by ancient trade" (ibid., 122). Such groupings in the Southeast Seram area, such as *seri-tahun* and *tutu* (sometimes rendered *tutup*, as in "cover" or "complete"; or *toto*, *tetu*, meaning "spine"), were, however, not always organizationally comparable. Some were federations of equals; others were semiautonomous groups in a hierarchical relationship within a larger semicentralized domain. Moreover, their existence and specific composition appear to have been in a continuous state of flux.

Into this scheme the well-known Siwa-Lima system of the western part of central Maluku and elsewhere (Van Fraassen 1987, 2:460–512; Jansen 1977 [1933]; Valeri 1989) fits only awkwardly. There is a residual acceptance by some local people that Southeast Seram is Lima in general terms, and certainly seventeenth-century refugees from Banda brought with them a preoccupation with Siwa-Lima identities (Ellen 1993:28). Moreover, political linkages to West Seram were predominantly with polities identifying with Lima; for example, the Raja Empat group connecting Kilmuri, Tobo, and Werinama (some sources substitute Mengeli for Tobo) with Lima Sepa in South Seram (Jansen 1928:490), but not to be confused with the better-documented Papuan Raja Ampat of Waigeo, Misool, Waigama, and Salawati. Keffing, because of the intermixing of both Siwa and Lima from Banda, sometimes describes its affiliation as "Siwalima." But this evidence is insufficient to permit any broad generalization of political significance, and it is easy to see how an inclination to make more of these facts than is historically justified, combined with "the application of pervasive dualistic principles," has permitted this particular reading. Similar difficulties emerge in overextending the concept of *pela* alliance to Southeast Seram from its Ambonese heartland. Certainly, some Southeast Seram polities have historical links with places in West Seram that can definitely be described as *pela* (e.g., Kilmuri) (Bartels 1977), and there is a kind of *pela* (*lidan*) between east-coast Seram villages and all of Kei, between Geser and the raja of Kilmuri, and between Amarwatu and Tual. However, such alliances do not necessarily exclude marriage—as *pela* must.

The tangible political resonances of those groupings called *tutu* and *seri-tahun* are very different from the vagueness of Siwa-Lima. The groups called *tutu* are, if we follow Jansen (1977 [1933]:104), of four kinds, each with a mathematical and geometrical value: *tutu tolu* (3: that is, 2 + 1), *tutu lima* (5: 4 [or 2 + 2] + 1), *tutu hitu* (7: 3 + 3 + 1), and *tutu siwa* (9: 4 + 4 +1). In each case, the final single digit mediates the entire class. However, I have not been able to locate any *tutu siwa* in Southeast Seram, though there is one case of *tutu waru* (eight). These alliances are not only known from the literature, but are also spoken of by contemporary peoples of the region in their oral histories, ritual, sung verse, and political rhetoric. It is easiest to describe what contemporary fieldwork yields concerning these groupings by dealing first with the Seram Laut–mainland Seram area and then the Gorom Archipelago.

A *tutu tolu* (union of three) links Geser, Kiltai, and Kilwaru. Along the east coast of mainland Seram *tutu tolu* include the groupings of Dinama, Kilbat, and Gah, linked by a single ancestor; Warus-warus, plus Sesar and Air Kasar (these last two are Buginese settlements that married into the royal clan of Buatan and are therefore incorporated by affinal linkage), and the three parts of the present-day domain of Kilmoi. These groupings still serve as a basis for invitations to life-crisis and new house rituals, as well as for recruiting labor on a reciprocal basis for public works of various kinds. There is also a *tutu waru*, linking eight settlements under the domain of Gah, and perhaps others.

In the Gorom Archipelago, according to the raja of Ondor in 1986, Gorom Laut (the island now generally known as Gorom) was originally divided into three dominant groups of allied domains: (1) *tutu tolu* (a three-clan group) centered on Amarsekaru and comprising Keliobas (providing the raja), Kelkulat, Hulihulis, and Loklomin, and the *tutu* of Rarat, Mida,

Amarwatu, Kotasiri, Kilkoda, and Miran (Buan); (2) a *tutu lima* or *liim* (five-clan group) centered on Kataloka and comprising the *samboi* (core clans) of Rumarei (providing the raja), Rumodar, Rumata, Rumbawa, plus the *tutu* of Samboru, Rumeon, Dada, Namalen, and Kinali; and (3) a *tutu tolu* (three-clan group) centered on Ondor and comprising the *samboi* of Gia-Kelilauw, Uiyara (the royal guard), Kates (the guardians of the wealth), and Kelikasa (the warriors), plus the *tutu* of Dulak, Dai, and Kelibingan. There was also a *tutu hitu* (group of seven) connecting Kilurat and Amar.

Rather different is the *seri-tahun* (*tahun* [people or tribe]) spanning the domains between Kwaos, Urung, and Keffing. According to myth, this originally was constituted through the marriage of a Keffing woman to a man from Urung and a man from Kwaos. Members of the group were expected to help each other in tasks such as mosque building and provide assistance in moments of conflict. Unlike *pela*, people from the three domains were allowed to marry; and boats continue to be named after this confederation. According to Haji Muhammad Sali Rumakat of Keffing, the confederation formed by the rajas of the five domains of Kianlaut, Kiandarat, Kwaos, Urung, and Keffing to organize against the Dutch was also described as *seri-tahun*. Whatever the combination of domains described as *seri-tahun*, and there are others, they always include the core three of Keffing, Urung, and Kwaos, and Keffing appears as some kind of primus inter pares.

2.5. Corporate Descent Groups and Property Relations

When not acting as agents of the Indonesian state, rajas are heads of traditional domains composed of a small number of patrilineal descent groups or clans *(etar)*, sometimes referred to by the widely understood Moluccan Malay term "soa." The minimum number of *etar* in any one domain is three, and in every case there is a strong tendency to distinguish autochthonous *etar* from groups of historically recent migrants (which may become *etar* in their own right over time). Van der Leeden (1983:82) used the terms "dynastic" and "nondynastic" clans to refer to this same difference in the Raja Ampat Islands. A list of some of the Southeast Seram autochthonous *etar* and their distribution is provided in Table 2.1. Autochthonous *etar* may themselves be conveniently subdivided into core *etar* (the *samboi*) and the rest. Thus, in Ondor the four core *(samboi) etar* are viewed as descendants of those ancestors spoken of in myth who originally came from the central mountains of Gorom. In addition there are eight other autochthonous *etar* *(etar alu)*: Pentang, Balili, Katotak, Makar, Kelbaun, Kelsuangi, Salamu, and Kilsodi. For Kilwaru, it is the sacred *kayur* tree that, through its four branches, gave rise to four core *etar*, one of them Kailen (the *etar* of the current raja), and the others, dispersing to each of South, North, and West Seram. Indeed, many domains claim the privilege of being the original center of creation; the dispersal of local peoples generates rival mythic histories

Table 2.1. The partial distribution of some putatively "indigenous" East Seram *etar*

Etar	Domain, Island, or Settlement	*Etar*	Domain, Island, or Settlement
Derlaen	Kidang, Garogos	Rumalas	Keta-Kwaos
Ena	Kilfura, Geser (Kilwaru), Kifar (Kilwaru), Maar, Kiltai, Kidang	Rumalolas	Kwaai, Kidang
		Rumalowa(k)	Rumatau, Kelu
		Rumalutur	Kiltai, Kwaai
Kastella	Aruan, Keffing, Kiltai, Kilberau (Kelu), Tarui, Tamher Timor	Rumandan	Keta-Kianlaut
		Rumarei	Kataloka
		Rumata	Samboru, Kataloka
Kelderak	Dinama, Terui	Rumatamerik	Dinama, Terui
Kelian	Geser (Kilwaru), Air Nanang, Namalomin (Kilwaru)	Rumau	Kifar (Kilwaru), Maar
Kelibia	Rumatau, Kelu, Kilfura, Namalomin (Kilwaru), Maar, Kilberau	Rumbati	Keta-Kwaos
		Rumbawa	Kataloka, Samboru, Garogos
		Rumboli	Aruan (from Mela)
Kelirei	Walang Tengah	Rumbou	Rumadan, Bati, Garogos
Keliwo	Kilfura, Kelu, Amarwatu	Rumdauer	Aruan
Kilei	Kilberau (Kelu)	Rumeon	Kwaos
Kiliwou	Kifar (Kilwaru)	Rumesi	Kwaai
Kilosa	Undur (Kilmuri)	Rumfeka	Kidang
Kilutur	Amarwatu	Rumfot	Dinama
Kwaai-Rumaratu	Kilmuri	Rumodar	Kilfura, Kataloka, Dinama, Garogos
Obas	Namalomin (Kilwaru)		
Ramaratu	Selagur (from Geser)	Rumoga	Bati
Rumadan	Rumatau, Kelu, Kwaos, Keffing	Rumoma(r)	Selagur, Amarwatu
		Rumonin	Keffing, Kilberau (Kelu), mythically from Onin
Rumadei	Kilfura, Keffing, Warus-warus, Kelu, Rumatau	Rumuar	Selagur, Urung (from Kianlaut)
Rumaen	Selagur, Aruan, Kianlaut, Kilwerane, Nama		
		Rumwo	Keta-Kianlaut
Rumakamar	Keta-Kwaos, Kilmuri	Rumwokas	Geser, Kiandarat, Kiriga
Rumakat	Kwaos, Keffing, Kidang, Garogos	Safua	Aruan, Kianlaut, Kilwerane, Nama
Rumakwaai	Amarwatu	Senaji	Guli-guli (from Ternate)
Rumalaen	Maar, Rumadan, Selagur, Kianlaut, Kilwerane, Nama	Waaroi	Kelu (from Tidore)
		Wokas	Urung (from Kwaos-Keta)

of legitimation. Thus, Kiltai claims to have once owned all Seram, until their rights were usurped by, or gifted to, various immigrant *etar*. Thus, for those on Kiltai who guard the collective memory, Kilwaru (*Wawa ria*) came originally from Gorom and was given land by Kiltai. Kiltai claims to have exercised suzerainty formerly (before the Dutch arrived) from Hatumeten in the west to Hutubongooi (near Bula) to the north and as far as Manawoka to the southeast. Similarly, Keffing gifted part of the island of Seram Rei to refugees (Kelu and Kwaai) from Seram Laut.

Table 2.2. Distribution of some immigrant clan names in Southeast Seram

Name	Origin	Distribution
Alkatiry	Banda (Arab)	Geser
Andi	Bugis	Kwaos
Bugis	Bugis	Kelu, Maar, Kilberau (Kelu)
Dertuban	Kei	Kelu
Hatala	Batumerah (Ambon)	Rumadan, Kwaos (fled the Dutch; formerly provided imam of Al Fatah mosque, Ambon)
Iskandar	Arabic	Kwaos
Lenhuat	Kei	Kelu
Maba	Tobelo	Kilberau
Mandar	Mandarese	Kwaai, Kelu, Kilberau (Kelu)
Rahanusun	Kei	Kelu, Kilberau (Kelu)
Sabandar	Syahbandar	Kilmuri
Siun	Salayor	Kelu
Sulawesi	Sulawesi	Kwaai, Kelu
Taip	Bugis	Geser (Kilwaru)

As well as autochthonous *etar* moving outward, most domains also contain immigrant clans (Table 2.2). In Ondor these are the Bugis clans of Dain Perani, Dain Dain Perati, and Wajo. Of course, the distinction between autochthonous and outsider, core and periphery, is one that is historically changing as various clans migrate, become extinct, or are progressively absorbed into the core. The way in which such real-time population movements create new political realities, which are in turn symbolically legitimized through myth, is what Platenkamp (1993:61) has called "the cosmological valorisation of historical events."

Each *etar* has a traditional headman *(mancialen)*, distinguished from the state-recognized "kepala soa" (now "kepala dusun"). In Kataloka the position of kepala soa is assigned by the raja to an individual for an indefinite period; the deputy of a kepala soa in Kataloka is called *warnemen* (Soselisa 1996:36). Some polities (such as Kataloka) also had kapitan responsible for organizing war parties, a position that is lacking in polities without a tradition of warfare (e.g., Warus-warus); and some polities also had an *anaklaen*, a council. There are other traditional roles, and various new ones imposed by the requirements of Indonesian government, which are sometimes combined with the old titles where there are functional similarities.

The notion of core autochthonous *etar* providing the raja is, on the face of it, somewhat at odds with another equally strong tradition, namely that of immigrant rulers. This is a widespread idea in the political cultures of island Southeast Asia; indeed the Dumézilian notion of "the stranger king" has been raised by some as a global structural principle in social formations of a particular kind (Sahlins 1981). Here, however, it is sufficient to say that it provides a principle of historical legitimacy, but also, in some cases, continues to influence current practice. Thus, the rulers of Amarsekaru came from outside, and Kiltai (Kastella) and other origin myths speak of Portuguese origins. At some point in the fairly distant past, the sultan of Tidore married the daughter of the raja of Kataloka; as "mas kawin" (bridewealth), the sultan gave Kataloka Usung, Buan, Rumanama, and Kulgoa. Warus-warus has family relations with Misool, and the kapitan of Kilkasa (Gorom) is descended from immigrants from Kisar.

But in addition to mythologized and not-so-mythologized histories of immigrant ruling dynasties, these islands have demonstrated the capacity to absorb thousands of foreigners over many hundreds of years. The entire Southeast Seram littoral, but particularly the core area, has been the locus of much interethnic mixing for centuries, showing various degrees of integration, precisely because it is a well-connected central place. The groups involved in these patterns of movement have included local peoples, migrating spontaneously for economic motives, as well as politically motivated relocations, prompted first by the Dutch and then by the Indonesian authorities. Mountain Alifuru have, as in many parts of Seram, moved to more accessible coastal locations, such as Mogosinis, a village in the domain of Urung, or Bati in the domains of Kiandarat and Kianlaut. Migrants from Kei Besar have relocated in the domain of Kilmuri and in the villages of Gauer in Kianlaut. And then there have been those drawn in by trade. The slave trade with New Guinea (of which more will be said later in this section) resulted in an influx of Melanesians who, through a relaxation in the conditions of servitude, have been absorbed. The mangrove village of Kwamar, for example, is said to have been peopled by Papuans, former slaves, and perhaps also returning mixed Serammer-Papuan settlers. More recently it has been a haven for Hadhrami Arab land settlers. Other Arabs migrated via Werinama to Guli-guli. Bosscher (1855:34–42) and De Hollander (1895) noted over a century ago the mixture of ethnicities in Kilmuri and on Seram Laut: Bugis-Makasarese, Tobelorese, Balinese, and Papuans. In some cases this history is only evident in clan names and mythic histories; in others it is part of a contemporary ethnic reality. And then there are the Butonese and Chinese. With the large inflow of immigrants over the centuries one perhaps would have expected a correspondingly diverse system of kinship. For the most part, however, immigrants have been absorbed into the general regionwide system. The only exceptions are recent immigrants in some of the larger centers (such as Chinese and Arab traders in Geser) and in villages of recent migrants (such as Butonese and to a lesser extent Bugis). Some of the implications of ethnic difference for the organization of trade are explored further in chapter 9.

We must now return to a consideration of some more formal aspects of Southeast Seram littoral kinship organization. *Etar* are composed of *rumara*, literally "houses" (e.g., Rumakat, Rumadan), bound together by common residence, consanguinity, and descent. The relationship between *etar* and *rumara* is a fluid (one might almost say a segmentary) one, and over time *rumara* may assume the status of *etar*, which is why so many have names prefixed by *rum-*. In turn, *rumara* or *etar* names may come to designate entire settlements (*wanu*), which may themselves contain various *etar* and *rumara*. In addition, *etar* may exhibit within themselves lines of relative seniority and subordination. Thus in Kiltai, the core *etar* Kastella is composed of two descent lines at the *rumara* level: Rumalaen (the larger and more senior) and Rumaokat (the smaller and more junior).

Present-day Southeast Seram descent groups—both *etar* and *rumara*—are not exogamous, and the rate of in-marriage is high; indeed it is preferred. Close kin who are excluded as partners are those fed from the same breast (*roh susu* [i.e., blood siblings or children wet-nursed together]), or a mother of a brother or the younger sibling of an existing spouse. Thus, marriage between cousins (*wini, hi-wini* = W, H, MBD, MBS, MZS, MZD, FBS, FBD, FZS, FZD), matrilateral or patrilateral, cross or parallel, is quite common. Such high rates of descent-group endogamy are partly due to the relatively small number of *etar* or *rumara* in any one place, bolstered by Muslim preferential marriage among close kin; though there are also customary notions that "blood should not go outside" (*rara sing aluar bolo*), and the low cost of such marriages is also a consideration (Soselisa 1995:51). Formerly, all marriages in Kataloka are said to have been within the *etar*, and within the *etar* often within particular descent lines, especially where core high-status *etar* are concerned (e.g., Tukwain within Rumbawa, and Wattimena within Rumarei). Of the 297 extant marriages recorded in 1986 for twenty settlements, 30 percent were within the *etar* (though not necessarily within the same settlement or domain). Soselisa (1995:51) reported that in Garogos in 1993 fifteen out of the forty-five extant marriages were within the *etar*. In Kwaos and Keffing in 1986, extra-*etar* marriages were largely between just three descent groups: Rumadan and Rumadaul, and between Rumadaul and Rumakat. Despite the tendency toward descent-group endogamy in *samboi* clans, inter-*etar* marriages between families of rajas from different domains are still common, for example, Kataloka with Kilmuri. A ruler, or someone destined to be a ruler, traditionally was required to marry the offspring of another ruler elsewhere or within his own *etar* and definitely not into another clan within the domain.

STRATIFICATION

Each domain in Southeast Seram was stratified traditionally into three classes: *matlaen* (the raja and his kin), *bala* (commoners), and *moi* (slaves), though Riedel (1886:154) recorded the terms *gahiin, mahun,* and *moi,* respectively. Thus, in Amarwatu, Rumakwaai provides the raja and Rumagutawan the raja's bodyguard. In Kataloka there are four royal *etar*: Rumarei (the clan of the raja himself); Rumodar, providing in the form of its leader a personal manservant; Rumbawa, providing a keeper of the treasury to advise on financial matters; and Rumata, providing warriors under the leadership of the *kobaresi* (or kapitan). In Amarsekaru there are also four noble *etar* (out of some thirteen) occupying a similar relationship. The stratification system restricts marriage choices, encourages endogamy, and takes on a regional dimension through marital alliances, particularly between the families of rajas.

Religious functionaries also hold positions within particular *etar,* and sometimes that of the raja also provides the imam. Religious functionaries, however, are less likely to be linked to core authochthonous clans. For example in the domain of Dai on Gorom, different core *etar* provide various secular and religious functionaries as follows: Kelerei, *matlaen* (raja), *kobaresi* (kapitan); Kelibai, imam (communal prayer leader); Adi, marbut (caretaker of the mosque); Rumasilan, khatib (preacher and mosque official); Kelian, modin (caller to prayer and circumciser). The allocation of religious functionaries in this fashion is not everywhere the same (some roles are combined in a single *etar)*, but in every case there was an expectation that succession to office would descend through the male line.

Below everyone else were slaves (*moi* or *arobi*). According to local oral tradtion, slaves were originally native Moluccans, generally obtained on mainland Seram, but all historic references and contemporary evidence suggest that for at least five hundred years they have been mainly of Papuan origin, obtained through barter. Slaves traditionally are distinguished between those exchanged or bought (*tebus*, redeemed or obtained as compensation) and others (*moi to-tous*), presumably captured in war. In much of the area a clearly identifiable slave class has disappeared, though it is still distinguishable in parts of Gorom, in Kiltai, and Keffing. Papuan ex-slaves are now widely employed as domestic servants, particularly in the houses of rajas. At the current time they are theoretically free persons, although they continue to occupy a semiservile position, living in poor accommodations, working as hewers of wood and drawers of water. They are often claimed to be physically distinct from the rest of the population (with characteristically Melanesian features), though there has been so much interbreeding that physical distinctiveness is no longer a really reliable indicator of slave status. It is still the case that ex-slaves can marry those of nonslave descent only with difficulty (indeed in the past they were not permitted to marry at all); neither can they in practice hold official and religious office. Though officially and legally equal with nonslaves, they continue to perform menial tasks. Slaves took their name and clan from their owners, and slave women often had children, *moi anak*, by illicit union. Slaves had separate *etar* incorporated into the clans of their owners. Mohammed Amin Kelian of Kilwaru was still able to recall in 1986 how his father had obtained Papuan child slaves in exchange for tobacco.

DISPENSION OF PROPERTY

For the land territories of each domain (that is, anything above the high-water line, or *baal*), we can begin by distinguishing village land, *baal wanu*, consisting of commonly held resources such as forest and rivers, from *baal etar*, clan land used for gardens (*um*), and from *baal sii-sii*, individual land (often plantations). Inheritance is usually through the senior male line. If there is more than one son, apportionment is at the discretion of the eldest son, though the eldest son usually receives the house. Landed property may pass through a daughter only if there is no son. Affines generally have rights of access to land (for example, a man can take produce from his wife's land) though these are never transferred formally at marriage. Land sale of any kind is rare. In Kataloka if you wish to sell land you must first obtain permission from the raja, and you are not allowed to pawn (*gadei*) or mort gage harvests of nutmeg or cloves and not allowed to sell land to Bugis, Makassans, and Arab or Chinese traders. Disputes over land between two domains or desa sometimes lead to armed conflict, as between Miran and Dai over the boundary in the center of the island of Gorom in the early 1980s. It is reasonable to assume that these rather inflexible features of land transmission in Kataloka are related to its overall scarcity. Certainly, arrangements on mainland Seram are more flexible, and we may assume in this respect a graded difference between the land-depleted archipelago and land-sufficient mainland domains.

Reef (*siaru*) and foreshore (*moti*) are usually regarded as being owned by a domain, with control vested in the person of the ruler or the *etar* providing the traditional ruler, rather than by individuals (though see Lapian 1981:2). Thus, the Kiltai reef is owned by the *etar* Kastella, and the raja is considered a kind of "tuan laut," lord of the sea. In Kataloka, on Gorom, maritime as well as territorial resources are effectively much more under the personal control of the raja. In the Geser-Gorom Archipelago more generally there can be little doubt that the absence of significant territorial resources, and the dependence of small domains on the production of sea produce for exchange over many centuries, has led to rights in marine resources being tightly defined and staunchly defended. Conflict has, therefore, been common.

The position with regard to the domain of Keffing on the island of Seram Rei is indicative of the complexities of tenurial issues with respect to reef. Keffing not only possesses the reef surrounding the island of Seram Rei but also that along the mainland Seram coast between the domains of Kwamar and Kwaos. With no sources of fuelwood on Seram Rei itself, this usefully provides inhabitants of the domain with access to as much mangrove firewood as they need, in addition to exercising control over sea produce. By comparison, the domain of Kelu on Seram Rei, which originally came from Kilfura on Seram Laut, has no reef of its own and no automatic rights of access (Figure 2.10). Nevertheless, over the years Kelu has obtained a series of entitlements that ensure a modus vivendi, though from time to time these have been disputed. We know that one such occasion occurred in 1840 with respect to the rights for opening and closing *sasi* (ritual regulation of the harvesting of resources, usually to ensure sustainable levels of extraction or to regulate amounts coming onto the market). In this case,

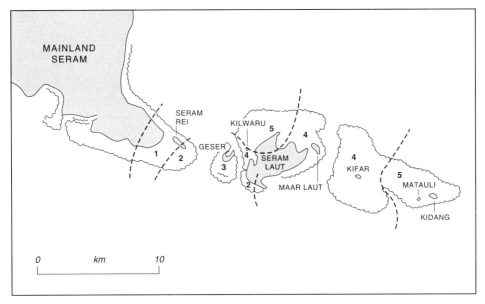

Figure 2.10. Reef ownership in the Seram Laut Archipelago, 1986: 1, Keffing; 2, Kelu; 3, Geser; 4, Kilwaru; 5, Kiltai.

the parties had sought a ruling from the Resident (colonial administrator) in Banda with respect to the tradition of imposing a *sasi* after the death of a ruler, which thereafter provided a baseline in other disputes.[6] We know this because a copy of that ruling is still in the possession of the raja of Kelu and resembles similar documents of colonial origin still held by rulers and used as evidence in disputes and as part of the paraphernalia of legitimating traditional authority (Ellen 1997). Another case, which first came to light in 1838, involved the "gezaghebber" (a village head temporarily recognized by the Dutch) of Kilwaru and the orang kaya of Kiltai, and concerned conflict over access to reef rich in agar-agar near Kidang. On that occasion, the judgment reached by Resident Lans on 14 August 1838 was that Kiltai owned the reef, though the dispute continued in one form or another for the best part of another hundred years. [7]

The underlying rule governing access (as in many other parts of Indonesia) is that free-swimming fish are a common resource but that sessile (apparently motionless) sea produce adhering to rock and reef, such as shellfish, trepang (sea cucumbers), agar-agar, and similar produce, are owned by the domain for which the reef is a territorial extension. The sea is not considered separate from the land, and a domain (in this sense a zone of political influence) consists of both land and sea. Problems occur where resources are irregularly distributed, and in particular when resources acquire a commercial value (that is, become commodities or "hasil laut"). Since the eighteenth century, at least, trepang, agar-agar, and various shellfish have become commodities in this sense, vital to the reproduction of these small island societies through external exchange. In such circumstances, ambiguity provides grounds for contention, conflict, and litigation, as where there are gray areas in defining edges of the reef or tidal zone. Complications also arise owing to the historic movement of local populations. As the cases just cited suggest, this often creates intricate and involuted patterns of resource entitlement and prohibition that provide reasons for disputes over many decades, even centuries. So although in theory it is possible for a Kilwaru *wean* or sero (a semipermanent fish trap of wood and bamboo fencing) to operate in Kiltai waters, in practice it is wise to seek some relevant authority; and conversely where rights are well established and understood, and political relations generally harmonious, though in theory permission to extract hasil laut might be necessary, in practice the conditionality is waived.

To show how some of these rights work out in practice it is instructive to refer to the case of Garogos, an inhabited cay that although located at the far eastern end of the Seram Laut reef is very firmly part of the traditional domain of Kataloka on Gorom. Outsiders wishing to fish on the Garogos reef require permission from the kepala soa, or sometimes the modin or khatib (that is, those who are accepted as representing the raja of Kataloka, whose reef it is, in his absence). It is also they who may open and close a *sasi* for trepang and other resources because Garogos is too far from Kataloka for the raja himself to make decisions. Local subjects of the raja do not require permission to fish or extract hasil laut, and guard the sea on his behalf, in the same way that he is expected to protect them when the occasion arises. People on islands near Garogos (e.g., Kidang), though part of a different domain, have secondary rights, acquired through kinship and marriage. Indeed, it is advantageous for people on small, resource-depleted islands (of which Garogos is an extreme example) to marry out, and this is often still quite consistent with the preference for clan endogamy, given the distribution of clans. People from other islands may enter, with permission of the raja, for the harvesting of specified resources. Other villages within the domain of Kataloka wishing to fish rather than extract hasil laut simply state their purpose to the kepala soa or raja. Those in domains of the Gorom group, other than Kataloka, need the permission of the raja or kepala soa, though permission is not required for waters off the reef. By contrast, if a Geserese *ang guik* (a small, open, plank-built boat that nowadays specializes in the fishing of the barred garfish [*neba, Hemiramphus far*]) wishes to work off Garogos, its owner must first seek permission. Then there are those who pay for access: commercial fishermen, villagers from other domains farther away in the East Seram area (e.g., Keffing), who especially come in the east monsoon to catch garfish in deep water. They must ask permission of the raja or the kepala soa, who then reports to the raja. They are required to pay for a period of say ten to twenty days (25,000–30,000 rupiah in 1993, shared between the raja of Kataloka and the kepala soa of Garogos, for their respective jurisdictions.) Finally, there are those from Ambon, Madura, Buton, and elsewhere (including businesses from Makassar or even Hong Kong), who must ask permission of the raja directly and also pay a fee. These are generally after "mamin," "garopa" (*Epinephelus* spp.), and other deep-sea export fish (Soselisa 1996:32–33). Conflict resulting from infringement of these regulations is common and in most cases is dealt with and fines exacted by the ruler of the domain or his representatives, without coming before Indonesian state institutions. But catching illegal fishermen is difficult, which is why locals say that they only really have control of reef, *moti*. Disputes over the illegal harvesting of fish from *lutur* (stone traps) are frequent, as between Samboru and Namalen in 1986.

There is, therefore, no sudden break between the rights of locals and outsiders, but rather a gradation between localities and domains, between insiders and outsiders, with no sharp divisions. Thus, marine tenure reflects other complex regional interrelations and the absence of overarching authority beyond the domain (that is, a web of rules and obligations binding polities and settlements together [such as *tutu tolu*], reflected in ethnicity, clan distribution, and so on). Similarly, the formal boundaries around domains are often cut across by kinship ties. Thus, Garogos, formally under the jurisdiction of the raja of Kataloka, has close descent and affinal ties with Kidang, under the authority of Kiltai, with reciprocal fishing rights. At the same time, Garogos people living on Kidang remain under the jurisdiction of the raja of Kataloka. Because Kidang has more agricultural land, it effectively subsidizes the diet of Garogos along genealogical lines. Garogos also has kinship ties—the common presence of the *etar* Rumakat—with Namalas and Maar on Seram Laut, and some of these clansmen visit Garogos for fishing and petty trade. Garogos also has kinship ties with Pulau Panjang, and here taro, manioc, and coconut are bartered for sea produce, though Panjang residents may also come to sell. Barter and sale are therefore not mutually exclusive and may be simultaneously engaged in. Garogos has permission from the kepala soa to collect firewood from Panjang or buy it from locals and timber for canoes. There are similar ties with Manawoka. Garogos people barter sea produce for sago flour (*bai*), sago leaves (for thatch), and *watu suat* (sago ovens) with mainland Southeast Seram, where they also buy canoes (Soselisa 1995:48–49).

The border between the claims of particular domains, where the intermediary area is deep sea, is the midpoint between islands. On Garogos people say that they can tell if they are in their own area by the *kedas*—these are basically local currents, not to be confused with *rurut*, major currents that connect the sea around major island groups (see chapter 6.4; and Soselisa 1996:32). *Trochus* (lola [*Trochus niloticus, Tectus pyrarimis*]), usually collected in the calm, clear seas of the west monsoon, is protected by *ngaam (sasi)* controlled by the raja. Similarly *nam kebi* is a *sasi* for trepang opened around March by the raja and imam. If there are enough trepang it may last for two months.[8] Apart from the obvious extraterritorial limits that a domain claims (usually those determined by the edge of a fringing reef), the width of sea claimed relates to what was in the past defensible (e.g., within the range of a cannon [lantaka, or *lilla*] shot), between four and five kilometers. Fishermen, on the whole, keep within the protective lee of the mountains. This same limit determines rights to salvage from wrecked vessels (the wrecking and sinking, particularly of small motor vessels, in the waters of Southeast Seram is a routine occurrence). When it comes to salvage, a distinction is made between coastal waters and the high seas (Lapian 1981:2), and beyond the coast the sea is regarded as a commons.

2.6. Fishing

This is a book about trade rather than fishing. However, because fishing is so important and complex an activity in the area upon which I focus, because both activities share a waterborne technology imposing similar kinds of constraints and offering similar opportunities, and because it connects with matters discussed in later chapters, something must be said about it beyond simply reporting its presence.

As befits a people of the sea, fish are caught using a large number of different methods: numerous techniques involving hand collecting, beating, and vibration, such as *sekeu*, *ker-ker*, and *tali kor* (Figure 2.11); spearing (*solo-solon*, a bamboo shaft with double-pronged metal head); weighted fish spears and harpoons (*ladung*); spearguns (*hanah ian*); harpooning (*soran*, *ter*, *acu*); various hook (*aul*) and line techniques; nets; portable and fixed permanent traps; and poisons (e.g., *tua* root [*Anamirta cocculus*], *simurut* root [*Derris eliptica*], and other roots, stalks, and vines). Sometimes techniques are combined. Thus, *tali kor* may involve the application of poisons and nowadays the incorporation of nets. What techniques are used and what resources extracted depends on seasonality, geography, lunar cycles,

Figure 2.11. Closing in to spear fish disoriented by *tali kor* vibration, Garogos, 16 May 1986.

tides, habitats, and animal behavior. Seafood of all kinds is extracted. Shellfish, crustaceans, octopuses, cuttlefish, squid, sea urchins, and sea cucumbers are collected, preferably during the east monsoon, though the best season for collecting from reefs is the west monsoon, with its *moti kei* (very low tides). Other invertebrates include various worms such as *lauer*, which can only be collected during March–April and November–December and then only for the seventeen to eighteen days of the new moon, when they rise to breed. Turtles, sharks, rays, dolphins, and dugongs (*roiin*) are hunted using harpoons: dolphins mainly when they get caught in nets, but dugongs deliberately at night during the east monsoon. The main dugong-hunting villages during the 1980s were Maar, Kifar, and Garogos. The meat is eaten locally and any surplus sold dried. The pelagic fish of the region are locally divided into those of the intertidal zone (*ian moti*), those of the reef (*ian watu*), and those of the open sea (*ian lau*).

Fishing with nets is a relatively recent innovation. The first nets were introduced to Keffing during the Dutch period, but as a widespread technique they date back no further than the Japanese period (1942–1945). Before that, plaited bamboo walling was used as a kind of net. Five main kinds of nets are used at the current time: the *fukat* (*huat*) *guik,* a large seine used in combination with *guik* boats for fishing for garfish; the *fukat subra*, a gill net used for flying fish, such as *Cypselurus nigripennis*; the *fukat watu*, a small seine used for all kinds of fish; the *jaring fukat,* for *Clupea,* herrings, and sardines; and the *jala selat* (*katula*), a throw or casting net. Throw nets may be used by solitary fishermen working along a beach, or when working in pairs from a dugout canoe. Night offshore reef fishing (*balobe* or *manyulu*), also from a canoe using a small net and lamp, and hauling in the net in the morning, is a common way of catching *ubi (Cypselurus poecilopterus)* during the west monsoon. Nets may also be attached to poles that are placed permanently in the reef, a technique similar to semipermanent traps discussed later in this section.

The most important single fish species for both subsistence and exchange is *neba*, Ambonese Malay julung (the barred garfish, *Hemiramphus far*). In season, this is caught in prodigious quantities in deep waters, both by individual fishermen and *ang guik* crews (Figure 2.12). It is not unusual for a solitary fisherman using a *fukat guik* to catch five hundred garfish in one night. With an *ang guik* and a minimum crew of twelve (only used in daytime), it is quite common to net ten thousand, and as many as twenty-five thousand with larger crews of up to twenty. Only a small proportion of such a catch can be eaten fresh, so the aim is to dispose of as many as possible as quickly as possible for drying or smoking. Garfish lay their eggs on the reef (*bas*), exhibiting a characteristic playing and jumping behavior. In the east monsoon they are large but limited in numbers; in the west monsoon they are more plentiful but not so large. Some people specialize in catching garfish using *ang guik*, though sometimes other species are caught using a canoe. Fishing times are determined by (a) lunar indicators (e.g., the *lauer* upon which the garfish feed hatch on the seventeenth and eigh-

Figure 2.12.
Threading garfish
after large catch
using *ang guik* boats
and nets, Geser,
Kampung Baru,
11 March 1986.

teenth days of the new moon and the sea cucumber *kebi susu* lays its eggs
on the twenty-seventh and twenty-eighth days of the moon, so ensuring
that the first three days of each new moon are good for fishing); (b) the
state of the tide and reef; and (c) the seasons, which in particular places create choppy seas or wave motion that restrict activity.

Hand-held fish traps (*dari*) come in at least four types, designed to catch
particular kinds of fish, and are made from rattan, liana, traditional fibers
(such as pandanus), and cotton or synthetic netting. There are also *wu*,
conical traps of plaited bamboo with necks that prevent the escape of
caught prey. These are used primarily by women on the reefs or in rock
pools at low tide and in shallow freshwater. Between the hand-held traps

and stone traps are *wean* (in Indonesian sero): semipermanent fixed traps made of wood and bamboo. These can only be erected in shallow water where there is sand and are constructed with the head (the trap) toward the coral reef and the foot (the mouth) toward the coast. They are only a temporary modification of the seascape. Permission is not required to erect them, and the fish are collected at low tide every day. *Wean* are probably of western Indonesian origin, though they were certainly present in the Seram Laut area by the seventeenth century, as attested by the map depicted in Figure 3.10. *Wean* currently are found off Keffing and Kiltai, but their effectiveness is limited by the disturbance of heavy motorboat traffic. Nevertheless, they do appear to be replacing fixed stone traps, to which we shall now turn.

Fixed traps are the most interesting and relevant for our purpose here because they represent a way in which humans have altered the shape of the microlandscape over many centuries. *Dabangat* (*watu*), for example, are recognizable as lines of stones parallel to the shore in the intertidal zone. They traditionally are used in conjunction with a net to seaward that is drawn toward the row of stones, thus trapping fish between the net and the stones, and are then retrieved by hand. Such devices can still be seen between Kilgah and Suru on the east coast of Seram. The second kind of permanent stone trap is the *lutur* (sero batu in Ambonese Malay), a structure of uncemented stones built out from the shore like a curved low jetty, or with V-shaped wings and a circular trap at the base of the V, or more simply a modification of naturally occuring reef pools achieved by moving loose material to form a barrier along the seaward edge to drive fish into the belly of the trap. In terms of collective effort, *lutur* represent a considerable investment, and some are probably over one hundred years old. They need to be renovated regularly, after wave damage in the east monsoon. Fish are driven into the closed end of a *lutur* and the entrance blocked with canoes. *Lutur* are used for various species of fish and also prawns, and may be up to 1 meter high. Low-walled *lutur* are used especially for a kind of trepang called *kebi susu*. There are *lutur* distributed along the entire mangrove coast of mainland East Seram between Air Nanang and Kwaos. In Keta Kwaos, for example, there are some *lutur* owned by individual *etar* and others by *rumara* (e.g., Rumalaen and Garogos). Soselisa (1995:113) reported eight on Garogos in the early 1990s, but only two were in working order at that time. They are treated as a kind of hereditary wealth with symbolic as well as practical utility, though few are built nowadays.

Though fishing is everywhere important, the techniques employed and levels of extraction vary from place to place, in some cases due to ecological constraints. For example, fishing in Kwaos and along other parts of the mainland is difficult, and this and the converse absence of vegetable foods and basic starch in many of the islands has sustained a classic fish-for-sago exchange that is examined further in chapters 7 and 8. There is also seasonal variation in patterns of fishing, as in Warus-warus, where

the east monsoon permits the use of sero, and the west monsoon is appropriate for collecting fish, crustaceans, and mollusks from the reefs and
intertidal zone. Although commercial fishing yields economic benefits for
some and is regulated through *sasi*-like institutions, it has not benefited
all. On Garogos and other small islands quite dependent on the import of
other foods, increasing commercial extraction of sea resources by both
locals and outsiders has led to increasing poverty (Soselisa 1996:28).
Though the fishing grounds around Seram Laut, for example, may appear
rich, the viability and sustainability of fishing is maintained only by
adopting a broad-spectrum strategy that involves traditional forms of regulation and many different techniques to ensure production under various ecological, seasonal, and social conditions. Paradoxically, fishing
underpins the livelihood of these small communities, in both subsistence
and exchange terms, but even here many are dependent on mainland
Seram for the very equipment to conduct it effectively. The practices of
drying, salting, and smoking fish are vital for communities that depend
on fish for income, because fresh fish cannot be marketed. Fishermen are
constantly making decisions about the strategies they should best adopt
given often competing needs. Thus, the incentive to spend time fishing
for sharks, which under the market conditions prevailing during the
1980s and 1990s yielded good cash returns for fins and tails, might be at
the expense of that fishing best suited to provide for home consumption.
As well as knowing how best to optimize the use of time and methods,
selecting strategies also involves choosing to be a member of fishing
groups (such as *tali kor* groups), investing in equipment, and choice of
fishing location. Fishing methods have changed radically over the last half
century, with the introduction of large nets, nylon line, and motorized
canoes. Though this has eroded traditional methods in places, traps and
even *tali kor* are still important, as marginalized fishing households seek to
survive the twin depredations of marine resource depletion and competition with commercial and more capitalized fisheries.

2.7. Subsistence Economy and the Importance of Trade

What I have said so far of Southeast Seram political organization, both of
the past and of the present, indicates a high degree of devolved control, a
large number of small independent units with few overarching power relations. That this pattern has existed over a period of at least five hundred
years will be substantiated in the next two chapters of this book. But if the
political organization might be said to exhibit—at a regional level—all the
characteristics of mechanical solidarity, then the whole is integrated
organically by a complex spatial division of economic labor, in which even
the most basic subsistence processes can be seen only in the context of
interisland organization. This is the key to understanding the cultural and

social uniformity of the area, its geographical extent, pivotal role in trade, and capacity to adapt to changing conditions, despite its political diffuseness. The small size of the domains historically has permitted quick, flexible, and locally effective responses in decision making that help counter the unpredictability accompanying relations with external powers, and has enabled more focused resource management in a capricious and marginal environment. Indeed, some of the distinctive features of political and economic organization in Southeast Seram are deliberate strategies developed over the long term to handle the consequences of resource and demographic pressure: exchange and specialization, and various collective arrangements for regulating extraction. In addition there is evidence of long-term out-migration from the center (e.g., from Kiltai and Keffing) to the periphery (e.g., Masiwang), reflected in the distribution of *etar* names, as well as continuing seasonal labor migration to Tehoru and other places during the clove season.

The East and Southeast Seram littorals, together with the Gorom Archipelago, represent the periphery of the area, are the least integrated economically with other parts of the system, and are less dependent on imports for basic subsistence. The picture is not necessarily reciprocal. By contrast, the central zone around Geser (Figure 2.1) exhibits a high degree of internal spatial division of labor and is economically dependent upon the periphery. In the Seram Laut Archipelago, only Seram Laut itself has sufficient land for cultivation, and this is restricted. The island settlements on Kiltai (Kiltai itself and Kilwaru) have access to land on Seram Laut, but this only supports meager plots of tubers, vegetables, and some fruit. The islands of Geser, Keffing, and Garogos have no garden land at all, and fuelwood, vegetable food, and sago (*suat*) have to be purchased from Seram Laut or brought in from the southern and eastern extremes of mainland Seram.

Human settlements built in such precarious localities are of two types: those that are almost entirely devoted to human settlement, with little vegetation, let alone gardens; and those with very limited agricultural land. Temporary fishing settlements on small islands and those that have become permanent (e.g., Garogos) fall into the first category. Kwamar falls into the second category. The gardens contain few crops, mainly bananas, *Vigna radiatus*, manioc, and chili, and are small and rudimentary (as in Seram Laut). Where there is soil on the larger islands it is often poor, and gardens are created on steep and rocky ground (e.g., at Kilfura on Seram Laut, Amarsekaru on Manawoka, and Ondor on Gorom). These conditions restrict the crops that can be grown and the yields that can be obtained. In such circumstances bitter manioc (*Manihot esculenta*, or locally *pangala*) is one of the few reliable cultigens, and it is hardly surprising that in the absence of sago it is manioc that is prepared in imitation (*suat pangala*) of the culturally more desirable sago. On mainland Seram, where garden land outside the mangrove area is relatively plentiful, gardens are vulnerable to pig predation due to the absence of systematic hunting by an overwhelmingly Muslim population. Despite elaborate fencing, gardening has, in places, been virtually abandoned.

However, there are some surprises. The settlement on Garogos is almost self-sufficient in fuel, relying on driftwood. On sandy atolls and banks, such as Geser and Kiltai, plants such as banana are grown by mounding, and in places young manioc roots are protected by old coconut husks, and crops are fed with seabird droppings (*tai manuk*) collected as fertilizer (*warat*). Kiltai supports a few fruit trees (durian, jambu, mango, and coconut), and has a few small, fenced gardens growing manioc and bananas. On Garogos, the shortage of fresh vegetables means that wild plants, such as *Sesuvium portulacastrum* (*menis laen*) and *Portulaca quadrifolia* (*menis ota*), have become critical. Small patches of wasteland provide grazing for a few goats.

None of the islands produces sago (*Metroxylon sagu*), the local starch staple, in any quantity, so this must be brought in from mainland Seram. Some is grown on Gorom, especially in the upper hill area, but this is not naturally reproducing and takes longer to grow because it is dry. Again, the shortfall is made up with sago brought from Seram. But a great deal of rice is consumed on Gorom, and manioc there is second or third in importance as a starch staple. Dry rice was once grown on Gorom, but expansion of nutmeg led eventually to complete dependence on outside supplies. All the sago in the central Geser area is easily accessible and owned; only that along the Masiwang is in any sense "wild." Other nonfood resources also have to be brought in, in particular firewood and construction timber. The village of Kwamar is a specialist producer of firewood, which it obtains from the adjacent mangrove swamps and exports to Geser. It is entirely dependent upon this commodity for exchange income. Seram Rei, though it has no land of its own, has rights in the mangroves that keep it self-sufficient in firewood. In exchange for all this the island settlements can offer two commodities to the periphery: one is fish, which it has in abundance in the shallow reefs; and the other is a market for agricultural products, which are then sold to larger markets outside the area.

Widespread resource poverty and striking asymmetries in availability have made local trade and specialization vital. In some cases the necessity to trade can be offset by resource substitution. Thus, a shortage of sago thatch on Kesui and Teor has led to some replacement with inferior coconut thatch, and in the Bula area even by the alang-alang grass, *Imperata*. In places starch from *Metroxylon* sago can be replaced with that from *enau*, the sugar palm (*Arenga pinnata*); *suat pangala* (sagolike porridge made from manioc) was mentioned earlier. Elsewhere, there is no option but to bring in goods from other islands. In addition, resource-depleted centers have come to depend on long-distance trade over many centuries. The rich reefs of the island settlements provide independent sources of export goods in the form of preserved fish for regional destinations (such as Ambon), and other marine produce: trepang; the seaweeds agar-agar (*Eucheuma edule*), and sangu-sangu (*Hypnea cervicornis*); hawksbill turtles, *eran* (*Eretmochelys imbricata*), collected for the carapace; edible green turtles (*henu, Chelonia mydas*); shark (*oi*) fin; *Trochus* shell; pearls; giant clams (falangaru: *Hippopus hippopus, Tridacna maxima, Tridacna squamosa*); abalone (*Haliotes asinina*); and the black-lip shell, japing-japing, all for the wider Asian market. From the mainland and the larger islands (Gorom, Manawoka, and Pulau Panjang) the principal export commodities are cloves (only recently planted in most places), nutmeg, copra, and coffee, and to a lesser extent nowadays forest products such as bushmeat and fruits. But more crucial has been the role the polities of the Southeast Seram corridor have occupied in mediating the trade between the western Indonesian Archipelago and the southwest coast of New Guinea. The defining characteristics of what I call the "Banda-Onin corridor" are indicated in Figure 2.1: a sea passage running northeast-southwest through the central zone of the Southeast Seram trading system and across the shallow reefs that connect the Seram Laut and Gorom groups. Involvement in this commodity trade has not only subsidized an ecologically and economically deprived area, but turned a marginal area into a historically crucial one in terms of global economic systems. The significance of this geographic configuration is expanded upon in subsequent chapters of this book.

3

A Conjectured History:
The Origins of a Trading Zone

[The sea] lies towards the east and according to the testimony of experienced pilots and seamen who sail upon it and are well acquainted with the truth it contains 7,448 islands, most of them inhabited. And I assure you that in all these islands there is no tree that does not give off a powerful and agreeable fragrance and serve some useful purpose.... There are, in addition, many precious spices of various sorts.... But they are so far away that the voyage thither is fraught with difficulty. When ships from Zaiton or Kinsai come to these islands, they reap a great profit and rich return. I must tell you that it takes a full year to complete the voyage, setting out in winter and returning in summer. For only two winds blow in these seas, one that wafts them out and one that brings them back.... From now on I will tell you no more of this country or of these islands, because they are so out-of-the-way and because we have never been there.

MARCO POLO, *The Travels of Marco Polo*

3.1. Environment and Trade:
The Banda System on the Eve of the European Period

Before the establishment of the Dutch spice monopoly in the seventeenth century, the non-European trade between the Moluccas and Java had been dominated by boats carrying spices and forest products westward in exchange for rice and manufactured goods. Vessels carrying exports sailed on the east monsoon (in April) via Banda and the south coast of Sulawesi to ports on the north coast of Java and returned on the west monsoon (in May–June) via the north coast of Bali and the islands of Nusa Tenggara to Timor, from where they struck northward to Banda (Figure 3.1). The run from Banda to Surabaya downwind with the east monsoon using a modern lambo, the sailing workhorse of the eastern archipelago, takes about fourteen days, and it is unlikely that voyages before the seventeenth century took any longer than this, although as we shall see, speed at sea was not necessarily a consideration. The seasonal reversal of winds (Figure 3.2) that

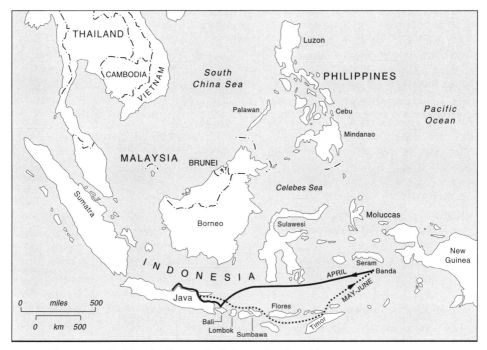

Figure 3.1. Traditional sailing routes between Banda and Java.

facilitated easy movement of maritime traffic is a product of the physical geography of the relatively enclosed seas of archipelagic Southeast Asia (Horridge 1995:135), which Coedes (1944:2) likened to some Asian Mediterranean (cf. Braudel 1949). In turn, that same physical geography was very closely linked to the kinds of sailing vessels and modes of navigation employed, an idea that is further developed in chapter 6. It is a pattern that has changed little since and is only beginning to alter now with the decline in the use of sailing vessels in the Moluccan trade. Its rhythms defined the parameters of the Banda system.

It should be borne in mind that in the Moluccas, and for large parts of insular Southeast Asia and Melanesia, short sea barriers are less limiting for humans than land barriers. The seas of the Indonesian Archipelago are mostly warm, shallow, and sunlit, with a rich and varied biomass. Although mud, shifting sand, and submerged reefs sometimes provide navigational hazards, the seas are not subject to frequent bad storms or strong currents and are well suited for easy communication. Moreover, the main east and west monsoon winds are ideal for sailing craft moving between the mainland and various lateral points of the archipelago (Urry 1981:2). Even for populations using simple vessels, small island groups are often better connected along coasts and across narrows and short stretches

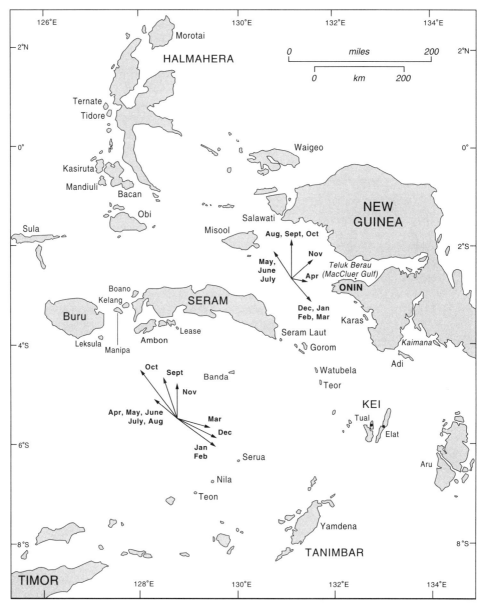

Figure 3.2. Wind direction chart for Arafura and Banda seas. Arrows show wind direction for the months indicated. Compiled from East Indian Archipelago Wind and Rain Chart, in Library of the Koninklijk Instituut voor Taal-, Land- en Volkenkunde, Leiden.

of open sea than are coasts with interiors divided by mountains, fast-flow-ing rivers, dense forest, and difficult terrain. Moreover, lowland coastal regions draining large upland interiors are often swampy, and their fore-shores are covered in mangrove. In parts of the Moluccas, islands rise pre-cipitously from the sea, and steep vegetation-covered slopes make coastal land travel awkward. In such areas, and also where forest, swamp, quag-mirish paths, and rocky and undulating surfaces prevent effective move-ment on firm land, intervillage travel may be along beaches. The littoral zone is particularly favored in this respect, but the availability of such routes depends on the tides. In the large islands to the west and in the Malay Peninsula, estuaries and river networks provide access to the inte-rior, but in the Moluccas such waterways are often shallow, full of rocks, liable to wet-season flash floods, and generally difficult to negotiate.

In the Moluccas the density of network connections has for a long time been infinitely greater along coasts and between small nearby islands than between the coast and the interior, and this has been closely linked to a high interdependency of local populations. By contrast, the most isolated and least dependent populations are those found in the interior and on highland peripheries. But although coastal connectivity within the small island groups of the Moluccas may well be high in terms of both human and nonhuman flows, as maritime distances increase beyond the 20-kilo-meter and 200-meter-depth frontiers (see Figure 6.1), so communication becomes technically more difficult and geographic barriers more resistant. As distance and sea depth increase separated landmasses become ecologi-cally more closed and some potential lines of closure more apparent than others (Ellen 1984).

I argued in chapter 1 in favor of a model of nested systems of exchange within the Moluccan area, in which at the lowest level the region can be seen as composed of relatively discrete local networks. At the hub of each network is a small island (or number of small islands) serving as a redistrib-utive center and point of articulation with the outside world: West Seram focused on Ambon, Aru on Dobo, Southeast Seram on Geser, and so on. The trading centers, or foci, show various degrees of dependency on their peripheries. The foci are generally very small islands that appear to owe their importance to their geographical centrality in the local trading area and having provided intrusive traders with good harbors and safe havens in otherwise hostile territory. Occasionally the reasons may have been environmental. For example, inhabitants of Keffing claim that the island of Seram Rei was first inhabited to avoid the mangrove swamp along the southeastern coastline of mainland Seram. But in this case one might ask why not settle at that point on the mainland where the mangrove ends. The ultimate historical reason is almost certainly more complicated than this and is probably largely political and economic in character: that an island among banks and shoals provided ready access to desirable sea prod-ucts, that land elsewhere was politically inaccessible, that anchorages were convenient and safe, and that Seram Rei lay in the immediate vicinity (the Seram Laut Archipelago) of what was already an important trading center. The reasons for settling on such small islands must have been strong because the disadvantages were often severe. Small islands such as Geser, Kiltai, and Seram Rei are flat, low-lying, tiny, and exposed coral atolls and banks, subject to high tides and frequent flooding, vulnerable to tsunamis and hurricanes, with virtually no possibilities for cultivation and with only brackish drinking water. Even Banda has no surface water apart from one stream on Lonthor, and although its soils suit nutmeg they are otherwise agriculturally poor. Moreover, in the early VOC period Banda suffered prolonged droughts, in 1620, 1630–1631, 1635–1636, 1660, and since (Loth 1998:69), as well as endemic and periodically catastrophic volcanic eruptions and seismic instability (Ellen 1987:48–50, 52).

There is oral historical evidence, as well as that of contemporary administrative boundaries, suggesting that in the past local domains rivaled for control of these small strategic islands. Islands with so little natural wealth, with the possible exception of sea produce, must be contrasted with powerful domains, such as Kataloka on Gorom, that also exported local nutmeg and had opportunities for subsistence cultivation.

Very small islands with no possibilities for cultivation were dependent upon the import of basic foods and materials: rice and manufactured goods from outside the Moluccas and other starch staples (largely sago), vegetables, fruit, and constructional and craft materials from other islands in the immediate vicinity. Such needs in a hypothetically pristine world might initially have been met through local trade, such as between Geser and Seram Laut. Geser, Kiltai, and Seram Rei are still dependent on the vegetable produce of nearby Seram Laut, and the economic significance of this island is reflected politically in the threefold administrative division between the polities (now pemerintah negeri) of Kelu, Kiltai, and Kilwaru, themselves places without agricultural land. But long-term requirements for trade objects to exchange for rice and manufactured goods, and the increasing scale of such trade and home consumption, led to the growth of a much larger periphery. In the case of Geser, Kiltai, and Seram Rei, it meant the incorporation of the eastern part of mainland Seram and parts of Teluk Berau and the Onin Peninsula of the island of New Guinea (Irian).

It now seems likely that the earliest and most important and enduring trade relations between the Moluccas and New Guinea have concerned forest products other than sago. Only with the introduction of nutmeg plantations in Banda and the rapid growth of its population did trade in sago from such distant places as Aru and New Guinea become necessary. In fact, the New Guinea sago trade may never have been significant over a long period, only at times of acute subsistence crisis. Certainly, it is not known from recent history. In other places, such as within the Southeast Seram network, sago was such a constant item of exchange that it was almost, as Tomé Pires suggested, "a kind of currency" (Cortesão 1944: 208–209).

By the time the Portuguese arrived in the Moluccas we can be certain that the Banda system existed and that the small islands around the easternmost tip of Seram were a significant part of it. We know from the *Hikayat Tanah Hitu* that within the domain of Hitu on Ambon Island, between 1450 and 1490, there were four groups of outsiders thought worthy of mention: from Java, Jailolo (on Halmahera), East Seram, and Gorom (Krause-Katola 1988:27, Manusama 1977). Indeed, Gorom was almost certainly more important than Ambon until the second quarter of the sixteenth century. But in what we now call the central Moluccas as a whole, Banda was the point of articulation with the outside world: drawing in commodities for trade from its periphery, which most importantly included Southeast Seram and Gorom, an area that in turn controlled the New Guinea trade, as well as produced its own nutmeg. At the same time, Banda depended on the periphery for its basic needs; sago and timber in particular came from Southeast Seram. By this time it is clear that the social structure of the polities of Southeast Seram had evolved to a point that would be recognizable today: small, centralized, (and probably newly) Islamicized polities of endogamous clans, in alliance through royal marriages and underpinned by slavery, the product of trade with New Guinea, trade with the West, and Malayo-Islamic influence; in short a creation of the Banda system itself. Some of the most compelling evidence for this is linguistic.

3.2. The Testimony of Language

It is convenient, and I think acceptably precise, to speak of Southeast Seram Littoral (SSL) as the language of the majority of inhabitants of what is currently the subdistrict of East Seram. The modern distribution of this language and its historic spread is an important thread connecting different parts of the argument in this book. For this reason, and also because the status of the language is not entirely uncontroversial, it is necessary to say a little more here.

Both J. T. Collins (1986) and Loski and Loski (1989:108) distinguished what they call a Seram Laut group of languages within which they include two subgroups: Geser-Gorom (alternatively Seram, Seran, Gorom, Goran, Gorong) and Watubela (alternatively Kesui, Kasui). The geographical distribution of these languages is shown in Figure 3.3. According to the Loskis (ibid., 124–125) Geser-Gorom and Watubela share a mean lexical similarity of 57 percent, and speakers of both languages agree that they share a common tongue. Moreover (ibid., 110), Geser-Gorom and Watubela have a 50 percent lexicostatistical relationship and Watubela and Teor-Kur (also considered a separate language) a 40 percent relationship. The Watubela language is spoken by 3,500 inhabitants of the Watubela Islands southeast of the Gorom Islands.

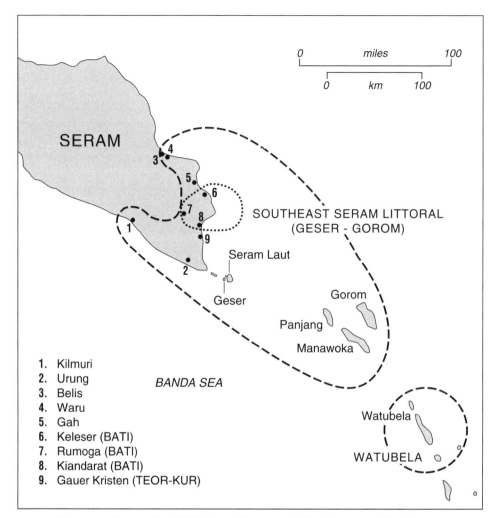

Figure 3.3. Geographical distribution of languages in East Seram, modified from Loski and Loski (1989:125, 129). The dotted line indicates the approximate distribution of Bati (Kiandarat)-speaking settlements. The dashed lines indicate the distribution of the two main variants (Geser-Gorom and Watubela) of Southeast Seram Littoral (SSL) outside those areas of the New Guinea coast where it is also spoken.

On the basis of phonology and reported dialect differences, the Loskis divided Geser-Gorom into two major dialects (Geser-Gorom and Bati), this latter spoken by some 3,500 people located in the mountains of the Seram mainland between Kiandarat and Keleser (ibid., 129). Geser-Gorom and Bati share approximately 80 percent lexical similarity. In the Loskis' view, there has to be a 70 percent or less similarity for dialects to be regarded as languages. J. T. Collins (1984) claimed that both Bati (which he called Kiandarat) and Kilmuri (the Loskis claim no basis for positing a Kilmuri dialect) substitute /ng/ for the /g/ in other Geser-Gorom dialects. The objective classificatory status of Bati might well be contentious, though modern residents and nonresidents alike assert its uniqueness, describe it as "*minak esi*" (mountain language), associate it with the Bati people who cling to many pre-Muslim traditions, and generally view it as a relict of some former, more localized language.

According to Loski and Loski (1989:126, 128) the Geser-Gorom language is spoken over a wide area in Southeast Seram and the Gorom Islands, southeast of Seram, by approximately 40,000 people. It is also a second language in many parts of eastern Seram, in the Watubela Archipelago, and in parts of southwestern New Guinea (Walker, in J. T. Collins 1986:125). Some of the people who speak Masiwang claim to be bilingual in the Geser-Gorom language (Loski and Loski 1989:124). Collins (1984:118) stated that Geser-Gorom "has diffused all along the northeast coast of Seram, both by the movement of Geser-speaking people who have established villages in that area, and by changes in linguistic allegiance in other villages, particularly in those villages settled some time ago by people originating from north Halmahera, for example, Silohan. The language of Hoti, a Seti dialect, is said to have been replaced by Geser as well."

On the basis of consistent phonological changes, the Loskis further subdivide the Geser-Gorom dialect into two subdialects: Geser (spoken on Seram and the islands adjacent to it) and Gorom (spoken in the Gorom Islands). For example, where Geser uses /h/ the Gorom subdialect uses /f/; where Geser subdialect uses /k/, Gorom uses /?/. In practice, distinguishing the two is messy, as, for example, in Ondor (generally Gorom dialect), where these same phonological shifts (here, Gorom > Geser) indicate membership of the family of the raja; thus dialect merges with a register associated with social class.

We must now look at the wider linguistic picture. J. T. Collins (1980: 28–29) tentatively divided Proto-Central Maluku into Proto-West Central Maluku and Proto-East Central Maluku. Proto-East Central Maluku is in turn divided (via Proto-Seram) into Nunusaku and East Seram (Figure 3.4). Elsewhere (1986), he presented a reconstruction of the languages of East Seram, all members of the Central Malayo-Polynesian subgroup of the Austronesian Phylum (Blust 1979). Collins (1983, 1984, 1986) further subgrouped all of these languages (except for Teor-Kur, which has closer affinities with Kei) to form Proto-East Central Maluku. He (Collins 1986) classified the Seram Laut group together with the Banda language in Proto-Banda, a daughter of Proto-East Central Maluku. The Bandanese language is no longer spoken in Banda, but survived after the Dutch invasion of 1621 in two villages on Kei Besar (Banda Elat and Banda Eli), where a modified

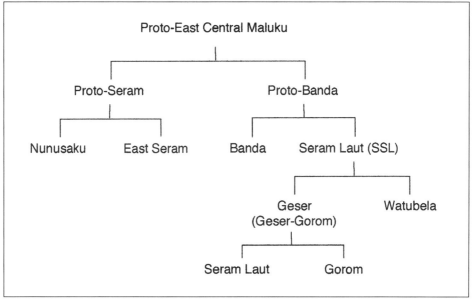

Figure 3.4. Genetic classification of SSL and related languages (after J. T. Collins 1984:122).

version (*tur wandan*) is still spoken (Collins 1986; Collins and Kaartinen 1998). The geographical position is indicated in Figure 3.5.

What is significant about this linguistic evidence in terms of the analysis presented here, especially given the physical isolation of Banda and its lack of endemic wildlife, is that it is almost certainly the case that Bandanese is an offshoot of a language (that which Collins called Proto-Banda) with its homeland somewhere in the Southeast Seram area, and most likely (given the direction of SSL expansion) in the vicinity of what is now Geser. Thus, it is plausible to treat the expansion of Proto-Banda to Banda and the later geographic spread of SSL as part of a single phenomenon: the emergence and evolution of a trading zone integrating the area of what I have called the Banda system. External evidence for the existence of this zone is found in the global trade in nutmeg, and as we have reports of nutmeg in the Mediterranean basin by the second millennium B.C. (chapter 1), we must presume that Banda was inhabited, and the trading zone operating in a form resembling that found at the time of the arrival of the first Europeans in 1500, by the beginning of the Common Era.

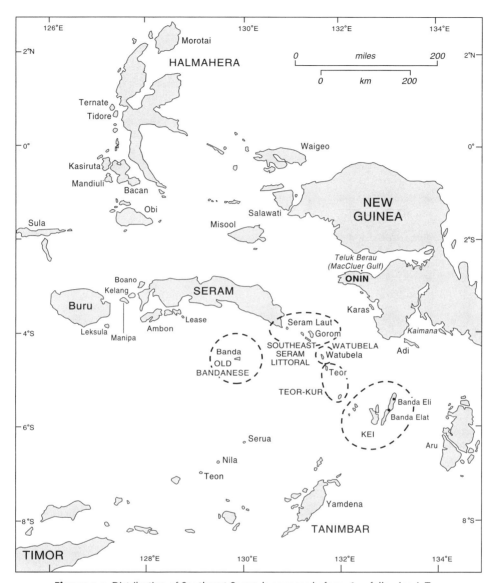

Figure 3.5. Distribution of Southeast Seram languages before 1621, following J. T. Collins (1986) and Loski and Loski (1989). Language names are written in CAPITALS. Banda Eli and Banda Elat are the two isolates where a variant of Old Bandanese is still spoken.

3.3. The Protohistory of Archipelagic Southeast Seram

Enough is known of the prehistory of Southeast Seram to conclude that it was an important trading zone before the arrival of the Portuguese. For one thing, trade winds and geography facilitated human motivation to exchange in particular patterns. For another, spices and other New Guinea products (such as bird of paradise feathers) were reaching the outside world, and these must have come through the Geser (Banda-Onin) or Halmahera corridors. Although most nutmeg (*Myristica fragrans*) came from Banda, Banda itself was dependent for its subsistence upon its periphery, which included Southeast Seram, and the Geser corridor was also the principal route by which long nutmeg (*Myristica argentea*) moved from New Guinea into the world system.

It now looks as though spice cultivation in places such as Banda and Southeast Seram must have been secondary to their emergence as centers of trade, as local trading communities dealing in spices produced elsewhere attempted to exercise more control over the production of the commodity. This, at least, appears to be the case for the Southeast Seram network and for Banda. Sixteen species of *Myristica* (the nutmeg genus) are recorded for the Moluccas, of which three are represented by two subspecies. In the normal way this species richness and a degree of endemism suggest that cultivated forms of nutmeg may have evolved locally (De Wilde 1990:233). However, we know also that for many centuries wild nutmeg had been coming from the forests of New Guinea via the trading polities of Southeast Seram. It seems likely that the emergence of Gorom as an important trading and political center was linked to the planting of nutmeg, both pala bundar (*Myristica fragrans*) and the less aromatic long nutmeg, pala panjang (*Myristica argentea*), brought from New Guinea (Flach and Tjeenk Willink 1999; Utami and Brink 1999). In turn, it is possible that the first nutmeg grown on Banda (pala bundar) was brought from Gorom. The original Banda nutmeg may have been pala panjang or the pala onin (*Myristica succedanea*) of the northern Moluccas, a species intermediate between pala panjang and pala bundar. Thus, the Banda system may have been a rational outgrowth and extension of a Southeast Seram system, linked to the planting of nutmeg in the Banda Archipelago, the growth of the islands as a general primary trading center for incoming traders from the West, and the consequent refocusing of other radial supply links. But in any case, the principal Banda–Southeast Seram artery remained for good geographical, navigational, and economic reasons.

Direct documentary evidence for the structure of the zone in the two centuries before 1500 is to be found in the Negarakertagama and in Roxo de Brito's manuscript (Van Fraassen 1976). The Negarakertagama, written between 1350 and 1389 in Majapahit, mentions five localities in the Southeast Seram region: Gurun (Gorong or Gorom), Seran (by which is probably meant only the easternmost tip of Seram, or the Seram Laut Archipelago),

Muar (which may be Maar or Kei, though Van Fraassen, following Rouffaer [1905, 1908, 1915], said that Muar is Hoamoal [in West Seram]), Wandan (Banda), and Wwanim (probably Onin, Wawani). Banda(r) itself is probably a term of Persian origin meaning "emporium," highly appropriate for the hub of a vast trading system (Purnadi Purbatjaraka 1961).

The de Brito manuscript (Boxer and Manguin 1979; Sollewijn Gelpke 1994) is a more substantial source. It indicates the existence of a thriving trading zone in the Geser-Gorom area, and its significance becomes palpable when we superimpose the places and routes mentioned by de Brito onto a modern map (Figure 3.6). However, the manuscript provides no names for localities in Southeast Seram that appear in later historic or contemporary records. In 1513 Tomé Pires wrote in his *Suma Oriental* that near Banda there are three islands: Seram, Arua, and Papua. Pires added that the inhabitants of other islands come to Banda to buy cloth: Tanimbas, Papua, Moluccas (Cortesão 1944:208–211). Banda is clearly seen as the central market in the region and the gateway to all points east.

When Antonio d'Abreu sailed from Malacca to reconnoiter the route to the Moluccas in November 1511, he was accompanied by a highly regarded pilot and cartographer, Francisco Rodrigues. They had to wait out the westerly monsoon at Guli-guli before sailing on to Banda, where Abreu purchased spices and from where he returned to Malacca. Rodrigues copied the locations of many islands from older Malay and Javanese charts onto folio 37 of his so-called "Javanese" map, which shows Timor, Banda, and Seram. The "Book" of Rodrigues is preserved in the Bibliotheque de l'Assemblée Nationale in Paris, dated at around 1513 (Sollewijn Gelpke 1992:243; 1995: 81, 84–85, 89, 97–98). On that map Guli-guli (Gully-gully) is clearly shown. Sollewijn Gelpke suggested that Rodrigues cut through from Guli-guli to Arnanen along a creek through the mangroves (Figure 2.5), and that it was this that gave his map of Seram its curious shape. He also suggested that by "Ceiram tem houro" Rodrigues meant Seram (which at that time was almost certainly a toponym restricted to Seram Laut or the Southeast Seram Archipelago) had gold. Written next to Guli-guli is a reference to the importance of Seram Laut as a trading center. From the Rodrigues map it is also clear that there was a monsoon route from a point to the north of Sumbawa to Buton, a second trade route from Sumbawa to Southeast Seram along the great arc of islands between them, and a third route from Southeast Seram to Halmahera. A map attributed to Pedro Reinel of about 1517 differs in some respects, but also clearly marks Guli-guli. New Guinea or Irian is first shown on a Portuguese map in 1558 as an island, but named Ceiram (Haga 1884, 1:11). The *Insulae Indiae Orientalis* of Jodocus Hondius (ca. 1635) follows this with "Ceiram Os Papuas" and to its southeast "T(erra) Cenaon," which from its position in relation to other islands must be Seram, a confusion also found in W. J. Blaeu and Hondius' map of 1624 (Figure 3.7). We can only assume that this confusion of Seram with the western part of New Guinea, a confusion that persisted into the

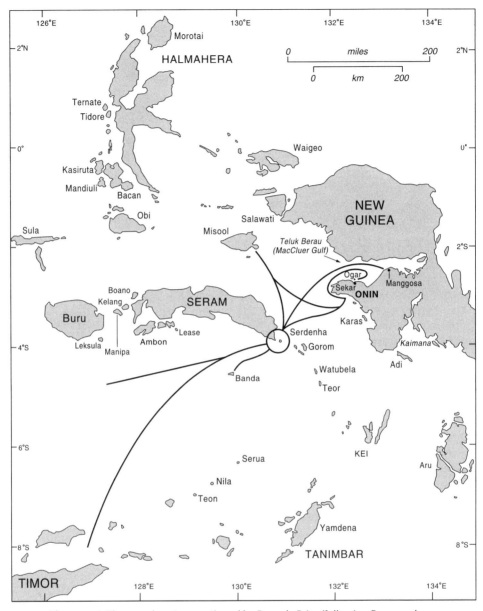

Figure 3.6. Places and routes mentioned by Roxo de Brito (following Boxer and Manguin 1979) superimposed on a modern map of the Moluccas and New Guinea.

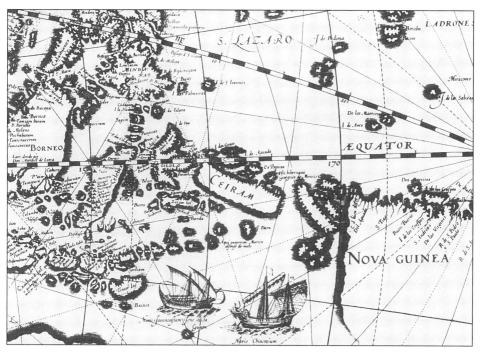

Figure 3.7. Part of the world map of Willem Janzoon Blaeu and Jodocus Hondius, 1624 (from facsimile dated 1977 in the British Library).

second half of the seventeenth century (Suárez 1999:168, 177, 212), arises from the use of the term "Seran" to refer to the Seram Laut Islands and the close association between Papua and the Serammers.

Much more revealing than the map, however, is the de Brito manuscript. De Brito spent from May 1581 to around November 1582 in the Raja Ampat Islands, in Teluk Berau (New Guinea), and along the North Seram coast, sailing under the Spanish flag (Sollewijn Gelpke 1994:125). The fact that he was in these places at all strongly suggests their contemporaneous political and economic links with Geser-Gorom. The original account was presumably written in Portuguese, though we only know of a Spanish version made in Manila around 1590. In this manuscript de Brito tells us about Serdenha (Sardenha, Cerdenha, Cerdeña) (Boxer and Manguin 1979:180), 30 leagues (approximately 165 kilometers) south of Misool, close by Seram; it has an islet, Citan (Kidang), nearby. For Sollewijn Gelpke (1994:127, 129), this is undoubtedly Seram Laut, and Serdenha is de Brito's corruption of Ser-Läen (sand harbor) in the language of Misool, the term used before the Malay Seram Laut became current. Boxer and Manguin (1979:180 n. 14) were more circumspect and said that it might also be Gorom.

De Brito described the population of Serdenha as comprising five thousand "wealthy merchants" (Sollewijn Gelpke 1994:130–131) and as basically egalitarian, though the Papuan king of Misool exercized some influence, periodically sending raiding parties. Serdenha possessed a stone enclosure (a fort) on a hill on its southern side above the beach, with towers and small guns. Artus Gijsels, the Dutch governor of Ambon between 1621 and 1634, described the walls of the fort on Seram Laut as 10 feet high and 10 feet thick and sketched other forts along the South Seram coast. Forts of a similar description have been found in the Raja Ampat Islands and on Teluk Berau (the MacCluer Gulf), especially in the area visited by de Brito. According to de Brito, the village was divided into eight parts, each with a head. Each year two of these heads led trading expeditions (presumably to Onin) while the rest stayed to defend the community (ibid., 132). Those treasurers who looked after trade goods received a cut in the takings of each vessel for their trouble, a sum also used to pay mercenaries from other villages when at war (for example, with Banda) and also for the redemption of hostages taken in raids by Misool islanders. At the time Serdenha had about six hundred small guns, but de Brito claimed that they did not know how to use them and kept them only for prestige.

For de Brito, Serdenha was clearly involved in trade with Onin, a name that originally referred only to the northernmost tip of the modern Onin Peninsula on the New Guinea coast (ibid., 130). Among the most important commodities acquired there was "massaya" (*Cryptocarya massoy*) bark, but it is evident from de Brito's description that Serdenha also obtained slaves and gold, all in exchange for (among other things) iron and gongs. These commodities were then traded on to Bali and Java, thus giving Serdenha an important role in regional redistribution. In 1510 Pires noted (Cortesão 1944:208) that massoi appeared to have been carried directly to Banda. It had probably been traded from Onin for many centuries and may tentatively be identified with "ting pi," mentioned by Rockhill (1913–1915: 256–257). The tree, which is killed in the process of harvesting, yields a volatile oil similar to cinnamon and has for hundreds of years been used medicinally and as a spice, cosmetic, perfume, and fixing agent for dye in various parts of Southeast Asia. We shall return to the significance of the massoi trade in chapter 5.

Serdenha is also reported as building ships that sailed to the "Timor" Archipelago (perhaps Timor, but this could equally refer to Kei or Aru), Nusa Tenggara, Bali, and Java. In Bali traders from Serdenha obtained gold and cloth and in Bima gold, amber, and wax; they also sailed to Marcho (probably Makassar) and Butung (Buton), where they bought gold, textiles, and cotton yarn, and to Tobungku (Tambuco), where they obtained iron. Together, this well describes the Java route (Sollewijn Gelpke 1994:132). The iron they exchanged for massoi in Offin, between Ugar and Onin (ibid., 135). The traders of Serdenha also handled *landa* or *landu*. As Boxer and Manguin (1979:178 n. 13) pointed out, this was almost certainly sago in

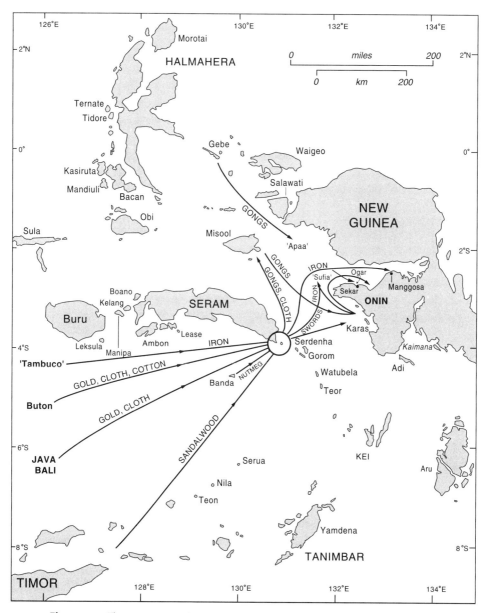

Figure 3.8. The movement of commodities eastward around 1581–1582 according to Roxo de Brito's account (ca. 1590), following Boxer and Manguin (1979:180–181, 185).

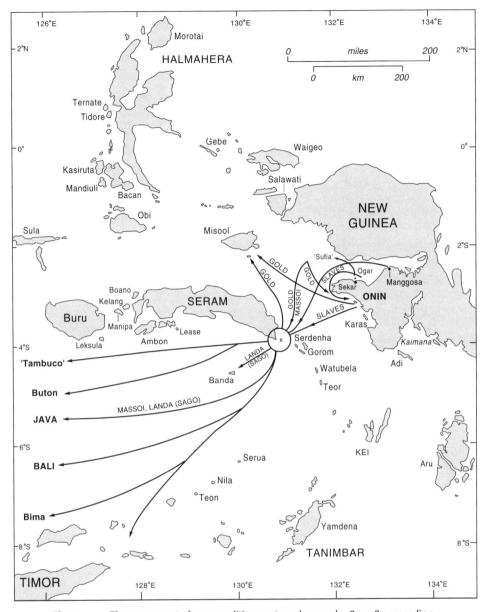

Figure 3.9. The movement of commodities westward around 1581–1582 according to Roxo de Brito's account (ca. 1590), following Boxer and Manguin (1979:180–181, 185).

some form, which was sold to Bandanese, who lacked a staple food (Sollewijn Gelpke 1994:135). Slaves were obtained from Sekar (today one of several settlements on the island of Kokas on the south coast of Teluk Berau); and the people of Onin are described as buying slaves that they sold in Serdenha, where they were used as garden labor on Kidang. In addition, according to Boxer and Manguin, Gorom and Seram Laut were already involved in the bird of paradise trade in the early sixteenth century (Figures 3.8 and 3.9).

Whatever we make of the detail in this partially speculative historical geography, such accounts demonstrate that archipelagic Southeast Seram was a place of some importance by the beginning of the sixteenth century. Certainly, the evidence is consistent with a fragmentary archaeology (Lape 2000). By the fifteenth century Chinese trade pottery, for example, was reaching Arguni on Teluk Berau (Swadling 1996:136). The physical relics of early contact are found in the form of Dongson drums (Kataloka-Namalen) and other bronzes, possible Majapahit Buddhist stupas and early Chinese porcelain, and Muslim Majapahit tombstones in Ondor and at Ilili on Watubela. The mosque of Namalen is said to incorporate stone from the pre-Islamic period. Glass armrings (*mamakur*) found widely in New Guinea and Seram are now known to have been introduced from the West (ibid., 206). By comparison, Ambon-Lease was relatively unimportant in East-West trade at that time; artifacts of Javanese and western Indonesian origin, bronzes, and Hindu-Buddhist monuments are found in Banda, Gorom, Kei, and even New Guinea, but not in Ambon-Lease (Van Heekeren 1958: fig. 1), with the exception of a Shiva figure from Amahai.

3.4. **Onomastic and Toponymic Traces**

When the Portuguese first arrived in the waters of Southeast Seram they found a thriving trading population conversant with Malay. Many of the toponyms they were given were in Malay or other nonnative languages, though it is difficult to gauge the extent to which such terms were part of local currency. "Geser," for example, is possibly Bandanese or Malay in origin (in which it means "to shift," "to move up"). This seems plausible, either as an evocation of the shifting banks and mangroves or as a reference to the way in which political centers and settlements shift from one place to another, and about which I shall have more to say in chapter 4. Before it was known as Geser, this island was called Lutur, an allusion to the resemblance between the stone fish traps that are so characteristic a feature of the area and the shape of this coral atoll, with its lagoon and narrow-necked entrance from the sea.

But the names of places given to the Portuguese by their guides and translators in Kei, Aru, and Onin were often in the local language of the Southeast Seram Littoral (SSL) and were not the names that the local inhabitants themselves used. This suggests that SSL was already widely used as a lingua franca. The Kei islanders, for example, called their island Ewab. Aru is derived from "*ar*" (water) and Kei from "*kai*" (trees), indicating that these places were distinguished on the one hand only by water and on the other only by trees. We also have the evidence of toponyms that the SSL area had already reached something approaching its current extent by the mid-sixteenth century, and it is a plausible hypothesis that spread of the language reflected political and economic expansion or its use as a medium of trade. Thus, many places on the Papuan coast were given SSL names, which became official toponyms for later traders, enshrined in Dutch maps and administrative documents (e.g., Tanjong Kafura and Kumawo [De Brauw 1854:210], Rumgaigar, Rumkai, Rumbati, Solat Len, and Tubi Seran [Haga 1884, 2:211; Hille 1905:261, 302; 1907:opp. 630]). *Kil* or *keli* (meaning either mountain or clan) occurs in many place-names along the Papuan coast, as in Kilbati, something that the Dutch explorer Keyts had noted in 1678. Similarly, Onin means "head" in SSL—Onin di atas being to the east as far as Kowiai; Onin di bawah to the west (Hille 1905:253).

There is some evidence also for the historical replacement by SSL of other languages: in the existence of isolated relict languages, such as Bati (Kiandarat), the known historical migration of mountain peoples westward, and the concentration of toponyms in recognizably archaic SSL on the southeastern tip of Seram and in the Seram Laut Archipelago, which we might reasonably suppose to have been the center of linguistic and cultural dispersion. Moreover, the name "Seran" itself derives from the indigenous names for the island widely known as Keffing (Seram Rei) and the Seram Laut Islands. For Rouffaer (1908) "Seran" is the archaic term for just one part of Southeast Seram, that part with many connections with Gorom, and only later became the name for the entire island. The phrase "Seran-Gorong" is sometimes found to describe the tip of the mainland and the entire southeastern archipelago (Jansen 1928:491). Over time the name Seram expanded to refer to the entire island, in a way that parallels the contemporary metanymic use of centers to denote entire regions, such as Dobo to refer to Aru as a whole, Tual to refer to Kei as a whole, and Geser to refer to East Seram as a whole (see chapter 9.8). For the Dutch, from the early seventeenth century onward, the inhabitants of the area (Oost Ceram), most specifically those of the Seram Laut Archipelago, were known simply as Serammers (Cerammers or Seranners). Today, residents of archipelagic Southeast Seram often refer to mainland Seram, using Malay, as Tanah Besar or Seram Besar (as opposed, that is, to Seram Laut). How the use of these toponyms relates to the local system of orientation and navigation is discussed in chapter 6. A similar process of semantic expansion of geographic reference can be seen in the way the toponym Maluku, and its various European cognates, began by referring only to the five clove-producing islands off the west coast of Halmahera, extended to encompass Ambon and its environs, and finally officially denoted an entire province.

Table 3.1. Current folk etymologies of SSL toponyms (including some *etar* names)

	Place-name	Gloss	Notes
1	Air Kasar	Brackish water	East coast Seram
2	Akat Padedo	(Drifting mangrove)	Kilmuri
3	Anger	Tree, *Alstonia scholaris*	Corklike wood; bark used medicinally; Kiandarat
4	Arnanan	"*Ar*" (water), "*anan*" (house) (Bati)	Kwaos
5	Artafela	Water forming a barrier	Kiandarat
6	Guli-guli	Water container	First recorded in 1511 by Rodrigues; Urung
7	Kelderak	"*Derak*" (thorny tree from which red dye is extracted)	Tarui (Dinama)
8	Keliolan	"*Olan*" (winding path)	Walang Tengah
9	Kiandarat	Land spring	East coast Seram
10	Kianlaut	Sea spring	East coast Seram
11	Kwamar	"*Kwa gamor*" (fetch the nipa)	Reference to *Nipa fruticans;* Urung
12	Liangtasik	"*Liang*" (spikey stone), "*tasik*" (sea)	"*Tasi*" (sea in Bati dialect); Kwaos
13	Namalen	Big harbor	Kataloka
14	Reiwanatu	Above the edge of the water	Tarui (Dinama)
15	Rumadan	Rumara Andan, house of Banda	Kianlaut
16	Rumbori	"*Bori*" (kind of fruit) (Ind.)	Semunit (SSL), Walang Tengah (Dinama)
17	Rumodar	"*Odar*" (kind of marine mollusk)	Dinama
18	Segei	River gravel	Amarwatu
19	Waru	Kind of tree (Ind.)	"*Daro*" in de Brito 1581–1582 (Sollewijn Gelpke 1994:131); east coast Seram
20	Warus-warus	Fine beach shingle, pebbles	East coast Seram

The importance of trade, the presence of outsiders, and linguistic expansion all suggest that we are already dealing with something more complex than the traditional societies characteristic of the interiors of the large islands of the Moluccas. Toponyms in Southeast Seram and the archipelago attest to the political and trading dominance of the inhabitants of the Geser-Gorom area from an early date (Table 3.1). In Table 3.2 indigenous clans (meaning those originating in the Banda–Southeast Seram area before 1621) are listed for seven SSL (Seram Laut dialect)–speaking domains. The prefix *rum* indicates a settlement, hamlet, or house, and also noteworthy are the references to distinctive topographic features (e.g. "*akat*" [mangrove]) and to geographical locations, most interestingly Onin (as in Rumonin and Rumai). From such data we may infer that early settlements

Table 3.2. Distribution of indigenous *etar* in seven Seram Laut–speaking settlements.

Etar	Kilfura	Keffing	Warus-warus	Kwaai	Kelu	Rumatau	Kwaos	Tarui
Rumain	■							
Ena	■							
Rumadei		■	■		■	■		
Basu	■							
Pompanua	■							
Rumadar	■							
Rumesi				■				
Rumaru				■				
Rumalolas				■				
Kelimala				■				
Rumalutur				■				
Kelibia	■				■			
Rumadan					■		■	
Rumalowak					■			
Waairoi					■			
Kasongat		■			■			
Rumonin		■						
Rumarotu				■				
Kotabanda		■						
Rumakat		■					■	
Rumadaul							■	
Rumeon							■	
Kastella		■						■
Mau		■						

were dispersed subclans or "houses" (*rumara*), although modern SSL kinship terminology—where we might reasonably look for fossil evidence of an earlier preference for cross-cousin marriage—is of no help (Table 3.3). In fact, what we find is an "amorphous" terminological system, generally generational and "Hawaiian" in character (Waterson 1986), with some variation in the application and extendibility of terms, and quasi-bifurcate by virtue of the number of descriptive terms. Until recently we would not have known what to make of all this. *Tete* is patently a recently introduced Ambonese Malay term, and we might expect influence from Ambonese Malay more generally given its progressive spread during the Dutch period. As we have seen in chapter 2, the preference for marriage within the group is certainly consistent with preferred Muslim practice, following Arabic custom, and I originally suspected that the introduction of Islam must have fundamentally changed both marriage practices and kinship terminology.[1] Though Islam may well have consolidated such tendencies, I now think we must look for other explanations.

Table 3.3. Geser-Gorom kinship terms

Reference No.	Term of reference	Gloss
1	Baba	F
2	Nina	M
3	Ana (urana)	S
4	Ana (wawina)	D
5	Tata	SS, SD, DD, DS, FF, FM, MM, MF
6	Toi, ali	yB, yZ
7	Kaka	eB, eZ, MBS
8	Mema, memara	FB, MB
9	Wowa	FZ
10	Baba ota, otak	FyB, MyB
11	Baba laen	FeB, MeB, MB
12	Nin natak, nin ota	FyZ, MyZ
13	Nin laen	FeZ, MeZ
14	Mema	Male relative of parent other than sibling
15	Wowa	Female relative of parent other than sibling
16	Nusi	FFF, FFM, FMF, FMM, MMM, MMF, MFF, MFM, SSS, SSD, SDS, SDD, DDD, DDS, DSS, DSD
17	Tokan	FFFF, etc.
18	Wan	FFFFF, etc.
19	Kula	FFFFFF, etc.
20	Wala	FFFFFFF, etc.
21	Wini	W, H, MBD, MBS, MZS, MZD, FBS, FBD, FZS, FZD; preferred marriage partner
22	Urana	H
23	Wawina	W
24	Dau, dauk	WB, WZ, HB, HZ
25	Dear	HW, WH
26	Ketan kurana	WF (Gorom)
27	Ketan wawina	WM (Gorom)

Note: Fieldwork by Ellen in 1981 and 1986 elicited some geographic variations, perhaps most strikingly between Bati and other Geser-Gorom populations, with, for example, more emphasis on specification of gender in same generation terms: thus *toi* (yB, yZ) > *toi balona* (yB) and *toi bina* (yZ); *kaka(k)* (eB, eZ) > *kakak balona* (eB) and *kakak bina* (eZ).

Part of the problem stems from the models that anthropologists working in eastern Indonesia have inherited from Van Wouden (1968 [1935]) and that have been recently modified and reified by Shelley Errington (1990). These are models based on the structuralist assumption that the "exchange societies" of this part of Indonesia are all variations on a single theme of alliance and prescription, and that where we find the situation otherwise it is (as in the case of the Christian Ambonese) the result of European influence or (as in the case of Muslims in Southeast Seram) the consequence of Middle Eastern custom that was part of the wrapping in which the gift of Islam was received in this part of the archipelago. Of course, on Seram and Buru we have evidence for both unilateral and bilateral prescription with bifurcate terminologies and characteristic equations of the type MBD = W for the Huaulu and Maneo (Hagen 1999; Valeri 1975–1976) or, for the Nuaulu, MBD = FZD, MBS = FZS, W = BW, D = BD, D = WZD, WBW = Z (Ellen 1978:51, and unpublished data); or H = BW, W = ZH, ZH = WB on Buru (Grimes 1993:116, 127). However, recent work by Grzimek (1991: 299–300) among the Wemale of West Seram suggests an alternative explanation. Grzimek found a loosely structured clan system with much in-marriage and a terminology essentially similar to that of Gorom-Geser. I suspect that these terminologies are more common than has been previously thought, that for centuries they have coexisted with prescriptive systems (much like the clinal distribution many now accept for Timor (Hicks 1990: 82–87), and that the Christian Ambon-Lease system reported by Cooley (1962) is much closer to that of the Alune and Wemale than previously thought and not a "transitional form" between matriliny and patriliny. We should, therefore, not see the contemporary pattern in coastal and Southeast Seram as a break with a prescriptive past, but rather a continuation of pre-sixteenth-century forms, modified slightly but altered and reinforced in their own ways by Christian and Muslim norms.

3.5. Folk Histories as Evidence

Folk histories, which merge with biography for the near present and myth for the distant past, have always represented a temptingly rich source to tap in reconstructing political development in the absence of written records, and quite properly there is no shortage of cautionary advice to those who are tempted to make use of them (Tonkin 1992; Vansina 1985). In the context of Southeast Seram, a major difficulty in interpreting oral history is its contemporary rhetorical use to bolster rival claims between antagonistic domains and their rulers, as to which is the most truthful, culturally authentic, or politically legitimate (Ellen 1986b). There is a great deal of competition between polities with traditional rivalries, as well as resentment over other people's versions of history. I therefore proceed here with considerable wariness.

One area where folk history is plausibly helpful is with respect to traditions of migration, and in chapter 2 I have already made use of such evidence in relation to the distinction between autochthonous and immigrant clans, and with regard to the tradition of claiming outside rulers. When we aggregate the stories that legitimate these customary beliefs, they clearly underwrite the importance of particular enduring trading and political relations. The most obvious of these is in relation to the significance of Banda. Thus, in the folk history of the raja of Kataloka, the person known as Wattimena (an Ambonese name) originated from Malaya, but came via Banda, first as an ulama to Tidore and then to Gorom. More generally, folk histories suggest political links and population movements in a regional context that go back well before the first documents were written. Many of these stories are enshrined in historical ballads known as *takunu*. These accounts conveniently divide thematically into three kinds: resettlement stories set within the Southeast Seram area, migration histories set within the general Moluccan region, and origin myths stressing the origin of particular polities in the migration of people from outside the Moluccas.

Local resettlement histories include many accounts of *etar* moving from the mountains to the coast (Kwaos, Kiandarat), and others of groups moving around in the archipelago to find land (for example, the migration of Kelu people from Seram Rei to Kilfura on Seram Laut before the arrival of the Dutch, or the fleeing of Kwaai to Seram Rei from Kelikwaai on Seram Laut). Stories of the second kind include the oral traditions of Hitu that assert that certain kinship groups can claim descent from a Goromese pattih, and another from Seram Laut (Van de Graaff and Meijlan 1856:76). This is consistent with the claim by Rijali (who must have based his account on earlier versions of these traditions) that one Ali Liang of Gorom visited Ambon (Mamala Liang) (Jansen 1928:492; Manusama 1977). A similar account is that of the Gilolo (Halmahera) prince Bakar, son of the king of Bacan, whose brother, around 1465–1480, became orang kaya of Lisabetta and whose sister Jamilu married Pattih Hatalion of Gorom (Valentijn 1724–1726, 1:94, 2:4–5 [in Haga 1884, 1:4]). Stories of the third kind include the tradition that Kilwaru was founded by Bugis from Sulawesi. At present, there is one family of recent and incontrovertible Bugis origin called Dain Tanga Wajo; the rest simply use Bugis as an *etar* or soa name, as in Mohammed Kasim Bugis (Table 2.2). Such stories add credibility to the long-term significance of Kilwaru as a trading center with links with South Sulawesi. Type-three stories also include accounts that are far more difficult to substantiate, such as the Kiltai version of a story that, through the myth of Angus and Ungus, asserts the establishment of a dynasty of Portuguese origin in Keffing and Kiltai, respectively. We shall examine some of this evidence again in chapter 4 to show how settlements and clans have shifted geographically in the Geser area, but for now we must return to the wider trading picture for the period before the arrival of the Dutch.

3.6. The Banda System in the Sixteenth Century

The appearance of Europeans in Southeast Asia had little initial impact on the volume and character of trade being handled in regional ports (Hall 1981:34). The Portuguese incursion in the early sixteenth century prompted the kind of response Asian traders would have adopted with any new customer or competitor. There was no disruption and still less domination of the complex, local pattern of commerce of which, in eastern Indonesia,

Makassar (Ujung Pandang) was the center; and the Portuguese were content to accommodate their own trading activities within this pattern, handling the same goods and following the same routes. For example, they hired local vessels for the Malacca-Makassar route and used mixed crews (Villiers 1981a:19). Trade continued to grow steadily. The needs of commercially oriented polities such as Aceh, Malacca, and Banda depended on bulk trade in rice, salt, and dried fish (Hall 1981:35; Reid 1993:39). In the Moluccas, bulk trade in sago must also have been important, and with the evidence of the de Brito manuscript we know that some was exported as far as Java.

These regional developments led to the emergence of local individuals (orang kayas) who obtained status and power from their position as endogenous economic middlemen or conferred on those in ascribed positions of authority more power by virtue of their control of the means of exchange. Banda consisted of a number of quasi-independent polities governed largely through leaders who acquired much of their power and authority through trade, though the extent to which such orang kayas might be said to constitute a class or their domains' states is a matter of some debate (Hall 1981:36). But in the larger ports, there were also functionaries who were subservient to local rulers who served as syahbandars (harbormasters). Syahbandar is a term of Persian origin meaning, literally, "king of the trading center (emporium)," rather than harbor. It is a term widely found in early sources for the Indonesian region (including for Majapahit). Though their precise function varied from place to place (Moreland 1920), they had a general responsibility for dealing with foreigners and interstate relations. An ancient Balinese code for Lombok specifies how relations with foreigners should be handled, how disputes should be resolved, how to repatriate ex-slaves, and how to deal with prisoners in transit. The syahbandar was a kind of diplomat or cross-cultural broker, who was able to issue travel and import permits, helped ships in distress, and contracted treaties with foreigners. In large ports (such as Palembang) different ethnic groups had their own syahbandar (Purnadi Purbatjaraka 1961:2–7; also Resink 1968:49–51). At the time of the arrival of the Europeans there were four such agents in Malacca, handling boats and their crews from particular places: one each for Javanese, Moluccans (meaning from Ternate and Tidore), Bandanese, and Palembangers. In the Moluccas syahbandar were known from Ternate, Tidore, Bacan, Ambon, and Banda. In Banda, from where we have a Dutch reference to their presence in 1599, they operated in Lautaka (Latetaha), Neira, Lonthor, Orantatta, Ratu, Kombir, and on Run and Ai (Van der Chijs 1886:1, 23).

The fall of Malacca in 1511 to the Portuguese, and following this the North Javanese ports, had the effect of shifting the focus of the Asian spice trade to Makassar. In consequence, the Muslim rulers of the Moluccas increasingly placed themselves under Makassan protection and fought with them later in resisting the Dutch (Villiers 1981a:16). Thus, events far away in the western part of the archipelago had far-reaching effects on local political and economic relations in the east. Merchandise from the east was brought to Makassar by Javanese, Malay, and Bandanese traders. The Makassans themselves do not appear to have engaged in much direct trade at that period, except for Banda, where the prince of Tallo kept an agent to maintain supplies of nutmeg and mace in exchange for rice and cloth. As for the Portuguese, they were unable to sustain their monopoly in the spice trade (in which one-third of Moluccan exports were theoretically reserved for the crown) and despite European demand sold most of their spices in Malacca. By 1605 Amboina and Banda were virtually free ports with traders from all over Asia (including Turkey) (Boxer 1969:61–62).

We know that by the time of the arrival of the first Europeans Banda had already been long dependent for food, fuel, thatch, and timber on nearby islands, mainly Seram (Loth 1998:67–68). Pires in 1515 spoke of sago going to Banda, and we have already examined the account of de Brito. In 1620 a junk and two great sampans containing sago from Aru beached at Kidang and were recovered for the VOC (C. F. van Fraassen, personal communication). There can be little doubt that as Banda grew in importance as a producer of nutmeg and as a player on the international scene, it became ever more dependent upon its local periphery to provide essential supplies and as a feeder of commodities for onward export. In this the Geser corridor played a key role.

3.7. The Seram Laut and Gorom Archipelagoes, 1500–1621

The arrival of the Portuguese is indelibly marked in the folk histories of Southeast Seram as the beginning of the modern world and of recorded chronological history. Sundry monuments are described as Portuguese, though where they are evidently European they are almost certainly Dutch. Kidang is said to be the site of armed conflict between Portugal and Kastella (Spain). The domain name of Keffing is said to be derived from the Portuguese "kepeng," meaning money, and it is the Portuguese who are said to have given the title "mayor" to the *matlaen* of Keffing.[2] However such social memories are interpreted, it is likely that at that period Keffing was in political ascendancy (see, e.g., Wurffbain 1931:91 [writing in 1686]) and may have been at the time of the first permanent settlements on Kiltai and Seram Rei. The Kastella dynasty must date from that period, though whether this reflected Iberian in-marriage, whether the name was given by the Portuguese or Dutch as a title, whether it was appropriated by the users themselves, or whether it was simply used to describe the rulers of Kiltai and Keffing by other local peoples impressed by their links with foreigners is unclear.

The Portuguese evidence is interesting, especially when taken together with later historic and ethnographic sources. It is obvious from de Brito that Serdenha was a major redistribution center before 1500 and the

Southeast Seram archipelago more generally throughout the sixteenth and early seventeenth centuries. It has not been possible to locate precise locations for Serdenha, which in itself may be revealing; though it is plausible that Serdenha is Keffing (a name of Malay origin, indicating its importance in trade), and that eventually replaced it. It is also possible that Serdenha was, rather than being a single place, a reference to the entire Southeast Seram Archipelago, including Seram Rei, Seram Laut, Kiltai, and Geser. The connections to the Papuan coast, and especially the southern side of Teluk Berau (Ogar, Onin, Sekar, Mangossa) northward to Misool in the Raja Ampat group and between Southeast Seram and Banda, which de Brito described so clearly (Figure 3.6), must have been important throughout the sixteenth century, and early Dutch observers such as Schouten (in 1602) confirmed the involvement of traders from archipelagic Southeast Seram over a vast area, encompassing the Raja Ampat Islands, New Guinea, Buru, and Timor (Swadling 1996:137 n. 6).

What is striking is that although Southeast Seram as a whole persists as a regional trading node between 1500 and 1900, at certain periods some domains are mentioned and not others, and the frequency with which they are mentioned also changes, suggesting fluctuation in the significance of particular places over time. What is evidently a common feature of Southeast Asian history may partly reflect the patchiness of documentary evidence, and the importance of particular places may be obscured by name changes, inadequate knowledge, and poor transcription, but as I argue in chapter 4, this feature may also shed light on the relationship between trade, local politics, and ecology.

Identifying ethnic, political, and geographical labels for this early period is not easy. One location mentioned frequently in sixteenth-century sources, after general references to Maluku, Banda, and Amboina, and that can be confidently identified, is Guli-guli (Figure 3.7) (Langren 1595, in Van Linschoten 1955 [1596]). Other places are more problematic. Thus, when the name Gorom or its cognates occur it is not unreasonable to assume that the contemporary island of Gorom is meant. However, before the late nineteenth century Gorom referred to the island now called Manawoka, and what is now Gorom was known as Gorom Rei. As the island of Gorom Rei became more important politically, and perhaps in response to administrative convenience, the qualification *rei* (land) was dropped (see chapter 6.4). Also, the toponym Gorom is sometimes extended to Pulau Panjang and Manawoka. For those periods when we know the domain of Kataloka to have been in political and trading ascendancy we may assume that Gorom was often equivalent to Kataloka. The term "Serammers" is more complex. We have noted that Seram, Ceram, or Seran initially refers in European documents to the extreme east coast of that island, together with the Seram Laut Archipelago. Much of the time it is not unreasonable to assume that Serammers refers to Seram Laut in the wider sense of including the domains of Kiltai and Kilwaru, and sometimes Keffing and much

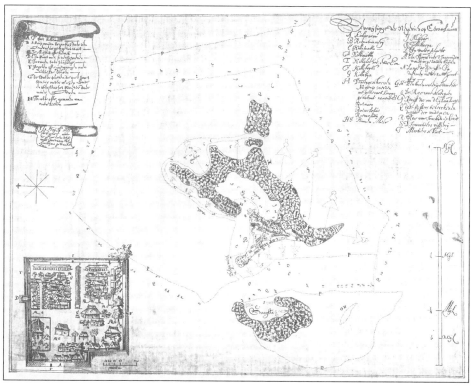

Figure 3.10. Seram Laut Archipelago in the early seventeenth century. Copy of a manuscript by Artus Gijsels made in 1889 and deposited in the map room of the Rijksarchief in The Hague (Koloniale Aanwinsten 170, 684056). The original is in the Landesbibliothek in Karlsruhe.

later Geser. The island of Seram Laut has few independent domains (possibly excepting Maar) that can be confidently identified for the sixteenth century, though Keffing, Kelu, Kilwaru, and Kiltai have all controlled parts of Seram Laut for various periods in their histories. Geser was probably uninhabited and of relatively little significance at that period and in the early seventeenth century was a place where firewood was exchanged (Reiner de Klerk 1894 [1756]:39). Urung, Kilmuri, Kiliban, Guli-guli, and Kilboi (between Tobo and Kilmuri) are all mentioned for this early period, but Keffing is undoubtedly the most important (Coolhaas 1968:13, 217). With the arrival of the VOC the data become more reliable. To defend their monopoly in the spice trade, from the 1630s onward the Dutch attached great significance to detailed intelligence concerning East Seram, and an indication of just what can be found in the archives is the map produced by Gijsels dated 1637 (Figure 3.10).

General accounts of Moluccan history for this period assume a significant political influence in Southeast Seram for the North Moluccan sultanates of Ternate and Tidore. Tidore was at war with Ternate from 1583. In 1628 Kimelaha Leliate claimed for Ternate the south coast of Seram, including Keffing. The east coast was claimed by Tidore as far south as Seram Laut and Gorom, and in 1572 the Tidore admiral Kaicili Salona is said to have controlled the coast from Waru in the north to Keffing in the south (Haga 1884, 1:12, 43). The same coast was still under Tidore influence in 1610 (ibid., 41). Archipelagic Southeast Seram was clearly an area of overlapping claims and of strategic importance to both sultanates on account of its pivotal role in trade. However, whether Tidore influence was really effective along those parts of the Onin coast where Serammers traded is doubtful. Keyts, for example, did not mention it, even indirectly through the activities of Serammers, and the position and mode of operation of the Serammers hardly indicates Tidore domination. Of course, it is possible that Tidore exerted influence only intermittently and indirectly, perhaps through raids by Misool Papuans along the Onin coast. But again and again reports in the Dutch archives throughout the seventeenth century indicate that Seram Laut was very much in charge of the Papuan trade in this area. This is supported by the linguistic evidence, for though SSL was well understood along the Onin coast by the time of Keyts (ibid., 120–122, 136), the language of Tidore was unknown.

3.8. The Banda System after 1621

Although the Dutch had been present in the Moluccas since 1600, they did not take a particular interest in Southeast Seram until after 1621, presumably because its traders were not seen to threaten Dutch interests. In 1621, however, the Dutch finally conquered Banda, most Bandanese fled or were murdered (including forty-five orang kayas [Reid 1993:274]), and the Dutch took steps to establish a monopoly in the production and trade in nutmeg and mace. The independent trade with Makassar ended.

Some Bandanese found refuge in Makassar and continued to play a part in its commercial life, particularly through utilizing their knowledge of the nutmeg trade (Tiele and Heeres 1886:17; Villiers 1981a:18). Some fled to the Kei and Aru Islands, but many also to Southeast Seram and Gorom (Brumund 1845:77; Van der Chijs 1886:162; Haddon 1920:110; Tiele 1886:315), taking advantage of the existing trading corridor and its political alliances. Indeed, Seram Laut and Gorom are reputed to have sent a flotilla of *kora-kora* (war canoes) to Banda in 1624 to evacuate the indigenous population that remained and to prevent further Dutch slaughter (Coolhaas 1975: xvii). Hanna (1978:55) estimated that of the original population of 15,000, no more than 1,000 survived in the archipelago, supplemented by a further 530 who were shipped back from Batavia where they had been stationed on the orders of Jan Pieterzoon Coen, who in 1618 became the first governor-general of the Netherlands East Indies. It is commonly assumed that this remaining population was predominantly female and that it is through them that the vestiges of the old Bandanese culture have been perpetuated down to the present. Wurffbain (Van den Berg 1872; Hanna 1978: 66) listed 560 native Bandanese in 1638 (291 of which were females and 211 enslaved) out of a total population of 3,843. Surviving Bandanese were, therefore, mostly enslaved and, moreover, required to transmit their skills to imported labor from New Guinea, Seram, Buru, Timor, and Borneo. In these inauspicious circumstances a new society was forged from free men and slaves drawn from as widely as Mozambique, Japan, Holland, Portugal, South Africa, and China, as well as from the Malay world (Hanna 1978: 62–63).

Those ethnic Bandanese who had fled to Southeast Seram settled on the small islands of the Seram Laut Archipelago and involved themselves in trade, the usual niche of migrants and refugees. In Guli-guli and Keffing, they became prominent in trading activities (Van Doren 1857:315; Knaap 1985), including the smuggling of cloves in violation of the VOC prohibition. Some settlements may have been predominantly Bandanese in composition, and on some early maps Banda-Keffing is marked. Other villages may have assimilated lesser numbers of Bandanese. Of those Bandanese who fled to Gorom, we know from Valentijn (Haga 1884, 1:43) that some sheltered in Rarakit on the east coast, known to the VOC as a hideout for "Papuan pirates." The Dutch made some punitive raids (Van Doren 1857: 315) in 1624 in the Southeast Seram area in an attempt to flush out the remaining Bandanese, but in the end gave up.

The evidence for significant Bandanese settlement in the Gorom-Geser area is overwhelming, despite the fact that the language did not survive here, but rather in two isolates on Kei Besar (see section 3.2). That the language is no longer spoken in any form may be because the Bandanese in Southeast Seram were too thinly spread in different settlements, partly as a result of preexisting ties of trade and marriage, and because of the existence of a dominant panlocal lingua franca—Southeast Seram Littoral. Had there been numerous local languages it might have had a chance. Also, Bandanese was more closely related to SSL compared with the languages of Kei and Aru. Indeed, in the early seventeenth century, the similarities between Bandanese and SSL may have been no greater than those between Gorom and Geser currently.

Apart from the sources just mentioned, the evidence for Bandanese settlement is mainly in the form of *etar* that are able to trace their origin to particular Bandanese villages (Table 3.4). Thus, in Guli-guli there is Kilu-anga and Lewataka. Haji Machsin Kilualaga claims that his family has been there seven generations, which is, however, disappointingly somewhat short of the number of generations needed to be consistent with the chronology. In other cases the *etar* names indicate more amorphous Ban-

Table 3.4. Bandanese clans in the Geser-Gorom area

Bandanese Clan	East Seram Location	Place of Origin
1 Kiluanga	Guli-guli	
2 Lewataka[a]	Guli-guli	Labatakka
3 Kasongat	Kelu, Keffing	= *kadang* (a blood relationship)
4 Soleman	Keffing	Selamon (Uli Lima)
5	Kelu (Keffing)	Namasawar[b]
6	Tobo < Kiltai (Kilwaru)	
7 Wakaringi-Lautaka[c]	Keffing	
8 Ruma[n]dan	Keta-Kianlaut	
9 Lautaka	Keffing	Namasawar, though Lautaka (or Nautaka) is a settlement on the north coast of Neira
10 Siwa	Keffing	Lonthor
11 (Kota) Banda	Keffing	
12 Andan-Lewataka	Keta-Kianlaut	

[a] Lewataka was a "chief raja" of Banda.

[b] Namasawar cannot be found on maps of Banda, though it may be Samar, a settlement on the south coast of Banda Besar.

[c] Wakaringi is a Bandanese term indicating persons coming from outside.

danese origins without specifying particular places (Andan, Kotabanda) or descendants of particular individuals (Lewataka). There are Rumadan *etar* in Keta, Kwaos, Kelibat, Gorom, and Miran (Gorom), suggesting either the movement of Bandanese from some original settlement on Seram, or independent settlements after 1621. According to Umar Norf Rumalutur, Rumalutur is an SSL corruption of Rumalonthor. *Lutur*, as we have noted, is a stone fish trap, and I think we must discount this as a dead metaphor, though the ingenuity with which people invent such, and their persistence, reflects the importance attached through folk histories to the Bandanese connection.

The links with Bandanese settlements are still maintained today (Ellen 1993), reflected in the attempts made by those tracing Bandanese descent or affiliation to confirm their links with Banda in the form of written documents. These include letters of authentification (Surat Pengasihan), in Malay or Indonesian, from villages on Banda in reply to requests from Southeast Seram villages for confirmation of a link or clarification of some disputed matter of tradition. A major preoccupation in this connection is the existence of a common symbolic linkage, in the form of membership of Uli (or Ur) Fito (seven), Siwa (nine), and, especially, Lima (five). In 1986 I collected a copy of a letter of this kind between Namasawar and the raja of Kelu (on the island of Seram Rei), dated 18 January 1890.[3] Such letters now exist only in typed form, probably having been copied in the 1950s or

1960s, which is some measure of the importance still attached to them. There are also the more substantial "Warta" (Communications), running to four sides of typed foolscap. I have a copy of one of these dated 5 October 1926, again from Namasawar, to the rajas of Kelu and Tobo (on the south coast of Seram) and the orang kaya of Kiltai. Occasionally, similar documents appear in Dutch as "Korte beschrijving" (Short Descriptions). I have a copy of one of these, undated, consisting of two sides of typed foolscap, that explains the Lima, Siwa, and Fito affiliations of Banda villages and their links with Southeast Seram. Geser, it explains, is mostly Siwa, though with some Fito; on Seram Rei only the Soleman clan (that is, those persons tracing their patrilineal ancestry to the Bandanese domain of Selamon) is Lima, the rest are Siwa.

In the course of a generation or two, there evolved a new social and economic system on Banda founded as much on precedent as on VOC prescription (Hanna 1978:64). After 1621, the Dutch were faced not only with the problem of how to maintain nutmeg production on the backs of a decimated population, but also with the same infrastructural problem that had faced the authochthonous Bandanese before them: how to feed the population. The introduction of the "perkenierstelsel," a classic plantation mode of production, which intensified land use and rationalized agricultural production, transformed both the pattern of settlement and the management of natural resources. The conquest had disrupted the entire economy and social organization; only the environment and nutmeg trees were left intact (Loth 1998:68). Apart from importing labor, and establishing the estates under the supervision of Dutch perkeniers, the VOC created a new geographical division of labor in which certain islands became reserved for firewood, timber, fruits and vegetables, and cattle production. To some extent the food problem was solved by imports from the West, but this hardly satisfied the needs of the newly created population of Javanese coolies with their Ambonese overseers. The only practical solution, paradoxically, was to harness the Banda system, more or less as it had existed before 1621 in service of the precolonial society, to supply the needs of a very different colonial economy. Thus, slaves on Banda ate sago imported from Seram, and the perkeniers and VOC officials ate rice imported from Java (Valentijn 1724–1726, 3:3, cited by Bokemeyer 1888:333). But for this arrangement to succeed, the Dutch had to mend their relations with the peoples of Southeast Seram and ironically the Bandanese refugees among them (Heeres and Stapel 1931:5, 93). To this end Van Speult negotiated on behalf of the VOC an agreement on 23 December 1624 with the orang kayas of Seram Laut, Keffing, Gorom and Guli-guli, Urung, and Kwaos (Coac) (Haga 1884, 1:45). Arrangements were made in 1633 for the VOC to be supplied with sago and other necessary commodities from Seram Laut and Gorom, and also Kei (Tiele and Heeres 1886:73). Very soon, the periphery supplying Banda encompassed Aru, Tanimbar, Kei, Southeast Seram, and parts of the Papuan coast (Van de Graaff and Meijlan 1856:192). Gijsels reported that by 1634 five or six large perahus (sailing boats) a year were going to Seram to obtain turtle shell, rice, beans, and slaves. By 1658 Banda was routinely importing sago, coconuts, beans, peas, parrots, and slaves from Southeast Seram (Keffing is a location mentioned), Kei, and Aru; sending in return textiles, iron, silver, and gold. Although the VOC had formally claimed Gorom in 1637, in reality any control was difficult to exercise. In the same year the first VOC treaty with a ruler on Seram Laut, Orang Kaya Baud, was signed, along with contracts with Keffing and Rarakit, which obliged people to trade only with the VOC and to report on smugglers (Riedel 1886:149–150). These contracts were renewed in 1650, 1661, and 1677 (Reiner de Klerk 1894 [1756]:37), though they had relatively little effect. Under similar treaties Ambonese were not permitted to trade with Southeast Seram, which only served to strengthen the Banda–Southeast Seram tie.

The VOC thus relied upon Southeast Seram, and yet it continued to pose a threat, both by challenging the spice monopoly and by interfering with what Polanyi (in Polanyi, Arensberg, and Pearson 1957) would have described as "administrative trade" and thus the efficient running of VOC settlements on Banda and Ambon-Lease. In 1649 the VOC met a legation in Ambon from the nine polities of Seram Laut, and De Vlaming visited Keffing. As a result the polities agreed not to grow spices. The VOC also secured agreement with the "king of Onin" that his subjects should not pick wild nutmeg (Haga 1884, 1:70, 72). In 1650 representatives from Gorom, Keffing, Kilmuri, Seram Laut, and Rarakit signed a further agreement with the VOC in Ambon covering such matters as repatriation of runaway slaves and the handling of Makassan traders. In practice, though, these agreements had little effect.

There was a lively trade between the Bandanese and local peoples of Southeast Seram and Gorom in long nutmeg, partly imported from New Guinea but partly grown in their own groves. The cargoes were smuggled out of the area. Rumphius reported that in 1632 twenty-eight foreign vessels, eight described as Malay, six Makassan, and the rest Javanese from Bantam, Japara, and Giri, were found to be smuggling nutmeg; in addition there were two sampans, one from Kambelo on Hoamoal and one from Mamala on Ambon (Coolhaas 1960, 1:398). We know that in 1633 Seram Laut and Southeast Seram generally were also involved in the illegal spice trade, with cloves being smuggled from Hoamoal, often handled by Makassans (ibid., 533). We have reports for the same year of Makassan vessels visiting Seram Laut, Kei, and Aru. Again, in 1637 Southeast Seram, and Seram Laut in particular, was visited by at least nine Malay, Javanese, and Makassan junks (ibid., 614). There is evidence of Javanese and Makassan trading in the Werinama area of South Seram involving Keffingers and Seram-Lauters (Van Doren 1857:316). Seram Laut continued to provide products from New Guinea to Bali, Southeast Kalimantan, and East Java, smuggling spices and trading turtle shell, pearls, bird of paradise plumes, damar, ambergris, massoi, and Papuan slaves. Most smuggled spices went to China and India. In return they obtained rice, guns, pottery, and utensils. In the periphery of Tidore, VOC restrictions led the Gamrange and Raja Ampat islanders to sell spices, slaves, ambergris, and turtle shell in Gorom, Kilwaru, Keffing, and Rarakit, often to Malay, Javanese, Bugis, and Butonese traders for textiles, iron, gunpowder, and lead, or in their absence to local traders who took the goods to Timor and Larantuka (Andaya 1991:94). Of all places, Rarakit was regarded by the VOC as the greatest problem, being both an illegal market and a haven for Papuan pirates (Haga 1884, 1:61). Indeed, much of the so-called "piracy" attributed to Serammers may actually have been the responsibility of Papuans (Coolhaas 1960, 1:402). This pattern continued for some sixty years, and even for 1704 we find *Generale Missiven* reports of Serammers (possibly meaning Seram Lauters in this context) and Keffingers handling illegal spices from the Papuan Islands and the Gamrange (Coolhaas 1976, 6:294).

The Dutch destruction of Banda and the imposition of a nutmeg monopoly stimulated planting on Gorom and elsewhere, and also the collection of wild Papuan nuts in an attempt to evade the monopoly. In response to what was perceived as illegal trade, and despite the existence of treaties, VOC forces began to take action. In 1645 the Dutch prevented Seram Laut trading activities in the Aru Archipelago. The first nutmeg extirpation ("extirpatie," or eradication) on Gorom was conducted in 1648. In an extirpation in the same year in Keffing, four thousand trees were destroyed, though this could not have been Keffing on Seram Rei and was probably on Seram Laut or mainland Seram. In 1649 there was an extirpation on Gorom, which was subjected to a further extirpation of one thousand trees in 1670 and another 137 trees, plus two hundred smaller stands, in 1748 (Reiner de Klerk 1894 [1756]:37; Warburg 1897:125). Further extirpations of Southeast Seram plantations followed in 1637, 1652, 1668, 1672, and 1674 (Van de Graaff and Meijlan 1856:76, 193). The VOC also sought to protect its interests by placing Company soldiers in places of strategic importance on a more permanent basis, such as Guli-guli, where in 1657 they built a small fort, "Oosteinde," with a garrison of 30 soldiers (Van de Wall 1928:214–215). In the early years of the extirpations (as is reflected in these figures) the aim was to destroy preexisting plantations; the smaller extirpations of the later years appear to have been to enforce unequal treaties with unwilling domains that had the temerity to violate the monopoly. For much of the second half of the seventeenth century, the VOC was effectively at war with the polities of Southeast Seram, and the most prominent among them was Keffing.

As for Tidore, there is no reason to think that its influence on the conduct of trade and political affairs of the peoples of Southeast Seram was any greater after 1621 than it had been before. The sultan may well have been responsible for occasional *kora-kora* raids on the coast of Seram and Gorom, such as that recorded for 1673 (Haga 1884, 1:136), but Tidorese influence was weak along the south coast of Teluk Berau and along the Onin coast. Rumphius followed Keyts in indicating that the Goromese and Seram Lauters largely had the trade to themselves, though they may have been afforded additional protection by the presence of Makassans (ibid., 140, 147). The picture that emerges is one in which Tidore operated through loose formal treaties of exchange at what we might assume to be the highest level and within a framework of notional terms of exchange, whereas the Serammers were much more politically devolved, operating at the individual and local domain level and determining exchange values without reference to higher authority. In this respect the Serammers posed similar problems for Tidore and for the VOC. It was only in 1705 that Tidorese authority over Keffing (and Gebe) acquired a degree of effectiveness, and this only as a result of Dutch recognition, providing an example of colonial powers bringing about through their own actions what was later to be accepted as the precolonial political dispensation (Ellen 1993).

3.9. Conclusion

By the end of the seventeenth century, the VOC had instituted some significant changes in the Banda system, but paradoxically these changes could only be sustained by relying on a preexisting framework of inter-island trade and division of labor. The political economy of Banda had been transformed,[4] but with the aim of maintaining a pattern of production and export that had preceded it and that was only possible because of an existing indigenous periphery to supply its subsistence needs. But one unforeseen consequence of this was to fuel the growth of Southeast Seram as an alternative trading zone, one that the VOC would find impossible to control. Indeed, the volume of trade conducted between 1621 and 1800 rivaled that carried out by the Dutch in the whole of the Moluccan Islands, which they directly administered (Swadling 1996:137 n. 7). And, as Andaya (1991:83) reminded us, the transfer of indigenous Bandanese expertise and contacts in this trading world acted as a stimulant in transforming archipelagic Southeast Seram into another competing commercial center, though the data presented in this chapter suggest that we should in no way underestimate the significance of native Seram trade before 1621. The Southeast Seram trading area itself cannot have been a Bandanese creation, as is sometimes suggested (e.g., Van der Crab 1862:62).

Another development that occurred during the early VOC period was the beginnings of significant trading involvement with the Moluccas and Southeast Seram by the peoples of South Sulawesi. During the later sixteenth and seventeenth centuries Makassar had become the commercial hub of the eastern islands and, in particular, the center of the spice "smuggling" trade in nutmeg and mace in defiance of the VOC monopoly (Sutherland and Brée 1987:2). Reports as early as 1632 show that Makassan vessels already equaled in number those of Malays in the waters around Seram Rei and Seram Laut, though Javanese vessels still predominated (Coolhaas 1960, 1:534; Tiele and Heeres 1886:203). Moreover, Makassan traders, along with the Javanese, were implicated in violating the VOC monopoly by bringing cloves from Luhu on the Hoamoal Peninsula of West Seram to Guli-guli for onward export. During the late 1630s Makassan vessels are regularly reported as laying in off Gorom, Guli-guli, and Keffing (Tiele and Heeres 1890:242, 297), and in 1662 we get the first evidence of Bugis at Rumbati in New Guinea (Haga 1884, 1:79). However, the kingdoms of Gowa-Tallo finally fell to the Dutch in 1669, and this marked the end of an era when Makassar dominated free trade in eastern Indonesia. One consequence of all of this—the Dutch monopoly, declining exports, and restrictions on production—was, strangely, to maintain preexisting local, intermediate, and regional trade networks in the Moluccas. As the significance of the Moluccas, and in particular Southeast Seram, receded in the fortunes of the colonial economy, trade continued for locals in many ways as it had done before the arrival of the Dutch, constrained only by the vicissitudes of geography and a sailing technology, an asymmetric distribution of vital resources, and a dependency on the Asian market.

4
The Political Economy of
a Conradian Space

En die van Goram soo hij kan,
Die wort er eenmael meester van
Enkrijgt hij dan veel rijkke waer,
Als elders heen in twintigh jaer.

He who comes from Gorom,
Will be the owner one day
And he will have more riches,
Than elsewhere be found in
twenty years.

SEVENTEENTH-CENTURY DUTCH VERSE QUOTED IN
A. HAGA, *Nederlandsch-Nieuw-Guinea*

4.1. The Vagaries and Testament of Historical Geography

In *An Outcast of the Islands* Joseph Conrad (1896:61) manifested his knowledge of the local situation by having Babalatchi argue that the time was coming to apply to the Orang Belanda for a flag "for that protection which would make them safe forever." For Resink (1968:316; see also Warren 1977), writing in 1959, Conrad's books well evoke the eastern Indonesian scene: for they "bristle with brigs and barks, schooners and proas, owned by shippers of many nationalities and manned by sailors from the four winds.... European-rigged ships [are] frequently the property of Chinese, Arab or half-caste owners...and most trade is in non-Dutch hands" (ibid., 319). One sign of the inroads that the Dutch had made by the early nineteenth century (though in this case perhaps unintentionally) was reflected in the role of flags to symbolize the secure conditions for the conduct of trade and to signal political allegiance. Thus, when Bik arrived in Dobo in 1824 (1928:41), he found Dutch flags being flown by Makassan pinisi, and there is no doubt that by that time flags generally had become an important means of signifying political submission and identity. The use of the Dutch flag has to be seen in the context of the widespread use of flags and pennants (*gici-gici*) in Southeast Seram at the time, well illustrated in those reproduced by Riedel (1886, plates XVII–XVIII, 133, 140) for eighteen polities in the area. Some of the flags portrayed by Riedel were still in use in 1986, hung on either side of the middle of a boat while at the stern and prow was flown the merah-putih (the flag of independent Indonesia) instead of the Dutch tricolor (Figure 4.1).

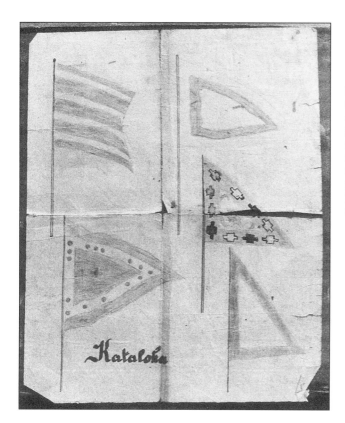

Figure 4.1. Pennants and flags of Kataloka as recorded on a document (estimated to be at least one hundred years old) in the possession of the raja of Kataloka in 1986 and reproduced with permission. Ellen 86-14-28. Compare with Plate XVIII in Riedel (1886:140).

By 1800 Southeast Seram consisted of a large number of relatively autonomous domains with a similar political organization and social structure, some large and influential in trade and politicking, such as Ondor and Kataloka, but most of them small. All were in competitive trading relations, waxing and waning in their political and economic fortunes, and bound through formal alliances and other allegiances with each other. The domains also increasingly provided space for traders from outside the area (Bugis, Arabs, and Chinese) settling in the Seram Laut area, on Gorom or Manawoka, usually moving in from Banda, and with whom local people (especially rulers) traded and who received protection in exchange for material resources and commercial opportunities. This essentially Conradian picture persisted until the end of the century.

Comparing the available historical data on these polities with what we have for the present day it is evident that there have been changes in the location and geographical extent of individual domains. Some, again domains such as Ondor and Kataloka, have remained important and more or less intact over the entire period. By comparison, Namalen on Gorom, which was independent in 1792, had by 1986 become part of Rarat; and of its various constituent villages, Dada had become part of Kataloka and Kinali part of Miran. Ainikke (Enneka) on Pulau Panjang, important in 1792, though not as important as Ondor and Kataloka, and perhaps in some sense politically subject to them, nevertheless operated protected franchises (*sosolot*s) along the coast of Onin and traded independently with Bali. It had ceased to exist as a separate place by 1986, and its once subject settlement of Buan had become part of Miran on Gorom. Kelikat (Kailakat), equally important in 1792, and still mentioned in 1862 by Van der Crab (1862:87), had also effectively disappeared by 1986; the settlements of Bas and Aran had come under the jurisdiction of Kilkoda. Nirang had likewise disappeared, though its subject settlement of Rarat had by 1986 become a domain in its own right. Mida, Amar(watu) and Dai all continued to exist though Mida lost Kilibingan to Dai. Van der Crab (1864: 531–556) reported that in 1862 the raja of Amar also ruled Manawoka, part of Gorom and Panjang. In particular, Amar had jurisdiction over Kailakat, Kiltalisa, Aran, Tinari, Baras, Rumatela, Kilsodiromesi, Katawawar, Romanana, Bawan, Kilgowa, Tonastalu, Ilor, Adar, and Ramandan. Amar even extended its authority to the Watubela Islands (Bosscher 1855:39), though in 1916 Watubela was withdrawn by the Dutch from the jurisdiction of Amar. Riedel (1886:147) reported that in the early 1880s the raja of Kataloka had authority over eight settlements, the raja of Ondor eleven, and the raja of Amar twenty-nine on Gorom, ten on Manawoka, and four on Panjang. At its zenith the influence of Amarsekaru extended to Kei and Aru.

Today the official jurisdiction of the raja of Amar (Figure 4.2) is confined to Manawoka. From the oral records we know of disputes over the ownership of the cay of Garogos, first between Amarsekaru and Kataloka and then between Kilwaru and Kataloka (Soselisa 1995:42). Thus, a very clear impression is left not only of shifting relations of tribute, subjugation, and alliance but, in some cases, the physical movement of settlements as well.[1] On top of this the imposition of indirect colonial administration further muddied the status of individual domains, not only by altering their boundaries but also by conferring or confirming titles of Malay origin that differentiated between rulers who had hitherto maintained the fiction that they were all equals (Ellen 1986). Thus, Van der Crab (1864:534–535) spoke of the Orang Kaya Ondor, but De Hollander (1895:502) said that Ondor, Amar, and Mida each had a raja.

The situation in the Seram Laut Archipelago was even more complex. In the 1820s there were, according to Bik (1928 [1824]:6, 9), an orang kaya and kapitan in Kelu, a mayor and kapitan in Keffing, and an orang kaya in Geser and Kwaai. Half of Seram Laut was under Kwaai. By the last decade of that century there was still a mayor of Keffing but a raja in Kelu, dividing the island of Seram Rei between them (De Hollander 1895:501). Although the raja of Kilwaru had authority over Geser and Kilwaru,[2] the raja of Kelu had control over part of Seram Laut but preferred to live on Geser (as indeed

Figure 4.2. Raja of Amarsekaru wearing ceremonial clothes of Dutch nineteenth-century origin, Manawoka, May 1986.

his descendants still do), where he could drink wine. Seram Rei consisted of Keffing, Kwaai, Kelu, Kotabanda, Pagar, Kotawau, and Kilberau.

In discussing the significance of particular domains, care must be taken to note the changing names for islands and settlements. The interpretation of old maps is a minefield, and it is hoped that we have moved on from literalist readings that see them as only more or less accurate (and progressively better and more objective representations of the world) as technical expertise in surveying and printing has improved (Wood 1992), to being reflections of complex social constructions. Of course, there are plenty of mundane sources of misinformation as well, such as copying errors and problems in communication between travelers and printers, in addition to the topography of parts of the Moluccas being still uncharted until considerably into the second half of the nineteenth century. Thus, as late as 1767

Tanimbar was sometimes located next to Gorom, rather than the 600 kilometers farther south that it should be.[3] Difficulties arise partly through changes in the conventional local usages and shifting spaces occupied by particular domains, but the position is further complicated by the ways in which different writers, colonial officials, and mapmakers refer to places. From the late nineteenth century onward, place-names definitively changed through official fiat to suit the convenience of colonial and post-colonial administration. Thus, before 1900 Pulau Panjang is often referred to as Suruakl (De Hollander 1895:502), a name also used by Riedel (1886: 146, opp. 177), who called it Gorongrei (also Wallace 1962 [1869]:277–278). One systematic source of confusion is the replacement of a local topographic naming system based on the mainland (*rei*): sea (*lau*) opposition. Thus, in older sources, what is now Manawoka is known as Gorom (sometimes Gorong) Rei, in contrast to Gorom Laut. Gorom Laut is what is now known simply as Gorom (De Hollander 1895:502; Riedel 1886:146). What confuses the situation further is the shortening of Gorom Rei on some maps to Gorom. Thus, two islands at different times in different written contexts are quite accurately referred to as Gorom. Similarly, at the tip of what we now know as Seram, we have the opposition between Seram (sometimes Serang) Rei and Seram Laut (Seranglao). In contemporary usage, Seram Laut remains though the name Seram Rei is not used for official purposes; the island is known metanymically by the name of its historically most important domain, Keffing (see also Bik 1928 [1824]:3, 7). Sometimes maps speak of the Keffing Islands, in the plural: Klein Keffing (Seram Rei) and Groot Keffing, the mangrove area on the mainland of Seram (Van der Crab 1862:57, 59). In contrast to both Seram Rei and Seram Laut, mainland Seram is often known to this day as Seram Besar or Tanah Besar.

Seventeenth-century maps in the Rijksarchief give us some idea of places that were important at the time. During the first decades of the seventeenth century Keffing and Seram Laut appear to have been primarily anchorages for Malay, Makassan, and Javanese trading vessels (Tiele 1886). On a map of 1651, based on information provided by Arnoldus de Vlamingh, only Seram Laut is marked among a number of small islands and banks off Southeast Seram that bear little resemblance to the actual geography.[4] Another seventeenth-century map in the Rijksarchief shows Keffing on the mainland of Seram, suggesting that it was once part of the wider mangrove area and that the domain of Keffing comprised both the mainland and the small island of Seram Rei.[5] As has been noted, Seram Rei was often described by the Dutch as "klein Kefing" (small Keffing) (see above and Bosscher 1855) in contrast to unmarked "Keffing," which referred to the mainland mangrove zone that now includes Kwamar. Guli-guli is consistently marked on the earliest maps. Maar appears on several maps and in the late nineteenth century is sometimes used as a synonym for the entire island of Seram Laut, on which it is situated (e.g., Riedel 1886:146). Maar currently is used synonymously for Seram Laut; it is the marked term:

implicitly Maar Rei, in contrast to the smaller island Maar Lau. On one map what appears to be Kilwaru is marked as Pulau Sarong, though with its sartorial allusion to the shape of an atoll, this may just be a reference to Geser.[6] In the 1680s Geser (Gisser) was claimed by Kilwaru, but is no longer itself inhabited.[7] On some maps Geser is shown but not named.

One late seventeenth-century map in the Rijksarchief provides us with some extraordinary detail concerning the mangrove area between Guliguli and Kwaos (Figure 2.5). But this map is probably less interesting for what it shows of the distribution of the mangrove itself (though this has clearly altered) than for what it tells us about shifting human settlements and political control. Thus, some settlements are marked on an inlet within the mangrove that no longer exist (Mattahenny and Matta Boelan), which is consistent with narratives suggesting that the mangrove was a refuge in the seventeenth century during wars with Tidore and the VOC (chapter 2.3). More intriguing, however, are the settlements marked on the island to the extreme east. This island cannot be other than Seram Rei or Keffing, yet neither of these names appear. Quay (Kwaai), Killeloehoe (Kelu), and Kullebia (Kilberau?) all appear more or less in their current locations (compare Figure 2.4). "Banda" is indicated, and this is presumably Kotabanda (the settlement of Bandanese refugees). Roema Samesit and Sumbacko have no obvious contemporary equivalents and must be assumed to no longer exist. However, Killetay must be Kiltai and Killewaroe must be Kilwaru, though both domains are now centered on the islet of Kiltai off Seram Laut. These may, of course, be errors, but given other circumstantial evidence (e.g., Kilwaru present both on Geser and Kiltai) this may indicate control by these domains.

In Keizer's map of between 1735 and 1747 (Figure 4.3) Rarakit is marked prominently on the east coast of Seram (disappearing by the twentieth century). Keffing is marked as a large island with its various polities and some clans clearly marked (Kasongat, Keliwalanga, Kelilla) and separated from the mainland by the "Keddakreek." There may be some confusion between Keffing and the mangrove area on the mainland, though Kwamar is clearly marked as part of this. Again, we may have evidence here of Keffing being part of the mainland mangrove area. Seram Laut is prominent, though Kilwaru is not marked as a separate island and there is no mention of Kiltai. In 1779 Geser and Seram Laut appear to have been the political centers of gravity as far as the Dutch were concerned, and the heads of these polities signed contracts renewing old agreements with the VOC to supply Banda with victuals, slaves, and manufacturing materials.[8] A proclamation on smuggling issued in 1824 by the Dutch authorities and addressed to rulers in the Amboina residency is quite specific in its mentioning of locations, but among the polities of the Seram Laut Archipelago only Gorom is mentioned, suggesting that at that time Gorom (Kataloka, Ondor) was in political and commercial ascendancy, while Keffing and Seram Laut and other places had been temporarily eclipsed.[9] In 1824, according to Bik (1928

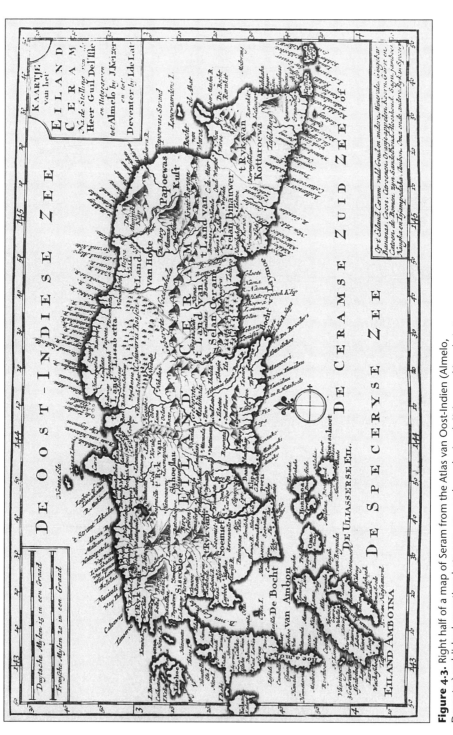

Figure 4-3. Right half of a map of Seram from the Atlas van Oost-Indien (Almelo, Deventer) published sometime between 1735 and 1747 by Jacob Keizer and Jan de Lat. Reproduced by courtesy of the Koninklijk Instituut voor Land-, Taal-en Volkenkunde.

[1824]:16) it was possible to walk at low tide along the beach from Keffing to Seram, along the south coast as far as Tobo and northward to Waru, and via inland paths over the mountains to Sawai. Wallace (1962 [1869]:277–278), passing through the area in 1860, spoke of, and marked, Kwamar as an island, and had much to say of Kilwaru as an important trading center but did not mention Geser, which he elsewhere mistakenly refered to as "Kissa" (ibid., 288). On another map, dated 1835, Geser is marked but not Kilwaru. On the other hand, another map of 1835 shows Kilwaru and Kiltai in their modern locations, Kelu and Keffing are placed on Seram Rei, Geser is marked, and both Kwamar Besar and Kwamar Kecil appear, all shown as part of the "afdeeling Banda."[10] Another map of the same date shows "Keilaka" marked on Gorom; Pulau Panjang is marked as "Klein Sallawatie Monowokken"; Geser is marked but not Kilwaru; Keffing, Kwamar, and Kwaos are all marked on the mangrove island.[11]

It is interesting that a map in the Rijksarchief dated 1872 also shows Keffing as a large island within the mangrove area (i.e., part of the mainland), with "Keffing" marked as a settlement inland along the sunge "vroeger straat Salila." The island also indicates Kilbroh (Kilberau), Killoe (Kelu), and Koewai (Kwaai).[12] Another map, which must be later than 1875 but reflects the position as understood for the 1860s (Figure 4.4), marks the mainland swamp as Keffing and Seram Rei as Klein Keffing; Geser is marked but not as a significant settlement. Such a configuration indicates some continuity in political geography, first evident at the opening of the European era. On the same map Kalmaru or Kilwaru is marked (but not Kiltai). In the Gorom group, Panjang is marked as "Salawattie or Soeroeaki" and on Gorom only Ondor and Kailakat are marked. On Manawoka only Dejrang is marked. In Baron van Hoevell's sketch map of 1894, the large island coterminus with the contemporary distribution of the mangrove area is named Kwamar, separated from the mainland by a wide and obviously navigable channel between Air Nanang and Guli-guli. By 1909 a map in the same collection provides the more or less correct contemporary proportions of Keffing and the adjacent mainland.[13]

4.2. Reconstructing Precolonial Political Systems

Although from the beginning of the seventeenth to the end of the nineteenth century the VOC, and after it the government of the Netherlands East Indies, succeeded in forcing temporary agreements on the rulers of Southeast Seram, these potentates and their domains remained more or less autonomous. Or, rather, until 1768 the VOC controlled the islands indirectly through its vassal, the sultan of Tidore, who in that year terminated the vassalage and returned the area to the VOC (Leirissa 2000:631). Only when the internal politics of the region affected the business of the VOC or the colonial state was there any attempt to interfere, and it is really

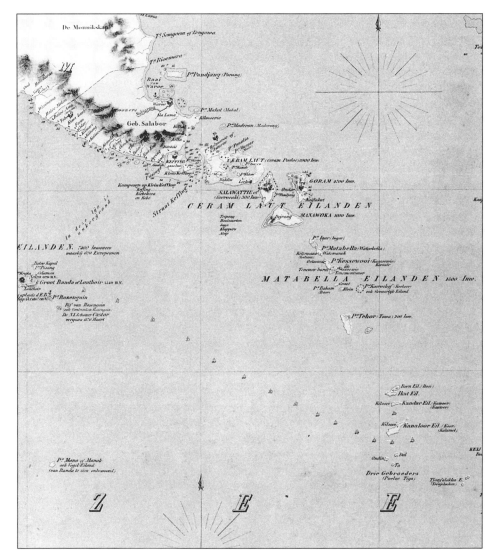

Figure 4.4. Part of Algemeene Land- en Zeekaart van de Asst. Residentie . . . Heer Dirk Heuting, by A. Guyot, 1871. Original in Koninklijk Instituut voor Taal-, Land- en Volkenkunde (photo C 11.1 sheet 2 [detail]). Reproduced with permission.

only then that the archives have much to say. What we learn is mainly intelligence of military significance—numbers of able-bodied men, names of rulers, estimates of quantities of firearms held—but the data that exist are sufficient to cast an interesting light on political organization. One such episode in the records that yields more data than most was prompted by the activities of the Tidore prince and culture hero Nuku. Between 1780 and 1805 Nuku consistently sought the support of polities in Southeast Seram in his rebellion against the Dutch and received it. In 1792, for example, having stayed for the preceding seven months in Waru, he moved to Ondor for the west monsoon, staying with his brother Mangoffa. From there he sought the backing of the raja of Maguindanao against the VOC, assisted by the raja of Kataloka. The flotilla consisted of one Goromese vessel under the command of Ancoda Bui Bale, one vessel from Kilwaru, two vessels from Kiltai, and one vessel commanded by Nuku himself.[14] The accounts we have (see, for example, Andaya 1993:220–239) suggest strongly not only the powerful political charisma of the person of Nuku but also the independence of the various small polities and the role of regional alliances in the pursuit of a common goal.

It is for the nineteenth century, however, that we can best reconstruct a picture of precolonial Southeast Seram society. This is mainly because the government of the Dutch East Indies (rather than the old VOC) had begun to impose its control over the area in more formal terms. For example, between 1817 and 1830, the Dutch reorganized the administration of the Moluccas. Southeast Seram was accorded special status through the appointment of a "Ceramische Bale," a Makassan based in Ambon with special responsibilities as a mediator with the islands (Leirissa 2000:632). More direct control was also achieved through the device of granting titles to local rulers and installing them as officers in the colonial administrative hierarchy (Ellen 1986b). By the middle of the century the system of titles was well established. In 1850 the Dutch established a permanent post on Geser, effectively incorporating it into the Residency of Banda. The demise of Banda, however, led to a change in the administrative structure. At that moment, when the old social order was effectively frozen, Riedel (1886: 147) reported the existence of eight polities with *matlaen* in archipelagic Southeast Seram, four in the Seram Laut area (presumably Kiltai, Kilwaru, Keffing, and Kelu) and four in the Gorom group (presumably Amar, Wisalen, Kataloka, and Ondor). However, there is evidence for considerable fluidity in the period immediately preceding this (for example in terms of [for the Seram Laut Archipelago] those settlements owing allegiance to Kelu and Keffing, and the degree to which Kwaai and Maar were autonomous domains; and [in the Gorom group] variation in the allegiance of some settlements to Wisalen rather than Amar, realignments following the disappearance of Ainikke and Kailakat as independent domains, and the status of Mida [Table 2.1]).

There is plenty of evidence of the often difficult relations between local rulers. Bik (1928 [1824]:10, 15–16) spoke of mutual distrust between Kwaos and Keffing, expressed through the persons of raja and mayor, and of conflict between the raja of Kelu and other heads arising from war between Kwaos and Kilberau on Keffing, for which Kelu had provided boats, gunpowder, firearms, slaves, and money. He also (ibid., 30) reported war between Kataloka and Amar, and between Ondor and Amar, concerning a settlement formerly ruled by Ondor but by then ruled by Amar (ibid., 19). Nonpayment of bridewealth (elephant tusks, gongs, and *lilla*) could also be a source of conflict between domains. The Adatrechtbundels (1925:197; also Kniphorst 1883:312) reported a case from 1853 in which the mayor of Geser had brought a complaint against the raja of Kilwaru through the Resident of Banda concerning who should receive anchorage fees ("ankergelden" in Dutch, "labu batu" in Malay) and how much, with respect to vessels moored between Geser and Kilwaru that stopped for drinking water. The fee paid to the raja of Kilwaru was 35 guilders, with a further 10 guilders for each month. Because of this, Butonese and Mandarese perahus preferred to anchor in Keffing waters where there was no tax and then bring their wares to Kilwaru and Geser (Van der Crab 1864:544). By comparison, anchorage fees on Gorom could be as high as 100 and 300 guilders per vessel, serving as a real deterrent for intrusive traders. It was Assistant Resident Bosscher who finally arbitrated in the Geser-Kilwaru conflict, as it was presented to him in March 1854 following a related dispute over the land border between the domains of Kelu and Kilwaru (that part coming within Maar) on Seram Laut (ibid., 546).

4.3. South Sulawesi and the Oriental Emporium

By the seventeenth century Bugis and Makassan traders had begun to develop important links with the Moluccas and Southeast Seram. Malay traders continued to be involved, but their role was eclipsed by traders of Sulawesi origin. Moreover, the next hundred years saw a major change in the economy of Southeast Seram, though not in the basic geographical structure of trade, nor in its social mechanisms. Until the sixteenth and seventeenth centuries the central commercial exchange in eastern Indonesia had been textiles for spices (Sen 1962), even though VOC attempts to maintain a monopoly position with respect to the spice trade were never completely effective. Wild long nutmeg (*Myristica argentea*), for example, were traded from New Guinea throughout the seventeenth and eighteenth centuries (Warburg 1897:128), some being taken to free ports in Borneo by Serammers, while cloves leaked out from domains such as Kilmuri. However, VOC policing of the spice monopoly, backed up by an efficient body of regulations, system of accounting, and commercial bureaucracy (Sutherland and Brée 1987:3–4), plus the damaging punitive extirpations of clove and nutmeg trees, were sufficiently problematic for the indigenous population of the Banda zone to seek alternatives to spices, at least after 1669.

In addition to the growth of Bugis and Makassan power in the western archipelago, and the "routinization" (though declining effectiveness) of Dutch maritime hegemony during the first half of the eighteenth century, the Banda zone had to adjust to other new forces, which themselves were facilitated by the VOC presence. These were the strong development of the

China trade together with the increased influence of Chinese captains in the shipping routes around Makassar, and increasing penetration by British and American "country traders," independent rivals of the English East India Company. Taken together, all of this led to two kinds of trade: one dominated by the VOC and Chinese (sea and forest products in exchange for Chinese goods) based at Makassar and another involving Wajo (Bugis) and Mandarese traders bringing imported textiles from the Strait of Malacca and bypassing Makassar and the VOC (Sutherland and Brée 1987:23). This was accompanied by a radical shift in the pattern and volume of ship movements. Trade between Makassar and Maluku, still vigorous in 1722, had declined or vanished by 1766. Also, in 1722, Maluku represented the most important trade out of Makassar in terms of registered tonnage, but this had dropped considerably by 1766 and vanished almost completely by 1786 (Sutherland and Brée 1987:14–15; H. Sutherland, personal communication). Between 1722 and 1766 larger ships were trading with the Moluccas, because the VOC explicitly prohibited those smaller boats considered suitable for smuggling. Nevertheless, by 1786 the few remaining ships trading with the Moluccas were, on average, much smaller.

Indian textiles, therefore, continued for many years to be the most significant import to the Moluccas from the West and the principal medium of exchange. Indeed, it can be said that the hand loom products of poor Indian weavers formed the basis of the mighty inter-Asian trade of the European companies and laid the foundation of their wealth and power (Sen 1962:95). However, textiles were, by the nineteenth century, being increasingly supplemented by opium, guns, and manufactured materials in exchange for sea and forest products, which in turn were used to purchase Chinese earthenware and porcelain, and metal goods, as well as cloth. The new involvement of the Chinese was occasioned by the demand for exotic produce, particularly sea produce. The principal interest was in trepang (sea cucumber, bêche-de-mer), and it was conflicts arising over ownership of trepang-bearing reefs that were one of the reasons leading to the direct involvement of the Dutch in the affairs of Southeast Seram during the early nineteenth century, where they were called upon to arbitrate in boundary disputes.

Another major development between 1750 and 1850 is that we begin to learn much more about the Papuan trade. Indeed, by the nineteenth century, Gorom and Seram Laut were being explicitly referred to in Dutch records as "schakeleilanden" (connecting islands) (Leirissa 2000:630). Though this trade had been going on for centuries, it seems to have grown during this period, partly in response to Chinese demand for exotic produce. It was organized by dividing up the coast between the various Southeast Seram polities into *sosolot*s, bays or anchorages in which one individual, descent group, or polity maintained a recognized monopoly in trade. The main items involved were barks, nutmeg, bird of paradise feathers, and slaves. Slaves had been a major export of New Guinea from the earliest period and had originally been taken by the Serammers for their own needs and were only later traded on to Banda and farther afield. With the development of seventeenth-century colonial society new needs for slaves arose, in Ambon and elsewhere. The decision by the VOC in 1689 forbidding the use of slaves from large tracts of the western archipelago increased demand in the east, where the freeburgers and Mardykers (freed slaves of Christian Asian origin) were licensed to supply the VOC, who relied on their extensive knowledge of local trade networks (Andaya 1991:83). Although local traders were initially excluded by the VOC from dealing in slaves, as with spices, they were soon able to evade the controls and to profitably restore their involvement (ibid., 88). The slave trade intensified again in the late eighteenth and early nineteenth centuries, this time partly in relation to processes of indigenous political centralization elsewhere in eastern Indonesia (Needham 1983; Reid 1983). However, by the middle of the nineteenth century the Dutch were already beginning to control the trade, although it persisted well into the twentieth century in a modified form.

4.4. Trade in the Banda Zone between 1700 and 1900

Even by 1650, less than thirty years after the Dutch conquest of Banda, the regularities of local trade had reestablished themselves with Banda Neira as the hub. The Dutch had engineered the restructuring of the trading system to suit their needs, and, if anything, Banda became more dependent for basic supplies on imports from Southeast Seram than it had been before 1621. Kei islanders (partly Old Bandanese) brought pottery and Serammers thatch, coconut oil, tubers of various descriptions, coconut, dried meat, maize, sago, pigs, goats, chickens, vegetables, new perahus (Bik 1928 [1824]: 97), and timber especially from Seram and from places as distant as Waru (Van der Crab 1864:548). For onward shipment from Kei and Aru there were edible birds' nests, various items of manufactured equipment, birds of paradise, imperial pigeons, and turtle shell (Buddingh 1860, 3:303–304). This dependence went beyond simply receiving incoming supplies but involved active attempts to ensure that supplies were available on a sustainable basis. Thus, in 1731 the VOC established a plantation of jati trees *(Tectona grandis)* on Gorom for use as timber on Banda and built a fort to regulate the trade. From the very beginning the Banda colony had relied on imported labor from elsewhere in the Moluccas and beyond, but because Southeast Seram had been a refuge for indigenous Bandanese and a constant irritant through their violations of the monopoly it was not seen as an obvious source of labor. However, by 1863 even Goromese were being employed on Bandanese perks, and marital ties between Gorom and Banda became common (Bik 1928 [1824]:3).

From 1650 to 1750 Bandanese perkeniers also branched out into regional trade, shifting slaves from plantation work to manning boats trading with Kei, Aru, and elsewhere: smuggling out nutmeg and mace; smuggling in rice, textiles, trepang, edible bird's nests, bird feathers, turtle shell, ebony, shark fins, and sandalwood. In particular, the perkeniers dealt in long nutmeg, generally considered inferior to round ones, but in demand in the Asian market and possibly used as an illegal makeweight for round nutmeg (Hanna 1978:79–80). Bandanese were also involved in the Ambonese mahogany and rattan trade with Seram and dealt in pearls from Kei and Aru and the oil, resin, and gum of *Ficus elastica* from other islands (Linden 1873:59). This led to the neglect of the nutmeg estates and reliance on subsidies available to perkeniers from the VOC (Hanna 1978:81–82). During the British interregnums (1796–1803, 1810–1817), instigated by the Napoleonic wars, perkeniers were further encouraged to engage in private trade, and the same period saw aggressive penetration of the area by country traders (English, Arabs, Chinese) (ibid., 92–93). Banda continued as an important center for handling onward goods; this role increasingly eclipsed nutmeg production. By the late nineteenth century, however, Banda was more and more replaced by Ambon as an import-export center (Heeres 1908: 343).

We have an excellent account of Banda as a redistribution center in a report written in 1797 by a British official, Robert Townsend Farquhar, who was there during the first British occupation (W. G. Miller 1980:41–43) and who usefully summarized trading activity in terms of seasonal variations. Farquhar noted that boats left Banda for Aru between the end of December and February carrying manufactured goods, rice, and sago in exchange for trepang, birds' nests, pearls, birds of paradise, turtle shell, and slaves, having first supplied all Bandanese needs. Small boats (perhaps an earlier version of the modern *ang kalulis* [see chapter 6]) were purchased in Kei for the Aru trade. The Tanimbar trade fell somewhat later, at the end of February or the beginning of March, and involved the exchange of manufactured goods for trepang and turtle shell. At the same time, Makassans and Goromese collected Tanimbar trepang themselves. Bandanese merchants with larger vessels (ibid., 50), wellmanned and armed, sometimes went to New Guinea for trepang (which was regarded as being of better quality than that available in the Moluccas), where they also collected massoi, karlie, swang, kuli sorie (all different kinds of valuable oleaginous and aromatic woods), long nutmeg, slaves, turtle shell, and pigeons. Eli and Elat (the two settlements of Old Bandanese on Kei Besar) were visited at the end of March, mainly for subsistence items. In the middle of April, small vessels went to Seram, Geser, and Seram Laut to buy goods that the inhabitants of those islands had collected in New Guinea. In exchange, the Serammers received "all kinds of coarse cloth commonly called Company's cloths" and brought coarse textiles to Banda for sale (ibid., 51). Bandanese vessels had usually returned from Seram and the southeastern islands by the middle of May and sold their purchases on to bigger merchants, who took them to Batavia during the first half of June. The trade with the southwestern islands (meaning mainly Timor) took place between the end of June and September, and surplus goods brought from Batavia were traded on to Ternate in August–September. During September and October Bandanese took rice and trade goods to Ambon in exchange for money (significantly, not sago). Hila (on Ambon) and Saparua supplied pigs, orembai (a kind of boat, similar to the *ang guik* [see chapter 6.2]), and other subsistence goods. In November Kei islanders brought coconuts, oil (presumably coconut oil), sago, and pottery. The whole year round vessels from the Seram Laut area and Gorom frequented Banda, though chiefly at the turn of the monsoon, bringing slaves, massoi, sago, planked timber, thatch, betel nut, coconut oil, yams, cockatoos, parrots of all kinds, birds of paradise, cassowaries, "and other curiosities." In exchange Gorom obtained mainly iron, textiles, and trade goods for the Papuan trade (Bik 1928 [1824]:16). Seram sago was reexported from Banda to Aru (and Kei) (ibid., n. 4), and a proportion of rice imported to Banda was reexported to Southeast Seram and the south-eastern islands (Quarles van Ufford 1856:136).

The peoples of Southeast Seram, Seram Laut, and the Gorom Islands, when not victualing Banda, maintained a vigorous independent trading posture as well as jealously guarding their political independence. For the Dutch in 1796 they were pirates, and the archipelago was generally regarded as a center for smuggling (Heeres 1908:308). But curiously, the trading success of the people of Southeast Seram between the seventeenth and nineteenth centuries, which in terms of volume of trade rivaled that of the Dutch, endured primarily because of expanding Dutch enterprise. Indeed, the extension of the services of the state steamship company, the Koninklijke Paketvaart Maatschappij (KPM), to the area encouraged part of this expansion (Broersma 1934; Leirissa 1981:56).

Close trading connections with Sumba, Sumbawa, Lombok, and Bali are evident between 1700 and 1900, probably mediated through Bugis traders on those islands, who also sent their ships to Southeast Seram. Some operated with Dutch passes, but most without. We have this on the testimony of one Juragon Yusuf, a trader originally from Bangka but proba-bly of Arab descent, who was engaged in the Seram sea trade at the turn of the eighteenth to nineteenth century (Leirissa 1994:106; 2000:631). Goromese traded directly with Bali; Amar in particular had close links with a Balinese princedom (Jansen 1928:491), reflected in modern oral history. There are traditions of a Goromese presence on Bali, together with people from Kilmuri (Van Eerde 1911:219). Jansen (1928:490–494; also Rouffaer 1915) suggested that the Goromese toponym and clan name Kenali may be a reference to the old Javanese Kadali. There were seven or eight vessels from Gorom to Bali annually in the early nineteenth century (Bik 1928 [1824]:36) and strong contacts also between Bali and Kelura (the raja allegedly being the head of a Sasak domain from Lombok [ibid., 14]). All villages under Ainikke (Enneka) traded with Bali, according to Bik (ibid., 13, 25). Serammer vessels going to Bali did so via Kei, taking mainly Papuan (long) nutmeg, massoi, some trepang, and bird of paradise plumes. Traveling south of Rosengain, the vessels stopped off at Nila, where they picked up sulfur that could be sold in Bali for two Spanish mats a pikul.[15] Serammers could obtain seven Spanish mats in Bali for a small cask of matting and rattan weighing 50 kati. Bik (ibid., 13, 25) also noted that formerly there had been direct trade with Java, with many people having been to Surabaya.

In the early to mid-nineteenth century, trade in Southeast Seram and the Seram Laut Archipelago was increasingly concentrated on the domain of Kilwaru (Kiltai Island). Much of the onward shipping westward and the trade with New Guinea by that time involved vessels from South Sulawesi, with Bugis based in Kilwaru bringing cloth from as far as Lancashire and Massachusetts. Bugis called in to refit and sort and dry cargoes. Van der Crab (1862:64, 71) reported that Bugis sailed annually from Kilwaru to New Guinea, each vessel returning with three pikuls of turtle shell, 700 pikuls of trepang, 700 pikuls of massoi, birds' nests, and birds of paradise. Bugis also bought sago (Van der Crab 1864:542). Ua Baweang, working for the Makassar-based Chinese trader Tio Inho, managed to fill the contents of his padewakang[16] for the return trip with 2,548 pikuls of mother-of-pearl, 6,554 pikuls of trepang, 10 *lillas* (a kind of cannon), and some pottery. On 14 August 1862 the vessel was wrecked on a reef just outside Geser. The people of Kilwaru are said to have brought ashore 2,962 mother-of-pearl shells, 601 plates, six lantakas and two mariams (other types of cannons), one blunderbuss, two anchors and chains, and a keris (dagger); the people of Kiltai and Kelu also retrieved salvage. Surprisingly, Ua Baweang is reported to have got his possessions back.

According to the firsthand reports of the Italian naturalist Beccari (1924:196), and unpublished archive sources,[17] by 1870 Kilwaru, which was often lumped with Geser because of the Kilwaru trading settlement on that atoll, rivaled Dobo in the Aru Islands in importance, with Geser the principal focus of commercial activity for the entire west coast of New Guinea. Goromese and other traders from the Seram Laut area brought Papuan produce to Kilwaru to exchange for cloth, sago, and opium. Beccari calculated that the import-export trade in Geser was worth in the region of a million florins a year. For Van der Capellen, writing of the early 1820s (1855:288), it was Keffing, along with Gorom, that controlled trade with Papua and Aru. It was his visit of 1824 that prompted the sending of Bik. The picture is not entirely clear, but it seems that the domains of Kilwaru and Keffing in particular oscillated in commercial significance during that time.

Serammers appeared to be gatekeepers not only as far as the New Guinea trade was concerned but also occupied a similar role with respect to Aru. Bik (1928 [1824]:41) spoke of the political control exercised by Goromese over Makassans and Chinese in Aru, providing them, at a price, with protection. Chinese came in small boats from Kei or Gorom and traded directly with the indigenous inhabitants of Aru, all onward trade then going through Banda (ibid., 43). Goromese, using vessels built in the

Kei Islands, voyaged annually to Kei and Aru and other southeastern islands, collecting trepang, in exchange for textiles, *lillas* or artillery, and also *tatumbu* (decorated nesting pandanus containers) (Bik 1928 [1824]:44; Van der Crab 1862:72), which were also an important export commodity for Watubela. Imports coming into the Aru Islands also included coconut oil, boats, and wooden bowls from Kei, and Goromese and Serammer traders also brought sago from Seram (Wallace 1896:132). Pearls were important, and agar-agar and turtle shell (Bleeker 1856:129–130). They dealt with Bugis and Makassan traders but sometimes took their commodities directly to Salayar, Timor, Bali, or Bantaeng. Makassans also traded arak (Bik 1928 [1824]:97). The Serammers brought gunpowder from Bali, which the Makassans obtained in Kei to use, along with gongs and elephant tusks, to trade on Aru. Although barter was the standard means of converting commodities, silver coins were also used when buying trepang on Aru (ibid., 45), though whether these functioned as a true medium of exchange rather than as just another valuable is not clear. In the east monsoon Goromese traded along the wider channels of the Aru Islands mostly for edible birds' nests (ibid., 58). Wallace (1962 [1869]:321–323) reported that: "All day long native boats were coming with fish, cocoa-nuts, parrots and lories, earthen pans, sirih leaf, wooden bowls and trays, etc., etc., which every one of the fifty inhabitants of our prau seemed to be buying on his own account . . . for every man on board a prau considers himself at liberty to trade, and to carry with him whatever he can afford to buy." But this apparent celebration of the free play of market forces was not without its downside. By 1853 opium smoking, arak alcoholism, and gambling had become social problems in Aru, with much conflict between traders of Sulawesi origin and backshore people. Some of the sources even suggest that the alcoholism was deliberately fostered to cement ties of dependency through debt (Spyer 1997:517). Goromese and Serammer traders bartered sago directly with Aruese for pearl oysters, trepang, and turtles, which were sold to traders in Dobo. From the 1840s onward, Hokkien Chinese began to replace Bugis and Makassan middlemen, with whom Aruese built up enormous debts (Ossewijer 2000:58). However, trade with Aru until the early twentieth century was mainly controlled by Serammers, Kei islanders, Goromese, and Bugis (Van der Crab 1862:91), though there were Japanese companies in Aru as early as 1912 involved in the copra trade, and Arabs and Australians involved in pearling (Broersma 1934:334).

The Geser corridor also served as a zone of redistribution for the mainland of Seram. Mountain villages such as Bonfia traded in sago and sago leaf thatch, salted bushmeat (usually venison), and other forest products, in return for manufactured goods, including textiles (Heeres 1908:353; Jansen 1928:493), although not all mountain peoples came to the coast. Trade was reinforced through political influence. During the nineteenth century Bati villages, for example, were allied to Kianlaut and Kiandarat, who in turn were under the influence of the raja of Kwaos and the mayor of Keffing (Bosscher 1855:34).

The heavy reliance of Serammers on intermediary trade, though to a much lesser extent the peoples of the Gorom group, was a continuation of their historic inability to produce sufficient food to meet their own needs. During the early nineteenth century Gorom and Manawoka could produce some sago, many kinds of tubers and bananas, watermelons, squash, and maize (Bik 1928 [1824]:27). Gorom, on the whole, was more productive than Manawoka, growing in addition to those things some rice (100–150 koyongs annually) and with many coconut palms, coffee, and sugarcane from which syrup was extracted (ibid., 36; Van der Crab 1864:531–556). Gorom was even in a position to export agricultural products to Keffing (Seram Rei) and Seram Laut, and thatch and coconut oil went to Banda (Ellen 1992:126). No rice was grown on Manawoka, and for a long time this had been brought from Java (Bik 1928 [1824]:28). Seram Laut was also considered by Bik (ibid., 14) to be very productive: some Serammers, though mostly Papuans and others that had been enslaved by Seram traders, planted rice, tubers, maize, sugarcane, and squash. What Seram Laut could not provide was said to be obtained from Gorom. Other islands were in a far worse position. All food for Kelu came from mainland Seram or Gorom; rice, tobacco, and red yarn (which women used for weaving) was imported from Bali (ibid., 16). Of particular importance for all the islet-based domains of the Geser corridor was the import of sago from mainland Seram (as part of the fish for sago exchange) and from New Guinea.

The overall carbohydrate and vegetable food deficit in archipelagic Southeast Seram was offset from the eighteenth century onward by increasing local production of exotic marine commodities and by craft specialization. The Seram Laut and Gorom groups (and also Watubela) had a vigorous iron smithing industry, producing parangs (bushknives) and klewangs (swords), which were exported to Kei, Aru, some parts of the Papuan coast, and even Java (ibid., 34). Seram Laut also provided other specialists, such as carpenters.[18] Boats were built in the more southerly islands, though larger vessels were bought from Balinese and Kei islanders (De Hollander 1895:501). Gorom and Seram Laut had been centers for textile production and export in the early eighteenth century (at which time VOC records indicate that they were certainly reaching Ambon) and probably even earlier.[19] This distinctive cloth is known in the literature as *ute-ute*. Riedel (1886:169) listed various kinds of *ute-ute* (or *ure*) from Seram Laut: *ure kait, ure nina, ure kamason bolin, ure bitnar, suta kefing, ure suta,* and *suta kelibia*. Nineteenth-century Goromese were also making their own dyes: blue from *Indigofera tinctoria*, red from *Morinda citrifolia,* and yellow from *Curcuma longa,* although we know from Valentijn that dyes were also being imported from Sulawesi and other places in the western archipelago by Makassans almost two centuries earlier. At the beginning of the twentieth century Gorom was still a center for weaving and export of *ute-ute* (where four could be purchased for 30 guilders), with dyes being obtained from Bugis, Makassans, and Arabs (Niggermeyer 1952:3883, 3892). By comparison, pottery was a weakly developed specialism; most pottery and potters still came from the old Bandanese settlements in the Kei Islands (Bik 1928 [1824]:29).

By the end of the nineteenth century the dominance of Serammers and Goromese in the New Guinea trade (as well as that with Aru) and in handling commodities that they themselves produced had already eroded. Makassans and Bugis had long been active. Increasingly, Chinese merchants came from Ambon and Banda, many settling. Trade was now mainly in the hands of Bugis, Chinese (including peranakan), and Arabs, most of them based on the atoll of Geser under the protection of the rulers of Kilwaru, Kelu, and Keffing. Other traders—Butonese, Makassans, and Singaporeans—are mentioned as settling on the northerly part of Seram Laut, under the protection of the raja of Kilwaru (De Hollander 1895:502).

4.5. Trepang and the Rise of the China Trade

The rise in Chinese demand for exotic produce, particularly sea produce, during the eighteenth century has already been remarked upon, and also the way this stimulated the junk trade centered on Makassar, with its vital connections with outlying areas of the eastern archipelago (MacKnight 1976; Sutherland 1989, 2000). The principal interest was in trepang, which remains a Chinese culinary delicacy. There was also interest in various algae, mainly agar-agar. Both were traded for imports from Amoy and Canton. Initially the Chinese controlled the trade between Makassar and China, leaving the Makassans and Bugis to harvest the produce themselves or obtain it from other producers. Much of the eighteenth-century trepang trade from the Moluccas was handled by Bugis, who dealt with local producers, and passed through Banda. Makassans tended to harvest the trepang themselves, either in the Moluccas or New Guinea or northern Australia, this latter probably constituting the largest fraction of the total exported through Makassar (MacKnight 1976:15). With the declining inability of the VOC to defend infringements on trading pass violations, Makassan and other trepanging activity in the Moluccas became more important (Sutherland 1989:463–465, table 3), and by the time Bik (1928 [1824]:8) observed Chinese on a perahu off Keffing and Kilberau buying trepang had become routinized. However, the newfound values attached to marine resources produced conflict over their habitats, and as the Dutch authorities gradually strengthened their administrative presence so they were increasingly called upon to arbitrate and settle boundary disputes on the trepang-bearing reefs surrounding Seram Laut and Gorom.

The techniques of trepang (in SSL, *kebi*) production and its organization in archipelagic Southeast Seram have remained largely unchanged for three hundred years, and it has continued to be important in the economy down to the present. Occasionally Bugis or others from Makassar (Ujung Pandang) bring mechanized equipment, such as that required for fishing deepwater trepang, but apart from that the following account describes the main processes.

There are about thirty types of trepang recognized in the Seram Laut area, and the main types collected are listed in Table 4.1. Names, on the whole, refer to appearance or habitat. Thus, *kebi metan* (trepang raja) is black (*metan* = black), and *kebi bas* (trepang gosok) is characteristic of the coral cays or tanusang (*bas*). Other names are less obvious. For example, *kebi sumu ratu* and *kebi sumu moi* are so named because the coloration of the first is likened to the clothes of a raja and the second to those of a slave. *Kebi daul-daul* (*daul* = cut) is locally eaten raw with lime and white pepper, after first removing the gut. *Kebi utuk* can be eaten with its gut, although care has to be taken to catch it in the right season and state of tide because it contains sand, which makes it unpalatable. The red parts of the *kebi kurit* that are removed during processing are used as bait for octopus. Otherwise, trepang is neither eaten locally nor used in any other way, being far too valuable a commodity.

Trepang (Figure 4.5) are gathered mainly in December from shallow waters by men and (in Kiltai at least) also women. The season is generally over by May. Small trepang can be collected at low tide in 60–90 centimeters of water, and in 1986 children were being paid 5 rupiahs for every small trepang (trepang meti) caught in this way. Larger trepang, such as trepang nanas and trepang batu, fetch higher prices and are obtained in waters of 7 meters depth or thereabouts. Divers wear goggles and pierce trepang with a spear or metal point (*acur*), afterward stringing them on a length of rattan or other cordage. Harvested trepang are accumulated in a canoe before coming ashore. Trepang in deeper water, up to 30 meters, are caught using a weighted harpoon and line (*darurat*), with a 60-centimeter head, although the darkness at that depth is a handicap. The wood used for the shaft has to be hard and heavy, so that it sinks, and on Kiltai is *tombe-tombe* (tomi-tomi). On a good day, six hundred trepang can be collected, working from first light to dusk.

The gut of the harvested trepang is removed and the meat is boiled and then dried. The gutting usually takes place on the edge of the sea so that the waste can be easily disposed of and the body cavity properly cleaned. The boiling eviscerates, thickens, and shortens the trepang. Trepang nanas, about 40 centimeters long when gutted, shrink to about 15–20 centimeters on cooking and drying. Trepang takes 3-4 days to dry in the sun (left either on matting or on some other suitable material on the ground, or placed on drying racks [*wadar-wadar*]). It will dry overnight using a wood fire dryer or smoker (*dafi-dafi* [or *dahi-dahi*)] *kebi*). On Kiltai, the fire is usually of mangrove wood brought from Seram Laut. The uprights of the dryer are about 50 centimeters tall, and the frame 95 centimeters long by 70 centimeters wide. On this frame is placed old bits of tin and oil drum tops, iron mesh, corrugated iron, or zinc to provide a hot plate and act as a tray to prevent water from dripping out of the trepang onto the fire. The metal tray

Table 4.1. Trepang types distinguished in Kelu (1981) and Garogos (1986), with historical notes.

Local term	Ambonese Malay Gloss	Riedel List (1886:166–170)	Scientific Name	Notes
Kebi metan, kebi raja	Trepang raja	Ebi metan	Holothuria (Halodeima) atra	
Kebi farai, kebi fati	Trepang batu, trepang besi	Ebi varai	Holothuria (Microthele) nobilis or whitmae[i]	White
Kebi kurit			Holothuria (Halodeima) edulis	
Kebi lelela	Trepang tai kokong		?Stichopus hermanni	Kong kong = loud dog bark
Kebi bas	Trepang gosok, trepang kebibas, ebi basa		Holothuria (Metrialyla) scabra	White; inshore, banks, shallow water
	Trepang pasir		Holothuria aculeata	White; inshore, banks, shallow water
Kebi susu(k) rou	Trepang susu, samandar alus		Holothuria (Theelothuria) spinifera	White
Kebi kaukena				White, inshore
Kebi gusi-gusi	Trepang guci		Holothuria (Microthele) fuscopunctata	Brown, with creamy brown markings
Kebi tamateun				
Kebi (de)duran, kebi duren	Trepang nanas, trepang duri	Ebi duduran	Thelenota ananas	Spiky
Kebi deduran metan		Ebi duduran metan	Stichopus chloronotus	
Kebi sisiar mahuti		Ebi sisir	Bohadschia marmorata	White
Kebi sisiar bintik		Ebi sisir	Bohadschia marmorata	White
Kebi masin (-masin)		Ebi masin	Bohadschia marmorata	White
Kebi utuk		Ebi utuk		
Kebi sarasa		Ebi sarasa		
Kebi tarangan			Holothuria(Microthele) nobilis or whitmae[i]	Harvested during season of south winds

Kebi bas lau			Outshore reefs
Kebi sika	Trepang tai kucing	*Stichopus horrens (variegatus)*	
Kebi sia	Trepang benung	*Bohadschia argus*	
Kebi darat			
Kebi futi			
Kebi rarawa			Colorful
Kebi sumu ratu			Dull
Kebi sumu moi			
Kebi bora-bora		Specimen unidentified	Small
Kebi daul-daul			
Kebi cera metan		*Holothuria (Halodeimna) edulis*	
Kebi tewer			
Kebi urat	Trepang talengkong		
Kebi mera		*Holothuria edulis or atra*	

Note: Identifications from Encyclopaedia van Nederlandsch-Indië, 1st ed., s. v. "Tripang" (following Koningsberger 1904) and Cannon and Silver 1987; and (based on photographic and cured specimens) by F. W. E. Rowe (personal communication).

Figure 4.5. Sorting trepang drying in the sun on a sheet of corrugated iron, Kiltai, 6 April 1986.

also prevents burning and makes the entire operation generally easier to handle. A larger *dafi-dafi* on Keffing was 90 centimeters high, 200 centimeters wide, and 370 centimeters long. Another on Kiltai was 60 centimeters high, 13 centimeters wide, and 150 centimeters long, with sides built up from logs. In 1986 there were *dafi-dafi kebi* also at Maar (used by Kilwaru traders), at Kwamar, and perhaps other places. The trepang is first cooked in an old oil drum for about twenty minutes, until the water is boiling. Most kinds of trepang can be cooked and dried without further attention, although *kebi farai* is first cooked briefly before removing the gut and then cooked fully. Similarly, *kebi bas* and *kebi bas lau* are precooked for about five minutes to allow removal of an otherwise intractable skin. Other varieties have their body ossicles removed at the time of smoking. This is generally done with the fingers although a knife may sometimes be used. It is then cooked again for about twenty-seven minutes. Alternatively the root of *ui ara* (a kind of wild yam [*Dioscorea* sp.]) is grated onto the precooked *kebi bas* in an old canoe or other suitable container and marinated before resuming cooking. After cooking, all kinds of trepang are dried over the *dafi-dafi*, a process that can be done overnight. Sometimes trepang will be salted after gutting and left to stand for a day.

The availability of different kinds of trepang depends on season and ecology. Thus, the trepang found on sandy bottoms, stone, mud, or coral all tend to be different. Trepang raja (*kebi metan*) is the most common type around Kiltai. *Kebi kurit* has to be caught at the right time and is found in only a few localities (e.g., Seram Rei, Kiltai, and at Rurura and Bokon along the beaches of Seram Laut). The most frequently harvested type in the Seram Laut area is trepang batu (*kebi farai*), though trepang nanas (*kebi deduran*) is also important. However, during the early nineteenth century Seram trepang was generally regarded as being of only intermediate quality, standing between that of Tanimbar (the best) and that of Aru (W. G. Miller 1980:51), and commanding between 14.16 and 25 rix dollars[20] per pikul.

4.6. The Impact of Dutch Administration

On the whole, the VOC had been content to leave the polities of Southeast Seram independent after the seventeenth-century wars, but there were, increasingly, ways in which that independence in matters to do with commerce was constrained. Serammers, for one thing, had to deal with the Dutch government in Banda to trade. We can see how this worked in a short letter dated 29 March 1779 explaining that the rulers of Geser and Seram Laut had entered into an agreement to supply Banda with slaves, sago, and so on at agreed government prices. The agreement gives VOC recognition to the captains and specifies the products in which it is acceptable to trade. The same letter notes that the arrangement continues previous agreements of 1763, 1768, 1770, 1773, 1775, and 1778.[21] The contracts made between the VOC and local rulers often included clauses requiring them to acquire navigation passes (zeepas) that afforded some protection against confiscation or molestation, though they were also an instrument of control. Between 1743 and 1818 regulations controlling shipping for VOC subjects became more stringent, involving a system of passes and annual sailing permits, and the concept of a Netherlands Indies flag of registry for those living in areas under direct Dutch control, who were compelled to fly the Dutch tricolor. However, the requirements for European-rigged vessels (50 percent of which were Asian owned by the first half of the nineteenth century) were tougher than for indigenous rigged ones (Knaap 1989:17). After 1816 coastal and interinsular trade in Indonesia was legally reserved for colonial shipping and that of friendly native powers. Between 1820 and 1850 Batavia and Semarang were superseded by Gresik and

Surabaya as the most important Javanese ports involved in the Moluccan trade, partly as a consequence of new Arab interest. The growth of Chinese and Arab tonnage was ultimately at the expense of the Europeans (Broeze 1979:252). There was, therefore, for a period an institutionalized "dual economy" of administered trade and informal trade, to use Polanyi's terms (Leirissa 1994:111). However, at the same time the tight control exercised in parts of the Moluccas subject to the monopoly was eased in 1853 when a number of harbors were declared free ports and the Moluccas made accessible to all flags, supposedly to counter the growing economic power of Singapore (Van der Crab 1862:22), although this status was removed in 1904, leaving only Southwest New Guinea within the Southeast Seram trading zone available for completely free trade. With the establishment of the Nederlandsche Handel Maatschappij (Netherlands Trading Company) in 1824 a new phase began (Knaap 1989:20), followed in 1852 by a government-subsidized packet-boat service (granted to the Nederlandsch-Indische Stoomvaart Maatschappij in 1865 and from 1891 the Koninklijke Paketvaart Maatschappij), though freight transport remained largely in the hands of private coastal traders (ibid., 22, 24). Given one of the general arguments of this book (concerning the resistance of traditional trading routes to change), it is interesting to note that even these new steamship services stuck to traditional sailing routes, going from Banda to Geser and then on to Sekar in the MacCluer Gulf (Beversluis and Gieben 1929:200; Bokemeyer 1888).

Apart from the early exploratory visits of Keyts and others, there had been little Dutch interest in either archipelagic Southeast Seram or New Guinea until the Napoleonic period. Both were significant only as the lair of pirates, though the population of Southeast Seram could hardly be regarded as insignificant, with a reported 80,000 souls for Gorom as opposed to 5,094 for Banda.[22] But the 1790s onward (the period of the Nuku insurrection) saw VOC activity against Gorom (Haga 1884, 1:324). Article 9 of the contract of 27 May 1824 with the sultans of Ternate and Tidore ceded to the Residency of Banda the easterly part of Seram, formerly claimed by Tidore: including Geser, Gorom, Kei, Aru, Keffing, and Seram Laut; also the southeast and southwest islands and that part of the mainland (Groot Seram) running from Tobo in the south to Waru in the north. This carving up gave jural legitimacy to the de facto situation created by traditional trade routes and political alliances.[23] P. Merkus, who was governor of the Moluccas between 1824 and 1828, sought to curtail Serammer trading activities with Bali, Sumbawa, Sulawesi, and so on, by establishing a scheme (1827) by which Serammers and Goromese could purchase goods on credit for sale in New Guinea and East Seram (Leirissa 1994:110). On 26 March 1826 D. H. Kolff sailed via Banda to Seram Laut and discovered what everyone else knew: that the Seram Lauters had a monopoly on the trade with the coastal inhabitants of New Guinea west of the bay of Lakahia, and that the area to the southeast was generally unknown (Haga 1884, 2:13). Merkus' scheme failed.

Another reason why the Dutch were concerned to bring Southeast Seram under more effective control was its involvement in the opium trade, which was considered a malign influence on the peoples of the territories that the Dutch did administer directly. There was a trade in opium in Southeast Seram as early as 1795 and also in Banda. By the mid-nineteenth century opium smoking had become a major social problem in places such as Seram Laut and Gorom, and trade in opium in the Moluccas had become very important (Bosscher 1855:39; Van der Crab 1862, 1864). In 1851 the value of the opium trade in Ternate exceeded that of all other categories of goods: 9,880 guilders compared with 6,800 guilders for bazaar items (Quarles van Ufford 1856:69). Beccari (1924:49, 248; also De Hollander 1895:501) reported opium smoking on Keffing in 1870; it was also widespread on Gorom (Kniphorst 1883:312), as well as on Banda in 1876. Trade in opium was widespread in Southeast Seram in 1896, and the alcohol and opium problem extended to Netherlands New Guinea by 1889.[24]

By the 1830s the Dutch had begun to impose their control over the area in more formal terms. Bik's visit had laid the foundations for this and there followed negotiations with the heads of the Southeast Seram polities in Banda. On 29 April 1824 it was formally proclaimed that the Residency of Banda would from that moment on "consist of the Bandanese islands plus the easterly part of Seram claimed by Tidore—from Tobo to Waru, Kei, Aru, Geser, the south east and southwest islands."[25] In this way, maintenance and reunification of the Banda system through the drawing of boundaries gave administrative recognition to an indigenous zone of trading and political influence. The method adopted by the Indies government to integrate the area rapidly into the Residency was, as we have seen, by granting titles to local rulers and installing them as officers in the colonial administration (Ellen 1986b). By the middle of the nineteenth century the system of titles was well established.

The decline and eventual demise of Banda, both in terms of its plantation economy and its function in the entrepôt trade, eventually led to a change in administrative structure, reflecting the changed circumstances. In 1814 the Residency of Banda had included Aru, Kei, and the southwestern and southeastern islands; the Residency of Ternate included New Guinea and Manado.[26] In 1866, after a period of unified Moluccan government from Ambon, administration reverted to the three residencies more or less as they existed during the VOC period, one of which was Banda (Leirissa 2000:632). In 1888 Banda was downgraded to an Assistant Residency, below Ambon and Ternate. Postholders based in Waru and Geser came under Banda, but the rest of the Moluccas was administered from Ambon. The Dutch established postholders in Geser for Seram Laut, Gorom, and Watubela and for the Kei Islands (Bokemeyer 1888:322). Further adjustments were made in 1925, extending the Amboina Residency to include southern New Guinea, as far as Digoel (Tanah Merah). The interior of New Guinea was added later. The Residency of Ternate, therefore, included Manokwari, Sorong, the Schouten Islands, and the Japen group, as far as Hollandia (Beversluis and Gieben 1929:101). Thus, the final ironic distortion of an earlier political reality was complete. Ternate, which had boasted no precolonial pretensions in New Guinea, became the administrative center for what had previously been a zone influenced by its rival Tidore, and the area once the exclusive trading territory of the domains of Southeast Seram was now administered by Amboina.

Moreover, the appearance of regular Dutch steamer schedules and the introduction of new maritime technology began to undermine the traditional trading supremacy of the Bugis. The niche they progressively vacated was partly filled by the Butonese sailing the Banda-Surabaya route in smaller vessels of European influence (lambos), and it was during this period that Butonese began to settle in Banda, which has remained a major center for Butonese boats, boatbuilding, and repairs ever since. By the beginning of the twentieth century Butonese were also settling on Seram Laut. Steamers took over from sailing vessels in the first decade of the twentieth century, and trade became more regulated. Ambon and Banda became less important than they had been before 1850. In the twentieth century the relative significance of exotic commodities destined for the Asian market declined, to be replaced by—in addition to nutmeg and cloves—rubber, coffee, copra, and damar (Broersma 1934:326).

In 1850 the Dutch established a permanent post on Geser, though they had planned to build a fort there as early as 1785, and from then onward it became effectively part of the Residency of Banda. According to Sterker (Kniphorst 1883:310), Geser had already become a stapling point for the whole of the southeastern archipelago, with Bugis coming from Makassar and Singapore with textiles, Balinese copper, rice, firearms, silver, and a great deal of opium. The establishment of Geser as an administrative post, formerly a dependency of Kilwaru (De Hollander 1895:501), marked a major change in the trade patterns. More Chinese arrived, such as the Tio Inho reported by Van der Crab (1864:542), Arabs from the Hadhramaut, and European traders (Ribbe 1892). With the arrival of steamships a government coaling depot was required, and in 1870 such was established at Kelwarit (Kilwaru?) (Beccari 1924:45) and on Geser in 1874. Geser had been pinpointed as a likely coaling depot in the early 1860s (Van der Crab 1864: 550) and was well established by 1876.[27]

In the early 1860s Van der Crab (1862:57) noted the independence of the rulers of the various autarkic polities of East Seram, but optimistically declared that they were becoming increasingly subject to Dutch authority. This view was starkly contradicted as late as 1874 by the Italian explorer G. Emilio Cerutti, who could report to the Dutch authorities that although Aru and Kei were claimed in the name of the Dutch crown and were from time to time visited by the Resident in Amboina, they were in fact commercially and politically quite autonomous.[28] From 1887 onward the government commitment to East Seram became evident in other ways (for example, in the establishment of a permanent military detachment in Geser

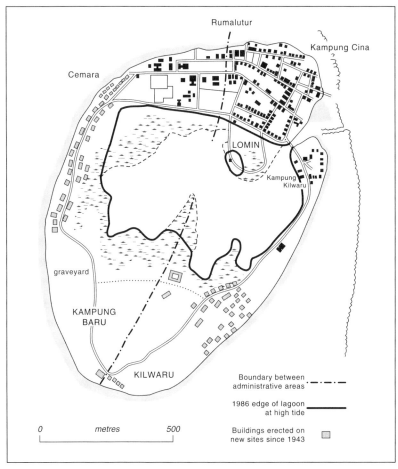

Figure 4.6. Geser Island. (Based on Map 9, Netherlands Forces Intelligence Service, No. 216a.) Latitude 3° 52–31' South, longitude 130° 53–50' East. The original was prepared in September 1938 and updated in 1943. It has been modified to accommodate changes up to 1986.

[Beversluis and Gieben 1929:135]). The Dutch also created a mayor of Geser, the third and last of which (the position is now one of raja), Mohammed Kelian, was installed in 1932 and was still living to be interviewed by me in 1986. The first permanent settlement on Geser was Kampung Kilwaru, formerly known as Kilwaru *tewu*, established on the promontory east of the mouth of the lagoon called Ge. Kampung Baru was founded around 1918; its native inhabitants had originally come from Keffing. When the Dutch expanded their settlement at Cemara, Kampung Baru moved to its current site. The Controller at the time brought in labor to reinforce the lagoon edges, and stones and coral from as far away as Teor and Wahai for the buildings and to extend the land surface. This gave rise to "Kampung Kockman" (though there is some doubt about the real identity of the administrator so memorialized), which after independence became Lomin (meaning "full"), or Kampung Tengah. Formerly the lagoon was larger, with more mangroves and mud fringing its edges (Figure 4.6). Today Geser is divided between the wards of Kilwaru, Lomin, and Kampung Baru, the latter standing on land owned by Keffing. By the 1930s the population of Geser comprised 200 Chinese, 20 Arabs, and 1,000 "natives" (Broersma 1934:341), and by 1986 had risen to 2,216. Geser in 1986, like Serdenha in 1520, still served as a major entrepôt in local terms, though the onward trade to New Guinea had declined significantly, as had the role of local Serammers and Goromese in trade, now dominated by intrusive specialist traders.

5
Southeast Seram and the Papuas

...at Gessir, a mere horseshoe-shaped, coconut-fringed atoll, picturesquely showing its surface above the sea at the east end of Seram ... the rendezvous of the Paradise—and other bird-skin collectors from the mainland of New Guinea, from Salawatty, Mysore, and Halmaheira, and of the pearl-divers of Aru; hither the tripang, tortoise-shell, beeswax, nutmeg, dammar and other rich produce from a multitude of islands is brought to be exchanged with Malay and Chinese traders, of Macassar, Singapore and Ternate, for the scarlet, blue and white cottons of the Dutch and English looms, for the yellow-handled hoop-iron knives, which form the universal small change of these regions, and for beads, glass-balls, knobs of amber, old keys, scraps of iron, and worthless but gaudy Brummagen.

HENRY O. FORBES, *A naturalist's wanderings ...*

From Waropine ... is said to be a long land stretch to the head of a river, a branch of the sea, which comes from the south coast of New Guinea. I have been told that the inhabitants of Ceram carry iron and other goods up this inlet, and trade with the inhabitants of the north coast, for Missoy bark ... they are said to deal honestly with the Chinese, who trade with them, and advance them goods for several months before the returns are made.

THOMAS FORREST, *A voyage to New Guinea ...*

5.1. Traders and Pirates

The rise in eastern archipelago trade in maritime commodities, and the increasing significance of traders of Sulawesi origin during the period between 1750 and 1850, was accompanied by another major change. We begin to learn much more about the peoples of New Guinea (the Irianese, or the Papuans,[1] as I mainly describe them in this context). This occurs not only because the Dutch and other European powers became more interested in the island of New Guinea for commercial reasons, but because the indigenous peoples of Southeast Seram expanded their existing trade as the Makassans and Bugis expanded theirs. It is perhaps not entirely paradoxical, as we shall see, that the geographical zenith of Serammer involvement in this trade coincides with a period of growing interest shown by outsiders.

Before providing further detail on the form of trade in which the Ser-ammers were involved, it is important to emphasize that the fluidity of population movement and of political influence was by no means entirely in one direction, namely from west to east. We know, for example, that Biak-Numfor seafarers made extensive trading journeys along the whole of the north coast of New Guinea and far into what is now eastern Indonesia, at least partly a consequence of environmental restrictions on eastward movement. In many places settlements of Biak and Numfor people were established, as on Halmahera and probably North Seram also (Kamma 1972:8); with others (people from the Onin Peninsula in particular) settling in Seram and Ambon-Lease. Papuans, probably of Raja Ampat origin (that is, from the Tidore "client" domains of Waigeo, Salawati and Batanta, East Misool, and West Misool), raided Gorom, Aru, Kei, and Tanimbar from time to time and attacked villages in Ambon-Lease throughout much of the seventeenth century (Rumphius 1910 [1687] I:87, II:65, quoted in Bartels 1977:97 n. 34; also 174). Such raids were often coordinated through the leadership of the *sengajis* of the Gamrange Islands, usually that of Patani, on behalf of the sultan of Tidore. Indeed, raids are reported as far west as Buton and Gorontolo in Sulawesi and even Java, all of which confirmed the reputation for "piracy" that the coastal peoples of New Guinea had during the early period of European contact (Andaya 1991:86; Kamma 1972:8).

5.2. Spheres of Influence and Forms of Contact

Although economic exchange between local populations and most points west had been going on for centuries (Bruyn 1962; Galis 1953; Galis and Kamma 1958) and had ancient roots, trade certainly grew from the mid-eighteenth century onward. There are Chinese porcelain and Indian coral beads reported archaeologically for as early as 1616 in Biak (Kamma 1972: 9), and as we have seen from chapter 3, there are written reports of cloth being exchanged for massoi bark as early as 1636 (Haga 1884, 1:70–71, 80); and Roxo de Brito had traveled up the MacCluer Gulf and reported Ogar, Sekar, "Sufia," and Manggwa ("Magusia") as trading stations (Boxer and Manguin 1979:184, 186). But to understand how this trade was organized from the sixteenth century onward (and perhaps before then) it is crucial to distinguish between two spheres of influence and forms of contact. The first is that associated with what I shall call Tidore Raja Ampat and the sec-ond that of Southeast Seram and the Gorom Islanders (Haga 1884, 1:2, 17). The sources suggest that these two spheres were to a considerable extent geographically discrete and operated according to, or were constituted through, different kinds of political relations (Figure 5.1).

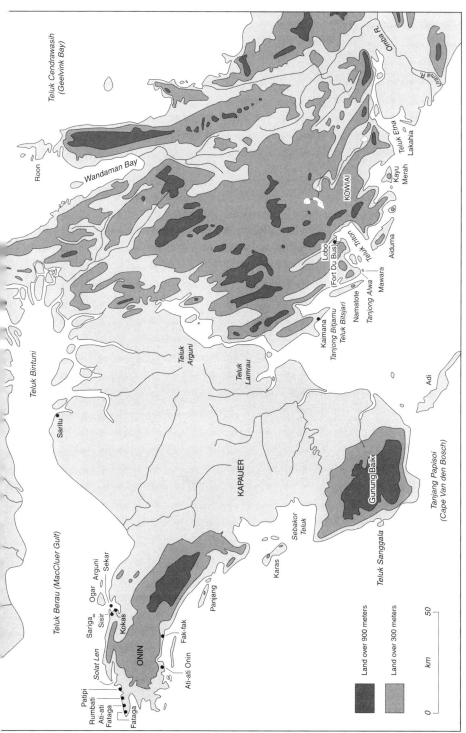

Figure 5.1. The Onin and Kowiai regions of Southwest New Guinea, showing main Serammer and Goromese trading areas and places mentioned in the text.

The Tidore Raja Ampat sphere extended at its zenith along the north coast of New Guinea as far as Biak-Numfor in Teluk Cendrawasih (Geelvink Bay) and south along the Bird's Head coast into Teluk Berau (the MacCluer Gulf). It also included Papuan settlements on the coast of Seram and other places north of Hote and Rarakit with close ties to Raja Ampat, particularly Misool (ibid., 2, 28). At least for the period under review here, outside of Tidore itself, it displayed a hereditary "raja system" of devolved centralized authority, in which rulers maintained their position through the control of trade, extraction of tribute, and the periodic use of force (Healey 1998: 339, 344; Mansoben 1995); in Polanyian terms a form of tributary trade. It is possible that Tidore influence extended even farther along the north coast of New Guinea, as there is evidence in the form of glass beads and bronzes from Lake Sentani and for indirect culture contact as far as Vanimo in present-day Papua New Guinea (Swadling 1996:206; C. Kocher-Schmid, personal communication). Indeed, this region shows evidence of very early contacts. For example, Haddon (1920:91, 129), in his study of outrigger canoes, showed how those of Northwest New Guinea are closely matched by a type he found in Halmahera and the Raja Ampat.

On the other hand, the Serammers and Goromese were involved in a different kind of trade from Teluk Berau in the north, south and southeastward along the Onin Peninsula as far as Pulau Karas and Pulau Adi. When Jan Carstenzoon reached Cape Debelle on the south coast of New Guinea in 1623, he found an island that, he said in his journal, some maps signify as "Staat Ceram" and others as belonging to the Papuas (Haga 1884, 1:36). We have already noted the influence of the language of Southeast Seram on local toponyms along the Onin coast; and, indeed, the lingua franca of this part of New Guinea, from Onin as far as Kowiai, had been Southeast Seram Littoral (or at least a pidgin combining SSL and the language of Onin (Van Hille 1905:253–254) for some centuries, and it was Serammer voyagers who commanded authority, provided an institutional base for trade, and served as political gatekeepers. On the coast SSL is still in use among a mixed Papuan and Serammer population.

From the eighteenth century onward Malay increasingly became important as a language of trade, but Tidorese (or for that matter the languages of the Raja Ampat [Van der Leeden 1983]) never appears to have been of any significance. The political arrangement on Onin and along Teluk Berau seems to have been quite different: the Serammers were concerned mostly with trading access rather than symbolic power, and operating at the level of relations with separate domains from Southeast Seram rather than as embassies from the court of a sultanate. Although there was sometimes conflict between Serammers and Papuans (as we shall see later), on the whole the former were approved of precisely because they traded rather than raided (Earl 1853:54). Our knowledge of the claims and history of contact for Tidore Raja Ampat is much better known, and it is instructive as well as overdue to focus on the activities of the Serammers.

In the area of Teluk Berau itself there was some overlap of influence between Tidore Raja Ampat and archipelagic Southeast Seram, and I shall return to this later. However, it is worth noting now the confusion in the literature regarding the extent of Tidore contact with this part of New Guinea, which has arisen as a consequence of simplified assumptions about the division of dependencies between the sultanates of Ternate and Tidore, and the difficulty of distinguishing between claims, authority, and an effective politico-economic presence. We have already noted in chapter 3 a comparable problem in assessing the control that Tidore exercised over the polities of archipelagic Southeast Seram. In New Guinea, as in Southeast Seram, European interpretations of local political realities seem to have had some effect on subsequent outcomes. Thus, the Dutch had renewed their treaty with the sultan of Tidore in 1733 despite his lack of authority in New Guinea. In the late eighteenth century the Dutch only allowed Chinese traders, from Ternate and Tidore, to trade in New Guinea, on the grounds that they would not trade for nutmeg. Chinese interest lay more in massoi, ambergris, trepang, turtle shell, pearls, parrots, and paradise plumes, which they exchanged for iron tools, cloth, beads, plates, and bowls. This VOC presumption and its consequences undermined the position of the Serammers in favor of Tidore and sustained the view that the Dutch had already formed: that Tidore effectively controlled all trade with New Guinea and exercised legitimate authority over it. Indeed, the Dutch were prepared to devolve absolute authority for New Guinea to the sultan of Tidore and even expanded the area under his putative jurisdiction. Similarly, the British contract of 1814 granted to Tidore territories that it had never really influenced, let alone dominated (Van Hille 1905:238), proclaiming the entire northern coast to be a legitimate "possession" of the sultan of Tidore (Haga 1884, 1:460). The Articles of Agreement drawn up with the British Crown in 1815 specified that "The whole of that central and eastern part of Halmahera . . . , together with the whole of the Papua islands, and the four districts of Mansarij, Karandefur, Ambarpura and Umbarpon [. . .], on the coast of New Guinea shall for the future be considered as the legitimate possessions of his Highness the Sultan of Tidore" (ibid., 460). In the same Articles, which bound Muhammad Jamanludien, the sultan mudah of Tidore, to recognize Muhammad Tahir as the "true and lawful sultan" (Article 6, to be precise), the sultan mudah undertook to solemnly promise "to refrain from all communication or intercourse, with the pirates; and . . . [to] . . . maintain no correspondence whatever with the chiefs and people inhabiting the islands of Mysore [sic], Goram, Ceram and Ceramlaut" (ibid., 462–463). The boundaries and rights of the domains of the sultans of Ternate and Tidore were laid down in the British contract of 1814 and subsequently endorsed by the returning Dutch authorities in relation to rights with respect to the movement of goods and services between various places. But there were no comparable contracts with even the then-dominant domains of Southeast Seram.

There were further contracts with Ternate and Tidore in 1824, which reiterated and strengthened the agreements of 1814 regarding areas of putative authority. The Dutch treaties of 1828 and 1848 gave Tidore authority over much more of New Guinea than it had hitherto controlled and cut right into areas under Serammer influence as far southeast as the Kowiai (Koiwai) coast. But after 1828 the area under the sultan of Tidore was no longer precisely specified in the contracts made. The area that came under Tidorese jurisdiction or direct Dutch jurisdiction in New Guinea during the nineteenth century was always vague (Swadling 1996:116), visiting Dutch administrators even confirmed the appointment of headmen on behalf of the sultan of Tidore in areas that were quite new to them. Tidore suzerainty over the area from Teluk Berau southward was, it would seem, in large part a self-fulfilling prophecy: Dutch and British administrative actions were based on fictional assumptions of the extent and quality of Tidore influence, eventually bringing to pass a situation that resembled what they had first presumed to be the case.

In practice, as far as the Onin region was concerned, the sultan of Tidore had no direct power at all, and the only effective indirect influence was through the quasi-client domain of Misool, the ruler of which he was expected to inform before taking any actions with respect to the local people. Beyond the area of direct interest to Misool and the other Raja Ampats, the coast was almost completely the protected trading zone of Serammers and Goromese. Despite Kamma's speculation (1948:179), there is no evidence that goods and tribute collected by Seram Lauters went to the sultan of Tidore on a regular basis. It is true that the Tidorese prince Ali defended a position at Tanjong Seli in 1850, the most westerly point of Notton, and another at Atiz, Wonim diatas, that had been under Tidore control since the end of 1848. It is also true that he visited the south coast at Kowiai and Kapia, that his name reached the "rajas" of Aiduma and Namatote (Namatota), and that he tried to claim the south coast in the Merkus region, where Fort Du Bus formerly stood and where there was no previous recognition that the sultan had any claim to authority. We know also that a representative of the sultan, a *sengaji*, spent six or seven months on Karas at the time of Van der Crab's visit (1864:532). But by that time Tidore could extend its claims to territory in the knowledge that it had the backing of the government of the Dutch East Indies, even though the authority of that government was only evident, for the most part, in the display of Dutch tricolors on Serammer and Bugis perahus (Haga 1884, 2:98, 311).

As we have seen, there were differences between the Tidorese and the Serammer spheres in terms of the form of political relations established, the general cultural context, and in particular their organization of trade. The Tidorese and Serammers differed profoundly in their mode of political operation. There had been formal political ties between ethnic Melanesians and Tidore as early as the late fifteenth century and perhaps much earlier. These had led to the creation of the four Papuan kingdoms known as the Raja Ampats (East Misool, West Misool, Waigeo, and Salawati and Batanta) as client domains of Tidore, probably sometime after 1534 (Elmberg 1968:128). Papuans were employed as oarsmen on Tidore hongi fleets (used for punitive raiding) to West Seram (Kamma 1972:8). Moreover, Tidore was in the habit of exacting tribute (for example, in the form of slaves) and raiding Papuan settlements when this was not forthcoming. This was still happening as late as the eighteenth century as far east as Teluk Cendrawasih (ibid., 215). There was much Tidorese cultural influence also (for example, in Biak, where the administrative division into districts was a Tidorese creation [ibid., 8–9]). The sultan of Tidore sought to extend his influence by the gifting of titles such as those of *sengaji* and *korono* (Haga 1984, 2:xvii). This was still an extremely common means of exerting power during the nineteenth century, with both Ternate and Tidore bestowing titles of Indonesian origin (Elmberg 1968:128), along with flags and a kind of official dress, the latter practices perhaps adopted from the Dutch. Serammers did not, as far as we know, do such things in quite the same way.

Of those stretches of the New Guinea coastline frequented by Serammers for trading purposes, it was the south coast of Teluk Berau and the northernmost part of the Onin Peninsula where there was most overlap with the interests of Tidore and where people were most harassed by the sultan's agents. Much of what we know about this conflict comes from the nineteenth-century records, and yet again we may assume that this reflects an increased boldness on the part of Tidore stemming, at least in part, from the legitimacy obtained through British and Dutch recognition of its claims. For example, the sultan created a number of "chiefs" on the basis of recognized Serammer trading areas, though later the Serammers regained their power to appoint chiefs there, though formally in name of the sultan (Elmberg 1968:129; Müller 1857:67). The raja of Rumbati in the 1870s was paying an annual tribute to the raja of Misool of cannon (three copper *lillas* and two small *lillas*, or lantakas),[2] who received it on behalf of the sultan of Tidore; in turn, other villages paid tribute to Rumbati (Robidé van der Aa 1879:304–305). On Pulau Panjang during the 1870s there was an agent of mixed Tidorese and Papuan descent who used to collect taxes on behalf of the sultan (ibid., 172).

Onin was also subject to Tidore hongi, but seems to have fared better than the Kowiai coast in the late nineteenth century. An 1874 hongi, led by Sebiar, raja of Rumasal on Misool, on behalf of the sultan of Tidore, imposed heavy taxes on Ati-ati and Rumbati, who had to supply fifteen slaves of each sex and their equivalent value in massoi, nutmeg, turtle shell, and other goods (Miklouho-Maclay 1982:443). Hongi fleets tended to avoid Karas and other islands frequented by Serammers and other traders, but those same traders feared hongi, and locals fled to the mountains. In 1850 Prince Ali (Amir) of Tidore raided Lakahia, enslaving one hundred Papuans (ibid.; Pouwer 1955:218). In fact, Tidore Raja Ampat raids, with their intention of intermittent subjugation, had quite an adverse effect on trade. The attempt by the sultan of Tidore to extend his influence led to the destabilization of the Kowiai coast and a deterioration in relations between coastal communities and also between coastal and inland communities, exacerbated by the free availability of guns. All this affected Serammer trading, and scarcely a year passed without someone being lost. Wallace reported that two Gorom perahus were attacked in May 1860 on the Kowiai coast and that a further fifty Goromese were killed in 1856 (Wallace 1962 [1869]:378–379). Instability and intervillage warfare continued into the 1870s (Miklouho-Maclay 1982:440–441).

5.3. *Sosolots*

It is in the early period of contact with the VOC that we first begin to learn something of a trading institution that is crucial to understanding the entire political economy of the region and in particular the success of Serammers in controlling the trade along the Papuan coast. This institution was a device for dividing up the coast between the various Southeast Seram polities, namely *sosolot*s: bays and anchorages in which one polity maintained a recognized monopoly in trade. In 1986 the term "*so solot*" still meant a kind of bay, a river mouth, or a stretch of coast where boats might enter. Between the sixteenth and early nineteenth centuries Seram Laut and Goromese traders were making annual visits to such places on the coast of Southwest New Guinea, from Salawati in the north to Utanata in the south, sailing annually according to the rhythm of the monsoons, departing with the northeast monsoon in February–March and returning home June–July (Bik 1928 [1824]:36).

The Dutch had early noted *sosolot*s. Even in the late seventeenth century the Serammers had discrete *sosolot*s ("sesolo") with exclusive trading rights on the Onin coast (Haga 1884, 1:103). Johannes Keyts talked of Laku, the orang kaya of Keffing, and the jurisdiction he had over part of the Papuan coast, through what he said the Keffingers called *sosolot*, the rule being that whoever planted their flag first had rights to trade, so that no others may come to trade, a right defended to the death (ibid., 102–103). One hundred and fifty years later, Van der Kemp (1911:386), writing in 1817, reported that Gorom, Seram Laut, Keffing, Geser, and other places in Southeast Seram all had established rights to trade along the Papuan coast, where they exchanged items of manufacture for massoi, trepang, and wild nutmeg. Both Bik (1928 [1824]:28) and Kolff (1927 [1840]:297) noted that particular "villages" traded with particular places, with Papuans carrying on trade only with those who visited them on a regular basis (Haga 1884, 1:121).

It does appear to be the case that the rulers (generically, *matlaen*) of the Southeast Seram domains had a special role in establishing and maintaining *sosolot*s. It is not only that such franchises were established in their name (following the functional simultaneity between a ruler and realm), but individual rulers appear to have played an active role in the trade, in a way reminiscent of the aristocrats of Kiriwana (Malinowski 1922). Bik (1928 [1824]:19) tells us that the orang kaya of Ainikke had his own trading place, and we know that in 1860 the raja of Manawoka traded in Papua (Broersma 1934:340). When Arsali was raja of Kataloka, the "other raja" (most likely the "raja mudah") spent half the year in Papua on trade (Van der Crab 1864: 535). Rulers certainly were more likely to command the wherewithal to mount trading expeditions and to have the slaves for boats and agricultural labor at home as well as the capital to purchase the goods. But it was not only rulers of the Southeast Seram domains (or at least not latterly) who had a *sosolot*, but commoners as well. These, we know, tended to be smaller and arranged through mutual consent.

We do not know precisely how a new political dispensation emerged, and it must have taken place at different times at different places, but it did so at the interface of contact between traders from archipelagic Southeast Seram. From early on selected individual natives of the various *sosolot*s were designated agents who could represent the trading interest of their trading partner or his domain and prepare for visits. Such persons had limited jurisdiction, but could sometimes create "subchiefs," and take commission on goods landed.[3] Unlike traditional Melanesian exchange partners, such as those described by Elmberg (1968:128, 203) for the Mejprat, such trade agents related to those with whom they exchanged in a hierarchic rather than egalitarian fashion, and marriage was permitted for agents but precluded for ceremonial exchange partners. The first Dutch traders to arrive found a system of advance payments being used by middlemen of mixed or immigrant stock who were termed "*papua*," using bush knives and low-quality cloth as a means of payment. From such beginnings a "raja system" developed, rather different from that associated with the Tidore Raja Ampat, involving conversion to Islam and relations of marriage with Serammer and Goromese trade partners. By the time we have adequate records in the seventeenth century, we can identify some nine such kerajaan (domains), the names of which recur again and again as significant operators in the New Guinea trade, right up until the beginning of the twentieth century: Rumbati, Patipi, Wertuar, Sekar, Arguni, Ati-ati, Fataga, Namatote, and Aiduma (Goodman 1998:437). Such local rulers, sometimes intermarrying, gained wealth and influence from trade and contacts, simultaneously participating in an external world of trade and an internal world of institutionalized competitive exchange (Andaya 1991:94; Healey 1998:345; Van Hille 1905:254–256). The raja of Lakahia in 1876 not only spoke SSL, but had visited Seram, Banda, and Makassar (Swadling 1996: 148).

Trade, it seems, was conducted in terms of fixed rates of barter exchange, without much variation. Local people undertook to supply traders with particular quantities of forest or marine products. Thus, gongs, copperware, amber-colored beads (Indian corals), and iron all had fixed exchange values with regard to each other (Kamma 1972:9). More will be said later about particular commodities, but the general pattern was the purchase of natural resources, such as long nutmeg, massoi, and pearl shell, against manufactured goods, such as textiles, ironwork, beads, peddling goods, and, at least latterly, also rice. Robidé van der Aa (1879:177) listed the following equivalences, which he says were fixed by the raja, for receipt of 1 pikul of nutmeg:

2 pikuls of rice	2 pieces of red cotton
2,000 pieces of sago	2 pieces of blue cotton
2 pikuls of iron	1 pikul of lead (presumably
2 pieces of patterned cotton	for musket shot)
1 piece of white cotton	

Temporary houses were built, apparently by locals for traders, during the annual visit. In most cases, products were supplied in the agreed time, but sometimes traders had to wait many years, and in some cases promises were never fulfilled. Seram Laut traders around Triton Bay in 1828 usually stayed between four and five months (Earl 1853:59–60; Kolff 1927 [1840]), though Miklouho-Maclay (1982:44) reported meeting a Makassan captain in 1874 near Namatote who had been waiting six years for goods.

But not only were Serammers frequent visitors throughout the historical period, they also settled. We know that in 1828 there was a Serammer colony at Abrauw or Uta, Kipia (Van Hille 1905:321–327). Such colonies became bases from which to establish new *sosolot*s. Thus Fak-fak traders moved to temporary camps at places such as Kulkadi (on the Sebakor Gulf), collecting trepang from surrounding coral banks and bringing it back to be processed. Shell was also brought and birds. De Brauw (1854:206) considered most inhabitants of Ati-ati to be Muslim; the animist Papuans lived farther inland. There were Seram Lauters permanently based on Karas and on Namatote by 1858 (Haga 1884, 2:370), the latter serving as a base for individuals from Kilwaru trading with mountain people.

For some three hundred years the main trading settlements were situated on the south side of Teluk Berau, the same area over which, as we have seen, Tidore most often sought to exert its power and where it sought to claim its authority. The main settlements were Ati-ati, Fataga, Rumbati, and Patipi, and it was in these places that Serammers and (by the early nineteenth century) other outside traders were based. The first two traded imported goods north of the bay (the Nattan area) around the rivers Kais, Kaibus, and Rumkai; Rumbati and Patipi went to Inanwaton and eastward to what is now Teluk Bintuni (Goodman 1998:437; Robidé van der Aa 1879:42). The coastal people of Teluk Berau themselves, rather than the Serammers, Goromese, and, later, Makassans, were engaged in most of this onward trade (Haga 1884, 2:81), though Forrest (1969 [1779]:113) reported stories from 1776 of Serammers exchanging iron for massoi in Wandaman Bay (separated from Teluk Bintuni by a narrow isthmus), where he also encountered Chinese traders. Goodman (1998:437) has suggested that this trading point might have been located on Roon and speculated on Serammer trading linkages southward to what is now Teluk Arguni.

Throughout the period documented in this chapter it was Kiltai and Kilwaru that always seemed to dominate the New Guinea trade (De Hollander 1895:502). Bik (1928 [1824]:38) reported that the "kommandant" of Kiltai was linked to Rumbati. The orang kaya of Onin traded with people from Gorom as well as from the Seram Laut Archipelago; the orang kaya of Fataga and Kilbati seemed to be under the influence of Keffing (Haga 1884, 2:112). Rarat was trading with Qwejay (Kowiai), Onin, and Karas (Carren), exchanging iron goods and cotton fabric, and Gorom (which must mean in this context Kataloka) traded on the islands of Samail and Karas (De Brauw 1854:208). Perahus reached Namatote from Aiduma on Triton Bay (ibid., 212), a trade that was entirely in the hands of Serammers (Haga 1884, 2:118). By 1833 trade in the Merkus region (ibid., 60–63) was under the influence of Seram Lauters in particular. The Kapia area, by contrast, was much used by traders from mainland Seram, but this decreased after more effective Dutch controls on the slave trade (Van Hille 1905:282).

So, it would seem that some stretches of coastline were exclusively associated with the *sosolot*s of individual domains, sometimes aggregated into contiguous areas, that represented the traditional trading prerogatives of particular islands; though elsewhere they were quite mixed, and in some areas increasingly intermixed with areas in which Makassans or Bugis traded or with general trading settlements, such as Fak-fak, where *sosolot* norms and rules of engagement did not apply. By the 1870s even Salawati in the Raja Ampat group, with all its historic links to Tidore, was serving as a trading post for people of both Ternaten and Goromese origin (Robidé van der Aa 1879:86). But even for the indigenous traders of archipelagic Southeast Seram, *sosolot* boundaries were not necessarily an impediment to trade in particular areas, because we know that Ondor used Papuan, Seram Laut, and Keffing captains on their vessels to give them access to places where Goromese were not otherwise allowed to visit.

The institution of *sosolot* was not always free of conflict, neither between Serammers and Papuans nor between different groups of Papuans and Serammers vying for the same trade. As early as 1680 we learn of enmity between Karas and Onin sufficient to halt the trade (Haga 1884, 1: 91, 128). As Europeans took a closer interest in the area, about one hundred years later, there are more numerous accounts of conflict. Bik (1928 [1824]: 38), for example, mentioned war between the raja of Rumbati and Patipi and Ati-ati, which prevented trade with the Serammers. To some extent this might also reflect an increased volume of trade and certainly increased competition between different groups of traders. In the 1850s Muslim villages along the coast are reported as being raided from the interior. Earl (1853:55, 57–58) reported Karas islanders raiding houses on Triton Bay. Wallace (1962 [1869]:379) tells us that regular Goromese traders along the Onin coast suffered frequent attacks, sometimes when there were arguments over trade. In 1856 fifty Goromese were murdered on Lakahia (Haga 1884, 2:107), the incident presumably being that which Wallace himself (1896:131) refered to when he spoke of the murder of the crews of two perahus, including the son of the raja of Kataloka. In 1871, along the south coast of Teluk Berau, Kapitua was at war with Sisir (Haga 1884, 2:210). In 1899 (or at the very end of 1898) a Guli-guli perahu was plundered on its way to Wamuka. As a result eight people died, including the orang kaya of Urung, which led to a feud between the two places (Van Hille 1905:317). There was still much local intervillage raiding along the Papuan coast at the opening of the twentieth century (Van Hille 1907:584, 596).

One can only speculate as to the causes of this conflict. Nonfulfillment of quotas might have been sufficient to generate hostility between traders and local people, a situation that we anyway know sometimes led to the fleeing of Papuan suppliers to the mountains. By the early years of the nineteenth century Papuans had acquired a reputation among both Moluccans and Europeans for "thieving" (Bik 1928 [1824]:36), and others described them as "treacherous" (Wallace 1896:130); though it is not unreasonable to assume that with a system of trade that relied on negotiation rather than subjugation, conflict might be understood (by the local population at least) as the pursuance of legitimate exchange by another means. Moreover, it is plausible that since we know of cross-cultural misunderstanding between Tidorese and Papuans due to radically different political cultures (Ellen 1986b), similar problems between Serammers and Papuans in terms of occluding economic cultures might have generated some of the conflict.

The records and oral traditions offer no trace of evidence for centralized political domination by any of the Southeast Seram trading domains. Instead, their heads simply established a monopoly along certain stretches of coast, which they were prepared to defend against traders from other domains who attempted to violate their patch. Thus, on the whole, they traded through influence, rather than ruling through domination. But although the Serammers, as far as we know, never sought to incorporate Papuans as subjects into some wider centralized polity, they did, like the Tidorese, introduce ascribed statuses for individuals who acted as their trade agents and forged alliances through marriage. Taxes were collected at irregular intervals by these representatives (cups, bowls, and copper rings) (Pouwer 1955:216, 218). As early as 1663 an orang kaya was reported for Rumbati and a raja of Onin engaged in trade with Seram Lauters (Haga 1884, 1:84). In 1702–1703 individuals in Ati-ati and Rumbati were being described as orang kaya, kapitan, and raja (Van Hille 1905:259), but whether any of these were settlers or indigenous Papuans is not clear. Interbreeding (and possibly intermarriage) between Papuans and Moluccans had been reported in 1581 by Roxo de Brito in the islands along the south coast of Teluk Berau (Sollewijn Gelpke 1994:135–136). By the early nineteenth century intermarriage was certainly a long-established practice. Bik (1928 [1824]:36), for example, tells us that the wife of the mayor of Kilwaru was from Ati-ati Papua Onin, west of Fak-fak. Adi had a raja by the middle of the century (Van der Crab 1864:533). By 1870 Karas had a raja mudah who visited Gorom and is described as being of Papuan physique but culturally Malay. Fataga, the "king" of Ati-ati, had a Goromese wife in 1880, and their son married on Seram Laut, returning to Ati-ati in 1899 (Van Hille 1905:260). From my own fieldwork, we now know that the clan of the current raja of Ati-ati is Rumakat, which as noted in chapter 2 is a descent line of Kastella in Kiltai. In this process of acculturation conversion to Islam played a significant role (Haga 1884, 2:81; Van Hille 1905:253–254; Robidé van der Aa 1879:319).

The *sosolot* system remained pretty much intact until 1900, undermined perhaps in those areas (such as along the south coast of Teluk Berau) where other traders had long been making incursions and where the political remit of Tidore had long held some sway. However, throughout the eighteenth and nineteenth centuries the system continued to expand into new areas to the southeast. As Swadling (1996:138 n. 9) suggested, the effectiveness of the *sosolot* system may indeed have been responsible for the Dutch failing to establish a trading foothold in this area until well into the nineteenth century. During the twentieth century the *sosolot*s retained some links with their earlier "owners" from Seram and Seram Laut. Even in 1902 the rajas of Ati-ati, Rumbati, and Patipi spoke only SSL, although other villages were bilingual in SSL and the local vernacular (Elmberg 1968: 129). Trade between Southeast Seram and Onin was still important in 1928 (Jansen 1928:492), though effectively ceased with Indonesian independence.

5.4. Regional Relations of Exchange

Produce acquired from individual *sosolot*s was sold on in different ways, depending on domain of origin, status, and customary networks. Some was sold locally in Southeast Seram or in other parts of the eastern Moluccas, some was sold in Banda, but some was also taken to Bali. Bik (1928 [1824]:19) tells us that the orang kaya of Ainikke (Enneka) sold produce obtained from his *sosolot* to traders in Ondor and Kataloka. Trade goods were obtained by Ainikke mostly in Ondor, often on credit reckoned in trepang, turtle shell, or other commodities (ibid., 36). Traders from other domains sold their produce to Bugis visiting, or later based on, Kilwaru or Aru. Goromese sold their trepang to Chinese traders or Serammers on Keffing, or sent their boats to Kei where Makassans stopped on their way to Aru (ibid., 26). Much produce (massoi, trepang, and wild nutmeg) was brought to Banda by Goromese, Keffingers, and Seram Lauters, where it was sold to Chinese traders or, increasingly as the nineteenth century progressed, to Ambon (Haga 1884, 1:312; Van der Kemp 1911:386). We have noted in chapter 4 how Goromese controlled the westward trade with Aru until the end of the nineteenth century. It is not surprising, therefore, that they also

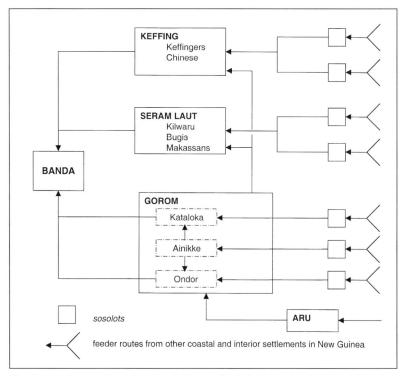

Figure 5.2. Schematic trading pattern in archipelagic Southeast Seram for the mid-nineteenth century, indicating movement of produce into and out of New Guinea. Note that certain polities that maintained *sosolots* did not all trade directly with Banda, but might use larger local centers who would then deal with Banda. Similarly, some Goromese trade was conducted with Keffing and Seram (Laut) rather than directly with Banda, where there were concentrations of outside traders, such as Chinese.

served as middlemen between the Papuan coast and Aru, supplying, for example, the shell arm bands worn by women (Bik 1928 [1824]:88). Few Goromese traveled westward themselves (Wallace 1962 [1869]:380–381). The pattern of this disposal of goods is schematically diagrammed in Figure 5.2.

In the same way that *sosolots* were only the alpha point for a complex set of subsequent trading linkages westward across the Banda zone, so from the point of view of Papuan participants they were the omega point of trading networks with ramifications deep into the interior. It is certainly the case that many commodities were extracted directly by the inhabitants of those stretches of coast along which particular Southeast Seram domains traded. But other *sosolots* were effectively no more than points of exchange, producing little of interest themselves to intrusive traders but nevertheless handling goods as middlemen from other points along the coast or inland. This was often true of the offshore islands. Robidé van der Aa (1879:167) was quite emphatic about this for Karas on the Onin coast, but it must also have applied to Arguni, Ogar, Sariga, and Sekar on the south side of Teluk Berau, and perhaps also Panjang and Adi, and Namatote, Mawara, Aiduma, and Lakahia in the Kowiai area. Sekar, in particular, is a minute island, no larger than Geser or Kiltai. Thus, these cases, yet again, demonstrate the way in which small offshore islands develop as trading centers, a situation reminiscent not only of Southeast Seram, but of Melanesia more widely.

Onin, in general, was a center for onward internal trade within New Guinea. Bik (1928 [1824]:13) described Papuan traders using between 150 and 200 small vessels at a time, coming from the east to Onin to sell sago, mussels, and stoneware bottles, which were then traded onward to Seram Laut. People on river mouths sold sago in exchange for massoi, which in turn was bought by Serammers in these villages (Robidé van der Aa 1879: 40). Along the south coast of Teluk Berau and in Onin generally there was little sago, and in large part it had to be obtained from people living along the north coast of the gulf, in exchange for red cloth (at the rate of one linso costa for 30 tumang of sago), wild nutmeg, some trepang and turtle shell, and iron implements (Van Dissel 1904:639, 640; Van Hille 1906:527). We know that in 1860 (Wallace 1896:129–130) Salawati and Misool were net exporters of sago; Serammers took it to sell as far north as Ternate. Sago, therefore, was a means of payment, as tobacco was later to be for birds of paradise as well as other commodities (Haga 1911:342). The Kasuri area was visited by perahus from Sekar (Van Hille 1907:556), and Waromge exchanged sago and slaves for trade articles with Rumbati. Near Konda there was a trading place for Ati-ati traders in 1905, who also operated in Teminabuam and Seremuk as bird hunters (ibid., 571, 624–630). In the same year there was a Serammer damar buyer's house on Senindara (ibid., 581).

The spread of the textile trade into the interior of the Bird's Head Peninsula appears to have come from both the west and south coasts. It appears to have reached the Ayamaru area, for example, from the south through the exchange relationships established between Serammer trade agents and local big men of Ayamaru origin, and some immigrant big men originally from Salawati (Miedema 1986:27). If kain timor reached the interior of the Bird's Head from the south coast (Miedema 1984:78; 1986:42 n. 3; contra Elmberg 1968), then the traders were almost certainly Serammers. These imported ikat cloths served as a medium of exchange in cycles of life crisis rituals (*popot*) and their associated feasts involving exchanges between wife-receivers and wife-givers in the Mejprat area. The items involved included Indian patola-patterned ikats, their wax-resist and block-printed imitations, and Indonesian ikats or cottons, kain bentenon (cotton-weft ikat), from North Sulawesi; and textiles from Sumba, Sumbawa, Timor, Roti, Tanimbar, and Seram, factory-made cloth and Indonesian sarongs of various origins. Kain timor was obtained by Serammers for trade in New Guinea from Bugis or Makassans and did not come from Timor direct. *Popot* leaders were immigrant trade agents who assumed the role of bride-givers and hosts. In 1957 a small ikat could be exchanged in the Mejprat area for ten pieces of white bark cloth, twenty skeins of *Gnemon* bast for one printed sarong or a small ikat, 20 pieces of white bark cloth for one large ikat, or one fully grown pig for eight ikat cloths. Before World War II one captured child could be exchanged for between one and four ikat cloths, depending on height (Elmberg 1968:21–23, 205, 246, 285).

Thus, Mejprat marital and genetic exchange was ultimately part of intraregional trade (ibid., 246). Traders from and agents for the Southeast Seram domains and officials of the remote sultanate of Tidore collected taxes in West New Guinea and in the case of Tidore tried to establish permanent authority. Biakers on the north coast left trade partners who were ultimately agents with different partners given by the sultan of Tidore (Van Dissel 1904; 1907:992–994, 1002). Despite innovative leadership roles developed under influence of coastal traders, the officials of sultans and their successors (Elmberg 1968:204), it was on this frontier that Malay assumptions of hierarchy met Melanesian notions of egalitarianism with interesting consequences, including evidence that one political culture found it difficult to fully comprehend the other (Ellen 1986b).

5.5. The Commodities of the Papuan Trade

The commodities involved in the Papua trade have varied over time. For the period before 1700, the goods moving westward to Tidore, the Raja Ampats, through the Geser corridor and the Gorom Archipelago, and into the markets of farther Asia tended to be diverse products of the rain forest. Particular products dominate the literature, and we must assume that this reflects in some crude way the quantities traded and their value. During the seventeenth century massoi and long nutmeg are crucial. However, the onward trade was not the same as the local trade, and Southeast Seram traders sought in Papua commodities that they consumed directly themselves, mainly slaves, but also staples such as sago. The movement of commodities eastward into Papua was mainly Indian and Indonesian textiles and Chinese porcelain, but also ironware and elephant tusks (Earl 1853:59–60). The textile trade was clearly long-standing; there is evidence for the import of glazed beads, coarse white calico, blue cotton cloth, and patola cloths from Gujerat from before 1500 (Elmberg 1968). Getting some sense of the volume of trade across the strait from Onin to Southeast Seram at this early period is not easy, though we can assume that many of the references to trade in long nutmeg in the VOC reports indicate produce of Papuan origin, and as already noted this trade was sufficiently significant to challenge the Dutch nutmeg monopoly and to invite punitive raids and extirpation. On one visit in the early seventeenth century Nicolaes Vinck found forty traders, mostly Serammers, involved in trade on the Onin coast (Haga 1884, 1:88).

From 1700 to 1850 we find an increase in the trade of marine produce, with particular attention being paid to trepang. Something has already been said in chapter 4 of the circumstances giving rise to the growth in the trade in maritime products in the waters of Southeast Seram, and its extension to New Guinea was a logical one because Serammers were already in command of the knowledge and could easily respond to increasing demand. The massoi trade had (as we shall see) become relatively unimportant by the mid-nineteenth century, though slaves were now part of an onward trade beyond Southeast Seram to other parts of the Indonesian Archipelago. The commodities moving eastward remained more constant: textiles and porcelain, though iron becomes of increasing importance. Let us consider the case of iron a bit further.

There is written evidence for iron technology in Triton Bay as early as 1606 (Kamma and Kooijman 1973:9). By 1793 the English were trading iron bars near Dorei in Teluk Cendrawasih. By the late nineteenth century the trade in iron (both manufactured items and bars for smithing) to New Guinea was substantial, though Papuan smithing itself was still limited to forging and reforging (ibid., 1–2). Von Rosenberg (1875:145) reported that between 1864 and 1869 ironware worth 26,858 guilders was exported from Ternate to New Guinea. Some of the iron products (especially parangs) were manufactured in the Moluccas and by Tidorese smiths on Tidore, Makian, and Kajoa, or in Seram, whose parangs were known widely in New Guinea as *sumberdain* (dain or lain, apparently meaning Seram in the language of Numfor). But much ironwork came from farther afield. From as early as the last quarter of the seventeenth century parangs from Tobunku, Belitung, and Karimata were reaching the MacCluer Gulf (Teluk Berau) and parts of the Bird's Head (Andaya 1991:91–92). But there was also trade within New Guinea and a reverse movement of worked iron back into the Moluccan area. For example, arrow points made in Biak are known from Waigeo (Kamma and Kooijman 1973:19). In 1872 forges are reported at various places along Teluk Berau (Van Dissel 1904:639, 640; Van Hille 1906: 527). Rumbati and Patipi appear to have acquired their iron-working techniques from Seram (Van der Sande 1907:237), though possibly also from Gorom-Kataloka.

During the 1820s between twelve and fifteen junks (elsewhere twenty to thirty Goromese vessels) were reported (Bik 1928 [1824]:36) as sailing to New Guinea for trade, and Kolff (1927 [1840]) noted that every year two or three traders from Seram Laut visited Onin. The coast of Teluk Berau continued to export wild nutmeg (Wallace 1896:130), as well as trepang; turtle shell; pearls; mother-of-pearl; karet (latex); birds' nests; bird of paradise plumes; the medicinal and aromatic belishay, pulasari, and rasamala (*Altingia norona*) woods; imperial pigeons; lories; and slaves (De Brauw 1854: 209–210; Haga 1884, 2:342). Birds of paradise were also coming from Kowiai, Karas, and Asmalas to the east, with Asmat people bringing to Onin birds, slaves, trepang, and pearls on between ten to twenty boats at a time to trade with the Serammers (Bik 1928 [1824]:38). Papuan sago, coconut oil, wood, thatch, and livestock were exported on to Banda on boats from Gorom, Keffing, and Aru. Gorom and Seram boats also took sago to Aru (Wallace 1896:132). In return, in addition to textiles, porcelain, and ironware, guns and powder become increasingly important at that time; Bik (1928 [1824]: 38), for example, noted that Kiltai had maintained rights to trade with Rumbati Papuans on payment of a cannon, four rifles, and two vats of powder.

By the late nineteenth century the imports had become even more varied. Serammers traded porcelain, cotton cloth, arm bands, copper goods, bush knives, ironware, opium, arak, firearms, and "Brummagen" of all descriptions (Beccari 1924:197; Forbes 1885:299; Haga 1884, 2:342; Robidé van der Aa 1879:43, 303). But in return, the export produce remained remarkably constant. Beccari (1924:79) tells us that Sekar and Karas still annually exported 2,000–3,000 pikuls of long nutmeg and also massoi, and that lawan (*Cinnamomum culiban*) wood—the trade in which is on record for the sixteenth century—was distilled into medicine (ibid., 240). The trade in Papuan "wortelhout" (*Pterocarpus indicus*) is mentioned for the first time, as is that in damar (Van Hille 1907:582). Thus, the character and items of trade remained remarkably similar, with only the traders changing and perhaps the significance of each commodity through time and from place to place.

After 1900 the pattern and volume of exchange begins to shift radically. In 1914 bird hunting by permit had been opened up to everyone, and hunters included Makassans, Chinese, Ternatens, Tidorese, Javanese, and Arabs, assisted by Papuans, in addition to some registered Papuan hunters and many local assistants (Beversluis and Gieben 1929:196–197, Broersma 1934:332–333). Kain patola, sirih-pinang, and kain timor all continued to be traded with New Guinea, and trepanging remained important, though now increased numbers of Moluccans also went to settle and cultivate land. In 1986 Sainuddin Tukwain Rumbawa in Samboru could remember his grandfather voyaging to New Guinea on the old kind of perahu, which he had never seen and which has now been replaced by the *ang kalulis*. Between independence and the TRIKORA episode, which led to the incorporation of Netherlands New Guinea (Irian Barat) into the Republic of Indonesia, trade was not officially permitted.

It is instructive at this point to examine the history of two rather different commodities: massoi and slaves.

5.6. Massoi Bark

The role of the Southeast Seram archipelago in managing the New Guinea trade in massoi bark, *Cryptocarya massoy* (Figure 5.3) was already well established by the time the first Europeans arrived. This is clear from the evidence of de Brito and others. Seram Lauters reportedly were involved in the massoi trade in the 1630s, at the time Dutch traders first sought out trade

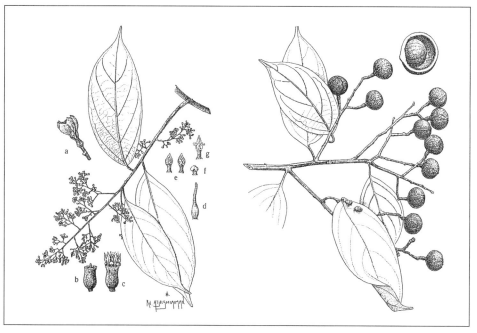

Figure 5.3. Flowering and fruiting branches of massoi, *Cryptocarya massoy* (Oken) Kostermans. Reproduced from Kostermans 1955:22–23.

on the Papuan coast, and in 1645 were bringing it to Banda from Onin and Adi. Artus Gijsels (governor of Ambon) reported that Kilwaru had sent nine *kora-kora* to Onin to procure massoi and slaves; between ten and twelve Seram Laut junks went to Onin to collect massoi in 1636 in exchange for swords, sago, and some gold (Tiele and Heeres 1890:2907). In other words, pretty much the same pattern existed as reported over one hundred years previously by de Brito. Indeed, the trade had not changed one hundred years later when we have a description from Rumphius in his *Herbarium Amboinense* (1741, 2:62; see also Kostermans 1950:435–437), who said that massoi previously came through the trade areas controlled by Seram Laut along the Onin coast. By the third decade of the seventeenth century the VOC was beginning to take a serious interest in the possibilities of being directly involved in Southwest New Guinea, once they had seen that the Seram Lauters were able to establish a profitable trade.

We know there was a division of the massoi and the slaving trade during the seventeenth century between two domains on Seram Laut. Seram Lauters voyaged via Gorom to the Papuan coast to "feed up" the natives and then collect massoi. *Toname-tomesen* (boxes made from pandanus leaves and the woody leafstalks of the sago palm) were traded from Gorom and Seram Laut to elsewhere (Haga 1884, 1:43). Rumphius (1856:125–127) reported the massoi and slave trade as being on the south side of Teluk Berau in 1684, involving mostly traders from Seram Laut and Gorom, in Buma Bati (Rumbati) and Satraga (Fataga). The western part of the coast was known as Papua Onin (sometimes called Woni) and the eastern as Papua Kowiai. Massoi grew on the alkaline soils of the coastal mountains as far east as the Omba (Opa) river, two to three days walk from the coast. Massoi trees were clear-felled and the bark removed. Thus, as supplies were exhausted in one area the trade moved to another (Swadling 1996:136). By the first half of the seventeenth century the main massoi area had already moved from Onin to Karas. Karas islanders themselves obtained massoi from between Arguni and Gunung Baik. By 1670 the trade had moved even farther east to Namatote on the Kowiai coast. Other islands such as Mawara, Aiduma, Kayu Merah, and Lakahia also became trading centers and some traders settled. In return, locals obtained poor-quality swords and hacking blades and cloth; palm sugar and rice were used as preparatory gifts. Enough massoi was collected to load one or two boats (between 60 and 100 pikuls, where a pikul was about 60.5 kilograms). Seram Laut traders continued to expand eastward along the southern Papuan coast until the Sultan of Tidore instigated hongi raids in 1850, which discouraged trade and had a devastating impact (ibid., 136 nn. 11–13).

In 1623 the governor of Amboina sent Jan Carstenzoon on an abortive visit to investigate possibilities for opening up the massoi trade, still entirely in the hands of Serammers. He got as far as Mupuruka on the Mimika coast before the captain of one of the vessels was killed. A subsequent visit in 1636 looked into reports by Seram Lauters of lignite deposits at Lakahia used locally for smithing. The leader of that expedition was killed at Namatote, and although the expedition continued along the Mimika coast it did not go ashore. Similar unsuccessful expeditions followed after 1650 in an attempt to purchase slaves along the Onin coast, which resulted in conflict with local populations. Another expedition by Johannes Keyts in 1678 to Onin and Kowiai led to the establishment of trading contracts at Fataga and Karas and involved the solemn distribution of Dutch flags, and visits to other places such as Adi and Namatote (Swadling 1996:138). Keyts made a contract at Namatote for massoi and for other products, including lignite from the then-uninhabited island of Lakahia (Rumphius 1856:125–127). Pressure from Seram Lauters, however, led to the breaking of the agreement, and six of the Keyts party were killed. Such a record of abject failure put an end to Dutch interest in the massoi trade and in trade with the Papuan coast generally for over one hundred years. The Bandanese perkeniers had more success in later years, but they too suffered major setbacks and faced competition from Gorom (Swadling 1996:138 n. 10).

The successful enforcement of the VOC monopoly on trade with Aru after 1645 probably forced Seram Laut traders eastward along the southern coastline of New Guinea in search of alternative sources of long nutmeg and massoi, as far as the Trans-Fly (Swadling 1996:154). The evidence for Serammer contact with the Trans-Fly is partly linguistic: SSL words such as "*turi*," (knife) or their close cognates can be found in the languages of Onin, Lobo on Triton Bay, Namatote and Wuanssirau on Etna Bay, and even as far as the Torres Strait, where they are all used for either iron or knife. There are also glass beads found in archaeological sites upriver of Kikori on the Gulf of Papua, one identified as being made between 1650 and 1750 and excavated from deposits dated between 1630 and 1770. The site is located on the main pearl shell trade route from the Torres Strait via the Papua Gulf to the highlands, and we also know that in 1606 Torres himself reported no local use of iron in the strait (ibid., 155–157). Finally, there is the evidence of local oral history, such as the Sido-Hido traditions of Southwest Papua, that "books" (surat, buku) were in circulation in the Trans-Fly before the arrival of Europeans (ibid., 158–159). It is this route that may have led to the introduction of tobacco, sweet potatoes, damar for torch making, and a new kind of sago pounder, especially since we do know that tobacco (for example) was introduced to Raja Ampat, Onin, Kowiai, and Mimika by Moluccans, who had obtained it from the Portuguese (ibid., 161).

5.7. Slaves and Slaving

Slaves have been a major export of New Guinea from the earliest period and had originally been taken by the Serammers for their own needs.[4] They may also have been traded on to Banda, where slaves were used in indigenous nutmeg production (Loth 1998:71; Villiers 1981b:729), and farther afield. With the development of colonial society new needs arose, in Ambon and elsewhere, and the seventeenth century saw an increase in the demand for Papuan slaves, many of whom may have been sold to the Dutch plantations in Banda (Andaya 1991:83). There is plenty of evidence in the VOC records of the late seventeenth century of slaving by Serammers along the Onin coast, including one report of a Misool vessel full of slaves off Karas destined to be sold on in Gorom (Haga 1884, 1:136). Kilwaru is reported to have dispatched about 10 *kora-kora* to Uring and Hotei on the Onin coast in an average year to obtain massoi and slaves, as well as cruising the shores of the northern Moluccas (Tiele and Heeres 1886:109, 244). Onin boats, mainly from the Rumbati area, regularly brought slaves to Gorom, where they were exchanged for the equivalent of twenty-five to thirty reals in cloth or Tobunku blades. In Rumbati itself between two hundred and three hundred slaves a year could be obtained, each at the cost of ten Tobunku swords (Andaya 1991:85). Indeed, Rumbati was an important center of late seventeenth-century slaving, supplied principally through the settlement of Rumakain at the mouth of the Kamundan River farther up Teluk Berau on the north bank (Wichmann 1909:107–112).

In the colonial Mail Reports of the nineteenth century we find extensive discussion of the Papuan slave trade, involving slavers from Raja Ampat and archipelagic Southeast Seram, with much detail on prices. Young and healthy slaves could fetch two "geras" and a coral and wood-handled knife, the same as ten Spanish mats (Bik 1928 [1824]:18–19). One trader from Seram, Danu Abdullah, working for Prince Mohammed Djin of Salawati, received 3,000 guilders,[5] but young Papuan slaves, often euphemistically described as "anak piara" (adopted children), exchanged hands for between 60 and 100 guilders each. Many went to Bali, Lombok, Bayon, and Labo Bua on Sumbawa. For the Serammers, however, Papuan slaves were not simply a trading commodity but an integral part of their own economy and social organization. On Gorom, in the early nineteenth century, slaves lived in the interior hills with their pigs, supplying their owners with two-thirds of their own production of rice (amounting to 100–150 koyongs a year), tubers, maize, sugarcane, and so on, all of which they brought to the coastal settlements of their owners (Bik 1928 [1824)]:35–36). Fishing on Gorom at that time was also mainly handled by slaves, as was the crewing of most boats (ibid., 13; Broersma 1934; Leirissa 1981:56). The extensive role of slaves in subsistence production released their owners to engage in more trade than might otherwise have been possible. Shortages of slaves in particular domains are reported for this period; Ondor, for example, had insufficient slaves to crew their vessels and had to take captain and crew from Kataloka.

One of the reasons why accounts of Serammer slaving increase in the early nineteenth century is due to Dutch concerns as to its morality. Bik, for example, resolved to report on the slave trade and recommend its outlawing (1928 [1824]:18–19). The number of slaves in Amboina decreased from 2,810 in 1837 to as few as 768 in 1855 (Bleeker 1856:139), and by the middle of the nineteenth century the Dutch were beginning to control the trade. The sale of slaves was officially banned in 1850. Slavery was abolished on Banda in 1860 and the trade monopoly in spices in 1864 (Hanna 1978:105), two facts not entirely unrelated because uneconomic perks (the nutmeg estates) had increasingly depended for their survival on cheap labor.

Shifting European attitudes toward slavery affected the economy of Southeast Seram; the mayor of Keffing complained about the prohibition on selling slaves on Saparua and Ambon, where previously good prices had been obtained. But at the very time slavery was under threat from Europeans the geographical range from which Seram Lauters were seeking slaves was continuing to expand. Thus, Haga (1884, 2:57) described the trade in 1833 between Mawara and Namatote in which slaves were mainly being exchanged for weapons and lead shot. Even in 1851 the slave trade was still buoyant in Southeast Seram and Gorom, which was considered by many to be its center (Van der Crab 1862:57); slaves were brought there from many parts of the archipelago, not only from Papua. Despite prohibition, Bugis and Serammers were still slaving on Karas and Kapauer well into the second half of the nineteenth century (Kniphorst 1883:338). In 1876 there are reports of slaves from Kilwaru en route to Bali, though six months later no slaves at all are reported. In 1881, Papuan men, women, and children were still being brought to Seram Laut and Gorom from the New

Guinea coast (ibid., 338–345). But by that time, groups more marginalized than the fiercely independent Serammers were involved, including the Bajau, whose "prejudicial dealings" (schadelijke praktyk) as corsairs were castigated by the governor of the Moluccas in a letter of 2 February 1887 to the governor of Borneo (Leirissa et al. 1982:112–118; Villiers 1983:53). Slaves continued to arrive in Gorom from New Guinea for perhaps four decades after that (Van Hille 1905:317), and were considered sufficiently valuable for owners to be found in the trading posts of Teluk Berau seeking those who had absconded (Robidé van der Aa 1879:42). Sainuddin Tukwain Rumbawa of Samboru could recall in 1986 that in Dutch times Papuan slaves were still being obtained for ringgit (money) and sirih-pinang.

5.8. Intrusions from the West: The Destabilization of the *Sosolot* System

Although we can be fairly certain that Serammers continued to play a significant role in handling the trade with Southwest New Guinea into the twentieth century, the importance of Melanesian commodities to traders and consumers farther west in the archipelago led to an early outside interest in these waters. As early as 1636, there is a report of the slaughter of a hapless Dutch party on Adi by Papuans (Haga 1884, 1:46). Having established themselves in the spice producing centers of the Moluccas, Dutch VOC traders were by the end of 1655 already going via Gorom to New Guinea to acquire slaves and timber (ibid., 70–72) and claiming parts of New Guinea as officially dependent by 1667 (Misool, Salawati, Waigeo, and Karas to the southeast). The raja of Onin had a representative on Gorom who went to the governor in Banda to seek help based on a 1664 agreement (ibid., 82), and the VOC even considered converting Oniners to Christianity to prevent them trading with Gorom. On 17 August 1678 (ibid., 106, 109) a contract was drawn up with Fataga and Kilbati permitting the governor in Banda to arbitrate in disputes, to fix the price of slaves and massoi, to arrange for goods to be collected for the whole year by the VOC in about June, and determining that the VOC alone was to receive goods. Local orang kayas were to trade with no one else. Understandably, the orang kayas were not entirely happy with this arrangement for long nutmeg, as few were available, and Johannes Keyts could confide to his journal:

Die hier handel drijven wil,	He who wishes here to trade,
Die hout Cerammer buijten spil.	Should the Serammers keep at bay.

The verse proved to be prophetic, and the good times were not to last. Influenced by Serammers who saw a threat to their *sosolot*s, the Dutch met heavy resistance on Namatote and elsewhere. In the end they effectively withdrew from serious participation in the New Guinea trade for almost two hundred years.

In 1656 the heads of Keffing, Kilmuri, Seram Laut, Rarakit, and Gorom were forced to sign a new agreement with the VOC in Amboina. Political instability continued in the entire Southeast Seram area, though the VOC tried to establish trade with Gorom again in 1659. In 1661 the orang kayas of Seram Laut, Gorom, Keffing, and all domains north and west of Guli-guli signed another treaty with the VOC and promised not to trade with Makassans, Javanese, or Malays, agreeing to exchange massoi only for VOC cloth. However, the VOC negotiators appear to have understood neither the particularities of local trade nor the differences between their own trad-ing culture and that of the peoples of Southeast Seram. Keffingers, for example, complained that the VOC had no right to violate their *sosolot* rights and trade along the New Guinea coast. Despite everything, spices, the main VOC concern, continued to find a market in Southeast Seram in violation of the monopoly the Dutch believed they had acquired (Haga 1884, 1:73, 78, 104).

Apart from the Dutch, other groups became involved in the Southwest New Guinea trade from the late seventeenth century onward (for example, Mardijkers in the Onin Karas trade [Haga 1884, 1:131]). Also, perkeniers from Banda are known to have been trading along the Papuan coast in 1746, violating Serammers, *sosolot*s and also the VOC monopoly, taking— most importantly—massoi and trepang, but also pearls, "red earth," other minerals, and roots (ibid., 237). Perkeniers were still attempting, and fail-ing, to trade directly along the Serammer part of the Papuan coast in the second decade of the nineteenth century (Bik 1928 [1824]:38). But by this time, certainly by 1814, the Bugis were also vying for produce with Seram-mers in places such as Ati-ati. By the mid-nineteenth century most of the Makassan perahus around Geser and Aru plied their trade onward to the New Guinea coast, returning to Geser in the southeast monsoon (Beccari 1924:62, 197; De Brauw 1854). Beccari (1924:58) reported ten Makassan per-ahus at Karas and Kapauer on the Onin Peninsula in 1870, as well as activity to the southwest in Kowiai. In 1871, vessels from Seram and Makassar were sailing annually to Karas (Robidé van der Aa 1879:314), and settlements along the southern shore of Teluk Berau, such as Ati-ati, comprised a cos-mopolitan mixture of Makassan, Bugis, Seram Lauter, Goromese, Papuan, and Ternaten traders, the latter active in bird hunting (ibid., 40, 179, 300, 304–305, 308). By 1860 Chinese traders had become directly active along the same coast and were beginning to take over the trade (Broersma 1934: 341). Ati-ati was the main base for Makassan trade in 1879 (Haga 1984, 2: 370), and in Fak-fak there was already a whole street of Chinese traders. There were also Kei traders, and Bugis traders were also reported farther up the gulf at Arguni. It is reasonable to assume that it was this ethnic mix that led to the increasingly important role of Malay in Papuan trading transac-tions and the virtual eclipse of Southeast Seram Littoral (Robidé van der Aa 1879:179, 300).

The arrival of Bugis, Makassans, Arabs, Chinese, and then the Dutch began at last to seriously threaten the monopoly of the Serammer's *sosolot*s (Haga 1884, 2:45, 55). By 1885 the Onin coast was still being served by vessels from Seram Laut and Gorom, but also by Bugis and Arab traders and in some places by vessels of the Nederlandsch-Indische Stoomvaart Maatschappij and later the Koninklijke Paketvaart Maatschappij (Van Hille 1905:248). By 1900, Kaimana, the trading center of Kowiai, possessed a raja, two houses inhabited by Arab traders, and a Nederlandsch Nieuw Guinea Handels Maatschappij store (ibid., 292). There were also Chinese and Arab traders in Kokas (or Sekar) and in Fak-fak (Haga 1911:342), and Butonese traders at the mouth of the Wirjager (Van Hille 1907:596). According to Mohammed Kelian, reminiscing in 1986, at that time Kokas consisted of Kelian and other Serammer clans, and the kepala desa of Sekar was one Mahomet Ruma Geser and that of Sisir Ugar A'alam; both men were "Papuan" Seram Lauters. It was they alone who were permitted to trade in paradise plumes and not the population in general.

It has already been noted that the attempt to impose the VOC monopoly in the early seventeenth century forced Seram Laut traders farther eastward along the south coast of New Guinea, probably as far as the Trans-Fly. Swadling (1996:157) suggested that the Serammers sought damar (*Agathis* bark and *Vatica papuana* sapwood) for lighting, though *Agathis* at least was available in plenty on Seram itself. By 1820 there were as many Seram Laut traders as far east as Namatote as there ever had been, at least since the seventeenth century. When Kolff (1927 [1840]) visited Seram Laut and Gorom in 1825 he found a regular trade going on between these Seram Lauters and the Namatote people. Some of the Seram Laut and Gorom traders married Papuan women and settled (Walker 1982:80). The first Dutch colony in New Guinea, Fort Du Bus, was established in 1828 on Triton Bay, just 24 kilometers east of Namatote. The Dutch made a treaty with the raja and afterward called in at Namatote on their patrols and for a time maintained a post there. The original immigrants from Seram intermarried with Mairasi people, the nearest neighbors to Namatote (ibid., 81); the raja exercised some influence over Arguni, Kamberau and Buruwai, as well as Mairasi. It is reported that he could call on settlements within a 100-kilometer radius of Namatote to come and serve him in various ways, such as by putting a new roof on his house, cleaning up the village for big occasions, and providing labor in other ways (ibid., 82). It was the raja of Namatote who, in 1850, also appointed a raja at Kapia (Kipia) east of Lakahia. Although Aru traders also visited the Mimika area for massoi, Seram Lauters and the raja of Namatote controlled the Kowiai coast pretty exclusively until 1898. The establishment of a post at Fak-fak by the Dutch led to Seram Laut traders and the raja of Namatote reducing their slave and armaments trade in the Kowiai area and strengthening their influence at Kapia in western Mimika. But the arrival of Chinese along with the new Dutch administration was to effectively bring to an end direct Seram Laut influence among Mimika people (Swadling 1996:149–150).

5.9. From a Serammer-Protected Trading Zone to a Colonial Mode of Production

The VOC had claimed parts of New Guinea as officially dependent as early as 1667, but these proclamations were never effectively translated into practical control until the early twentieth century. In 1828 Fort Du Bus was built at Triton Bay on the southwest coast; it was demolished in 1836 and the garrison relocated to Wahai in North Seram (Swadling 1996:142). Nevertheless, the Dutch attached increasing importance to the eastern outposts of the Indies, especially when their authority was challenged by Britain and Germany (Beversluis and Gieben 1929:22). Biak was colonized in 1916, the Raja Ampats by 1921, parts of the Bird's Head and the southwestern coast (including Fak-fak) between 1926 and 1929 (Soedjatmoko et al. 1965: fac. 358). Australian, Japanese, and Chinese *Trochus* and pearl fishing around Aru and New Guinea (Merton 1910:12, 18) was increasing, quite unregulated and the source of some conflict, as was bird hunting on the mainland,[6] with similar consequences. All this provided the Dutch with incentives to tighten up the administration of a zone they had long claimed and an excuse to fill a power vacuum.

With the establishment of a Dutch post in Fak-fak in 1898, the influence of Seram Laut traders and Islam declined, and that of Christian missions and the Chinese grew (Swadling 1996:149). As elsewhere, the arrival of the Dutch in New Guinea had particular administrative and social consequences: they created kepala kampung, but also followed Serammer practice of creating hierarchies of chiefs with Malay titles, such as raja, orang kaya, mayor, and kapitan. The consequences were sometimes not those intended, because the Melanesian system of achieved leadership was very different from the ascribed leadership acceptable in the Moluccas (Ellen 1986b; Elmberg 1968:20), and sometimes titles became family names (Kamma 1948:182). Ironically, Dutch administration enabled natives to make effective contact with commercial and financial services provided by the colonial state; native producers obtained access to credit facilities that weakened control of Chinese traders (Allen and Donnithorne 1954:218) and that of those Serammers who continued to trade in a traditional fashion. The setting up of coastal government villages also led to the increasing availability of cloth valued in local ritual exchanges. As a demonstration of their power, the Dutch were not beyond destroying or confiscating textiles involved in the traditional trade that underpinned exchange cycles. Pouwer (1957) reported 205 pieces of cloth being destroyed in the Teminabuam district, 365 in Ajamanu, and 314 in Attinjo.

Although Serammers continued to trade along Teluk Berau and southward along the Onin coast as far as Kowiai throughout the first half of the twentieth century, the greatest volume and value of trade was increasingly associated with Chinese and to a lesser extent Sulawesi traders. Indeed,

Chinese were already effectively replacing Bugis as the dominant intrusive trading group by the late nineteenth century. It is true that during the first three decades of the twentieth century Goromese maintained their earlier reputation as smiths in New Guinea and Geser carpenters were also in demand, but their traditional trading role steadily declined. Then there was bird hunting. Mohammed Kastella of Geser received his nickname "Kaimana" because he lived between the ages of 2 and 12 in New Guinea where his father hunted bird of paradise, but this ended with Indonesian independence. Voyages to New Guinea by Serammers were by now as much a matter of maintaining kinship links as motivated by trade alone. In 1986 Abdullah Rumatar of Samboru on Gorom could well recall voyages by *angbot* with his father when he was young to visit relatives on Karas. Inter-marriage continues to sustain relations between places in Southeast Seram and New Guinea with historic linkages, and Goromese traders working out of Kataloka, whether ethnic Goromese or other (including mixed) ethnic origin, still focus on the traditional *sosolot* areas, which for Kataloka were Karas and Adi. But by the 1980s *sosolot*s were of no significance in themselves. There was no way in which Serammers could morally or practically ensure their monopoly and, moreover, the growth of trading and administrative centers along the coast, particularly Fak-fak, and Kaimana meant that Papuan coastal settlements, most of which themselves had no permanent traders, were much more inclined to trade directly in these places or with itinerant traders working from Papuan centers, rather than rely on visiting Serammers. By the same token, traders working out of the Southeast Seram Archipelago themselves increasingly preferred to trade with larger centers such as Fak-fak rather than small remote settlements in traditional *sosolot* areas.

Trade between archipelagic Southeast Seram and New Guinea reached a historic low after Indonesian independence in 1945, because Onin remained part of Netherlands New Guinea until 1960. Trade was not officially permitted, though there was, of course, smuggling, a black market trade, and low-key maintenance of family ties. Many short-term Bugis and Butonese migrants returned to their homelands during that period. Sainuddin Tukwain Rumbawa mentioned to me in 1981 that during those years his father would voyage to New Guinea to buy tinned milk and margarine, where it was much cheaper than in Geser and because Fak-fak was considerably closer than the alternative, Ambon. The grandfather of Badaruddin Sohilau of Samboru sold sago, tobacco, and *Areca catechu* in New Guinea at that time also. After the incorporation of Netherlands New Guinea into Indonesia as Irian Barat (and later Irian Jaya), traditional trading links were reactivated but were never again to be a really important source of income for traders operating from Southeast Seram, even though motorization, and in particular the appearance of the ubiquitous "jonson," reduced voyaging times dramatically.

5.10. Continuity and Decline in the Papuan Trade

Although present-day trade between various Moluccan centers and New Guinea is a shadow of what it once was, it is not entirely insignificant. The Papuan coast can still be conveniently divided into that part incorporated within the periphery of a system focused on Ternate and Tidore and that part incorporated within the periphery of the Banda system; the two represent the main historical portals for New Guinea imports and exports. Within the Banda system itself, the secondary centers of Geser, Gorom, Tual, and Dobo are the most important. The traditional export pattern of forest products and slaves is no longer operative, though long nutmeg remains significant; and the reciprocal movement of textiles has completely ceased. More important is the coastal trade in copra and hasil laut (sea produce): trepang, lola, batu laga, shark fins, and agar-agar, most of which finds its way out of the Moluccas via Geser and Gorom. In 1986 the most important commodities coming into Southeast Seram from New Guinea were nutmeg, damar, some medicinal barks, eucalyptus oil, and yellow-breasted bird of paradise plumes (cendrawasih kuning), although trade in the latter was technically prohibited. In return, rice, manufactured goods, and cash move to the New Guinea coast, as well as local salt fish (especially to Fak-fak), dengdeng rusa (dried venison), chickens, sugar, paraffin, coffee, and even sand. There is still a trade in sago, in the lemping (biscuit) form, from Seram to New Guinea, in which in recent years at least one Kataloka man has been involved, and much of which goes to Fak-fak by sailing vessel where it purchased by resident migrant Moluccans. There is less demand for sago in Sorong, for instance, where there are fewer Moluccan residents.

The tendency to trade in settlements where there are kinship links or with places that have preestablished links with particular Serammer settlements provides just a bit more than an echo of the old *sosolot* system. Papuan localities that are of special significance to traders in Southeast Seram include Misool, Fak-fak, Arguni, Kokas, Popalab, Raja Ampat, Waigama, Karas, Kaimana, and Adi. All settlements are now of mixed Papuan and Moluccan stock, and SSL remains the lingua franca. The kepala desa of Sorong, for example, is Ali Kastella, who derives from the Kiltai branch of this clan; the raja of Ati-ati Onin is Haji Abdullah Basdui of Geser. However, there is no longer any clear commodity or exchange pattern to the trade, which is for the most part of short term and opportunistic. People from Warus-warus and elsewhere go to Misool to collect lola in the east monsoon. One Kwaos man recently spent some years cutting timber in New Guinea, and to some extent the trade in material goods has been replaced by a trade in labor. Norf Rumalatur, who now lives in Geser, used to accompany his parents to Kaimana when he was young, where his female relatives were tailors. Residents of Kiltai were still buying trepang, lola, agar-agar, coconut, and nutmeg in New Guinea in 1981. Abdurahmin

Warnangan, a trader now based in Kataloka, whose life history is summarized as Case 6 in chapter 9, collects antiques (porcelain and similar), lola, and batu laga from Kaimana, Pulau Adi, and Pulau Karas. Indeed, other Goromese traders often go to New Guinea for lola, nutmeg, and dugong. A trader operating from Kiltai, who owned a motor dalam, used to take copra, cloves, lola, and coconut oil regularly to Sorong and Fak-fak when prices were higher than in Ambon. And sailing boats also were used in the same flexible and opportunistic way in the 1970s.

6
Boats and Boat Handling

I boarded an *ang kalulis* bound for Afang early in the morning of 4 May 1986 at the invitation of its crew: the brothers Sadaruddin (who had built the boat), Sahari Rumau, one of their mother's kin, and Arogi Rumakei. All came from Inlomin on Manawoka and were planning to buy sago in Afang. If the price was not right there, they were intending to go on to other places, such as Kilbon or Kilmuri. Bitorik and Undur produce a small *tumang*, or cask, of sago, but the Sadaruddins prefer a larger one. The *ang kalulis* was reckoned able to carry a cargo of 400 large *tumang*, worth 200,000 rupiah. Such large *tumang* bought on the mainland of Seram for 500 rupiah each could later be sold in Gorom for 1000 Rp. We departed Geser at 9.21, polling and ghosting out over the reef into a steady Northeasterly wind North of the atoll, with a fluttering mainsail head to wind. The crew had departed Inlomin early the previous day and had arrived in Geser at 11.00 the same morning. At about 10.00 a.m. we bore away, the mainsail filled on the starboard tack and the jib was hoisted, enabling us to make a direct course for Kwamar. A little while later the jib was sheeted in enabling us to sail closer to the wind. We started off with a northeast wind coming from astern (*torat*). We then tacked with an oncoming North wind (*sokar*). When sailing direct from Gorom to Banda, I was told, you make use of *haluan selatan*; if sailing via Geser to Banda you use *haluan barat*. The lateral rudders were employed to balance the force of the sails, in order to keep on the desired course. At night, the Sadaruddins navigated by compass, or by the stars. When it is dark or cloudy, winds suffice as indicators. At 10.59 the mainsail and jib eased away to starboard, taking advantage of the East wind again. We continued on a zig-zag course South of Seram Rei and the Southern coast of Seram, as far as Guli-guli, taking advantage of the shifting wind. At 11.41 we changed tack again, and at 12.07 set the sails to starboard. As the wind was light and variable, it was not regarded as a "proper" or "true" wind. At 12.10 we changed tack again. A little while later the trailing *lepa-lepa* (canoe) was hauled on board to prevent drag. We finally arrived in our destination at 5.00 p.m. Guli-guli has a good harbour, with a deep channel passing close-up to the settlement.

ELLEN, *Field notes, 1986-6*

6.1. Boat Technology in the Moluccas

To say that trade generally depends upon the conveyance of commodities from the point of production to that of consumption is to state the obvious. Yet anthropological studies rarely pay attention to what is self-evidently a crucial technological and interpositionary process with ramifying social dimensions. In Southeast Seram all movement of goods of any economic significance has always been waterborne. Moreover, it is clear from the preceding chapters that our understanding of patterns and processes of trade here, as in the wider Moluccan region, is crucially linked to what we can discover about the possibilities and constraints associated with the use of boats. In this chapter, I consider the linkage between boats and the Southeast Seram trade nexus, not simply as exemplary and reified objects of material culture that might justify an examination in their own right, but as the material extrusions of a complex technology, which *connects* equipment, boat craft, and social organization, as well as the consequences of social, ecological, and economic processes.

If we look at the evolution of boats in the Moluccas in very broad terms, we can trace five lineages: that for the *lepa-lepa* or dugout canoe, which only in the last decades has seen major modification to accommodate the outboard motor; that for the *kora-kora*, a powerful and readily maneuverable multirower vessel used for war but with considerable storage, which effectively became extinct by the nineteenth century (Tan 1981:4, 10); that for the indigenous plank-built boat; that for the European-style sailing vessel; and that for the Chinese-style vessel. As far as we can tell, at the opening of the European era, the first three of these were mainly used for trade: what I shall call the proto-*lepa-lepa*, the *kora-kora*, and variations on an indigenous plank-built boat. The main forms show the influence of design intended for oar propulsion, or paddles: long, narrow craft with double outriggers. Alternatively there were slightly smaller craft, wider and shallower, with low gunwales of uniform height, double-ended hulls, and high, vertical stern posts (often decorated). In both cases sails only supplemented oar propulsion. In hull construction tension binding replaces ribs in both cases. *Kora-kora* of the early sixteenth century were plank-built vessels for the transport of large cargoes of men and materials (MacKnight 1980:124–125). Sails were of matting and ropes of rattan (De Bruin Kops 1854:23), though iron nails had been introduced for some purposes during the seventeenth century (MacKnight 1980:120). In terms of constructional features and techniques both suggest a center of dispersal in Sulawesi and the southern Philippines around 1000–500 B.C. Larger nonlocal vessels owned by Malays and Chinese were only occasionally visitors. Of all boat types, the outrigger canoe plus tilting sail technology undoubtedly represents the earliest and most enduring Austronesian solution to the engineering challenge of long-distance and flexible maritime communication (Horridge 1995:141).

Up until the mid-nineteenth century there had been little change in sailing boat design since 1500. Today, the old styles of boat described in the preceding paragraph (both in terms of rig and hull) have almost entirely disappeared. Only the *lepa-lepa* retains most of the older features. The last 150 years have seen the demise of the *kora-kora* and the traditional plank-built boat, while introducing forms heavily influenced by European design. Thus, in 1870 61 percent of registered vessels were "indigenous rigged" (as opposed to European rigged), representing 22 percent of the total tonnage. Until 1870 steamships constituted an unimportant part of the merchant fleet (Knaap 1989:18), but by 1907 they represented 83 percent of all vessels and 32 percent of the tonnage. By around the same time (1911–1912) European sailing vessels had largely given way to steamships. However, sailing vessels of "the indigenous variety" managed to hold their own, despite not competing with steamships and motor vessels on speed. Motor vessels represented 3.5 percent of total tonnage in 1915 and 24.5 percent in 1938 (ibid., 23). There is confusion in the literature as to what is meant by "European-rigged vessels," which sometimes refers to European and sometimes to indigenous vessels with European features, but the figures must surely be about right. The confusion reflects an interesting process of hybridization, which we must now discuss.

During the late nineteenth and early twentieth centuries, the indigenous plank hull and the European style underwent major interbreeding. This process gave rise to a large number of boat types in Southeast Seram that many now think of as indigenous: the *ang guik, ang kalulis,* and *angbot.* These last two fall within the stylistic range of what is known more widely in Indonesia as the "lambo" or "perahubot." The *angbot* in turn has adapted to motor in the form of the "kapal motor" and "perahu layar motor." Changes to the basic lambo form have continued throughout the second half of the twentieth century. For example, the Gunter sloop fore-and-aft rig (layar lambo) has since about 1960 been replacing gaff rigs, which came in about 1920; the "pinisi" rig has become important since 1890; and the bow since 1945. According to Horridge (MacKnight 1980:120), copying foreign hull shape has led to structural weaknesses, with the new form not supported by an appropriate method of construction; but there is no doubt that these hybrid forms have proved extremely resilient in economic terms. Because most government statistics (both colonial and postcolonial) do not distinguish between the various types of larger sailing vessels described in this chapter, I have used the generic term "perahu" to cover all of them.

The introduction of steamships after 1850 was only one reason why users and builders of local sailing boats sought to innovate. Traditional perahus suffered also from the opening of the Suez Canal (which increased the number of steamships) and in competition with Dutch, Arab, and Chinese ships displaced from the Java trade (Dick 1975, 1:75). These pressures probably stimulated the adoption of fore-and-aft rigs and improvements in the outfitting of perahus that occurred in the second half of the nineteenth century. The KPM (Koninklijke Paketvaart Maatschappij) was formed in 1891 and greater political stability and administrative and economic consolidation encouraged an increase in the routes covered and frequency of services. Perahus became, increasingly, feeder vessels to these main routes. From 1903 to 1940 there was a steady decline in the number and capacity of perahus in most Indonesian ports (ibid., 77), and they did not benefit from the trade boom in the outer islands before World War I and the 1920s. The depression of the 1930s, however, brought about something of a revival, as did the economic difficulties during the World War II and after Indonesian independence. Indeed, the 1939 perahu tonnage entering Surabaya exceeded that for 1903. In 1935 there were 345 registered perahus of 10 cubic meters or above in Maluku, and by 1956–1957 there were 357. In 1935 small perahus (up to 100 cubic meters) constituted 99 percent of all trading perahus; medium perahus (between 100 and 200 cubic meters) and large perahus (between 200 and 500 cubic meters) were just 1 percent. However, between 1940 and 1960 there was an increase in perahu size, though the total metric capacity remained the same, which probably reflects a decline in the average number of annual calls (ibid., 71). Perahu trade thrived in the 1950s and 1960s under conditions that motor shipping could not withstand: the KPM had been expelled, and smuggling was stimulated by foreign exchange regulations and political instability. Perahus were independent of imported materials (they did not need spare parts), placed few demands on infrastructure, and were not affected by harbor congestion and poor facilities. They were also unhampered by bureaucracy (licensing, freight controls, official routing, and military requisition). In short, they were self-sufficient, labor intensive, and unregulated. Indeed, perahu shipping remains virtually unregulated today; owners only have to renew their registration each year with a harbormaster's office. Only after 1967 did perahus once again come under serious competitive pressure from motorization and steel-hulled shipping (ibid., 81–82).

6.2. Types of Sea Craft, Their Range, and Uses

In Figure 6.1 a continuous line has been drawn at a distance of 20 kilometers from the coast of all inhabited landforms, a distance that corresponds approximately to the practical limit imposed by the use of small dugout outrigger canoes by present-day Moluccans. This limit depends in part on the distance of the horizon, which may vary between 4 and 188 kilometers but is generally no more than 60 kilometers. The physical demands of handling a small craft, the location of fishing grounds, the duration of journeys between nearby islands, and perceived weather hazards also affect patterns of use. However, as a rule, small outrigger canoes keep well within sight of land. Traditional multioared and long-hulled plank-built boats, on the other hand, as well as sailing boats of imported design, are not nearly so

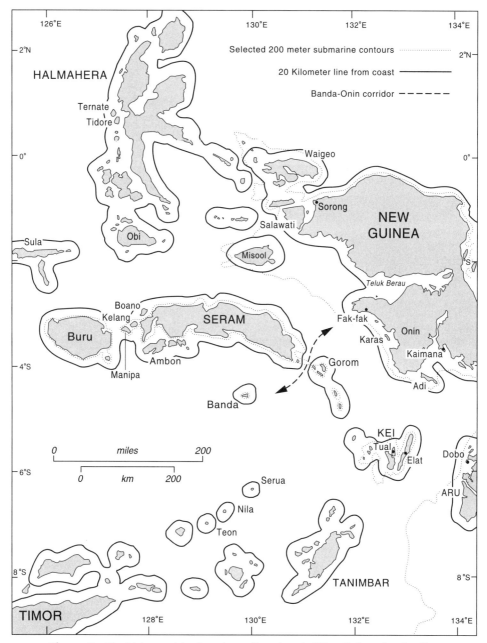

Figure 6.1. The Moluccan islands and an adjacent part of New Guinea showing the relationship between selected 200-meter submarine contours and the 20-kilometer line from the coast.

limiting. Their capabilities are well known, although subtypes and individual craft are extremely variable in design and size, which may have a significant bearing on performance. The dotted line on Figure 6.1 marks the 200-meter depth contour. Both lines encompass island groups within which we might reasonably expect local settlements to be highly connected, an expectation that is confirmed in chapter 7.

I wish to suggest that at least as far as Southeast Seram is concerned, and perhaps more widely, there is a good correlation between type of boat, the kind of trade in which it is involved, and range of operation; and that this is related to geography and environmental variation. It has already been noted in chapter 1 that there are a number of significant structural differences between the Ambon and Banda systems. Although the Ambon system might be said to reproduce itself internally quite adequately by relying only on small coastal craft, the Banda system involves major sea crossings. This has meant the employment of larger vessels, nowadays for the most part belonging to intrusive trading groups. In the Banda zone, the evolution of a social and economic system depending on movement over greater maritime distances required a corresponding greater diversity of boat forms and different proportions of one type to another. Thus, we may agree with MacKnight (1980:117) that "the design and use of ships are governed not only by their various functions but also, in part, by relevant environmental factors and, in part, by specific cultural traditions and innovations." Ships cannot be studied in isolation from the people who build them and sail them, nor in ignorance of the places where they are built and the seas on which they sail.

Sailing vessels currently used in trade within the Banda zone or between centers within the zone and the outside world are (excluding rafts, tenders, and fishing platforms) of four types:

1. Dugout canoes, with and without outriggers and sails (*lepa-lepa*, *ang tiang*, perahu semang, leb-leb, sampan, koli-koli) (Figure 6.2);[1]
2. Small, open, plank-built boats (*ang guik*, orembai, *kora-kora*), which may be sailed or rowed using a steersman and twelve or more rowers;
3. Larger, single-sailed, plank-built sailing vessels with a deck and cabin (*ang kalulis*) (Figure 6.3);
4. Still larger plank-built vessels (*angbot*, lambo, perahubot) (Figures 6.4, 6.5).

Some indicative measurements of these vessels are given in Table 6.1. As one might expect, there is, generally speaking, a higher ratio of boats of all kinds to people in small, isolated island settlements such as Kidang and Keffing than in settlements on the Seram mainland or even on the larger islands such as Gorom and Manawoka.

Table 6.1. Key dimensions (in meters) of different types of vessels recorded in Warus-warus, Kilfura, Kwaos, and Geser in 1981 and 1986

Type	N	Length Mean	Length Range	Beam Mean	Beam Range	Depth Mean	Depth Range
Lepa-lepa	21	5.07	3.43–9.32	0.53	0.40–0.80	0.35	0.30–0.55
Jonson	6	8.56	7.40–11.20	0.96	0.70–0.118	0.85	0.80–0.94
Ang guik	3	8.59	8.73–8.45	1.75	1.50–2.00	1.00	1.00
Orembai	2	13.00	12.00–14.00	2.50	2.50–2.50		
Ang kalulis	4	6.16	5.25–7.50	2.33	2.25–2.50	1.30	1.30
Angbot	6	14.06	7.32–18.29	3.12	2.74–3.50	1.32	0.80–1.83
Angbot pante bebek	1	16.00					
Angbot pante kadeira	1	23.00		1.78		0.80	
Perahu motor	1	12.19		3.66		4.57	

Note: The size of the *lepa-lepa* has not changed much in 100 years. Zeevisscherij (Anonymous 1882:360) reported them as being about 6 meters long and 0.75 meters beam.

Figure 6.2. Dugout canoe (*lepa-lepa*) pulling away from Geser on return journey to Rumadan on the Seram mainland. The cargo is sago thatch and pandanus boxes. April 1986.

Figure 6.3. *Ang kalulis* between Geser and Guli-guli. May 1986.

Figure 6.4. Lambo (*angbot*) moored in a creek near Samboru on the island of Gorom. The stern is the pante bebek variety. February 1981.

Figure 6.5. Repairs being made to Butonese lambo at Pantaseru, on Banda Neira in the Banda group. March 1981.

VESSELS OF TYPE 1

These are essentially short-range coastal and fishing craft, but may be used for short interisland voyages, as within the Banda and Kei groups, between Southwest Seram and Ambon-Lease, or Geser and Seram Laut. The simple dugout canoe (*lepa-lepa* in SSL) is made from a single piece of wood, of various sizes, used either with or without a sail, and nowadays also for the most part without the customary double outrigger. When a sail is added to a *lepa-lepa*—usually a single sail of a gaff, Gunter, or leg-of-mutton type—it is called, at least in Gah, where I have heard it described as such, an *ang keru*. Occasionally, one sees tilted rectangular sails. However, the *lepa-lepa* may sometimes be enlarged by adding planks to the sides and sometimes, as in Kilwaru, by adding a *kalulis* prow (see later in this section), when it is known as a *lepa-lepa kalulis*. Used for fishing, but also by villagers for bringing small quantities of products for trade (fish, sago, green vegetables), it is widely owned. In Warus-warus every house has a *lepa-lepa*; on Garogos every household except two has one, but some households own more than one. It is ideal for shallow waters with their reef hazards and for the short distances between islands in the Seram Laut Archipelago and is frequently used in combination with the punting pole (*doan*) as much as the paddle (*wosa*). Butonese from Seram Laut marketing food on Geser rely entirely on this means of transport. It is also highly suitable for maneuvering through the narrow shallow channels of the mangroves that lie between Kwamar and Arnaman, with their many hazards and uncertain way finding. The current upper distance limit of the *lepa-lepa* appears to be about 240 minutes or between 10 and 18 kilometers, say from Aruas to Kwaos or Rumadan to Geser. Formerly, the distance would have been much farther, but inroads have been made by motorization and it is no longer considered appropriate to sail or paddle longer distances in such a small craft.

Dugout canoes with double outriggers (*ang soman, ang tien, ang tiang*), which are still frequently found and are characteristic of West and central Seram, are less common in the east and no longer seen in the Seram Laut archipelago. In 1981 I saw no outriggers in any village between Warus-warus (where formerly they had been common) and Kwaos on the east coast of Seram, though there were many in Artafela, between Kwaos and Kilgah. Where outrigger canoes do occur they are smaller bodied than the *lepa-lepa*. Why they have disappeared in Southeast Seram is unclear. They are obviously unsuitable for narrow channel navigation and are said to get in the way when fishing for tuna. On the other hand the persistence of double outriggers in West Seram is claimed to be due to the fact that they are very handy, light, and stable craft, sufficient for the general purposes of a fishing community.

VESSELS OF TYPE 2

Vessels of type 2 have broadly the same range as the *lepa-lepa* but a larger capacity and are more useful on longer distances within the range. For more extensive trading voyages boats built of planks have been in use for many centuries, basically of the Moluccan orembai type. Early examples possess the double outrigger, as the *kora-kora* still does, and we may assume that the original prototype took this form. The outrigger is generally thought to be unnecessary on larger, more stable craft and for this reason may have been discarded in the orembai (Haddon 1920:129). In Southeast Seram the *ang guik* (*guik*, lit. "weighing water," to pull along) is the main example of this type, easily distinguished by its high prow and stern posts. It is primarily a fishing vessel, used particularly for ikan julung (various hemiraphid genera), though sometimes it is used for the same range of duties as the *lepa-lepa*. *Ang guik* are known to have been used for trips as far as the New Guinea coast. If the weather is windy with high waves, an *ang guik* requires a minimum crew of twelve: two men to look for fish and to dive over the side to look underwater, six men to row, and four to pull in the catch. It is this crewing requirement that determines the minimum size of the vessel. Crews can be as large as seventeen, but all are related through kinship. Sometimes a Gunter rig is employed. The *ang guik* is used in combination or rotation, and some individuals have as many as four. The *ang guik* is currently mainly distributed between Keffing and Kwaos, and num bers have declined over the last sixty years.

VESSELS OF TYPE 3

In the Moluccas, vessels of this type—locally called *ang kalulis*—are restricted to the Southeast Seram–Kei area. They have a larger capacity and range than types 1 and 2 but are unsuitable for long-haul journeys between the Moluccas, Sulawesi, and Java. They are used mostly on middle-distance interisland journeys between the islands and the mainland, between Geser, Gorom, Watubela, Teor, Kei, Tayandu, Aru, and the Papuan coast, and are the traditional mainstay of the fish for sago interisland trade. They are used for both passengers and cargo and occasionally used for fishing, turtle hunting, and collecting agar-agar.

Ang kalulis hulls were in the past lashed together using fiber fed through carved lugs on plank interiors, a technique that seems to have disappeared in Kei during the 1940s; boats were only being built on an intermittent basis after that. Since 1945 almost all planked *ang kalulis* have been fitted with fixed wooden ribs (gading) and are between 4.5 and 14 meters in length and with between five and eight planks. There have been changes in materials too: ropes formerly were of coconut husk (tali utis) and gemutu (tali nauk), and rectangular sails were made from sago leaf sections or matting, or karoro (sacking, sorat pisang from Java). Now polypropylene is used mainly for ropes, and for the sails (both gaf and Gunter) the replacement is cotton canvas and polypropylene cloth (or sometimes polyethylene sheets). Lateral rudders or paddles (cangkilan) have generally been replaced by a centerline rudder. The smaller version (*ang kalulis mafun*) can be smaller than the *ang guik,* as found in Kilfura. When fitted with outriggers, a deck, and a shelter (as observed in Warus-warus) the *ang kalulis* is sometimes called *ang tiang.*

VESSELS OF TYPE 4

The type 4 boat (*angbot,* lambo) is used for many of the same duties as the *ang kalulis,* but also for larger cargoes locally and for long-distance trade, as between Banda and Gorom, and between Geser and Gresik or Surabaya in Java. It is basically a small sloop or ketch-rigged boat or cutter, with a rig (gaff sails and jib, or main and mizzen) and hull that are essentially modern. Most have single masts (though some have two, and I have observed three such based in Banda of about sixty tons each) with a single head sail extending to the end of a tripartite bowsprit. They sometimes have a small cabin, though more often have a hull of low freeboard with raised sides roofed over with timber or a midship housing over the hold. Depending on the stern, Southeast Seram lambos are known as either *angbot* pante kadeira (lit. "chair end", or transom) or *angbot* pante bebek (lit. "duck end"). These latter are the most common. *Angbot* pante kadeira are now rare in the Banda area (though I have seen them off Run) and are regarded as less stable in rough water. When loaded, a pante kadeira pitches in a sea, and waves splash against the square stern. The rake of the stem is considerably greater in vessels from Seram than is found in the Butonese lambo.

The sloop rig first appeared in eastern Indonesia around 1930, changing from sliding gaffs to the more convenient Gunter or Bermuda rigs in the last four decades. The hull has a straight stern and stern posts set at an angle to the keel and, in most cases, a square stern design with a central rudder. A lambo seldom carries more than forty tons of load, and the rare larger vessels usually have two masts. Lambo is now a general term for small, single-masted sailing trade boats using a center rudder, with a sharp or square stern. Butonese lambos, judging from constructional features and from the proportion of English-derived partonyms, were plausibly based on pearling boats originating from Australia (Horridge 1979).

Relatively few *angbot* are owned by indigenes of Southeast Seram or for that matter immigrant Butonese. Norf Rumalutur in Geser owned a one-mast *angbot* in 1986, though there have never been many *angbot* based in Geser. There are no Bugis boats, though there was one Mandarese boat in 1986. Husin Sinjai of Kiltai possessed an *angbot* in 1986, taking a crew of five. Soselisa (1995:140) reported two *angbot* on Garogos in 1994. In Samboru on Gorom there were two *angbot* in 1986, though there had been five until the 1980s, owned both by locals and Butonese and often hired to

Table 6.2. Age and tonnage of lambos in Banda Syahbandar register for 1978

Age in years	Number	Tonnage	Mean capacity (m³)
20	4	80	23.51
17	1	17	67.12
15	10	24	26.59
12	2	—	21.85
10	13	130	31.6
9	4	36	20.22
8	7	56	27.9
7	5	35	50.49
6	3	18	19.1
5	12	60	26.20
4	5	20	41.4
3	1	3	52.67
2	1	1	19.6
1	1	17.71	57.6

traders. One was owned by Abdullah Rumatar. The other was owned by Badaruddin Sohilau and was six years old in 1986 and had not been used for two years. Until recently he had been using it three times a month. However, Banda has been for the last 100 years, and continues to be, the center for lambos.

Table 6.2 shows the age and tonnage of the sixty-nine lambos registered in Banda in 1978. The minimum capacity of all vessels registered was 6.30 square meters, the mean 37.73 square meters, and the maximum 86.89 square meters. There was one perahu layar motor, of less than 100 cubic meters. What is remarkable here is the range in sizes. The average age is 8.34 years, suggesting an increase in building during the 1970s; twenty were five years old, twenty-three up to ten years old, twelve between ten and fifteen, and nine over twenty years old. Forty-eight were owned by persons with Butonese names (e.g., La Ade), five were owned by persons with Arabic names, and one owner had an obvious Geser name (Rumfot). The others were varied, but include ethnic Chinese with Indonesianized names (e.g., Subuh Sun). Only one person owned more than one registered craft. However, not all of the registered vessels are operational (for example, only twenty-five to thirty-five of the sixty-five lambo registered for Banda in 1981); and (no doubt) not all vessels operating in the Banda zone are registered.

6.3. The Social Organization of Boat Use

Almost all *lepa-lepa* and most other sailing craft domiciled in Southeast Seram are owned by villagers, who may occasionally rent them out. Only a few are owned by full-time merchants or captains (Appendix 2). Ownership and shipwrighting tend to run in families. In the family of Badaruddin Sohilau in Samboru, for example, there have been *angbot* owned and used over many generations, though his paternal grandfather had a pante bebek rather than the now more common pante kadeira. Boats can go through many owners, and one I observed in Guli-guli had had five owners. Apart from local ethnic Serammer specialists, boats are owned and chartered out most visibly by Butonese, either Butonese from Sulawesi or Butonese based in Banda. On occasion, Butonese may themselves charter lambos.

Perahu shipping involves four main roles: owners (bos), captains (nakhoda), crews, and traders. We can add forwarding agents in the case of some long-distance trade. The roles of captain, owner, and trader may be interchangeable, and all roles may be interrelated through family ties. In economic terms, most perahus are small family businesses, with most roles other than crewing combined in a single person, or when two persons are involved dividing the labor between one person responsible for the craft itself and the voyage (the captain), and another handling cargoes and port facilities (Dick 1975, 1:82, 102). The navigational skills and commercial knowledge of a captain (nakhoda or tuan perahu, *ar* in SSL) are vital to profitability. They have little formal education and acquire their expertise from an early age. The problem for the perahu owner is to ensure that he receives his proportion of the earnings. A close kinship link with the captain may secure this and a general advantage of running and crewing a trading boat using extended household members is that the profits are not dispersed. Away from home a captain is an independent manager, and ownership is kept functionally separate from day-to-day control. Where owner and captain are separate there is a tendency to underreport earnings to the owner. These problems of control cause perahu ownership to be extremely fragmented. It is preferable for a captain to be his own owner and vice versa, but then owners of single boats are vulnerable to loss and damage (ibid., 102–107). Many owners in the Banda zone, including Southeast Seram, rent their boats to (mainly Chinese) traders. Kepata Kelirei, for example, the raja of Dai on Gorom, chartered his *angbot* to a Chinese trader in Kataloka in 1986 to transport oil from Bula, at a rate of 400,000 rupiah a voyage.

Crew size and composition vary according to type of vessel, tonnage, length of journey, and capital. *Ang guik* require a minimum of twelve crew to meet the requirements of fishing. *Ang kalulis* can be managed with a crew of four. I have seen *angbot* in Geser and West Seram with crews of between four and ten, and in Banda with crews of between five and seven. The crew of motor vessels is not much larger, if at all. One Geser-based motor laut consisted of an owner, a captain, and eight hands. Kinship and ethnic representation is equally fluid. Locally owned *ang guik* and *ang kalulis* tend to be crewed almost entirely by kin. Yusuf Mutahu Al Hamid of Geser crewed his *angbot* in 1986 with men from Geser, not necessarily kinsmen. Butonese lambo crews from Banda (for example, Run) consist predominantly of family with some nonkin. Lambo crews on the Surabaya run may be either local Moluccans or Moluccans accompanying Butonese. Motor vessels have a higher proportion of Butonese in the crew, though the *Nusa Indah*, plying between Ambon and Geser in 1986, had large numbers of Bugis.

Cargo is handled and stowed by the crew, for which they receive no payment other than food. In small locations perahus may be unloaded by the crew; in larger centers (such as Geser) gangs of laborers are employed who carry loads on back and shoulders. The tuan perahu (or owner) receives 25 percent of the profit on a small perahu, or 50 percent on a larger perahu (roughly above sixty tons). Payment to an *angbot* crew in 1986 was such that if the total profit on a voyage (say Kiltai to Tual) was 200,000 rupiah when the cost of food had been deducted, then each of the eight crew members received about 12,500 rupiah once the owner had taken his share. In 1981, on this basis, crews on voyages from Warus-warus to Fak-fak and Ambon received 15,000 and 25,000 rupiah, respectively.

But boats not only require effective social organization to transform them from concepts to material constructions, to transfer their ownership and use from person to person, and to render them useful at all; this can only happen if the boats themselves are socialized and anthropomorphized. Boats, especially large ones, with all the invested work and physical capability they represent, are powerfully condensed symbolic expressions, projections of the home settlements from which they hail. The most visible daily instance of this is in naming. Arsad Rumonin of Geser called both of his *ang guik Sala Lekum* (Safe Greetings). *Lepa-lepa*, by contrast, tend to be given Indonesian (or even English) names: say, *Mini Indah, Rencana, Ocean Star,* or *Taman Ria*. Almost all of these are fitted to take outboard motors (in other words all are jonsons). The investment and status that accompanies ownership of such vessels is comparable with that of plank-built boats, and naming reflects this. An *angbot* in Samboru was called *Tutup Tolu*, and one in Kiltai *Pulau Pasir*. Motor dalam and motor laut operating between Ambon and East Seram and within the East Seram area have names such as *Guna Ganda, Sinar Cemerlang*, and *Nusa Indah*. In the perahu register of Banda for 1985 most of the names are also in Indonesian, though a few are in Butonese. Apart from the obvious status considerations, these boats are in a very real sense interethnic, transcending locality, and the use of the national language and lingua franca may ritualize this quality.

Ritual is an intrinsic part of traditional seafaring, not only in the naming but also at the production stage and throughout use. Rituals of boatbuilding are well described for various parts of Eastern Indonesia (Barnes 1996:241–249, G. E. P. Collins 1937, 1940; Horridge 1978, 1979, 1986; MacKnight 1980; MacKnight and Mukhlis 1979; Southon 1995). In the Banda zone and throughout the Southeast Seram Archipelago, from the cutting of the timber to the launch, boat construction is punctuated by and facilitated through ritual. Offerings are made to the spirits of the land, and there is a blood sacrifice of a chicken on completion of the keel and the final opening of a boat's eyes. Foods and stimulants are applied to the timbers as they are shaped and fitted as offerings to the ancestors; traditional medicines are lodged between the planks to protect the boat from damage. "Sick" completed boats that malfunction are also treated with such remedies, and repair is as much a ritualized process as initial building.

For the *ang guik* ceremony of keel laying in Keffing (*fakarifi tian tua*) and for the launching (*fakarifi faka dulu)*, a chicken is sacrificed over the boat, followed by a feast. This is the same ceremony at which the name is given. The boat is compared with the human body (the keel is equivalent to the spine or the cross beam of a house, the ribs or frame to the ribs of the body or rafters of a house, and so on), and the *fakarifi* (ceremonies) are seen as its rites of passage. These symbolic linkages reflect a widespread form of anthropomorphization documented for different construction practices in other parts of Seram (Ellen 1986b, 1988a, 1990; cf. Barraud 1985), and so it is no wonder that a complex metaphorical language connects the coming into being, morphology, and use of people, boats, and houses (Barraud 1985; Southon 1995:100, 116, 120). In Banda, when the first plank (garboard) is fixed to the keel a white chicken must be sacrificed and two depa (the length between the fingertips of both arms spread out sideways) of white cloth given to the builder, and when the boat is complete another similar sacrifice and transaction are made. Indeed, the costs involved in building a boat involve the ritual means of production every bit as much as the physical work. Other payments include small amounts of gold to be placed in a boat's "eyes," a parang, a one-fathom (depa) length of fishing line to represent the measuring rod, a plate, and a gong or plate to symbolize a bailer. Divination for the best time for voyaging, to forewarn planners of dangers or when actually faced by imminent danger from storms or currents, involves navigators uttering Koranic verses (cf. Tan 1981:2–4).

6.4. Orientation, Navigation, and Sailing

People relate to their environment by socializing it, and the way they negotiate their way through it is by using concepts, imagery, and language that draw heavily on social and cultural experience. When this combines with a history in which physical forms have been systematically and incremen-

Table 6.3. Toponyms for selected maritime features in the sea around Garogos, Nukus, and Kun, as described by fishermen from Garogos (Soselisa 1996:31)

Name	Gloss
Watu ngada	*Watu* = stone, rock; *ngada* = *Lutjanus gibbus*; meaning that this stone is the "house" or resting place of this fish
Tuha lean	*Tuha* = kind of tree, *lean* = big; a log from this tree was washed up at this place and sticks out
Watu roti	*Watu* = stone, rock; *roti* = two; two big stones exposed at low tide that mark a concentration of *lilia* fish (*Balistoides viridescens*) and *gohu* (*Lethrinus* sp.)
Lian kapal lean	*Lian* = rock, *kapal* = boat (Indonesian), *lean* = big; reef shaped like a boat; the location of many *surwaki* (the sea urchin *Tripneustes gratilla*)
Lok tigurun	*Lok* = pond, *tigurun* = a kind of goldband goatfish
Lutur dak	*Lutur* = stone or coral fish trap, *dak* = personal name of individual who originally constructed the *lutur*
Niu lalabor	*Niu* = coconut palm, *lalabor* = distance between; from this point can be seen a line/clump of coconut palms planted on Garogos
Taiwan	Place where several years previously a Taiwanese boat went aground
Watu mansia	Stone (*watu*) that resembles a human (*mansia*)
Siaru henu	Reef (*siaru*) which resembles a turtle (*henu*)
Watu otan	large stone (*watu*) surrounding which are found many *otan* fish (*Epinephelus* spp.)

tally reshaped by human activity (deliberately and inadvertently), such as recounted in chapter 2, it is little wonder that in matters of orientation, navigation, and seacraft it is difficult to draw a boundary between the natural and the cultural, the actual and the metaphorical, the practical and the symbolic. The giant octopus that is believed to live at the mouth of the Masiwang in a deep, black pocket and that is able to consume an entire *lepa-lepa* and its occupants is as much a hazard to be negotiated as any reef or squall.

The most obvious way in which nature is socialized is through the lexicon that we apply to it, and the construction of such a linguistic framework to map onto geographical experience is a universal cognitive imperative. Proper names help us discriminate between particular unique features, and generic features are registered by using the same noun wherever the feature occurs. The first imperative applies as much to seascapes as to landscapes. For example, in her description of Garogos, Soselisa (1995:71–74, appendix 3; 1996:31) listed a number of toponyms given by Garogos fishermen to features of the sea around their island and between Kun and Nukus. Thus, *watu ngada*, meaning the stone (*watu*) of the *ngada* fish (*Lutjanus gibbus)*, in this context refers to the home of this fish. Similar names recorded by Soselisa are listed in Table 6.3. Some common SSL terms for generic landscape or geomorphological items are listed in Table 6.4 (see also chapter

Table 6.4. Terms for features of maritime geography in Southeast Seram Litoral

Term	Gloss
Arlena	Large river
Bas	Sandbar or cay, *tanusang* in Ambonese Malay
Ena	Sand
Esi, utan	Forest
Gelar	Area between shallow sea and deep sea
Keli, ukar	Mountain, hill
Kil	Cape, promontory, *tanjong*
Labuan	Harbor
Lawena	Beach
Liku	A deep place (within the mangrove area, usually at a confluence of channels)
Malaman	Deep sea
Malaman paskali	Very deep water
Moti	Shallow sea with underlying reef (green or light blue water); intertidal zone; low tide
Moti dekar	Dry reef
Moti-moti	Reef (rocks) that are exposed at low tide
Nama arat	"Sea edge," beach; see also *gelar*
Nama metan	"Black sea," deep sea, open sea
Siaru	Reef, where coral rises in the sea
Sikaru	*Tubir*, channel
So solot	Waterway through the mangrove area; anchorage; a passage; a place where boats can pass (in the mangrove area); a safe haven; a stretch of coast; a bay
Tansoa	Point at which beach sand meets the water; waterline
Tasik	Sea (water)
Wanura	Island
Watu kusar	Rocks that stick out of the water

2.2). There is nothing especially remarkable in the existence of such terminologies, but because some words refer to features that have a special cultural or historical significance in a Southeast Seram context, and because many enter into place-names and names of kinship groups it is useful to provide some account of them here.

So, lexica of proper and generic names combine, change, and recombine to provide a powerful, detailed, and culturally specific way of describing, referring to, and locating places, spaces, physical processes, and phenomena when engaged in fishing or navigating. If we compare, for example, place-names in Southeast Seram Littoral and their Malay equivalents, it is apparent how SSL reflects some fundamentally different ways of thinking about the same geographic spaces. Thus, "*Onin*" is used polysemously to refer both to what is now officially designated the Onin Peninsula and to Irian or New Guinea more generally. Rather differently, *"Seran"* in SSL refers to the islands known as Seram Laut (*Ukar Seran* or *Laukau*) and Keffing or Seram Rei (*Seran Rei*) in modern Moluccan Malay, but excludes mainland Seram (*Ukar Laen*), whereas the cognate term "Seram" in Malay includes the island of Seram, but excludes Keffing. More generally, SSL toponyms increase in areas where this has become the language of trade, and the subsequent rise in the importance of Malay is in turn reflected in the way Malay toponyms have eclipsed many local ones, both in the practical language of traders and sailors and in the official designations of the state found in maps and administrative documents.

Another way in which landscapes and seascapes are molded in the cultural imagination, and features related one to another and to an individual person, is through a kind of intuitive topology; that is, some kind of system of spatial deixis or geographic orientation. Right (*wanan*) and left (*ubalit*) are used in SSL only for the displacement of objects in the immediate vicinity of the body. Similarly, although cardinal directions exist (e.g., *warat* = west) they are not important.

The SSL system of deixis (cf. also Yoshida 1980) is best understood in terms of three concentric spheres circumscribed around the omniscient speaker-hearer. For objects, places, and persons within the smallest sphere, apart from the oppositions right and left, the contrast most usually employed is a variation on the "to the above"–"to the below" (keatas–kebawah, in Ambonese Malay). On Geser, for example, direction is expressed as either *ata* or *wawa*: *na ata* indicates movement toward or in the direction of the old and original settlement (as in *aku kutagi ata Lomin*), as well as "upward"; and *wawa* away from the center (as in *aku kutagi wawa kampung baru*), as well as "below." Anything away from the center is also *muri*, "in the back," or dibelakang in Ambonese Malay; and to the front of something, *boa*. In this system, Kilwaru is also *ata* from anywhere on Geser, suggesting that "the above" refers not simply to an objective spatial center, but to a historical and symbolic one as well. Thus, we have *aku kutagi ata Kilwaru* (I go to Kilwaru [from Geser]) and *aku kumuri ata mari Kilwaru* (I come home from Kilwaru). In this context *tagi* is "to there" and *mari* "to here." Soselisa (1995:50) suggested that when residents of Garogos use *ata* with respect to Kataloka it is, at least in part, because that is where the raja is; and that when *wawa* is used for Onin, it is because in former times that was the source of social inferiors, slaves. Indeed, *ata* and *wawa* are used as directionals in relation to relative symbolic and political centers quite generally. Similarly, *boa* (to the front) and *muri* (to the back) refer not simply to physical space, but to a specific quality of that space. So, suggested Soselisa, for inhabitants of Garogos, the island of Kun is "the back" because it is uninhabited, and Garogos itself is the "front" because it is inhabited. This can be a source of some confusion for locals as well as outsiders. Thus, on Seram Rei, Keffing (near Seram) is *wawa*, and Kelu *ata*.

In Seram, as elsewhere in Indonesia, a major axis of orientation is mountain-sea (see, e.g., Ellen 1986b, Taylor 1984). On mainland Seram this is often expressed using "to the above" in contrast to "to the sea," for example as in *aku saka ata Bati* or *aku dudu lau Kwaos (aku kumarin burebat)*. Alternatively, especially at points outside mainland Seram, the contrast is in terms of *rei* (big land, Seram, landward) and *lau* (sea, small Islands, seaward), as in *aku kutagi lau Geser* (from Keffing), *aku ka na rei Keffing* (from Geser), *aku muri lau Geser, aku kana rei Kwaos*, or *lau Kilwaru*, "over there on Kilwaru" (from Seram Laut). In the context of the Gorom group, the island of Gorom is *rei*. Though hardly much larger than Manawoka, it has come to be politically dominant.

In judging what directionals to use, the juxtaposition of various kinds of relative oppositions has to be weighed in relation to the geographical distance involved and scale of movement. Thus, in the second concentric circle it is easy to locate apparent contradictions, or assume that there is a complex fixed system of directionals in operation. In fact, the choice of modes of expression is all rather flexible. Traveling from Geser to Kilmuri (that is, to the west or northwest) or from Kwaos to Geser is *na wawa* (sometimes contracted to *wa*), as in *aku mau kusobal wawa Kilmuri*; to travel in the opposite direction (east or southeast) is *ata* (as in *Geser kami tagi atakan*, "we go to Geser"); but to travel from Urung to Geser (that is, also to the east or southeast, but much closer) is *lau* (lit., to the sea). From Geser to Urung (that is, from south to north) is *aku ka na muri Urung*.

To travel to Buru is (*na wawa* or *lau*) *aku asal ata mari Geser*, "I come from Geser" (*muri* = back, return); to Onin, Misool, and all parts of New Guinea from Geser is *ka na wawa*. To Ambon from Geser is *aku mau kusobal lau Ambon*. To sail to Banda from Geser is definitely *lau* (*aku mau kusobal lau Andan*); to Ambon may be *lau* or *na wawa*, depending on the route (e.g., via Banda or hugging the south coast of Seram). To sail to Dobo, Kei, or Tanimbar is *ka nata* (*aku mau kusobal ata Kei*). How these directionals are applied differently for Geser and Ondor (Gorom dialect), and why, when assumed to be part of a single system with simple logical properties, they appear confusing (Barnes 1988) is summarized in Figures 6.6 and 6.7. It is easy to see why some interpreters and locals alike might find it convenient to infer from the frequency of usages that *ata* is "sunrise," east and south, or southeast, and that *wawa* is sunset, west and north, or northwest. Most of the differences can be explained with reference to preferences for use of different oppositional contrasts given relative geopolitical, symbolic, and geographic realities. Thus, that Kataloka should be *wawa* for Ondor and Ondor *wawa* for Kataloka is very easily explained given competing political centers and a history of antagonism. However, even given the semantic exegesis in the preceding paragraphs it is difficult to account for why *ata* is always the directional for Kei, Tanimbar, and Aru. It is interesting that anything outside what I have designated the Banda zone (such as Sulawesi, Java, Europe, or even [for some reason] Tarui, high up on the east coast of Seram), is *nabuar*

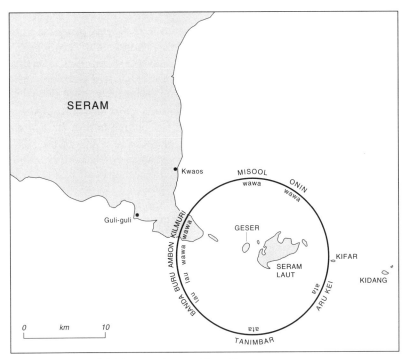

Figure 6.6. Spatial deixis, as understood from Geser.

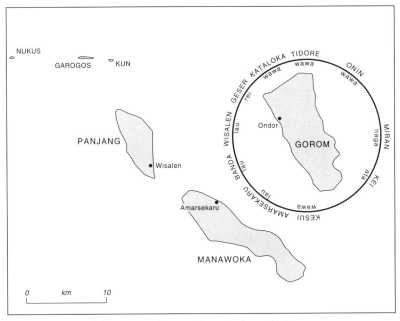

Figure 6.7. Spatial deixis, as understood from Ondor and Miran.

(or *bo* in Gorom dialect), as in *aku mau kusobal bua Jakarta*. Here, *bo* refers to places far away. Thus, *ata* is always away from the mainland. There are other differences between Gorom dialect and Geser. The use of the term *"rei"* is one. The term *"naga"* for "over there" is used in Ondor when directing toward Miran or other places on the northwestern coast of Gorom, on the other side of the hilly spine of the island. In Miran itself, *naga* is used for places due north along the east coast of Gorom. *Naga*, then, is confined as a directional to places "over there" on the island, but not beyond it. In other respects the directionals in Miran are much the same as in Ondor. On Manawoka and Pulau Panjang the directional *naga* is said not to be employed, except that I have heard it used to refer to Wisalen (on Pulau Panjang) when traveling from Amarsekaru (or Manawoka).

Any form of navigation must begin with a model of fixed points in space and their relationship to each other, and with the body that is in motion between those fixed (or in some cases moving) objects. This is why terms for different kinds of geographical features, toponyms for unique places, and a system of spatial deixis provide the basic calculus. But in addition to these there are other natural forces the predictable patterns of which are an essential aid to navigation using sailing boats: namely the movements of the sun and stars, the tides, currents, wave motion, and the winds. Navigation in the Geser-Gorom Archipelago is essentially a dead-reckoning system (one depending on position being calculated entirely on the basis of distance and direction traveled since the last known location) and one that depends on the specific characteristics of local maritime geography that I have begun to outline here. In this it is hardly unusual (see, e.g., Gladwin 1970: 144), as, indeed, is the combination of other techniques upon which it relies: the regular motions of heavenly bodies; the reading of wave motion and patterns; wind strength, quality, and direction; cloud cover and movement; the occurrence of particular seabird and fish species and their behavior; the distribution, type, and depth of reef; the location and visibility of terrestrial features and the water itself, its currents, temperature, depth, transparency, color, and other characteristics—all used in different ways at different times in different places. As Gladwin (ibid., 146) observed for Pulawat, "no one set of observed phenomena will suffice to guide a sailing craft under all the conditions it will encounter at sea." The account here cannot deal fully with the intricacies of navigation and piloting, as, for example, Ammarell (1999) has recently done for the Bugis of the Sabalana Archipelago, but it is helpful to summarize some details to reinforce my argument that an understanding of boats as material artifacts cannot be divorced from the knowledge of their use, no more than it can from the purposes for which they are employed and the social relations into which they enter. I deal here summarily with tides, currents, winds, waves, and astronomical features.

Tides and currents are not the same thing. However, in seas subject to tidal streams (diurnal oscillations in response to the gravitational pull of the moon) or currents (which generally run in one direction all the time, except when seasonally induced), an allowance must be made for these movements of the water. A blue-water sea current is referred to in SSL as *rurut*, which is also used for tide. Thus, *rurut* is generically a body of water moving in a definite direction: *rurut tonu* is high tide; *rurut moti*, low tide. When low- and high-tide currents meet we get a *rurut kedas. Rurut bail-bail* is a circular (turning, revolving) current, more extremely a whirlpool, usually located at a point where two currents cross or merge. There are basically two constant-directional currents identified in the Geser-Gorom area: the *rurut Onin* (Onin current), which moves from the west and southwest (Banda) toward the northeast (the Onin Peninsula of New Guinea), and the *rurut Andan* (Banda current), which moves from Onin in the northeast, west along the south coast of Seram, and southwest toward Banda (that is, in the opposite direction). The configuration of these currents is influenced by local geography, and Figures 6.8 and 6.9 show the appearance of these in the Geser and Gorom areas, respectively, as they are understood by local fishermen and sailors. The branches of these directional currents (in either direction) running between Kiltai and Geser and Seram Rei and Geser (marked A and B in Figure 6.8) are known, respectively, as the *rurut otak* and the *rurut laen*. The latter is claimed to be the stronger of the two. I should emphasize that these are folk representations, not data taken from technical manuals.

There are three basic winds (*mar*): the *mar tenggara* (the southeast wind), the *moda mar* (northerly wind), and the *timur mar* (easterly wind), and these roughly correspond to the prevailing winds at different times of the year. In the Geser-Gorom Archipelago, the *moda mar* (sometimes called *angin modara*) is the wind that comes from the mountains of mainland Seram, a cool morning breeze caused by the different speeds at which temperature adjusts on land and sea. Sailing from Kilwaru to Geser the *angin selatan* was a side wind, sometimes *tarangan alus*, a smooth southern wind. The *warat paling kaforat*, the westerly wind, is the strongest, with the strong east monsoon wind, *angin timurlaen*. Winds are also classified, irrespective of direction, according to their strength. Thus, *maleman* is a slow or moderate wind, *angin riut* a sudden unexpected wind, and *angin kaforat* a fast wind. Thus, there is a correspondence between the major directional currents and deixis, though no correspondence between deixis and wind. Of the various forces upon which sailing and navigation depend, it is wind that is thought to be manipulable through magical means: gongs and large conches (*tau uri*) are used to summon up the wind during calms.

Waves (*wala walau*), of course, are caused by the wind, and discriminating different kinds of waves is important in judging sailing conditions. During the east monsoon waves are represented as coming from the east, in the west monsoon as coming from the west. Short waves are known as *wala walau kubat*, long waves as *wala walau malas*; large breakers as *sesesar*, really large waves as *soar babak*, and waves that are continuous, not breaking, like

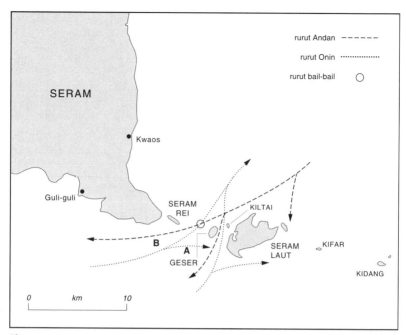

Figure 6.8. Main currents as understood in the Seram Laut group. Based on data obtained from Arsad Rumonin, Geser, April 1986.

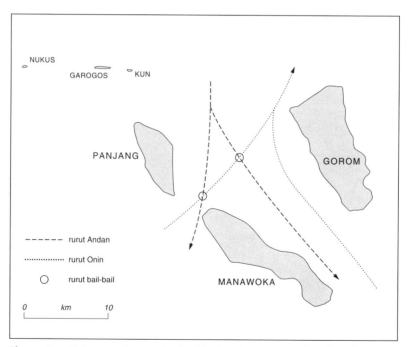

Figure 6.9. Main currents as understood in the Gorom group. Based on data obtained from Badaruddin Sohilau, Samboru, May 1986.

mountains, are *kulu-kulu*. Wave motion (by which I include swell patterns created by crosscutting effects) is important in navigation.

Both the moon (*ulan*) and the stars (*utuin*) are used in night navigation. Other than the moon, the most important constant feature of the night sky employed by sailors is *tirutuin* (the ikan gabus star, a fishlike spiky ball), the Southern Cross, which can be used as a fixed point regardless of the season and around which other constellations rotate. Other star groups are indicators of specific seasons. The appearance of the Pleiades, *buak hung* (or pinang rangka), usually heralds the east monsoon, but when seen at sunrise signals the onset of the westerly monsoon. The *utuin suveilat* (the net star) is also a sign of the east monsoon, though when the *ori hari* (the shark star, in the southern part of Scorpius) is visible it signifies that the heavy seas of the east monsoon are at an end. Other stars serve as *elat Andan* (meaning "the sign for Banda") used when steering a course to Banda, and others the *elat Onin*, when steering a course in the opposite direction.

Nowadays, all the techniques so far mentioned are supplemented by the use of the compass, even on an *angbot* and other larger plank-built vessels.

6.5. From Sail to Motor Power

Although the adaptation of European styles of rigging and boatbuilding marginally improved the performance of local sailing craft, it neither markedly affected the character of trade nor the shape of trading networks. The introduction of motorized vessels did both, although intermediate and long-distance trade remained mainly in the hands of sailing vessels until well into the postwar and postindependence period. The first motorized vessels to frequent the Moluccas were the KPM packet ships in the 1880s. These introduced regular schedules, had a larger cargo capacity than earlier vessels, and were not constrained by winds and currents. However, they did introduce new problems, such as the provision of adequate fuel.

Of motor-powered boats, the most ubiquitous in the Geser-Gorom area today is the jonson (or motor jonson; motor tempel). This is a flexible vessel basically constructed from a *lepa-lepa* hull modified to accommodate an outboard engine. In addition, a regular *lepa-lepa* can have an outboard motor fitted to it (pok-pok). Jonsons are adapted by raising the height of the sides and streamlining the bows. They come in various sizes and can perform duties of vessels of types 1, 2, and 3. At the local level, changes since 1945 have been wrought mainly by the introduction of the jonson. It was first introduced on a significant scale during the 1960s, but had a marked impact on local trade only with the availability of cheaper Japanese kerosene-powered models in the 1970s. The first jonson in Warus-warus, for example, was acquired in 1975. Official figures, never entirely reliable, show a steady motor tempel increase in both Banda and East Seram throughout the 1970s, though with much higher levels of ownership throughout the latter (Statistik Tahunan Kecamatan: Banda 1977, 1978 and Seram Timur 1982). This is not surprising given the population differences between the two subdistricts and their relative affluence during that period. Other reports suggest a steady increase in the number of fishing boats with motors during the early 1980s, increasing from 261 in 1980 to 460 in 1982. However, it is never entirely clear what kind of boats are being referred to, though we can probably assume them to be motorized *lepa-lepa* for the most part. The statistics divide them, unhelpfully, into "small," "medium," and "large" (ibid., Seram Timur 1982:33). Also, we know that hulls and engines are often quite separate, with far fewer engines in circulation than hulls.

Jonson ownership, though growing, is restricted. On the one hand are the traders who use them for transporting cargoes; on the other there are the more wealthy villagers (for instance, the rajas of Kiltai and Dinama) who rent them out or charge a fare to passengers. Almost all villages have some kind of jonson link. There are few villages of any size that nowadays do not have access to such craft, rapidly reducing journey times on short coastal trips and between nearby islands, and thereby increasing market integration and dependency. Given the size of the initial investment, "bodies" or hulls (*bodi*) are much more common than the outboard motors themselves, which are often owned by (usually Sino-Indonesian) traders and rented or loaned to others. This was the arrangement the raja of Kwaos had with a Chinese trader in 1986. Conversely, owners of outboard motors may hire a body of a particular size as and when another trader needs it. My own figures for 1986 are not complete for the entire area (Appendix 2) but suggest that the official subdistrict figures are not wildly misleading.

Jonsons generally have a crew of three: one person to steer, one at the prow to punt and act as lookout and guide (especially through reefs and mangroves), and one to bail (often a small boy). Occasionally, crews may consist of just two, but the lookout is vital given the hazards that floating wood, discarded nets, and similar flotsam and jetsam pose for propellers and fast-moving hulls.

Outboard motors were mainly, in 1986, 15-, 25-, and 40-horsepower Yamaha and Suzuki engines, capable of between 10 and 15 knots. The eponymous Jonson was itself an American engine, but because it ran on petrol alone was generally thought too expensive. Most motors start on petrol and run on kerosene. The cost of 1 liter of kerosene in Dinama (35 kilometers north of Geser, where prices are most competitive) was 350 rupiah in 1986; 40 liters were required for the return journey to Geser. One liter of petrol was 600 rupiah, and 2 liters were required for the return journey to Geser. In addition, 3 liters of oil was needed at 1,500 rupiah a liter, making the total cost of fuel 19,700 rupiah. In the same year, on Kiltai, adjacent Geser, one bottle (about 1 liter) of kerosene was 200 rupiah or as cheap as 125 rupiah if bought in quantity. Elsewhere 1 liter of kerosene could be bought for 275 rupiah, 1 liter of petrol for 600 rupiah, and 1 liter of oil 1,250 rupiah. A single journey from Geser to, say, Suru would need forty bottles of kerosene, 2 liters of petrol, and 2 liters of oil, at a total cost of 11,040 rupiah. Soselisa (1995) said that a jonson journey from Garogos to Geser needs 25 liters of kerosene, which at 450 rupiah a liter in 1993 came to 11,250 rupiah. By comparison, a pok-pok needs only 4 liters of kerosene at 1,100 rupiah a liter, a cost of 4,400 rupiah for the trip.

Motorization has also given rise to a number of other hybrid kinds of vessel. Outboard motors are being fitted to small plank-built hulls, giving rise to the ubiquitous motor jonson lambo. These tend to be larger and more expensive to build and run than regular jonsons. Ownership, there-fore, is increasingly falling to larger (mainly ethnic Chinese) traders with greater capital to invest and away from the control of small traders and peasants. Small motorboats (rather than jonsons) were also beginning to make an appearance in the 1980s. In addition, there are locally built diesel craft based on the perahu layar motor (perahu motor) template, a sailing boat with basically the same hull as a perahu layar, but with auxiliary diesel power. These are owned mainly by Sino-Indonesian traders based in the larger centers, such as Ambon, and having other trading interests. Such craft are used for the most part in long-distance trade.

Then there is the kapal motor, motor laut, or motor dalam, the "cart horse" of trade between island groups and passenger ferries. These are wooden and steel-hulled vessels of between 100 and 500 metric tons that can be grouped into the official category of "Pelayaran Lokal." The ferries operating between Ambon (mainly Momokeng and Tulehu) and Geser fall into this category. In 1986 there were three in regular service: the *Sinar Manis* (nine years old), the *Cemerlang* (two years old), and the *Purnama* (four years old); the *Nusa Indah* occasionally plied between Banda and Geser, and the *Bintang Makmur* between Geser and Sorong in New Guinea. The *Sinar Manis*, to take just one example, was built at Asilulu by Butonese shipwrights using traditional techniques for the hull with a modern super-structure. It typically runs from Momokeng to Geser, then to Kataloka and Ondor on Gorom, to Kesui, perhaps stopping off somewhere else to pick up timber, and then back to Geser and Momokeng. In 1981 it had recently had a three-month refit in the Ambon dock. It is based in Momokeng, near Tulehu, from where most of the Geser boats depart. The *Sinar Manis* is owned (among other boats) by the brother-in-law of Kino Atmojo, who runs the shop that is the contact point for boats in Momokeng and who also has a house in Geser. Atmojo, a second-generation Chinese born in Surabaya, had lived in Ambon for seven years by 1986, marrying into an Ambonese Chinese family. For comparison, the *Bintang Makmur* is owned by a local Ambonese, and the perahu motor *Hutai Indah* by mayor Rumalu-tur of Kiltai. There has been an increase in Sino-Indonesian ownership of these vessels since 1967.

Finally, there are steel-hulled vessels, which show no hint of vernacular influence. These are mainly PERINTIS ships—the Moluccan subsidiary of the state-owned PELNI, which operates the Ambon-Banda-Geser-Tual run, and variations on this, to accommodate major ports in other parts of Maluku Tenggara, in much the same way and along the same routes as the old KPM ships before them. The number of visits from ships to East Seram ports increased from twelve in 1973 to forty-seven in 1977, with a proportionate increase in the number of passengers and the tonnage of cargo shifted, though compared with modern international shipping the vessels used are technologically old-fashioned and labor intensive. For local traders, however, the freight rates charged are often prohibitively expensive and, moreover, those who use them have less control over routes and timing than those who hire a perahu or perahu motor.

So sailing vessels continue to be important. In 1980 they constituted 19 percent of registered arrivals and departures at Ambon harbor, 33 percent in 1981 at Mamokeng also on Ambon Island, 44 percent at Banda Neira in 1984, 40 percent at Geser in 1985, and 32 percent at Kataloka in 1985 (Kantor Syahbandar data). But although sailing boats still account for a significant proportion of local and long-distance traffic, they were during the 1980s fast giving way to motorized craft. By comparison with the rising figures for jonson and motor dalam ownership and trade, perahu layar at anchor in Ambon harbor decreased from 741 in 1977 to 364 in 1979, and docking increased from 173 in 1977 to 327 in 1979. Kapal motor anchorages changed from 635 to 626 and dockings from 254 to 213 during the same period (Port Information Ambon 1980:38). Motor vessels are not always an advantage (they are expensive, cannot be negotiated through shallows, are more prone to technical faults through their complexity, have a shorter working life [ten years compared with the forty years of a comparable sailing vessel], and are more likely to sink), but they are more independent of seasonal and wind conditions and are, for the most part, faster. The effect of their introduction has been to accelerate the integration of peripheral villages into market centers, but also to undermine the structure of older trading networks (through the development of routes ordinarily denied to sailing vessels) and the geographical division of specialist production. But the effects and scale of motorization have been uneven; local traffic has been more affected than intermediate or long-distance trade and central areas more than peripheries. Thus local trade in Piru Bay and between Ambon and the Lease Islands is now heavily motorized and well connected with major market centers (particularly Ambon), and the Southeast Seram area is less motorized and correspondingly less integrated. The jonson has mainly affected local networks, though in an area where much trade is in high-value products it is occasionally economical on longer journeys, such as to New Guinea.

Sailing vessels are much more cost-effective where time is not a crucial factor (though where ability to predict length of passage may still be) and for cargoes that do not command high prices or profit margins, such as recycled oil drums, empty bottles, worn-out tires, and scrap iron. Goods carried by perahu tend to be bulky, safely carried as deck cargo, of low value, or fragile (Dick 1975:86, 100). There is also a certain irony in the fact that perahus are sometimes the vessel of choice for transporting the oil, from Bula to Kataloka for instance, for the very motorized craft that appear to threaten their continued existence. There can be no doubt that sailing vessels of many kinds have shown great flexibility in adapting to changing circumstances and still supply an important service complementing modern shipping and motorized vessels. This is true generally in the archipelago and certainly continues to be so in the Banda zone. Sailing boat trade provides an excellent example of the resilience and viability of small businesses in modern Indonesia.

7
The Structure of Contemporary Trading Networks

7.1. Modeling Trading Networks Using Distance Centrality and Connectedness

Geographers, archaeologists, anthropologists, and graph theorists have all attempted measurements of centrality in trading networks, using various approaches derived from graph theoretic analysis and central place theory (Brookfield with Hart 1971; Hage 1977; Hage and Harary 1991:87; Hagget and Chorley 1969; Irwin 1974, 1978a; Smith 1976). One of the underlying propositions of central place theory applied to trade is that suppliers are typically mobile when the range of a good (that is, the distance that consumers are prepared and able to travel for it) is smaller than the supplier's threshold (meaning the distance that encompasses sufficient demand for their survival). This is what one might expect to occur in uncommercialized areas, such as archipelagic Southeast Seram. With commercialization, demand is predicted to rise, increasing consumer range and thus allowing the trader to become sedentary and permanent central places to come into existence. Until demand is sufficient to support permanent traders, marketing must remain dispersed and periodic (Smith 1976:16). Although in Southeast Seram, with its historical involvement in long-distance trade, we might expect centralization to have taken place long ago. In fact, what we find is much more complex: a degree of centralization in the Seram Laut area, though of a very diffuse kind, with relatively low populations (much lower than central place theory would predict), a mixture of vendors traveling to buyers' settlements and the reverse, a degree of locational specialization of production driven mainly by geographical and ecological constraints, and flexible general trading by middlemen. Indeed, since the 1970s a number of critics have begun to question the usefulness of a theory that cannot predict, especially one that makes some quite untenable assumptions, such as the existence of an isotropic landscape and perfect information (ibid., 24). Similar questions arise concerning the effects of topography, history, and system level on applications of graph theoretic models. Hage and Harary (1991:174), for example, conceded that the Micronesian landscapes that they consider are more "perfect" than most and elsewhere network structures may be affected by variations in coast-line, altitude, and terrain; and that many if not most trade networks are subsystems contained within larger, more global systems (Brookfield with Hart 1971:317). However, topographical distortions of network patterns are a problem for central place theory models of the Christaller-Lösch kind, in a way that centrality models based on graph theory are not, because they make no assumptions about ideal landscapes. Indeed, the notion of cen-trality in graphs is quite different and should not be confused. Even though some trade networks may have long and complex histories, Hage and Harary (1991:175) claimed that they should nonetheless be amenable to graph analysis, the point being not to insist exclusively on situational fac-tors or on social, political, and cultural factors in accounting for the domi-nance of a community in a network, but to assess the importance of the former. The history and socio-spatial character of the archipelagic South-east Seram trading zone pose special challenges to attempts to describe and explain it in theoretical terms.

Island groups are defined here as being equivalent to the level of local trading spheres or zones described in chapter 1. Thus, we can speak of the Seram Laut, Gorom, or Banda groups in this sense. The systemic properties of these trading zones and networks have arisen from a combination of environmental, technological, economic, and political forces. However, the technological changes in transport reviewed in the previous chapter have meant that trading routes are no longer entirely constrained by the conditions for using sailing vessels effectively.

Appendix 3 lists all settlements serving as administrative centers for desa (formerly negeri) in the East Seram subdistrict, as they existed in 1986. Only the Watubela group has been excluded, because by eliminating this group, as we have seen in chapter 2, we are left with an area that closely corre-sponds to the distribution of native speakers of SSL. Ideally, this appendix should have listed all settlements, not just administrative centers, but to have included them would have involved complicated matrices of central-ity, and anyway there is a strong intuition that desa centers serve as a good proxy for all settlements included within them. We are, of course, interested in mapping centrality and connectedness for a historically continuous period. It is true that the boundaries of contemporary desa do not always accurately match the colonial negeri or traditional domains that preceded them, and in some cases modern administrative centers are actually differ-ent from the centers of domains that preceded them (e.g., Pancalang for Amarsekaru and Argam for Ainikke). But again the match is judged suffi-ciently close for general centrality measurements of current settlements to reflect the historical situation, though as we move backward in time we would expect the fit to become increasingly problematic. Column five of Appendix 3 gives the distance centrality index (D) and column six the rank order for a matrix based on shortest distance. From this it can be seen that the lowest values, and therefore the most central places, are in the vicinity of Seram Laut, whether we look at individual settlements or desa measured from their administrative center. These are the areas described in the literature as being most active in trade and where there are a greater proportion of individuals involved in trade. In other words, centrality is positively, though not inevitably, correlated with seafaring, as demonstrated by Hage and Harary (1991:89) for the Carolines, by Hage (1977) for the *kula* ring, and by Irwin (1974) for Mailu, among others. The difference between the locations considered in these other studies (though not Mailu) and archipelagic Southeast Seram is that they are entirely insular systems where economies of distance are less constrained by topography.

Columns seven and eight in Appendix 3 give the distance centrality index and rank order for a matrix of the same places based on distances that are calculated on the basis of adjustments to make the distance traveled (the actual voyages) more realistic. Basically, these figures reflect assumptions of coastline and island "hugging." A comparison between these rankings and those based on shortest distance is instructive. In terms of the most central places the differences are slight, though they lead to a reordering of most central places: Kwaos, Kelu-Keffing, Geser, Kianlaut, Kiltai-Kilwaru, instead of Kelu-Keffing, Kiltai-Kilwaru, Geser, Kwaos, Kiandarat. The most significant differences are for Kiandarat and Argam, where for topographical reasons the distance economies of direct distances over those routes that hug the coast are greatest. Another practical problem to be considered in attempting measurements of centrality is that it is possible to travel from most places on the mainland or islands directly to Geser and from most places to every other place without stopovers.

The structural advantages of Geser, Kelu-Keffing (the island of Seram Rei), and Kiltai-Kilwaru (the island of Kiltai) in network terms lie in their neighborhood (that is, all points in a network graph adjacent to the particular point of interest). Thus, the neighborhood of Geser in Figure 7.1 is Seram Rei, Kiltai, Kwaos, Kwamar, Guli-guli, Kilfura, and Maar. This graph covers approximately what I have called the "central area" of the archipelagic Southeast Seram system and the northeast-southwest passage through it, the Geser (or Banda-Onin) corridor. The graph is, of course, selective, both in terms of its boundaries and its locational content. I have decided, for example, to draw the boundary at Guli-guli along the south coast of Seram and not Urung; the boundary along the east coast at Kwaos and not Air Nanang; and the easternmost boundary along the farther coast of Seram Laut, and not at Kifar or Kidang, say. This is arbitrary up to a point but is broadly consistent with the historical evidence summarized in chapters 3, 4, and 5 and with an interpretation of contemporary boat movements and ethnography, suggesting that this area has more connecting of its parts than any individual parts have connections with the outside. In terms of selectivity within the parameters of the graph, I have included all historically important places and then aggregated those that were close to each other. So, Kiltai and Kilwaru are merged, as are all the settlements of

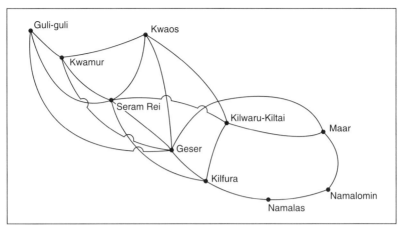

Figure 7.1. Graph indicating sea-lane connections between places in Seram Laut Archipelago.

Seram Rei, as are Kwamar Besar and Kwamar Kecil. The points in the graph have then been connected on the basis of ethnographic evidence of the sailing routes between the locations. On the basis of the links displayed in the graph in Figure 7.1 (which is not to scale), I have estimated real space voyaging distances between each node in the graph, which have been used to calculate the centrality index for each node (Appendix 4).

The centrality index ranking immediately confirms what a more informal reading of the evidence suggests: that Geser, Kiltai, Kilwaru, and the Seram Rei settlements are the most central, all with extensively overlapping neighborhoods. This advantage was enforced through good harbors. It is consistent with the "shifting centers" described in chapter 4 and also the ability of these places to control trade (Hage and Harary 1991:89). However, distance centrality data do not explain why, of the Seram Rei domains, Keffing is the most frequently mentioned in the historical sources consulted; why Kilwaru appears more significant over the same time frame than Kiltai; and, perhaps most important, why Geser did not assume any political significance until the mid-nineteenth century and the arrival of the Dutch. It is also difficult to predict social hierarchy and political domination over network peripheries on the basis of favorable location data. For Hage and Harary (ibid., 92–93), given the necessity of interisland exchange and the restriction to certain sea-lanes, any island that can control communication between other islands is in a powerful position to demand tribute and other payments. Some islands, they argued, have more potential for control than others by being on a higher proportion of geodesics between all other islands. This is the basis for the *betweenness* definition of centrality, betweenness being "the frequency of occurrence of each point on the geodesics between all pairs of points in the graph," an index for the potential for controlling communication. In the case of archipelagic Southeast Seram this was deflected by the importance of the Geser corridor and the Gorom group in mediating trade between New Guinea and the rest of the world to the west.

If we refer to Figure 7.1 and look at the various possible shortest paths between different points, we find that there are a large number of cases where there are three equal geodesics (say, with three or four vectors) but with the middle vector different in each case. Thus, traveling from Kwaos or some other point on the mainland to a place on Seram Laut (such as Maar, Namalomin, or Namalas), Seram Rei, Geser, and Kiltai are equally substitutable in terms of betweenness. This also reinforces the shifting center hypothesis.

Another interesting case of the shifting center is with respect to the Gorom group. Although too far deflected to the southeast to meet the ideal conditions of centrality and connectedness for the area as a whole, the connectivity data (Figure 7.2, Appendix 5) predict that several places facing inward on the three islands of Gorom, Manawoka, and Panjang could provide viable centers, other things being equal, and historically Amar (first at Amarwatu, then at Amarsekaru), Ondor, and Kataloka have all been centers of the first order for considerable periods of time. The connectivity and environmental data that are consistent with these places as centers only provide the backdrop, of course, and it is micropolitical events that have determined the specifics. The most recent of these is the shift of the economic center of the Gorom group from Amarsekaru to Kataloka. In 1972 it was suggested to Raja Wattimena by Sumarko, then the administrator of Ambon port, that because the government was sponsoring the building of a pier traders should now be allowed to settle permanently in his domain and that this would be beneficial to local development. The first shop opened in Kataloka in the same year. This was the Toko Kembung Raya, which had moved from Amarsekaru. Formerly Amarsekaru had been a more important trading center than Kataloka. Although Kataloka had the better harbor and the island of Gorom was more populous, a succession of conservative rajas had consistently refused traders permission to set up establishments on a permanent basis. From 1927 to 1972, successive rajas had pursued a policy of prohibiting traders to settle, believing them to be a disruptive force, who would, among other things, interfere with local women. During that period the economy of Kataloka relied largely on farming, though it had access to sea produce of commercial importance on Garogos. No local people could be described as traders and none owned an *angbot* or *ang kalulis*. In 1986 Raja Wattimena could recall Pedang Macau, who had peddled goods from one place to another on Gorom before returning to his base in Amarsekaru. Before 1972 there were two or three shops in Ondor and five or six in Amarsekaru. Indeed, Amarsekaru appears to have been the main trading center in the Gorom group, where during the colonial period Dutch KPM vessels used to call in, traveling from Ambon to Banda, Banda to Amar, Amar to Fak-fak, and returning via the same route.

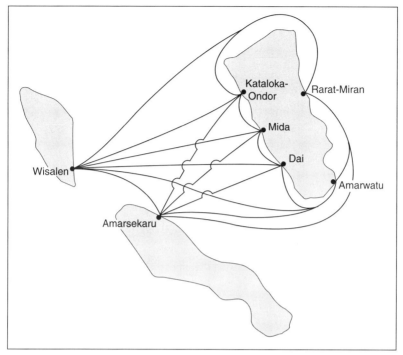

Figure 7.2. Graph indicating sea-lane connections between places in Gorom Archipelago.

7.2. Conceptualizing the Spatial Movement of Goods

Trade in locally produced commodities can be sorted conveniently into three categories: goods that are consumed within a local network (or perhaps in adjacent ones), those that are traded between island groups (intermediate), and those that are part of long-distance trade to Sulawesi, Java, or elsewhere. Commodities consumed within a local network include sago, pottery, vegetables, fish, palm sugar, timber, firewood, and alcoholic beverages. Within each zone different localities specialize in different products for trade and the local circulation of those products, either radially through the center or laterally within the periphery, all of which serve to integrate the area as a complex social and economic system. Thus, the Banda islands as a whole have no need to import palm sugar, firewood, vegetables, and fish, although no one settlement within the group is completely self-sufficient. But although the circulation of commodities maintains integral systemic properties within each trade zone, trade also occurs between zones. Thus, timber (and, previously, large quantities of sago) is generally imported to Banda from Southeast Seram and Gorom (Kolff 1927 [1840]:287), whereas Kei pottery was exported (after 1621) both to Seram and to Banda. The circulation of such commodities integrates Kei, Banda, and Southeast Seram into a wider intermediate system, both laterally (between localities of more or less equal political and economic significance) and radially (focusing on secondary and primary centers).

Trade in commodities of the third kind—nutmeg, cloves, exotic forest products such as edible birds' nests, trepang, pearls, turtle shell, and so on—only serves to integrate center with periphery (Seram Laut with Geser, Geser with Banda, etc.) or various points on the periphery through the center, because the demand is not local and is only mediated through traders operating from central places.

Termini are of two kinds. First of all there are those that are generally self-sufficient but that are the source of products desired elsewhere: in local centers, other parts of Indonesia, Asia, and Europe. Before 1900 all interior mountain villages on Seram would have fallen into this category. Highland termini were variously involved in the export of damar resin, timber, rattan, useful barks (such as cinnamon and lawan), dried meat, deer antlers, bird plumage, and wild cloves (cengkeh hutan). Because such termini were self-sufficient in a material sense is not to deny that the objects that they received in exchange (red cloth, patola, ikat, porcelain) represented a form of congealed value very necessary for the maintenance of local exchange and ritual cycles (Ellen 1979; Elmberg 1968). The second kind of terminus is one whose very existence is dependent on a wider trading network, secondary rather than pristine. An example of this is the Garogos reef, a settlement exporting fish, trepang, lola, and batu laga via Kataloka and Geser. Despite having to import all of its vegetable food, starch staples, and timber (even much firewood), Garogos has grown from a temporary to a permanent settlement in the course of the last thirty years.

Secondary and primary centers can also be classified into those that are basically self-sufficient and those that are utterly dependent upon others. Examples are found in Kataloka (on Gorom) and Geser, respectively. They can also be distinguished according to whether or not they are also centers for spice production. I indicated in chapter 1 the general historical relationship between spice-producing centers and starch-subsidizing peripheries, and I also discussed, in chapter 3, how it now appears that spice cultivation at such centers may have been secondary to their emergence as centers of trade. The significance of the Geser corridor, for example, first appears to have arisen through trade in a variety of natural products from New Guinea, only one of which was wild nutmeg. After 1621, however, it challenged the VOC monopoly not simply by continuing to trade in long nutmeg, but by planting the commercially more attractive round nutmeg as well. We can model the wider Banda-focused system (Figure 1.2) as a logical development and extension of a Southeast Seram system.

7.3. Trade within Island Groups

The close geographical proximity of certain islands and their economic interdependence means that not only are there boat movements between them every day, but some individuals cross the short stretches of water involved once a day or more. On Kiltai and Seram Rei someone from every household visits Geser every day, and all households own a *lepa-lepa*.

Table 7.1. Provenance of locally produced items in Geser market, 5 April 1986

Commodity	Latin Name	Island of Origin	Place of Origin
Chili	*Capsicum frutescens*	Seram Laut	Talang Baru
Coconut oil	*Cocos nucifera*	Seram Laut	Talang Baru
Shallots	*Allium cepa*	Seram Laut	Talang Baru
Cane sugar	*Saccharum officinarum*	Seram Laut	Kilfura
Cucumber	*Cucumis sativus*	Seram Laut	Talang Baru
Maize	*Zea mays*	Seram	Kwamar
Manioc (cassava)	*Manihot esculenta*	Seram Laut	Talang Baru
Manioc leaves	*Manihot esculenta*	Seram Laut	Talang Baru, Kilfura
Sagu lemping (*suat*)	*Metroxylon sagu*	Seram	Air Nanang, Kilaba, Kiandarat, Anger
Banana	*Musa paradisiaca*	Seram	Kwaos
		Seram Laut	Talang Baru
Coconut	*Cocos nucifera*	Seram Laut	Kilfura
Turmeric	*Curcuma aurantiaca*	Seram Laut	Talang Baru
Mung beans	*Vigna radiatus*	Geser	Geser
Kangkong	*Ipomoea aquatica*	Seram	Aruan, Talang Baru
Lime	*Citrus aurantifolia*	Gorom	Kataloka
Star fruit	*Averrhoa carambola*	Seram Laut	Talang Baru
Pawpaw	*Carica papaya*	Seram Laut	Talang Baru
Durian	*Durio zibethinus*	Seram	Talang Baru
		Seram	Ainena-Urung, Kilgah
Firewood		Seram	Kwamar
Suami (fermented manioc cake)	*Manihot esculenta*	Seram Laut	Talang Baru
Pandanus leaf mats	*Pandanus connoideus*	Seram	Kiloba
Kacang buncis	*Phaseolus vulgaris*	Seram Laut	Talang Baru
Lapur-lapur (rice packets)	*Oryza sativa*	Seram Laut	Talang Baru
Waya ikan		Seram Laut	Kilfura
Sago	*Metroxylon sagu*	Seram Laut	Ketepang
Pawpaw flowers	*Carica papaya*	Seram Laut	Sebrang

Table 7.2. Voyage times within archipelagic Southeast Seram

From	To	Type of Transport	Time (in minutes)	Date
Kilwaru	Geser	Jonson	15	January 1981
Kilwaru	Geser	*Lepa-lepa* (sail)	15+	January 1981
Kilfura	Geser	*Lepa-lepa* (paddle)	22	April 1986
Kwaos	Air Nanang	Jonson	26	May 1986
Kilwaru	Keffing	*Lepa-lepa* (sail)	30–60	January 1981
Geser	Talang Baru	*Lepa-lepa* (paddle)	42	April 1986
Keta	Kwaos	*Lepa-lepa* (sail)	60	April 1986
Geser	Kilmuri	Jonson	60	January 1981
Warus-warus	Kilgah	Jonson	60	February 1981
Garogos	Kataloka	Jonson	60	May 1986
Geser	Kianlaut	Jonson	60	April 1986
Kwaos	Geser	Jonson	60	April 1986
Air Nanang	Geser	Jonson	65	May 1986
Kataloka	Garogos	Jonson	75	May 1986
Kilmoi	Bati-Saiye	Foot	90–120	February 1981
Geser	Warus-warus	Jonson	180	May 1986
Kataloka	Wisalen	*Lepa-lepa* (sail)	120	May 1986
Warus-warus	Kilgah	Foot	120	February 1981
Ondor	Geser	Jonson	150	April 1986
Geser	Garogos	Jonson	150	(Soselisa 1995:12)
Geser	Gorom	Motor laut	240	February 1981
Keta	Kwaos	*Lepa-lepa* (paddle)	240	April 1986
Keffing	Waru	Sailing boat	270	(Van der Crab 1864:548)
Geser	Kilmuri	*Ang kalulis*	660	January 1981
Garogos	Kilgah	*Ang kalulis*	3 days	(Soselisa 1995:168)

Butonese women come early in the morning to Geser from Seram Laut to sell green vegetables in the market, the source of virtually all fruit and vegetables on Geser. On Geser there are no limes or chilies and only enough coconuts for home consumption. The development of Geser as a multipurpose central place has eclipsed the direct trade between other nearby villages and rerouted it indirectly through Geser. Thus the inhabitants of Keffing in the past could obtain the food they needed through exchange with nearer villages, but nowadays prefer to travel to Geser, where there is more competition, more choice, and because it is often a destination for other (for example) administrative business and because they themselves wish to maximize their selling opportunities. Some idea of the pattern of origins of food on sale in Geser market can be gathered from Table 7.1, which lists types of food and their provenance for just one day in 1986. What is interesting to note about the provenances of these goods is that none is more than sixty-five minutes traveling time by jonson, and most are no more than forty-two minutes by *lepa-lepa* (Table 7.2).

The vessels used for such trips are now generally jonsons for all distances, though punted or sail-driven *lepa-lepa* may serve for shorter trips. The loads are extremely variable in types of cargo and overall weight. Indeed, in over twenty-five years of fieldwork in the Moluccas there is little I have not seen carried by *lepa-lepa* or jonson. An average jonson is capable of carrying at least three passengers, two or three sacks of nutmeg, living plant material, small animals, empty plastic bottles, and empty petrol or paraffin drums. Larger vessels, such as the *ang kalulis* and *angbot*, may also be used for this varied cargo but generally for more specialized purposes, such as transporting nutmeg from local producers in Kataloka to traders in Geser or to fetch firewood from Panjang and Manawoka to Samboru.

7.4. Trade between Island Groups

Most boat movements between island groups follow patterns that are consistent with what we know historically. Thus, in 1980 most registered boat movements into and out of Banda involved Geser, Tulehu, Fak-fak, Ambon, Surubaya, Kataloka, and Tehoru (Table 7.3), in decreasing order of importance. Of the sixty-four total destinations for boat movements from Banda

Table 7.3. Registered boat movements in and out of Banda Neira, 1980 (Kantor Syahbandar Register, Banda Neira)

Place of Origin/Destination	No. of Reported Boat Movements
Geser	75
Tulehu	62
Fak-fak	44
Ambon	43
Surabaya	35
Kataloka	34
Tehoru	25
Makassar	9
Air Kasar	8
Wetar	7
Locations with six movements during the year: Selayor, Undur, Afar	18
Locations with four movements during the year: Pulau Tuju (Ambon), Saparua, Kesui	12
Locations with three movements during the year: Bima, Tial-Ambon, Passo, Momake, Belis, Kilbat	18
Locations (43) with two or less movements during the year	51
Total	439

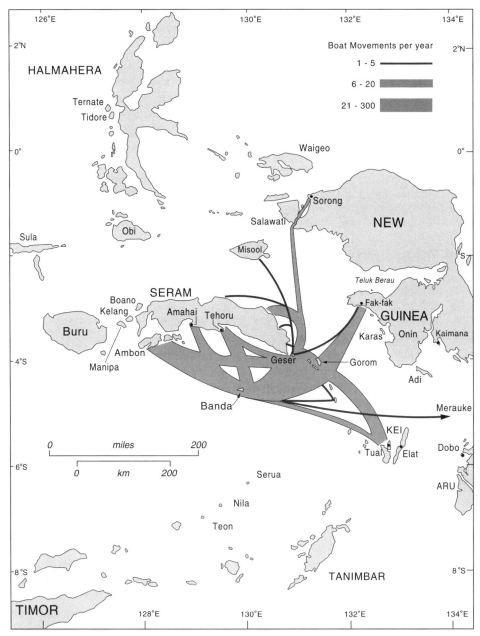

Figure 7.3. Density of registered boat movements in Southeast Seram region. Simplified representation based on Syahbandar reports for Geser (1985), Kataloka (1985), and Banda (1980).

in 1981, eighteen involved Southeast Seram links and two New Guinea, together constituting 31 percent of the total destinations. Of a total number of 435 voyages, 117 involved places in Southeast Seram and 66 New Guinea, together constituting 42 percent. In 1984, most registered boat movements in and out of Banda Neira involved Ambon, Geser, Tulehu, and Amahai, in decreasing order of importance. Of the seventeen recorded places involved in boat movements focused on Banda in 1984, five (29 percent) involved places in Southeast Seram and New Guinea. Of the total number of 202 voyages for which we have data, 51 (25 percent) involved places in Southeast Seram, Banda, or New Guinea. Similarly, for Kataloka in 1985 most movements involved Geser, Fak-fak, Tual, Bula, and Ambon. Of a total of twelve places involved in registered boat movements focused on Kataloka in 1985, four were in Southeast Seram, Banda, or New Guinea, constituting 33 percent of all places. Of the total number of 350 voyages registered in Kataloka for the same year, 196 (56 percent) involved places in Southeast Seram, New Guinea, or Banda. In 1985, most registered boat movements in and out of Geser involved Kataloka, Ambon, Bula, and Banda, in decreasing order of importance. Of the twenty-two recorded places involved in boat movements focused on Geser in 1985, nine were in Southeast Seram, Banda, or New Guinea (41 percent). Of the total number of 375 voyages for which we have data, 173 (46 percent) involved places in Southeast Seram, Banda, or New Guinea. The point is made graphically in Figure 7.3.

There is a strong seasonal pattern to boat movements between island groups, even for the workhorse diesel ferries (motor laut) that operate between Ambon Island and Geser. Motor vessels such as the *Sinar Manis* run from Tulehu to Geser, then on to Kataloka and Ondor, to Kesui and/or Teor, perhaps stopping off somewhere to pick up timber, and then back to Geser. This is the basic route, but particular itineraries vary with demand and season. In Geser, for example, the peaks for boat movements are September and February, and the troughs June–August and January (source: Office of Camat, Geser, 1980). Kino Atmojo, who owns some of the diesel ferries operating between Tulehu and Geser, told me in 1981 that sometimes there were four boats a week, but that this depends on the general trading situation and on the weather. By 1986 all Geser boats were going from Ambon city rather than Tulehu or Waai, an example of increasing centralization and bureaucratization, all departing (officially at least) at 10:00 P.M. The greatest number of departures, either to Tulehu or Ambon, occur in the clove season, when there is greatest demand for freight export and disposable income to allow people to travel. The time taken (Table 7.4) depends again on the weather, but also on the technical efficiency of individual craft (that is, during the period of this ethnographic study, the condition of the *Sinar Manis,* compared with the *Cemerlang* or *Purnama*). As can been seen from Figure 7.4, the February peak coincides with the first peak of copra and clove production, though the match between boat

Table 7.4. Voyage times between various Southeast Seram locations and locations outside the area

From	To	Type of Vessel	Time (in hours)
Samboru	Onin	*Ang kalulis*	12 (minimum)
Kataloka	Pulau Karas/Adi	Jonson	7 (minimum, 4)
Warus-warus	Fak-fak	Jonson	8
Dulak	Fak-fak	Jonson	12
Ondor	Banda	*Angbot*	12 (minimum, 48 maximum)
Geser	Tulehu	Motor laut	18
Geser	Waai	Motor laut	20
Geser	Ambon	Motor laut	18–22
Seram Laut	Banda	Sailing boat	36–48
Seram Laut	Ambon	*Angbot*	84–96

Note: All data are for 1986, except final two lines, which are from Bik (1928 [1824]:3).

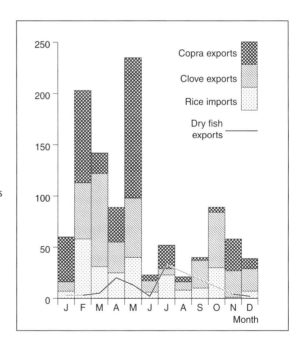

Figure 7.4. Fluctuation in import-export loads for selected commodities (in thousands of kilograms) by month, Geser, 1980. Dry fish exports are shown as a line graph where 10,000 kilograms on the bar chart scale = 1,000 kilograms. (Source: Office of Camat.)

movements and bulk weight of imported and exported goods is only approximate. This is explained in terms of the difficulty of matching harvests, nautical conditions, and optimal selling times.

Motorized craft, except in the clove and nutmeg seasons, return to Ambon or Banda with relatively little cargo and mostly passengers. The same is the case with sailing vessels. To take some actual examples: a lambo taking cement to Geser might bring back trepang, and another taking a cargo of paraffin from Tulehu to Gorom will return empty but with passengers, and Butonese who take sago to Ambon-Lease from Southeast Seram may come back empty from Buton itself. Some vessels carry a single cargo (say, parang blades from Binonko); others a combination of cargoes. Another might voyage to Ambon with passengers but be otherwise empty, though on the return voyage have picked up sago from Seram. Perahu are officially not permitted to carry passengers, but despite the regulation this remains relatively common in the Moluccas.

In 1981 official records listed copra, nutmeg, mace, lola, and trepang as the most important exports of the East Seram subdistrict. Lola increased from 23,000 metric tons in 1973 to 48,000 in 1977, and trepang decreased from 3,000 tons in 1975 to 1,270 in 1977. An increase in registered fishing boats from 147 in 1973 to 375 in 1977 probably reflects increase in population and in export of fish. Nutmeg production was 571,000 metric tons in 1971, rising to 718,000 in 1973 and 940,000 in 1976. It declined to 161,000 metric tons in 1977, rose to 520,000 in 1980, dipped to 250,250 in 1981, but rose dramatically again to 940,500 in 1982. Throughout this time the proportion of round to long nutmeg was appropriately 20–30 percent. The official export of timber rose from 10,300 metric tons in 1975 to 25,500 in 1977. There was also a threefold increase in passengers carried between 1973 and 1977. Copra production declined from 408,300 metric tons in 1971 to 268,000 in 1973, but rose again to 472,800 in 1980, and declined to 62,600 in 1982. Cloves declined from 48,600 to 43,000 metric tons between 1971 and 1973, but by 1980 had risen to 731,250, 482,370 in 1981, and 694,630 in 1982. Coffee, a new commodity, became important after 1974. The most important imports by weight are rice and sugar.[1] Trade between island groups is considered later in this chapter with reference to specific products.

In terms of total boat movements, the trade between archipelagic Southeast Seram and Banda (and onward from Banda) is still the densest in the zone (Figure 7.3). Most of this is entrepôt trade, using Banda as a staging post. However, Southeast Seram (particularly Kilmuri) remains important in supplying Banda with timber, sago, and coconut, though some sago and much other food now comes from Ambon and West Seram. As we have seen from chapters 3 and 4 (also Ellen 1979:68), sago imports to the Banda Islands (from Southeast Seram, Gorom, and to a lesser extent from Kei and Aru) have been quite considerable at various times in the past. Even thirty or forty years ago sago imports must have been more significant than they are now. Most sago arriving in Banda currently comes from "Geser" (sagu serang) and Gorom, usually brought by Butonese based in Banda. However, very little sago is currently imported to, or consumed in, the Banda Islands; the main staples are locally grown manioc and imported rice. No sago currently appears to be exported from the Aru Islands either (although it is traded from the New Guinea mainland to Dobo), nor from the Kei Islands.

There is some internal sago trade in the Kei group, but the main starch staple there is *enbal*, a variety of bitter manioc. The reasons for the decline in the Banda sago trade must include its price compared with rice and other starch staples. One *ikat* or laka of twenty small sagu lemping (biscuits) from Geser cost, for example, 150 rupiah on the island of Ai in 1981 (compared with 50 rupiah on Geser itself), and a small tumang (cask) 500 rupiah (compared with 250 rupiah on Geser). Also significant must be the demise of Banda as a source of trade objects for the periphery, the declining significance of the nutmeg trade, and the decline of the estate system since 1940, all of which have necessitated a shift back from plantation silviculture to subsistence horticulture and fishing. With this has come the planting of more starch staples.

7.5. Long-Distance Commerce

In 1981 Badaruddin Sohilau of Samboru on Gorom could still recall his grandfather taking an *angbot* stacked with sago to Bali. However, by the time of that recollection long-distance sailing routes between Java and the Moluccas had long been dominated by Butonese vessels and the motorized traffic along the same routes by predominantly Chinese traders. As we have seen in chapter 4, the Butonese had acquired supremacy with the decline of Bugis involvement in trade east of Sulawesi. But because the Butonese have tended to concentrate on lambos of less than 50 cubic meters this has meant that a carrying vessel (that is, one used or hired out to carry cargoes from A to B) is not as profitable as a trading vessel (that is, one that peddles between settlements). To make economic sense in the carrying trade, vessels of 200 cubic meters or more are desirable (Dick 1975:100). This, then, has tended to dictate patterns of operation.

In general terms, cargoes comprise either bahan pokok (general cargo) (that is, standard items of low value such as rice) and barang kelontongan (mixed peddling cargo). There are three types of general cargo trade: activity where freight earnings are less important than profits on resale; "carrying on inducement," calling in at ports on journeys in the hope of securing cargo or journeys to places where vessels might obtain freight; and "liner trade" where larger vessels carry 25 tons of bottom cargo (sugar, salt, cement—but not rice) and assorted goods on top (ibid.). This latter mode of operation is of less relevance to the contemporary situation in the Moluccas, and Southeast Seram in particular. Although long-distance trade using sailing vessels is still of considerable importance, there is a long-term decline not only in the volume of cargoes and number of movements, but in the value of the goods involved. Far fewer of the major merchants either use or own sailing boats, and the cargoes are of an increasingly marginal kind (such as empty bottles or oil drums).

Sailing vessels currently used in the long-distance trade are either based in Buton itself (that is, in Southeast Sulawesi) or in the Moluccas, where they are mostly (though not exclusively) owned by traders of Butonese origin. The vessels operating routes between the Southeast Seram area and other major centers and operating the Seram-Banda-Java run mainly belong to owners domiciled in Banda and the Buton Islands. According to the 1978 Banda register, sixty-nine vessels were in that year operating from Banda, mostly owned by people with Butonese names (forty-five) and the remainder by a mixture of Arab and Chinese and other local owners. Only one vessel was owned by someone from East Seram (Rumfut). All of the vessels were classified as lambos, and all except one was a sailing vessel (this was a motorized perahu). The average age of vessels was nine years (a minimum of one year and a maximum of twenty) and the average size was 31.32 cubic meters (a minimum of 6.30 and a maximum of 86.89).[2]

In the months preceding April (and between March and May), vessels from Buton (often empty) sail to the Moluccas in search of cargoes to take to Java, putting in at various places along the coast of Seram. During this (the east monsoon [musim timur]), the Banda Islands become quite deserted by the local Butonese male crews, who move out to seek cargoes of wood, nutmeg, copra, and trepang in South and Southeast Seram (Tehoru, Geser, Gorom) and occasionally as far away as the New Guinea coast. The cargoes are then taken westward along the south coast of Seram, Tulehu, Ambon, and Buru (usually Leksula) and across to Buton (especially Wana, Wanci, and Bau Bau); the last stage of this voyage takes about six days and six nights. Crews may remain in the Buton "home" settlements for some time before sailing on to either Surabaya or Gresik via Salayor (a voyage of about two weeks' duration), where the cargoes are discharged. Boats may spend between twenty days and one month in Java before returning with rice, cement, and other manufactured goods via Bali, Lombok, Sumbawa, Flores, the north coast of Timor, and then striking north to Banda. There are variations on this basic route. Vessels returning to Banda may stop off at places such as Babar and Wetar to pick up water and food, and vessels based at the large Butonese settlement at Leksula travel directly north to Buru, avoiding Banda altogether. The entire round-trip is made once or twice a year; traveling either way it may take between fourteen and twenty days. However, traveling east in the east monsoon may take up to one month, compared with two weeks for the west monsoon.

Though most of the boats and crews are Butonese (there are some native Moluccan crew members), the cargoes are largely owned by Chinese traders. During the east monsoon (around May) traders on Banda travel to Surabaya to sell cargoes and buy goods for the return journey. Nowadays they may either accompany the vessels that carry their cargo, ship or perahu, or fly. They are generally back in Banda by July. A similar pattern obtains with traders based in other centers in Southeast Seram. During the west monsoon the sailing conditions allow them to go to Ambon, but no farther. As Dick (1975: 86) explains, by mid-April there are large numbers of perahus awaiting cargoes and instructions to make the voyage to Surabaya, but traders are reluctant to consign goods until the East monsoon has arrived, at which point they can reasonably calculate the period of time for which they will require credit and the freight rate that they can afford, taking into account prices in Makassar and Surabaya and the cost of transport. If the perahu makes a quick passage, then the profits will be high; if the passage is slow, then there will perhaps be a loss. An owner captain has to see a short-term balance of payments, if not a profit, and the unit of account is the voyage. Only big owners can afford to run a deficit on a particular voyage, on the assumption that this might be made up subsequently. Profits are distributed as follows: the person who advances the capital receives 50 percent and the crew (including the captain) receives equal shares of the rest. Costs, such as harbor taxes, gifts for officials, and the ship's share of one-twelfth, are deducted beforehand. In some cases the total proceeds are used to buy new goods.

Evers (1988:94–95), who looked at Butonese traders operating in Moluccan waters from the Buton end, reported 169 lambos owned by people on Wangi-wangi. Captains and crew working the Moluccan routes generally know the headman of villages where they trade. Orders are often placed in advance, and long-lasting relationships develop. Some traders buy or rent land in the villages of their trading partners, establishing clove or other plantations, practices that in the past have often triggered patterns of migration, as in the case of Seram Laut. Evers considered as an example the case of Haji Ibrahim of Pongo on Wangi-wangi. Haji Ibrahim owns a twenty-ton lambo that he and his crew built for themselves. In January 1983, with a crew of six and borrowing some cash from relatives, he sailed for Banda with a cargo of household goods, cement, and textiles bought in Surabaya on a previous voyage. After ten days they arrived in Banda but decided to go on to Gorom and Watubela, where they traded their mixed merchandise for nutmeg. By mid-April, at the start of the northeast monsoon, they had 12 tons of nutmeg and 1 ton of mace. They took six days and nights to return to Wangi-wangi, stayed with their families for ten days, and then continued to Makassar, taking a further two days:

> When they contacted Chinese traders in the market they were dismayed to learn that the price of nutmeg had dropped considerably. After haggling and waiting for two weeks they decided, after long deliberations among the crew, to cut their losses and to sell at a lower price. . . . They had bought 15 ton of nutmeg at Rp 175 a kilogram, which they had to sell for Rp. 150 a kilogram. Losses due to price fluctuations occur occasionally, but usually profits are made and distributed. . . . In this case the total proceeds were used to buy new goods, among others rice, cement, household goods (. . .) and fashionable furniture. With this cargo they returned to their home

village . . . without, however, discharging it. In June they set sail again and arrived after four days and five nights at Pulau Dowora at the southern tip of Halmahera. Here they started to trade their goods around the villages on the various islands for about four months. Because of the earlier loss they decided not to buy any spices, but to return to their village. . . . They arrived safely in the first week of November, hauling the sailing ship up onto the beach for repairs, distributed their profits which amounted to about Rp. 25000 per crew member and dispersed. (Ibid.)

For a different economic analysis of a series of lambo voyages based in one Butonese settlement in Southeast Sulawesi see Southon (1995:78–88).

7.6. Trade in Different Kinds of Commodities

In terms of the commodities involved it is convenient to divide contemporary trade in archipelagic Southeast Seram into five kinds: the fish-for-sago exchange, trade in other subsistence products, trade in maritime export products, trade in tree products, and trade in locally manufactured goods. Bulk food imports and industrially produced goods from outside Southeast Seram are excluded. This division is not perfect, but it does provide a useful framework for organizing the accompanying data. Locally, a clear distinction is made between hasil laut (sea produce) and hasil darat (land produce), which provides a basis for specialization both among producers and traders. In general terms, the trade in tree products is rising at the expense of maritime products, and most important among these until the late 1980s was cloves. In the account that follows I have used English terms for products when it is likely that these are widely known and thereafter used the Indonesian or Moluccan Malay terms that predominate in commerce (e.g., lola or batu laga).

FISH-FOR-SAGO EXCHANGE

The mainstay of subsistence trade in archipelagic Southeast Seram is the classic fish-for-sago nexus. Before Geser became a permanent colony of nonsubsistence traders and administrators, exchange of sago for (mainly dried) fish was conducted entirely through barter, the specific mechanics of which is explored in chapter 8. The introduction of money changed this, though barter remains a major medium of trade between Bati villages in the interior of Seram and coastal villages, and between the villages of the large sago-producing areas of Southeast Seram and the fishing islands of Seram Rei, Kiltai, Geser, Garogos, Kidang, and Kifar, and even farther south in the Gorom group.

  The main sago-producing and export areas are on mainland Seram, currently particularly Warus-warus (where it is the second most important trade product), Kiandarat, Kwaos, Gah, and the domain of Kilmuri (especially the Dawan area), which has the largest reserves. Most sago is planted and owned but may sometimes be collected (by, for example, highland Bati) from the extensive area of noncultivated palms found in the Masiwang swamp forest basin. In most cases, however, palms are more accessible, being no more than 1.5 kilometers from a village, and in theory available all year round for trade, though heavy rainfall may interfere with levels of extraction.

Overall, most of the archipelago is a net importer of sago and a net exporter of fish. There are, however, exceptions to this apparently complementary ecological division of labor. Thus, of the islands, Seram Laut exports small quantities of sago to Geser, as does Manawoka. There are small groves of sago on Gorom, and not only are Dai and Miran self-sufficient in sago, people even come from elsewhere to purchase it, and small quantities are traded along the New Guinea coast. But although in the past Gorom as a whole may have produced sufficient sago for local needs, expansion of nutmeg plantations has eliminated suitable land. On the mainland, too, there are exceptional sago-deficient areas, especially Kwamar, which because of its physical isolation in the mangrove area has had to make special arrangements for access to sago and garden land in other parts of the jurisdiction of the raja of Urung. As has been noted, some sago is still traded beyond the Geser-Gorom zone, to Banda and New Guinea, and also to Saumlaki in Tanimbar. There is even direct export from some localities on mainland East Seram (such as Dinama) to Jakarta and Surabaya, which is said to yield profits of up to 40 percent. This has echoes of the ancient trade reported for Bali and Timor (Broersma 1934:339).

Sago is produced for trade in two forms: as tumang, casks of damp sago flour (*bai*) bound in sago leaves, and as lemping (*suat*), biscuits cooked in an earthenware oven (Figure 7.5). The Geser tumang is smaller than its Ambonese equivalent; the former weighs 6 kilograms and the latter 15. Large tumang, of similar size to those produced in Ambon-Lease, are also found locally in Kilmuri. The east coast of Seram produces mainly small lemping and tumang, as does also Bitorik and Undur on the south coast. A small tumang from Warus-warus cost 250 rupiah in 1981 (elsewhere 350 rupiah) and a large tumang 500 rupiah. There are also two kinds of lemping. A small variety is traded as an *ikat* of twenty biscuits that weighs eight ons (800 grams), and an *ikat* of twenty biscuits of the larger variety (as, for example, is produced in Kilfura) weighs about 2 kilograms. In 1981 an *ikat* of the smaller type cost 50 rupiah, and the larger 100 rupiah; by 1986 the former was 100 rupiah and the latter 500 rupiah. Most of the sago trade within archipelagic Southeast Seram and between this area and Banda and New Guinea is in lemping, but there is also some tumang trade. Some localities specialize in producing either tumang or lemping, a specialization that must be a response to the demands of the trade. In 1981 Gah special-

Figure 7.5. Sago biscuits (*suat*) drying in the sun, domain of Ondor, Gorom, 20 May 1986.

ized almost entirely in lemping, and Warus-warus mostly lemping but some small tumang. Similarly, localities vary in their preferences in terms of sago consumption; sago porridge (pepeda), for example, is rarely eaten in Kataloka, perhaps through force of circumstance, and in Namalomin there is a general preference for large tumang and therefore for trading with the south coast rather than east-coast villages of mainland Seram.

Particular island settlements have customary links with particular sago-producing areas. Individual traders and places on the mainland maintain long-term links with settlements in the archipelago, such as Inina with Geser, Gah with Kilwaru, Kiltai and Kelu with Kwaos, Afar with Garogos, Keffing with Air Nanang, Kilfura with Bitorik, Samboru with Dawan, Air Kasar with Kataloka, and so on. Kwaos, despite exchanging fish with a number of sago-producing localities and despite being situated on the coast, experiences regular fishing shortfalls and therefore also exchanges sago for fish from Keffing and Namalomin. Farther up the east coast, mountain Bati villages exchange sago for fish from Warus-warus and Kilmoi. Some places, such as Kilmuri, rely on selling sago for their main source of cash and also export (via Butonese traders) directly to villages in the Ambon-Lease group. But, as the following case illustrates, traditional relations between sago-producing and fishing villages may also be extremely sensitive to market-related conditions:

> In May 1986 Sadaruddin Rumakei and his brother from Namalomin voyaged to Seram to acquire sago. They first went to Afang, where there was little sago available, and only small tumang rather than the larger ones they preferred, and those too highly priced. They then moved on to other places—Kilbon and Kilmuri—where they were able to buy tumang for 500 rupiah each, which they later sold in Gorom and Kesui for 1,000 rupiah. Their *ang kalulis* can carry a

cargo of 400 tumang (that is worth some 200,000 rupiah). With an average wind two journeys can be made a month. Between months five and seven winds tend to be good; and with a good wind it is possible to voyage three times a month. With a good wind, if you depart Gorom early in the morning, you can be in Afang by afternoon, and need only be away for two or three days. One tumang can provision a large family for two days. The preference for larger tumang, and also the inhibitory factor of distance means that most sago is bought from south-coast villages. (Ellen, field notes, 1986)

Fish-for-sago transactions can take place in three ways: (a) sago purchasers may travel to production localities, (b) sago producers may visit sago-deficient areas, or (c) the trade may be entirely in the hands of middlemen. In each case different kinds of barter and cash exchange may occur, sometimes simultaneously.

Consumers from sago-deficient areas travel to production locations, mainly on mainland Seram, situated in a wide arc stretching between Waru in the north and Kilmuri in the south. For example, residents of Kilwaru collect sago from Gah using their own boats. Goromese going to Seram to obtain sago often buy fish on Garogos on the way. Some consumers simply barter or purchase with money sago that has already been processed. Some consumers may have preexisting rights to sago palms in particular areas, through kinship or affinal links. Thus, Arsad Rumonin of Geser Kampung Baru has sago at Kianlaut (Kau Islam) and Kilmuri (Wolo). Some people purchase trees and process the sago themselves. Transportation is varied. Individual households may collect enough for themselves utilizing a *lepa-lepa*. Others use an *ang kalulis* or *angbot* (for example, Kepata Kelirei, the raja of Dai, or Badaruddin Sohilau of Samboru) to fetch not only a large supply for themselves and their kin, but sufficient to trade with at home or on the route home. Those who process the sago themselves usually pay the owner of the tree by giving him three out of every ten tumang produced (the ratio is 7 to 3). Others still may purchase entire trees and hire local people to process it. This is common in Kelu, where local people claim not to have the technical expertise to harvest sago. In this situation the person hired receives three tumang out of every ten produced. Therefore, where a purchaser has to pay both the owner and a processor, almost half that produced may be lost in payment to others. Most palms yield between ten and twenty tumang, but a large tree can yield as many as fifty. Where sago is processed immediately into lemping, 1 meter of palm trunk is reckoned to yield 1,000 small lemping, and two men working from 7:00 A.M. to noon can cut sufficient sago for 2,000 lemping.

Sago may also be hawked around the islands by mainland Seram producers, using their own vessels or hiring Butonese boats that they accompany (for example in Kilmuri and Selor). In 1986 a vendor from Kilmuri paid transit costs of 200 rupiah per large tumang, though he received 1,000 rupiah for the same tumang sold in Ambon or Saparua. In the Ambon-Lease villages sago from Southeast Seram is sold directly to the public, and in Ambon and Saparua markets to traders. In this way Kilmuri sago in 1986 was being sold not only in Ambon and Saparua, but also on Gorom, Pulau Panjang, Geser, and Manawoka, though not Seram Laut. Tumang sago is the most important source of cash in Kilmuri; between eighty and one thousand large tumang (at 5 kilograms a tumang) are carried at a time depending on the size of the vessel.

Much of the middleman trade has traditionally been in the hands of local people on the small islands between the mainland and Gorom (for example, the fishermen of Kidang), who use the traditional vessel for this trade, the *ang kalulis*. However, this is a niche that Butonese have increasingly moved into. Butonese buy sago directly in Warus-warus and take it to Surabaya, as well as taking lemping to Bula, Gorom, Kesui, and Teor. In addition, some sago (and dried fish) is distributed through general retail outlets, usually those owned by Chinese dealers also involved in the regional dry fish trade to Ambon and the sago trade to Banda.

In addition to the trade in sago flour, there is a lesser trade in other sago palm products: thatch (atap) and the woody leaf stalks (*alaba*, gabar-gabar), both still used extensively for house building in the Moluccas. The trade in both of these, though, much decreased during the twentieth century, and in places where the trade in thatch was once important for export (e.g., Kilmuri) it had effectively ceased by 1986. There is still some export from Kiandarat and Kianlaut to Geser of both thatch and woody leaf stalks, but this too has declined. Some thatch continues to be exported from Seram to Banda, but the supply cannot meet demand, making it expensive even by comparison with corrugated zinc roofing. In 1981 a one meter piece of thatch cost 50 rupiah and one hundred pieces 5,000 rupiah. A small house would need about two hundred pieces (10,000 rupiah) and a larger house about one thousand pieces (that is, 50,000 rupiah), allowing for the necessary large overlap in both cases.

TRADE IN OTHER SUBSISTENCE PRODUCTS

In addition to fish exchanged directly for sago in the Southeast Seram zone, there is an independent fish trade (fresh, dried, and salted) both locally and for export farther afield. Thus, Geser consumes more fish than it can itself harvest and relies on imports of fresh fish from, mainly, Kiltai and Seram Rei. The most important fish of trade is the barred garfish (*neba*, ikan julung). Julung is a speciality of Keffing fishermen and sometimes Amarsekaru and Gorom. If Keffing fishermen make a large catch they may drop part of it off on Garogos, where women will get about a third of the amount they agree to take to smoke. Alternatively, a woman who takes four *waya* of *neba* (Figure 7.6) for sale will get two for herself. The distribution mechanisms for julung are explored in further detail in chapter 8. In the

Figure 7.6. Frame (*waya ikan*) of palala fish (*Selar boops*), for sale in kiosk in Elat market, Kei Besar, 16 March 1981.

Gorom group, Amarsekaru is perhaps the most important center for fish production, particularly julung, though Pulau Panjang is also a net exporter of fish of all kinds, to Kataloka.

Outside the Southeast Seram area, smoked and salt fish is exported to Werinama, Tehoru, Masohi, Ambon, and elsewhere, being taken either by the producers themselves or by itinerant traders, operating from owned or hired perahu or traveling on scheduled ferry services. Of those settlements involved in the direct julung trade Kilmoi is prominent. Alternatively, fish is purchased locally by traders from those places. The pattern does not appear to have changed much since it was reported by Van Bruijnis (1933:53) for the first decades of the twentieth century; he mentions traders from Keffing, Waru, Hote, Kilgah, and Kilwou selling fish directly in Ambon and the Uliassers. Until the collapse in the market in cloves during the 1980s, this was largely a trade of the clove harvesting season in these parts of the southern Seram littoral, when potential buyers are flush with cash. Despite the costs of preparation, salt or smoked fish can command a better price and profit than fresh fish, which must be sold quickly. There is a high demand for *tehar* (*Lethrinus ornatus*) and *ngelngeli* (ikan kakatua, *Scarus* sp.) as salted fish. Ikan teri (anchovy) is the next important species in interisland trade after smoked julung and is caught nearly every day on Keffing. Salted fish is sold by Garogos fishermen to middlemen living on the island or directly to people on Geser, Gorom, or Fak-fak. Salt used to be made locally but is now imported, a vital ingredient for salt fish. In Ambon market in 1981 I found smoked julung and also ikan kakatua from Geser and maki (herrings) from Warus-warus, plus Butonese traders from Geser selling whale meat at 2,000 rupiah a kilogram.

In section 7.3 I have already touched on the volume and breadth of local interisland trade in fruit and vegetables in the Seram Laut Archipel-ago and adjacent parts of the mainland. Geser, Seram Rei, Kiltai, and the smaller reef settlements of the Seram Laut arc (Garogos, Kidang, and Kifar) are obviously the main importers, and the main exporters are Seram Laut and the immediately adjacent coastal settlements of mainland Seram, as far north as Kianlaut and as far west as Undur. This is obviously a pattern that goes back centuries, though we might expect political and economic shifts in the archipelago to have influenced the details. In the last one hun-dred years, the pattern has been affected by the increasing centralization of emporium trade and administration on Geser, and the way the Butonese settlements of Seram Laut have come to dominate supply to Geser. What is striking, however, is the small role of mainland Seram in supplying these food-deficient areas in produce other than sago. Part of the reason for this is the intervening mangroves, which means that the nearest realistic sup-pliers are an hour or more away; but another factor is wild pig predation on mainland gardens, which in some cases has led to virtual abandonment of horticulture but which in many reduces surpluses over what is required for local consumption to a minimum. Finally, there are the costs of travel, which often make the marketing of produce with such a narrow profit mar-gin uneconomical.

Although self-sufficient in most fruit and vegetables, the Southeast Seram Archipelago, unlike most local trading zones in the Moluccas, does not produce enough palm sugar (from *Arenga saccharifera*) for its own needs. Some is produced locally (for example, in Kwaos) but is hardly traded. Most is imported from Bula, Masohi in South Seram, Ullath on Saparua, or even Makassar. An alternative sweetener, honey, is exported from Kilmuri and Afang. Cinnamon is exported from Kwaos.

Apart from food, the other significant item of daily need upon which the food-deficient center is dependent is firewood. This is mainly man-grove, an excellent slow-burning, high-temperature fuel that also makes high-quality charcoal. The principal suppliers, not surprisingly, are those settlements on the fringes of the mangrove area: to some extent Air Nanang, but predominantly Kwamar, whose entire economy rests on the export of firewood by virtue of an absence of sago and a shortage of land suitable for cultivation. Mangrove is cut green into logs roughly 6–8 cen-timeters in diameter and 213 centimeters long, which were being sold for about 250 rupiah each in 1986. The bark is removed and sold separately as a much cheaper fuel. Alternatively, branches are sold by the *panga-panga* (pile), with one hundred cut pieces costing around 100 rupiah. It is difficult to judge to what extent extraction of mangrove for fuel is sustainable, but there is evident depletion of mangrove fringes on Seram Laut and long-term historical evidence to suggest that formerly the mainland mangrove system was much more extensive than it is now; indeed once incorporating what is now the separate island of Seram Rei. For those poorer, fire-wood-deficient islands that stretch out eastward toward Gorom, such as Garogos, fuel is obtained as driftwood, from the uninhabited islands of Kun and Nedin, and sometimes collected with agreement from Panjang.

There has almost certainly been a historic decline in the significance of trade in forest products on mainland East Seram, partly due to a fall in demand and partly due to the relocation of former inland settlements that once relied on this trade along the coast. Damar and rattan were, for example, important in the first three decades of the twentieth century (Van Bruijnis 1933:54). A little damar was being harvested around Suru and Keta in 1981, much less according to local collectors than had been harvested by the previous generation. Warus-warus exports some rattan to Geser. In some places, timber extraction is significant. Timber, for example. is the second most important trade product in Kilmuri and is dominated by buyers from Banda, Tehoru, Ambon, and Saparua. Timber is the fourth most important cash earner in Warus-warus, most of which is extracted on commission from outside traders and transported on Butonese-owned vessels to Ambon and New Guinea, though some is marketed by local people. Timber is imported from Urung to Geser for local use. The timber situation in the Gorom Archipelago is more complex. Gorom itself is timber-deficient and must, for example, import large kayu besi for house building from Seram, though there is some trade in timber from Amarsekaru to Ondor and even export of timber from Gorom to Pantaseru in the Banda Islands for boat building.

Of the nontimber forest products, the one consistently mentioned by traders in 1981 and 1986 was dried meat (dengdeng), most of which is venison. Much of this comes from inland highland settlements and is exported through Warus-warus, Urung, Guli-guli, and Kilmuri. Kufar (in the Masiwang area) and Bula export to the New Guinea coast. Some moves through Geser, destined for Ambon, but most goes directly to Ambon, where it is a feature of local markets. Dried pig meat (dengdeng babi) is exported from Gauer-Kristen directly to Ambon, to avoid offending Muslim sensibilities. We find the same kind of markup between fresh and dried meat as we find with fish (500 rupiah per kilogram for fresh venison as opposed to 1,500 rupiah for the same of dengdeng). The same logic applies: the fresh product has to be disposed of quickly, which forces the price down, despite its greater desirability as an item of consumption.

TRADE IN MARITIME EXPORT PRODUCTS

The trade in maritime export products is mainly a speciality of the central zone and the islands to the southeast. Even there production for exchange is patchy. In Ondor there is little maritime produce, though Kataloka includes the important reefs around Garogos.

The harvesting of trepang has already been discussed in chapter 4, so I shall restrict myself here to just a few remarks on its geographic distribution and role in contemporary trade. Trepang is particularly important for Kelu (where it was the second most important commodity by total value in 1986) and in Keffing, Kilwaru, Kiltai, Kilfura, and other places on Seram Laut. Although there is said to be plenty of commercially extractable trepang off parts of the mainland coast, it is not an important commodity there, except perhaps for Urung. The reason for this may simply be the marginal benefits that other commodities attract. The jurisdiction of Urung over trepang-bearing reefs extends to Kwamar, and an arrangement between the rajas of Keffing and Urung allows the people of Keffing to collect along its shores. Kiltai can collect on Kilwaru reefs, because there are not enough people in Kilwaru to do it. On Gorom, some trepang is collected from the Samboru reef, though most is collected on Garogos, which is, as we have seen, part of the domain of Kataloka, though physically part of the Seram Laut reef system.

The cured produce is sold either directly to itinerant traders or through the Chinese traders of Geser, who sell it in Ambon. In Kilwaru in 1981 trepang was fetching between 800 and 2,000 rupiah a kilogram. In the same year local traders were paying Keffingese 500 rupiah for 1 kilogram of large trepang (approximately four trepang to the kilogram) and 400 rupiah for one kilogram of smaller trepang (about eight trepang to the kilogram). A lot of the price variation depends on the species of trepang offered. In 1986 children using borrowed tackle were selling trepang batu for 500 rupiah each to a Kiltai owner of a *dafi-dafi kebi* (trepang dryer). On Garogos in 1986 *kebi sisir* and *kebi metan* were commanding 400 rupiah each. Local traders such as the owner of Toko Danny in Geser often have an arrangement with a merchant in Java. Traders coming from Jakarta leave a storage container (*makala*), which is filled and later collected. The trepang is sometimes taken straight to Jakarta. Although the Toko Danny trader could get 2,000 rupiah for 1 kilogram of *kebi deduran* in 1986, he could get 4,000 rupiah for the same if sold to a visiting Javanese trader. *Kebi metan, kebi farai,* and *kebi futi* were even more profitable in 1986, at 8,000 rupiah a kilogram. In the same year traders were paying 3,500 rupiah per kilogram of *kebi bas* and about 7,500 rupiah for a kilogram of *kebi farai*. A century earlier Riedel (1886:166–170) reported nine marketable types of trepang from the waters around Seram Laut. It is interesting that the first three of these, in declining value, are *kebi metan, kebi farai,* and *kebi deduran; kebi bas* comes in at number nine. Thus, apart from the rise in the significance of *kebi bas,* this suggests a remarkable constancy in the marketable types and their relative prices (Table 4.1).

Although trepang prices were good in 1986 there is an evident decline in the trade reflecting decreasing availability of the most desirable species. Moreover, many traders in Geser will not handle it, as they say they have neither the special skills nor the capital required. The demand has risen since 1980, and since 1988 the number of types of marketable trepang has risen from five to twelve. Problems of availability have encouraged use of *sasi*, ritually sanctioned closed and open seasons, which ration access while the population is restored. In 1986 a *sasi* trepang was operating in Keffing and also Kelu-Kwaai. An enormous amount was being processed on Keffing in April 1986, for as long as the *sasi* remained open.

The shell of *Trochus niloticus* (lola, *lolak wawina*) and japing-japing (black lips, *sika dafi*, asa rak, a kind of mother-of-pearl) is particularly important for Kilwaru, Garogos, Gorom, Kilfura, and other places on Seram Laut (from where it is taken directly to traders on Geser). In some places, such as Kelu, lola and japing-japing meat is eaten; the animals are harvested from a depth of 7 meters, boiled, and dried for storage. Lola is one of the most important trade items in Kilwaru, Kilfura, and Amarsekaru and on Gorom, Panjang, Watubela, Teor, and Kesui. In Kataloka, lola is taken from a particular area once every three years and then only if the shells are above a certain size. In 1981 1 kilogram of lola (approximately two mature shells) earned Keffingese 800 rupiah. In 1986 lola was yielding 18,000 rupiah per kilogram for producers on Garogos, but dropped to 7,000 per kilogram in 1992 after an attempt by the government to curtail production to conserve the resource. The Toko Harapan Baru in Geser was buying lola at 1,700 rupiah per kilogram in 1986 and japing-japing at 1,000 rupiah a kilogram. *Lolak urana* (*Tectus pyrarimis*) fetched 300–500 rupiah per kilogram in 1992 (Soselisa 1995:173). Batu laga or green snail (*argas*) is as important as lola on Teor, Watubela, and Kesui; and mata bulan shell (white eye, various species of *Turbo*) is harvested regularly in Gofa (near Urung) and Amarsekaru and on Teor, Kesui, Watubela, and Panjang. In 1981 batu laga in Ambon was fetching a higher price than lola: whereas 1 kilogram of lola could yield 1,000 rupiah for a trader from Southeast Seram, 1 kilogram of batu laga could yield as much as 2,500 rupiah. In 1986 the white eye from the New Guinea coast was fetching 1,000 rupiah a kilogram in Kataloka. Abalone (*Haliotes asinina*) is important locally (for example, on Garogos). Demand rose after 1983 to 6,000 rupiah a kilogram and in 1992 stood at 18,000–20,000 rupiah, rising to 28,000 in 1993. One kilogram represents about one hundred to two hundred shellfish, though for trade the meat must first be removed from the shell, salted, left to stand for between 0.5 and 2 days, boiled for up to an hour, and dried in the sun for another 2–3 days. The shell is also sometimes sold. Giant clams (*Tridacna* and *Hippopus* spp.: *falangaru*) are also collected for trade in Garogos.

Various kinds of seaweed are important as food and in commerce. In the 1920s annual agar-agar (variously *Gracilaria lichenoides, Eucheuma spinosum,* and *E. edule*) production in the Geser area was in the region of 100,000 kilograms a year (Beversluis and Gieben 1929:188). It continued to be important during the period of World War II, but had declined dramatically by 1981. This may be due partly to demand, but certainly (despite *sasi* regulation) also to overextraction and harvesting by pulling out entire plants rather than by simply harvesting the uppermost filaments. By 1981 the Departemen Perikanan and LIPI (Lembaga Ilmu Pengetahuan Indonesia [Indonesian Institute of Sciences]) had attempted to reestablish agar-agar beds in the vicinity of Kiltai by planting it in special receptacles, but these had already been broken by the time of my first fieldwork. By 1986 most of the agar-agar beds had disappeared.

The main agar-agar–producing locations are Keffing, Kilwaru, Garogos, Geser, and Seram Laut. It is now, however, only collected occasionally to order, usually on Garogos. December is the agar-agar season, and once harvested it is dried for about three days, steamed, dried again, washed in seawater to draw out any remaining salt through osmosis, and dried yet again for another four days, by which time it is white. The costs of preparation for sale are therefore high and entirely the work of women and children. Prices in 1992 ranged between 250 and 500 rupiah a kilogram, but seaweed generally in the last decade of the twentieth century was in little demand (Soselisa 1995:148).

A related alga, sangu-sangu *(Hypnea cervicornis)*, is finer and smaller than agar-agar and is less widely distributed. It is collected mainly during the season of predominantly southerly winds and prepared by drying for three to four days, soaking in lime and saltwater, washing, drying again for another four days, and forming into balls for sale. In 1992 it was selling at between 100 and 150 rupiah a ball. Other sea plants (not all algae) have local value as food, especially in vegetable-deficient areas. There is *keor* (a kind of sea grass or rumput laut) found along sandy coasts, gorogan (*girogan*, a seaweedlike herb with small bladders), *beribun, lumut-lumut* (a kind of sea lettuce harvested in the west monsoon), *kakinu ain* and *latar* (other edible seaweeds eaten raw with pepper and lemon), and *samu-samut* (eaten locally mixed with cinnamon and sugar), which I have seen being processed in Kilwaru.

Turtles are important in many places, both the soft-shelled edible turtles (*henu*, tuturuga) including the leatherback (*fenu kotan tulu* = "three backs"), *Dermochelyes coriacea,* and the green turtle (*henu*, tuturuga), *Chelonia mydas*; and the hard-shelled turtles, the hawksbill, *Eretmochelys imbricata*, and the loggerhead, *Caretta caretta* (*eran*, keran, keran guar, *kura-kurafenu*), valued for their carapace. Turtling is mainly an activity of the west monsoon and, for export purposes at least, focused on the Seram Laut area (especially Kilwaru, Maar, and Kilfura) and around Garogos and Kidang. There is also evidence of less significant opportunistic harvesting for trade elsewhere, even as far north as Warus-warus on the mainland coast. Buying and selling mainly takes place in Geser or Kataloka, though transactions may also take place elsewhere between local producers and traveling (particularly Butonese) traders. Both types of turtles are purchased by Butonese, who take them to Buton, Bali, and Surabaya (often live, packed in ice).

The meat of soft-shelled turtles is dried by traders and sold as dengdeng. Green turtles are brought by Garogos fishermen to Kidang, where they are penned until a buyer comes, previously Butonese from Wanci in Southeast Sulawesi. Edible turtles of 63 centimeters width may fetch 17,000 rupiah and those less than that 8,000–10,000 rupiah. In Geser, where they are eaten, they cost between 5,000 and 10,000 rupiah each in 1992, depending on size (Soselisa 1995:178). Scutes are often removed from the living hard-shelled turtles through the application of heat. In 1986 a large hawksbill in Kilfura fetched 50,000 rupiah. Prices in 1992 ranged between 5,000 and 150,000 depending on the pattern. The shell fetching the highest prices is patterned hawksbill or soft young shell (*fenu galepang*).

There are a few dugong (*Dugong dugong, matabulan*) around the coasts, mainly in the area between Seram Laut and Garogos, living off sea grass beds. Dugong are hunted from Maar, usually in the west monsoon, using harpoon, often once they have been trapped in a sero. The tears (air mata) command a price as Chinese medicine, either neat or mixed with wangi-wangi (perfumed coconut oil). The ivory is sold immediately or carved into smoking pipes. The meat is not eaten locally.

Shark fins and tails are important in a few places, such as Kilwaru and Garogos. The tail of the white shark (*oi kulfeit*) fetches the highest prices, and *oi serasa, oi dom,* and *oi wasilu* (the hammerhead: *Sphyrna* sp.) are also traded for their fin. The fin of *oi gagaji*, the sawfish (*Pristiopsis* sp.), is rare, mainly being found in the muddy estuarine waters of the Masiwang. As the price rises, fishermen catch shark in preference to other species. It is, of course, the prepared tail and fin that command highest prices, dried and sold to traders in Geser or Gorom. The market in shark meat varies locally, but when prices are low, as they were in the late 1980s, it is reckoned to be hardly worth harvesting. Hammerhead fin was fetching 20,000 rupiah a kilogram in Ambon and Makassar in 1986. By contrast Soselisa (1995) reported that in 1992 three days' shark fishing on Garogos yielded 1–2 kilograms of fins, earning more than 100,000 rupiah, much more than the same investment of time in trepang collecting.

TRADE IN TREE PRODUCTS

From at least the beginning of the European era the dominant arboricultural crop of the area, both in plantations and in terms of imports from non-cultivated trees in New Guinea, has been nutmeg. Nutmeg is currently an important export crop (both long and round forms) in Kilgah, Kwaos, Dinama, and in the islands of Gorom. There is little nutmeg in Amarsekaru, nor on Watubela, Teor, and Kesui, though the raja of Amar had a nutmeg grove in the 1920s that was mortgaged to Njio Kik Tjien in Amboina to the value of 20,000 Netherlands East Indies guilders (Jansen 1928:491). On the mainland the season tends to be April–May; in the Gorom Archipelago, November–December. In Kataloka one sack of nutmeg weighs about 85 kilograms; in Ondor in 1981 it was approximately 70 kilograms. In 1972 1 kilogram fetched about 600 rupiah, but by 1980 it was down to 150 rupiah (with mace at 400 rupiah per kilogram). In 1986 round nutmeg was, however, fetching 4,500 rupiah and long nutmeg 3,300 rupiah per kilogram. The long nutmeg is slightly less valuable partly because it is more difficult to break open cleanly.

Cloves have seen a remarkable expansion in the last thirty years, and in many places on the mainland it was replacing nutmeg and copra as the most important export crop up until the late 1980s. As nutmeg prices fell, people started to plant cloves. Warus-warus was during the 1980s one of the most important producers, where the harvesting season falls in July. In Kilmuri and Kwaos (where it was the most important commodity) it is in June. Elsewhere it is August to September. Chinese traders based in Bula and Geser, as well as itinerant Butonese, visit Warus-warus to buy the harvest. Cloves are also important on Gorom and in Ondor and in the 1980s were the mainstay of Chinese traders in Geser and Kataloka. Cloves were less important during that time in Watubela, Teor, and Kesui. Sometimes local people took their own cloves to Geser and Ambon, where they got a higher price. Few traders in Sorong were ever interested in buying cloves. In 1986 cloves were fetching 55,000 rupiah per kilogram. One clove tree yields about 10 kilograms, and on average in Ondor each person has two hundred trees. Thus, between 1981 and 1986, cloves could provide a household with between 0.5 and 3 million rupiah a year. Similarly, in the clove season many outsiders (e.g., Bandanese, and Butonese from Buton) would move to Tarui, where hundreds of perahus could be seen at that time of year.

We know that copra was being exported from East Seram to Ambon via Banda just after World War II. However, it was not an important export crop in the area during the 1980s, even along the mainland coast. Indeed, there was even a shortage of coconut oil in Kwaos during the same period, with few palms and many of those old. Copra is of some significance in Ondor and on Pulau Panjang. The only curiosity in this pattern is that because all inhabitants of Kilwaru have gardens on Seram Laut, copra there (and in Namalomin) was the most important trade product during the 1980s. In 1986 1 kilogram of copra purchased from a producer cost a trader about 170 rupiah (one sack took 80 kilograms). Coffee is important along parts of the mainland coast (for example, in Kwaos and Warus-warus), where it is the third most important crop. The month of harvest varies as one moves north along the coast, being April–May in Kwaos, April in Kilgah, and March in Warus-warus. Little East Seram coffee reaches Surabaya; most is consumed in the subdistrict or exported to the New Guinea port towns.

TRADE IN LOCALLY MANUFACTURED GOODS

Petty commodity production has historically been important for the islands of Southeast Seram (for example, metalsmithing). There are black-smiths in Kilgah, Amarwatu, Remui (Teor), and Gauer; silver- and gold-smiths in Sesar and silversmiths also in Kilwaru, Kilmoi, Keffing, Kesui (Amarlaut), and Dulak (Gorom). All central Moluccan silversmiths originate from either Iha or Kulur on Saparua, except in Ambon where many are Chinese and some Makassans. There are nineteenth-century reports of gold having been found in sand near Afang, taken to the island of Maar (Seram Laut), and there smelted by Bugis to make armbands (Van der Crab 1862:156–157).

In some areas, particularly on the mainland, where suitable clay is available, there is limited pottery production, mainly of sago ovens (forna, *watu suat*), which cannot easily be acquired elsewhere. These ovens are traded throughout the Southeast Seram area. They are produced by women in Kilgah (from where they are traded into the upland Bati settlements), in Kilmuri itself and in other villages of the domain, in Rumeon, Kiandarat, Dinama, Kilbat, Gah, Warus-warus (though not actively traded), and in Suakil and Kataloka on Gorom. The reason for the particular asymmetry in types produced and a general underproduction is that historically this is an area supplied by Bandanese potters, before 1621 from Banda itself and after the exodus of ethnic Bandanese from other places, most notably from Elat in the Kei Islands brought by the producers in their own *angbot* or *ang kalulis*. Pots also used to come from Kaur (Lengur, on the border between the Kei Kecil and East Seram subdistricts). Bik (1928 [1824]:97) regarded this pottery as the best in the archipelago, and in 1849 sixteen thousand items of Kei pottery are reported to have been imported into Aru (Bosscher 1853). Kei islanders were still bringing pots to Kataloka for sale in 1981 but have not actively traded pots on any scale in these parts since the late 1970s. In 1986 there were still Kei pots in use in Guli-guli and Kwaos, and between Kilgah and Suru on mainland Seram. Occasionally, pottery from Ouh on Saparua is found, as well as large water pots of Chinese or Thai origin, brought by Butonese.

The weaving of textiles for export, important until the late nineteenth century, has now effectively ended in Southeast Seram. Some woven cloths (*ute-ute, uri*) and fishing nets are made in Dai and Ramadan on Gorom. Black-patterned baskets produced in Kelilau and Warus-warus and decorated baskets with lids (*tahalasi*) of Bati origin are traded widely within the area and certainly as far as Gorom. Wherever the materials are available there are local basket-making traditions. Thus, Goromese make a variety of baskets themselves (including carrying baskets). There is also a local trade in pandanus mats (tikar) from, for example, Warus-warus, and in rattan furniture from Kilgah. The celebrated *dom* baskets described in some of the early accounts of regional trade, made of pandanus and decorated with cowries, are still produced in Amarsekaru but not widely traded. In some ways, the decline in this traditional trade matches that in *ute-ute*.

7.7. Ecological and Geographic Divisions of Labor

The data presented on commodity production and movement in this chapter show that the systemic properties of the local trading pattern derive partly from asymmetries in production linked to the differential availability of natural resources, combined with the growth of manufacturing and trading activity in places that though resource-deficient are often strategically located in trading and political terms. There is, in other words, an ecological and geographic division of labor. Some places specialize in marine produce, others in wetland produce (sago and mangrove), others in plantation crops. But across this variation runs another axis in terms of what in ecological terms might be described as niche width: some places have access to diverse niches and are able to subsist on and export a broad range of products (they permit broad-spectrum strategies); others rely on a narrow range of biotopes and have to subsist on and export a narrow range of products (they are limited to narrow-spectrum strategies). Although in practice there is a continuous distribution of commodity breadth from one end of the spectrum to the other, it is helpful to distinguish three types of settlement: those relying on a narrow range of trade products, those relying on a medium range, and those relying on a broad range. Of the first, Garogos depends on trade in trepang, fish, and lola in that order; Kwamar on fishing, firewood, and some coconut; Keffing on julung in particular and trepang; Kiltai on lola, agar-agar, and trepang. In the middle group are places such as Kilwaru that have access to marine resources but also some significant terrestrial trading products; or on the mainland places such as Bati Saie or Kwaos that have access to a small range of terrestrial products and either no marine produce or produce that is very limited. In the case of Kilwaru copra, lola, trepang, agar-agar, and fish are all important, in that order; in Kilfura copra, lola, trepang, turtles, and fish; in Kwaos there is tradable sago, nutmeg, cloves, and formerly damar; and in Bati Saie sago, cloves, nutmeg, coffee, rattan, timber, and damar. In the third grouping are places such as Warus-warus, which can rely upon a wide range of commodities: cloves, coffee, timber, some nutmeg, fish, and turtles; Kilgah, which has cloves, nutmeg, coffee, and relies rather less on fish; or Kilmuri, with extensive sago, timber, some pottery, and cloves. Kataloka on Gorom must also be placed in this category, indicating that it is not mainland domains alone that command the greatest diversity of commodities. In 1980 the officially recorded exports out of Kataloka were 507,271 kilograms of long nutmeg with seed and mace intact: 119,843 kilograms of separated long nutmeg, 262,693 kilograms of long nutmeg mace, 62,900 kilograms of round nutmeg, 4,170 kilograms of round nutmeg mace, 18,710 kilograms of clove heads, 10,584 kilograms of clove stalks, 2,970 kilograms of *Trochus*, 490 kilograms of batu laga, 61,645 kilograms of nutmeg, 7,460 kilograms of kemiring (*Aleurites moluccana*, candlenuts) and 800 kilograms of ikan julung.[3] In crude terms, domains and settlements within domains falling into this latter category are regarded by local people as among the most prosperous.

7.8. Trade Networks and Commodity Flows in Modern Southeast Seram

A clear property of the Southeast Seram trading zone, the wider Banda system, and most other trading zones identified for the Moluccas is that despite the presence of crucial central places linked to the outside world, they are dependent locally upon highly connected peripheries, which provide for great system flexibility and resilience (Ellen 1987). Thus, if there is a shift from point A to point B in the periphery in terms of the production of a particular commodity, and even if point A were to disappear entirely, the system as a whole is sufficiently robust for the rest of the structure to adjust and remain intact overall, especially where the points on the periphery exhibit a weak division of specialization. Indeed, the implications for the center may be barely registered in terms of flow of resources. Moreover, the more vectors a center has to go through to obtain its primary products, the better protected it is from local perturbations in production, including environmental changes. But crosscutting ties also exist between points at different degrees of distance from the center. Thus, rather than the connections between the center and the periphery functioning as simple symmetrical dendrites, it is more like an asymmetric network. Such crosscutting ties increase the connectivity of the system but by permitting at the same time direct feedback from the periphery to the center, or vice versa, may be instruments of destabilization. Moreover, the ties that a center has with various secondary centers and the ties that those centers have with points of production are not equally significant. This introduces further vulnerability and must be set against other offsetting vulnerability-reducing features of the network.

The twentieth century saw four major changes in the structure of this system and the technical organization of trade: greater centralization, the diminishing of interior-coastal trade on Seram, the decline of the Papuan trade, and more direct, faster, and more frequent connections between centers and the periphery achieved mainly through the replacement of sail by motor. It is possible to specify these changes in the character of networks in formal terms based on detailed voyage analysis, network matrices, and commodity flow data.

We can identify a number of economic forces that have destroyed or concealed the more obvious systemic properties of historic trading networks in Southeast Seram. On the import side, the accessibility of a wide range of cheap manufactured goods through improved long-distance trade has killed off much local trade and local productive specialization. Radial routes have become emphasized at the expense of lateral ones (for example, leading to further centralization in Geser and less direct linkage between, say, Guli-guli and Kataloka). Stated formally, there is a reduction in the overall connectedness of the networks on the periphery, less clear definition of the boundaries of older local systems, and more direct connections between centers and distant places that bypass earlier stopovers. This latter is partly a reflection of motorization but also of the increase in the volume of trade and movement of people. Thus, where formerly vessels would travel from A to D via B and C, the pattern is now more likely to be direct connections between A and B, A and C, and A and D. The availability of imported rice in the center has led to a decline in the local trade of other starch staples, and local pottery is being replaced by plastic and metal alternatives. Even cheap vegetables and roots brought in from Java and Sulawesi are undermining local trade. In short, the economy is showing all the classic symptoms of a familiar form of underdevelopment. Increasing economic centralization has been accompanied by political centralization. Administrative pressures have encouraged the use of particular trade routes and centers. Remote populations on the periphery have been forced to move nearer the centers (e.g., Teon, Nila, and Serua to South Seram [Figure 1.2]) and inland mountain villages to the coasts of the larger islands (e.g., Bati, Bonfia).

Having said all this, cargo movements by perahu, by which we mean here mostly lambos, are grossly understated, being responsible for considerable fractions of the trade in timber, copra, primary produce, sand, salt fish, fertilizer, and so on. Of these, timber is by far the most important commodity in Indonesia as a whole. In 1972 at least 20,000 tons of copra was shipped by perahu from Maluku alone to Surabaya and Gresik (Dick 1975, 2:90–92).

The export trade in spices is also changing. The Moluccas as a whole are less important for the production of nutmeg and cloves than they used to be. Although up until the late 1980s cloves were being planted more widely in the Moluccas, on the periphery as well as at the centers, cloves and nutmeg are being increasingly grown in others parts of Indonesia. During the 1980s, clove trees were being increasingly planted at the expense of nutmeg, because the prices obtainable per kilogram were higher. Thus although nutmeg used to be the exclusive cash crop on Gorom, since 1950 clove production has gradually outstripped the production of nutmeg. However, the slump in the clove market by the end of the 1980s must have shifted the balance yet again.

The trade in sago, slaves, and forest products that maintained Banda at the center of the southern Moluccan nexus has virtually disappeared, and some traditional links in the system have been severed. The production of nutmeg and its relative market price have declined, and kenari and nutmeg trees are even being replaced by manioc and potatoes. The perkenier system ended with World War II, and the estates have declined further under Indonesian nationalization. Butonese have replaced Bugis merchants. Today Banda has become more of a trading base than a major center of production, occupying an increasingly more marginal position, with landless peasants relying on selling small quantities of nutmeg to monopolistic government corporations or trading dried fish, lola, cloves, cinnamon, and kenari nuts to private merchants, destined for the Ambon market. Despite improvements in communications, Banda has remained poorly placed to supply the Ambon market with its most abundant resource, fresh fish. But even with these changes it is still possible to discern systemic properties in the Banda zone. This is partly because Banda itself is so deficient in many of the products that it needs (timber, thatch, coconut), which can still be obtained most easily from Southeast Seram and other points east. It is also partly because Banda still maintains its role as a base and pivot in the long-distance sailing trade. That it lies in an advantageous geographical position and provides excellent harbor facilities is a fact that has not changed for five hundred years and still determines its economic options.

But if the wider Banda system shows signs of disappearing, the local zones of which it is composed maintain a higher degree of systemness: the Kei Islands (focused on Tual and Elat), Aru (focused on Dobo), and, most striking, archipelagic Southeast Seram (focused on Geser). Here the classic features of the fish–sago–export product nexus remain and provide an excellent opportunity for the investigation of trading patterns that were once found more widely. But more important than the geographical constraints that keep particular trading routes and networks alive is the social embeddedness of small-scale trade (peddling) in the production system of this part of Indonesia over the long term. As Evers (1988:91) put it: "The forms and customs remain stable over long periods of time, but the configurations in which they occur, the articulations with other forms of trade, and the relative significance change over time."

The interisland exchange network described here has, therefore, "simultaneously ensured the common survival and encouraged the differential economic and political development of its constituent" parts (Hage and Harary 1991:101), though the Southeast Seram networks are more like Melanesian ones than those modeled by Hage and Harary for Micronesia, being based on short voyages and political devolution rather than long voyages and political hierarchy. Looked at from a graph point of view of actual sea-lanes, within the Geser-Gorom sphere the central zone between the southeastern tip of mainland Seram and Garogos (what I have called the Geser or Banda-Onin corridor) represents a constricted bottleneck through which all journeys between the Gorom group and mainland Seram have to travel. Similarly, boats following the Andan currents to the southwest to Banda or northeast on the Onin current to New Guinea are bound to pass

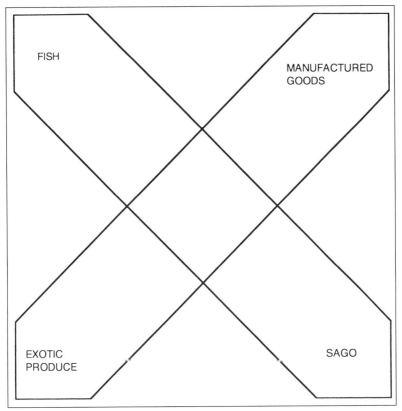

Figure 7.7. The diagonal exchange nexus of the Banda-Onin corridor: the south-west-northeast exchange axis of externally derived commodities against the north-west-southeast exchange axis of local subsistence goods.

through Geser (Figure 7.7). The Geser area is, therefore, a kind of plexus, a chiasma in terms of local sailing routes. Boats hugging the coasts, sailing eastward or southward, and boats coming from the southeast hugging the islands all meet or cross at Geser. We thus have a diagonal exchange nexus: the southwest-northeast exchange axis of externally derived commodities against the northwest-southeast exchange axis of local subsistence goods.

8

The Social Instruments of Trade in
Late Twentieth-Century Seram

"Other things being equal," the marketist says, the economy will perform as the model predicts. The facts seem to be first, that economies rarely perform as the model predicts; "other things" never are equal. And then secondly, it also seems fairly clear that those other things—the institutions, moral evaluations of goods and relationships, symbolic orders—are not random or arbitrary, but are patterned, coherent within reasonable limits of tolerance, and are consequential ...the slogan is "other things are never equal, and are always patterned." Consequentiality is located not in the working of economic laws, but in the social rules of power, symbol, convention, etiquette, ritual, role and status.

J. DAVIS, *Exchange*

For a part of the Asian trading network that has for so long been dominated by global market forces, traditional modes of distribution and exchange in archipelagic Southeast Seram might seem to be remarkably resilient. In part, however, this is to fail to recognize that in many other parts of the world system, impinging on global bulk and commercial trade, the position is much the same, even at the hubs and in the homelands of money exchange and capitalism. And to say so is to do no more than assert much in the substantivist and culturalist position of modern economic anthropology (Davis 1992; Gudeman 1986).

In this chapter I outline the basic organizing principles and social institutions of trading behavior in the Geser-Gorom area as these existed during the fieldwork phase of this project, in the early 1980s. I begin by saying something of the kinds of exchange and distribution that are to be found, arguing from first principles in relation to the general conceptions as to what constitutes that cultural behavior that we describe as "trade," paying special attention to the enduring role of barter, and exploring the different kinds and levels of activity and the social units through which they are realized. I discuss something of the processes involved in conducting transactions, particularly in relation to risk management, obtaining and giving credit, and determining prices, and conclude with an account of the regulatory framework within which all this takes place, both customary and at the state level. In the succeeding, penultimate, chapter, I look at traders as persons and as members of kinship networks and of ethnically labeled groups.

8.1. Exchange, Distribution, and the Definition of Trade

We can get a good sense of how traditional production-based distribution works by examining what happens to a catch of *neba* (ikan julung, the barred garfish *Hemiramphus*) caught using *ang guik* boats and associated techniques. On arriving on the beach, the catch is first divided in half, between "the net" (that is, the owner) on the one hand and the rest of the crew on the other. Thus, if a catch comprises one thousand fish, which is by no means unusual when encountering julung shoals, five hundred go to the net and five hundred are divided up among the rest of the crew. As we saw in chapter 6, the crew of an *ang guik* is variable but is never less than twelve, the minimum size necessary to perform the required technical operations. Assuming a minimum crew of twelve, a further 4.5 parts are added to obtain the actual divisor. This is because, in addition, one part goes to the owner of the sail, two parts to the owner of the boat, one part to the captain (*tenasi*), and half a part to the boatswain. This gives 16.5 parts in all, and 16.5 into five hundred works out at about thirty fish each. If, as is often the case, the net, the boat, the sail, and the captain are one and the same, then the extra shares combined accrue to him. The captain is the person who looks after the *ang guik* and is not always the owner. On one occasion Arsad Rumonin in Geser divided his own share as owner into lots of two hundred, which he distributed to various households for smoking. In return for this each household kept sixty fish (which were then distributed along lines of kinship and affinal obligation), and the residue was returned to Arsad for sale. With large quantities of julung it is imperative to move them through the distribution network quickly or to preserve them through smoking (*dafi ngaitor*). Fish that are not to be immediately consumed are made up into bamboo racks or frames (*waya*), each of twenty fish and weighing approximately 1 kilogram).[1] These are tied together into an *ikat* of ten frames. In 1981 a *waya* could be bought in Geser for 300 rupiah, and an *ikat* on Keffing from an Ambonese trader for 3,000 rupiah. Soselisa (1995:80 n. 7) reported that people purchasing fish on Garogos could still do so in 1992 for 300 rupiah a *waya* and for between 3,000 and 4,000 rupiah an *ikat*. A trader from Geser will buy any surplus of smoked fish prepared in this way and send it to Ambon. Fresh julung are threaded in tens onto pieces of bamboo. A plastic bowl full of threaded julung was sold in 1986 for 500 rupiah. Despite these precise figures and measures, in general quantities are treated as though they are approximate, always erring on the side of generosity to avoid any accusation of meanness on the part of either vendor or buyer. With other fishing techniques the distribution varies slightly. In *tali kor* (chapter 2.6) a third goes to the owner of the equipment, and the rest is shared among the members of the group. So, if an owner is also a member of a *tali kor* group, he gets two shares. This is the default position. The proportions may vary if this has the unanimous agreement of the members of the group. If one thousand fish are caught, three hundred go to the owner of the *tali kor* and the remaining seven hundred are divided among the helpers. Child helpers get a token payment of one fish each (cf. ibid., 162).

In the ikan julung example, the motivation for distribution, beyond the off-loading of produce the value of which will diminish the longer it is retained, is twofold. The first motivation, and the one that a shared morality places above all others, is to meet kinship expectations of gifts of food that themselves secure a delayed payment in kind at some future date. The second motivation is to obtain other goods that are needed, or cash to purchase necessities at some later date. Because the fresh produce diminishes in value the longer it is kept, this is only possible through some form of preservation—in this case smoking. It is conventional to think of trade as only the second of these forms of transactions, but I want to suggest that in formal terms there is really little difference between them, and in substantive local terms the similarities may actually be reinforced. In the abstract notation of exchange that we owe to Marx, the second form of transaction-can be represented as:

$$C_1 \rightarrow C_2 \qquad \text{(barter), or}$$
$$C_1 \rightarrow M \rightarrow C_2 \quad \text{(commodity exchange);}$$

and the first can be represented as:

$$C_1\,(t^1) \rightarrow C_1\,(t^2)$$

In this equation the commodity (though not necessarily the exact content) remains the same, but there is a time lapse in its return.

Another specific episode evokes well the social embeddedness of distribution and expresses the same logic somewhat differently. Yusuf Anudato and his wife Mariam of Geser traveled to Kianlaut in April 1986 in their jonson to visit his affines and her family. The journey took about one hour. They made stopovers at three places, including Kwaos. In each place they delivered no goods, but nevertheless left with enormous quantities of sago and dried fish, pandanus mats, and durian. The fish had been heaped upon them as they were trying to leave each place and not only by those who were close consanguines of the woman. In this case the perishability of the product was not an immediate factor (except perhaps in the case of the durian), and such potlatchlike generosity is largely explained as a strategy for storing up economic indebtedness on as great a scale as possible so as to ensure at least an equivalent return when the donors make a reciprocal trip to Geser. Such behavior is simultaneously a vindication of the power of the gift and of "moral accounting."

Most fishermen, subsistence agriculturalists, and sago producers in Southeast Seram are engaged, in addition to *hangu* (home consumption), in all forms of transactions just described. Barter (*tuar*) and commodity exchange (*tanak*) are often a means of disposing of inadvertent surpluses (as frequently happens in fishing), though the production of surpluses for exchange—sometimes through producers denying themselves what they might otherwise consume—may be a deliberate strategy to obtain other desired commodities or cash to engage in some form of delayed consumption. This is common also where there are local seasonal surpluses of fruit, such as durian. But barter may also be a means of coping with debt in the absence of cash, such as when shopkeepers will allow producers to take goods in advance of payment and at a later date settling up in kind (for example, in terms of trepang). Most will also, from time to time, engage in a fourth kind of transaction, namely:

$$M_1 \to C \to M_2$$

Thus, many people on Kidang purchase more sago than they themselves intend to consume, because in a sago-deficient area it is a convenient store of wealth that will increase in value during times of shortage, when it can be sold at a profit. Similarly, some small traders will take advantage of short-lived seasonal surpluses (we might use the durian example again, the marketing of which is very price-sensitive) by buying up a product in one place and selling it elsewhere at a profit. This is what was happening in February 1981 when an *ang kalulis* from Warus-warus showed up in Sesar to buy durian to sell in Geser.

Local producers engaged in such transactions distinguish between those that occur within the context of genealogical networks and are heavily constrained by kinship morality (urusan keluarga) and those that, although often conducted through the idiom of kinship, are in fact with professional traders with no imputed consanguinial links, where the constraining morality, though no less real, is much weaker (perjalanan dagang). Nevertheless, such a distinction cuts across the actual forms of transaction, both permitting barter or sale within the same domain or adjacent domains.

8.2. Barter: Fish for Sago

In the case of the distribution of the ikan julung catch described in the first section of this chapter, produce moves through several persons rapidly according to relatively unambiguous rules until it is either consumed directly or has been sufficiently preserved to permit more leisurely modes of exchange. In most cases nowadays this is through the market mechanism mediated by cash. But the role of cash in transactions is relatively recent. Wallace (1962 [1869]:321) reported that in the eastern Moluccas of the mid-nineteenth century money was unknown, with valuables, "knives, cloth and arrack forming the only medium of exchange, with tobacco a small coin."[2] We would understand this as barter, but as Wallace at least witnessed it, it was barter within the context of the market: the price was determined ultimately by the maximization strategies of both vendor and buyer within certain understood limits. To be more precise, Wallace (ibid.) recognized haggling when he saw it, "every transaction . . . the subject of a special bargain and the cause of much talking." Barter of this kind—where the notion of money (if not actual cash) is used to mediate the transaction—continues to be very important, especially in settlements where very little physical cash is in circulation or as a means of debt repayment to traders and shopkeepers. This is barter as a disguise or surrogate for money exchange, as "a solution to the problem of money" rather than the other way round (Humphrey and Hugh-Jones 1992:2, 4) .

But there is another kind of significant nonmonetary barter where prices (equivalences between quantities of different goods) are fixed, and this is a kind of barter that seems to constitute an identifiably different sphere of exchange. Both forms may take place among people related through kinship or between trading partners in villages traditionally linked through barter, though the second is restricted to such contexts. This is the form that underwrote *sosolot* loyalties along the Papuan coast and that has been briefly described in chapter 5. Let us take the particular case of Garogos to penetrate some of the rules and practices associated with barter of both kinds during the last two decades of the twentieth century.

Within archipelagic Southeast Seram, Garogos has traditional relations of barter with, among others, Kilgah, Selagur, Kilbat, Anger, Panjang, Gorom, and Manawoka, determined mainly through links of kinship and affinity, though these in turn often reinforce long-standing historical links. Outside the Geser-Gorom area, Garogos barters with Bandanese for taro and manioc (cassava) and with Butonese for salt (Soselisa 1995:166). There is a preference to barter with friends rather than strangers, because this engenders trust and helps to maintain the bond, important where exchanges at any one time are not of agreed equivalence. With strangers there is much bargaining of exchange rates. Soselisa (ibid., 157, 167) reported that on Garogos the following may also be obtained through barter: bananas, cassava, cassava biscuits (*suat pangala*), taro, coconut, sweet potatoes, durian, kenari, betel leaves, areca nut, pandanus mats (*ali-han*), and bamboo culms (*karawatu*). Barter is also used, in preference to cash sale, to dispose of low-priced fish, such as rayfish, which seldom circulate through the cash sphere.

The dominant form of fixed equivalence barter is fish-for-sago exchange, the locational and ethnographic context of which was described in chapter 7.6. As far as can be ascertained, money is neither used as a measure of equivalence in fish-for-sago barter nor as a medium of exchange, though in a region where both fish and sago can also be measured in monetary values we must assume some leakage in the flow of information between spheres of exchange that has some influence on the process of valuation. In Kwaos in 1986 one small tumang was being exchanged for two ekor (tails) of salt fish or one hundred small lemping for one *waya* of julung (twenty fish). On Garogos dried shark meat, dried ray, salted and baked fish, dried octopus, roast sea urchin (ten to fifteen cooked urchins form a *kour*), dried clams, and occasionally dried dolphin meat are bartered against, principally, sago flour *(bai)* in sago leaf tumang *(raun)*, other sago products, or sago-related items, such as earthenware ovens *(watu suat)*, sago leaves *(barem)*, and midribs *(alaba)*, although these latter are usually acquired through gifts along kinship lines. But, to a lesser extent, this kind of barter extends to other goods, though what is of interest is the boundary between commodity transactions that are mutually agreed to be acceptable through traditional barter ratios and those that are not. Thus, there is a lively barter trade between bundles of sago leaves used to manufacture thatch *(barem)* and salted or dried fish, though woven sections of sago palm thatch *(bangkalan)* must usually be purchased for money. In Kwaos, for example, one *waya* of julung is reckoned as the equivalent of one *pang* (cupa) of coffee (half a kilogram). The barter system has been extended to firewood and other commodities and also occurs as part of the negotiations for the payment of large shipments in the lambo trade.

Soselisa (1995:168) described barter as it operates on Garogos. It is predominately a male activity involving journeys to Seram, Gorom, or Panjang or journeys by people from those islands to Garogos. It is significant to note that Geser does not appear to be involved in this kind of barter. Boats used include *lepa-lepa*, sometimes motorized, *kalulls* and *ungbot* (lambo). Members of a barter expedition may include family, household members, other kin, or neighbors. The links are predominately with geographically separated consanguines but sometimes other acquaintances as well. The host will also seek out others in the village who may wish to barter with his guests. This serves to ensure that those involved in the exchange will be fair and share a common view as to rates of exchange. Where kin are involved there is less insistence on reaching equivalence in values. People say that what you give is up to you, but just give. Each party tries to be generous, in part to ensure the perpetuation of the relationship. Value is calculated nowadays by estimating the monetary value of the goods. Thus, if one salted *tehar* fish is agreed to cost 200 rupiah and one tumang of sago 1,200 rupiah, then the exchange rate is 12:1. Sometimes the calculation of values is less certain and responds to supply and demand (for example, in the durian season).

Some specific barter exchange rates recorded for Garogos by Soselisa are given in Table 8.1. This shows variation in the exchange rate for the same item. Though sago is universally cheaper on Seram than on Gorom, the rate is determined less by geographical location than by the conventions adopted by the network of people routinely engaged in the barter. Sometimes barter is used when there is no cash market for salted fish or when the cash price is low. There is also barter between local producers and commercial traders or their agents involving exported produce against manufac-

Table 8.1. Barter exchange rates recorded by Soselisa (1995:170) for Garogos

Product	Exchanged for
1 tumang of sago	5 large (40 centimeters) fish
	10 medium (20 centimeters) fish
	1 large piece of ray
	2 large octopuses
	10 small octopuses
	10 giant clams
	10 *kour* of sea urchins
2 tumang of sago	12 fish
1 small tumang of sago	1 *waya* of *neba* fish
	(approximately 20)
5 small laka (*ikat*) of sago biscuits (1 laka = 20 pieces)	1 *waya* of *neba*
4 small laka of sago biscuits	5 fish
1 *watu suat* (earthenware sago oven)	5 large fish
1 bundle of *barem*	2 large fish, 5–10 small fish
1 bundle of *alaba*	5 fish
1 bundle of bamboo	1 large fish
1 bunch of sirih leaves and 10 betel nuts	2–5 small fish

tured goods. Thus a middleman may accept four sarongs, or twenty-two sacks of sago flour, for a kilogram of abalone. Although barter is increasingly being replaced by sale of maritime products to entrepreneurs, at least as long as cash continues to circulate in increasing quantities in the periphery and at the same time holds its value, many people still say that it is quicker and more convenient to barter fish for sago on Seram (a single dyadic exchange) than to do a money-mediated exchange twice in Geser or in some other centralized trading locality. We might speculate that the crisis in the Indonesian economy since the late 1980s has only confirmed for local people the advantages of money-less transactions.

It is important not to generalize about barter. Before the relatively recent arrival of full cash payment and a cash mentality, it was, apart from gifting and theft, the only form of economic transaction. But to say this is to say little, for, as we have seen, even in the contemporary world the forms that it may take and the reasons why particular forms are encouraged are diverse. Viewed in a regional context, barter requires—unlike quick and dirty money exchange that needs only minimal social contact and shared values—continuing social relationships. It is this necessary institutional infrastructure that helped historically to integrate sea and land in an area with little political centralization, linking producer with producer, and that demonstrates the importance of securing *sosolot* loyalties through long-term norms and expectations. Barter involves mutual payment, and simultaneous barter might seem discontinuous and unstable, but relations of barter are themselves institutionalized in Southeast Seram: exchange taking place with known people and at known times and in known places and according to agreed rules; credit implies trust and expands the possibilities of barter. As Humphrey and Hugh-Jones (1992:9) put it: "barter creates its own social relations which can exist in a wide range of political situations" and which in the Geser region provide stability between independent polities and which historically provided for the same along the New Guinea coast. In barter goods are dissimilar (and so are therefore not the same as gifts), and the process is egalitarian. Each transaction is in "perfect balance," creating equality out of dissimilarity (ibid., 11). However, the Serammer evidence does not support the view that barter sustains "reciprocal independence" rather than the "reciprocal dependence" of gift giving (Gregory 1982:42). Instead, barter involves relationships and not merely goods, balance in contrast to the dynamic asymmetry of gift giving (Humphrey and Hugh-Jones 1992:13, 18). People on Garogos regularly give seafood as gifts to a potential father-in-law in marriage negotiations (Soselisa 1995:165). Textiles in Onin mean something very different from textiles in Bali, Gujarat, or even for Goromese traders; similarly, long nutmeg means something very different in New Guinea, Banda, and Amsterdam. To use Appadurai's (1986:4) phrase, they dwell in different "regimes of value." But within the Southeast Seram area, sago and fish are in the same regime of value. Barter can maintain the difference between different regimes of value and spheres of exchange, whereas money may lead to their eventual incorporation into a single regime.

8.3. Kinds of Traders and the Units of Trade

The exchange and distributional strategies so far discussed, though linked to particular social roles, are not markedly confined to any one category of trader, which might otherwise be inferred from how people talk about trade or how we might find it convenient to represent it. The main exception is where the role of trader also embodies the role of producer, as in the julung case, or in many instances of fish-for-sago barter. Having said this, however, we can usefully identify five generic kinds of traders operating in the Moluccan region:

1. Those who only occasionally trade the produce of the domestic unit, usually locally;

2. Those who regularly trade their own produce, usually locally, but sometimes taking the produce to more distant market centers;

3. Those who regularly trade their own produce and engage in some middleman activities;

4. Petty merchants relying on small capital, usually owning small shops (kios, toko), and where trade may occasionally be supplemented by some production where this is possible;

5. Major merchants relying on considerable capital, usually owning one or more shops (toko) and often with capital invested in transport and sometimes land. They may also sometimes have a stake in productive enterprises.

Traders in category 1 are exceedingly rare these days but in the past must have constituted the most common form of involvement for subsistence producers on the distant periphery. With any kind of regular commitment to cash crops, such as nutmeg, traders must be classified in category 2 or higher. Terminal points (such as Garogos or Bati Saie) in trading networks are usually composed of traders in categories 1, 2, and 3 but may sometimes have one or two resident petty merchants, depending on the size of the settlements. Local trade is that conducted within villages or between nearby villages, usually to dispose of small surpluses or make up day-to-day deficits. Everywhere, small items including fresh fish, fruit, and vegetables are peddled within the village. Alternatively, rice, sugar, cooked food, fresh food surpluses, and manufactured sundries (cigarettes, salt, matches, soap, and so on) are sold from pondoks (lit. "huts")[3] or private houses, or from boats on the beach. For example, Makmur Rumatar has a pondok in Arou (Miran) on Gorom that is looked after by relatives; its stock is bought from Chinese traders in Kataloka. On Geser, local people obtain fresh food directly from Seram Laut producers and from producers on the mainland in this way. In terms of volume of transactions, most trade is probably of this kind: direct barter or cash payments between consumer and producer of fish and sago. The kinship basis of local settlements at this level means that much disposal of surpluses and the making up of deficits is done through gifts or requests on the basis of generalized reciprocity. In the subsistence sphere, most center-periphery trade is conducted by producers directly selling their sago either in the center or on other parts of the periphery, or selling it to full-time traders. Again, much distribution occurs within the context of kinship relations and therefore is not trade in the usual sense, even though the distances traveled to achieve this may be considerable. As we have seen, residents of Geser make frequent visits to Seram, where they collect sago and other products from their relatives.

Trading in categories 1, 2, and 3 is therefore that most likely to involve production-based barter and to involve certain patterns in the division of labor by gender. Women, for example, predominate in the marketing of small quantities of food produce either through kiosk (kios) or pondok outlets, in markets or along path sides. Nan Kelian, for example, was born in Geser around 1950 and in 1981 had for some years run a dry-food kiosk at the market. Women, however, tend to be more involved in hasil laut than in hasil darat, especially where smaller quantities are involved (e.g., of trepang). By contrast, men preferentially hunt and trade in high-price resources (such as shark), as well as plantation crops such as nutmeg. These male strategies are also those that involve the greatest risk, both in terms of subsistence effort for yield (say, in shark fishing) or in terms of price fluctuation (nutmeg or cloves). The upshot is a pattern in which, in poorer households especially, less-risky female activity often subsidizes high-risk male activity.

Middlemen or petty traders (in categories 3 and 4) have single-stranded relations with the major merchants of category 5, though they characteristically relate to other traders and producers through multistranded relations (Soselisa 1995:189). They occupy a crucial pivotal position, bridging two conceptual worlds with their separate logics and moralities. Traders in other categories experience this duality and disjunction, though few to the same extent. There are material advantages: for example, a local middleman may use the capital of a major merchant in making purchases, though he can supplement this by buying goods with his own money. To an extent he is a trader's agent or anak dagang, though he can act with a degree of independence. Fishermen may sometimes become anak dagang for periods. Small traders from outlying places may stock up with goods from larger shops in secondary or primary centers, being unable to afford the expense of buying in Ambon or Surabaya. Thus, on Gorom, traders in places such as Miran and Namalen stock up in Kataloka. Such traders sell in small quantities, partly because this is what people demand and can afford and partly because vendors cannot afford or risk keeping large stocks of anything. Thus, the characteristic fare of small Geser pondoks in 1986 were newspaper twists of sugar at 100 rupiah each, tea at 50 rupiah each, and similar handling of salt and pepper.

On Garogos, middlemen are a recent phenomenon. In the past Garogos traded mainly with Geser Chinese merchants (who mainly handled the hasil laut) but had to take their produce directly to Ambon, Tehoru, Sorong, Fak-fak, or even Surabaya, because there were no such traders in Kataloka, the domain of which Garogos is a part. Even in the early 1990s Garogos fisherman were buying coconuts on Panjang Island for 75 rupiah each and selling them as far away as Fak-fak for 250 rupiah, using the imam's angbot, who in return received the boat's share (Soselisa 1995:79). Chinese traders were finally permitted access to, and residence in, Kataloka during the 1960s, replacing mainly Butonese. So, nowadays local producers are decreasingly likely to be involved in long-haul trade, which has become the specialism of full-time traders in major centers. Soselisa (ibid., 164) described one middleman (Hasan) who goes to other islands to buy agricultural products, such as copra or nutmeg. Some middlemen become kepala soa or acquire other political appointments because of their role as middlemen. Middlemen are dependent on traders for capital and access to markets, but they provide market information to other producers, introduce new equipment and new commodities, act as agent for the raja, and generally serve as go-betweens with serious social responsibilities, such as lending money, supplying basic necessities, and mediating with the outside world and the market (ibid., 99). Middlemen use their own kinship networks to attract custom for a particular merchant, for which they may in return receive credit and a share of the profit. But anak dagang seldom become pedagang (that is, full traders).

Petty merchants resident in peripheral termini are almost always immigrants and usually of Bugis, Butonese, or Chinese origin. In all cases their small numbers involve a degree of integration into the local community, especially where this is facilitated by greater cultural similarity, although isolated traders usually maintain kinship, marriage, and social ties with their families in trading centers. In secondary centers such as Amarsekaru or Kataloka, merchants in categories 4 and 5 are usually present in sufficient numbers for them to form an identifiable community, although they are seldom able to reproduce themselves locally without marrying out of their immediate ethnically labeled group. The ethnic dimension to trade is taken up at greater length in chapter 9. Secondary centers may have a few merchants with capital assets sufficient to run boats, but they usually also have strong links with primary centers. Only in primary centers does ethnic identity become a dominant organizing principle in trade, a function of demographic scale. Geser traders or traders in other large centers may keep middlemen or agents in local settlements to organize collection of produce so that it is ready when a trader arrives (such as along the New Guinea coast).

The physical and organizational infrastructure that accompanies the division of labor described in this section is conveniently divided into pondok, kios, toko, marketplaces, and shopping districts. In this classification, marketplaces can be seen as physical assemblages of pondoks and kiosks, and shopping districts as areas of spatially adjacent shops. Those small part-time retail outlets I have described above as pondoks are particularly numerous in the larger centers (Geser, Kataloka), where they are not simply the means of disposing of producer or household surpluses but may become business vehicles through which products may be specially manufactured or brought in for resale. In Geser many pondoks are owned by Bandanese. Kiosks are more permanent structures, requiring some capital to get established, and are more enduring as retail outlets, carrying a larger stock and with a larger turnover. Typically, they are run by members of existing trading families starting out in a particular location or by other small merchants whose longer-term objectives may be to open a shop. By contrast, a pondok may be run by ordinary villagers who may have no long-term goal to increase their involvement in trade. In organizational terms the distribution is continuous (small kiosks are indistinguishable from larger pondok and larger kiosks from small shops). However, there is an official governmental set of distinctions that is imposed (somewhat artificially it must be said) on this continuum of scale and to which I return at the end of this chapter. For one thing, the number of retail outlets is in a constant state of flux, especially at the level of kiosk and pondok.

The usual definition of a shop (toko) is a retail outlet where the owner sells goods, usually for cash, that have been acquired at a lower price or produced in-house. In Southeast Seram, as in all of Indonesia, there are many that conform to this definition, but very many that do not. In general, shops are usually named and are (a) invariably general stores with very little specialization and (b) (often quite literally) the "front" for more general trading operations. On the whole those who run them are petty or major merchants who use a shop as a physical base for their wider activities. Economically the shop broadens the base of the business and provides more security; socially the shop is often the instrument through which more general trading activity can be instigated and furthered—a form of advertisement. Shops open for long hours, especially at night, a pattern that may seem cost-ineffective given the little retail business that is often conducted during those hours. However, long opening hours provide a service that is expected by customers, are in part a consequence of a high degree of competition between shops offering an almost identical stock, and serve as a context in which general trade can be most effectively conducted. Most shops are owned by Chinese families and a few by Arabs; Bugis and Butonese generally tend to have sufficient capital to run only a kiosk. It is rare to find shops run by local people, for reasons explored further in the next chapter, and the one shop in Warus-warus is a rare exception in this respect. In 1986 a shop in Kilgah was owned by a local and rented to a Chinese trader in Geser. But the franchise had been subcontracted to another local person; the trader visited only periodically to check on the operation and collect produce.

We know of the existence of periodic markets in designated places organized exclusively by women on Banda before 1621 (Loth 1998:76), but such institutions currently are not important in most of the Banda zone. On the whole, they are restricted to larger urban areas founded on Dutch administrative posts elsewhere, such as Ambon, Tual, or Fak-fak. Marketplaces may once have existed where there are now groups of shops, but in general the units of redistribution and exchange are much more diffuse and devolved. There is no marketplace in Kataloka and the small market in Geser serves more as a backup than as a central point of redistribution, mainly being there to serve the administration on Geser. Only in Geser, Kataloka, Ondor, and Amarsekaru are there a sufficient number of aggregated shops and kiosks to justify the recognition of discrete shopping districts. The Geser market is a small purpose-built structure, with about eight kiosks and harian traders (those paying at the daily rate for a patch) squatting in the passageways. Two kiosks sell clothing and two sell general groceries including fresh produce from Seram Laut, which lands directly on the beach behind the market. In February 1981 the market had a large amount of sagu lemping, which on this occasion came from Kwamar;

coconut oil from Guli-guli; ikan julung from Keffing; bean shoots, rice in banana leaves, fried bananas, and many other vegetables from Seram Laut; and some cooked food and eggs from Geser itself. For an inventory of produce available in the same market during one spot check in April 1986 see Table 7.1.

8.4. **Calculating Risks and Arranging Transactions**

Traders in all categories continually have to estimate the comparative risks of buying at a particular time and selling at another. As far as we know, it has ever been thus for traders operating in Southeast Seram. What has changed is the speed and form of transport, the rapidity and quality of price information, and the degree to which trading culture has been formalized through government bureaucracies. For some commodities the risks are easier to estimate than others. We have noted, for example, the case of fresh fish, for which there is only a small local cash market. The main calculation here is how to balance a maximum catch against low demand and the requirement to dispose of a product that will deteriorate very rapidly if not consumed. The risk-reduction strategies in this case are twofold: first, mechanisms embedded in kinship and affinal relations that allow rapid local distribution, immediate consumption, and expectation of return in equal measure as a result of someone else's surplus; and second, smoking or salting to preserve the fish to enhance its shelf life. This latter is a good strategy because it means that the fish can be stored until prices rise, and dried fish always commands higher prices than fresh fish. Alternatively it can be bartered for sago at a rate that is always known to be constant. But calculating risks is seldom a simple zero-sum game. Consider, for example, the data presented in Figure 7.4: the official Geser figures for the monthly export by weight of copra, cloves, and dry fish (mostly ikan julung) and the import of rice. For this part of Indonesia, these are good economic indicators.

Let us begin by taking the example of cloves. The clove season varies in Southeast Seram, but it is mainly between June and October, depending on locality. Producers tend not to hang on to their crop to secure a higher price, so this season sees a rise in the number of local voyages, a sudden release of cash into the economy, and an upswing in consumer demand. However, during the 1980s there were two clear peaks in the export of cloves from Geser: February–May, and to a lesser extent October. This pattern is partly determined by price fluctuation in Ambon and other centers importing East Seram cloves, reflecting harvesting seasons in different places, and partly the buying strategy of the kretek (clove cigarette) companies who purchase most of the cloves. Thus, traders have to juggle all of this information to minimize their risk and maximize their profit. When prices are low, selling cloves through the government cooperative organization, Koperasi Unit Usaha Desa (KUUD) may be advantageous. For example, in

February 1981 Henke Bula (Case 7, chapter 9) received an extra 300–400 rupiah per kilogram by using this channel, but if he had bought from the local KUUD in Geser at that time he would have had to pay 700 rupiah per kilogram extra. The situation regarding copra is much more straightforward, though the seasonal pattern of exports is the same. The pattern for dried fish is simpler still, because there is a clear ikan julung season (the east monsoon) and the market is regional, mainly Ambon, though there are four visits a year from Banda to barter fish. Thus, the peaks of export are April and July. Rice imports show no clear pattern, with much month-to-month oscillation. Remarkably, most trade in the key export commodities takes place between April and September. Although this avoids the cyclone season of December–February and is the time of year most conducive to efficient sailing patterns, it is also the season of high rainfall and rough seas brought by the east monsoon. As we have seen, for over five hundred years most long distance trade has been confined to the period April–June.

One major consideration in avoiding risk is what constitutes an acceptable degree of specialization. In general, traders at virtually all levels attempt to diversify their activity to buffer against shortfalls and low profits in any one commodity, spread the overall risk, and speculate on good prices. On the other hand this has to be set against the fact that effective dealing in any one commodity requires a particular range of contacts (both buyers and sellers) and good information. Such factors lie behind a common division between traders into those who deal in a mixture of hasil darat and hasil laut and those who tend to avoid hasil laut altogether. Thus, there are occasions when the temptation to diversify has to be resisted because of the inability to secure a steady supply. In 1986, for example, the Hadhrami Arab Alkatiry at the Toko Danny in Geser had an arrangement to send trepang to a trader in Bandung who also wanted shark-liver oil, but because he saw so few sharks he could not produce a regular consignment and had to refuse the offer. Much of the hasil laut trade exists to supply Chinese consumers, so it is Chinese traders, or those with Chinese connections, who have both knowledge of the product and of the market. But there are even many Chinese traders who nowadays avoid hasil laut, such as Lie Wa Sung, a second-generation Chinese merchant in Geser, who (despite a father who was active in the trepang trade) himself only handles shark fins in addition to hasil darat; and Lie Ching Heng, who runs a kiosk in Geser dealing mainly in cloves, nutmeg, sago, and coffee. Moreover, specialist trading also requires good and reliable credit facilities to ride the troughs in commodity price oscillations and a spatial strategy that involves either complete mobility to seek out produce wherever it is to be found or location in a sufficiently large and accessible central place so as to attract custom. In Southeast Seram, this latter option restricts specialist traders pretty much to either Geser or Kataloka. On the whole, therefore, only where traders have firmly established themselves as major merchants in the larger centers can they afford to take advantage of niche marketing.

The risks associated with transactions can be reduced by reliance on a common morality or culture of trade. I shall return to the general issues of trust, security, and morality later in this chapter and in chapter 9, but one condition necessary for this culture to flourish needs to be mentioned here, namely agreement on basic rules of conduct and exchange. Thus, if there are no mutually agreed standards of value, trade, though not impossible, will constantly be a drawn-out process of negotiation from first principles. We have paid some attention already to the conventions of barter, and the use of money also relies on shared notions of denomination and value. Similarly, different commodities may generate different units of measurement and be essentially local. Thus, the main measure of fish in Southeast Seram is the *ikat* (or string). As we have seen with dried ikan julung this refers to an approximate number of fish, which presumably reflect a constant weight. In other cases, however, the *ikat* may consist of variable numbers of fish, even different species of fish, but be of about the same overall weight, weight in this case being judged by sight rather than by accurate measurement. In the same way, sagu lemping are measured in terms of laka and *ikat*: one laka is equivalent to twenty lemping and twenty-five laka equivalent to one *ikat*. But in Southeast Seram lemping come in different sizes, depending on the custom obtaining in the area of manufacture or the size of the clay oven (*watu suat*) used (chapter 7.6). One ikat of small lemping (as produced, for example, in Kianlaut) could be bought in Geser in 1986 for 300 rupiah; the larger variety (say, from Kilfura) commanded twice as much. However, for bulk international and cross-cultural trade to flourish, although merchants may use local units of measurements locally, they must convert into standard measures acceptable more widely or face confusing arithmetical conversions and risk taking a loss. Historically, common standards and units of value usually have been determined by the most influential intrusive trading group. Thus, the influence of Chinese is shown in weights and measures still used throughout Indonesia: for example, pikul (62 kilograms, a load that can be carried by one person) and kati or cupa (approximately 617 grams) (Quiason 1981:10; also Ellen 1979:71–72 n. 3, in relation to the spice trade).

Another factor is transport, especially where sea journeys are involved, and the longer the journey the higher the risk. The risks involved are various. There is the risk of losing a cargo, which can be a very real one (chapter 2.5), and there is the risk of not being able to sell a cargo at a price that will command an acceptable return. Transport charges, however, reflect speed of delivery rather than safety and to a lesser extent the value of the cargo. Therefore, the cost of a perahu is less than that of a motorized perahu, which is less than that of a motor laut, which is less than the freight charge of one of the major shipping companies. In 1986 the cost of sending one cubit of timber from Guli-guli to Flores on a perahu was 30,000 rupiah, or less than 15,000 rupiah if the cargo was only going as far as Banda. This would have cost approximately 40,000 rupiah if a motorized vessel had been used. In 1981 the cost of sending cloves by perahu from Geser worked out to 2,500 rupiah per sack (sac or karong) where each sack consisted of approximately 60 kilograms. The trade-off complexities exhibited in the perahu-borne long-distance copra trade are nicely exemplified by Dick (1975:99):

> Small perahus prefer to carry only their own cargoes, carrying and trading at the same time. This applies particularly to the Butonese who trade between Gresik and Maluku with *lambo* of less than 50 cubic meters. Arriving in Gresik with a copra cargo, a captain asks the ruling price of copra from one or two neighboring perahus before approaching a trader, who balances the value of the copra cargo and the freight payable (calculated even though a perahu is carrying its own cargo) against a shipping list of goods desired in exchange. Invariably the trader is someone with whom the captain has an established relationship, because it is known from bitter experience that those who seek the highest price for their copra are fair game to be cheated. The bargain concluded, a perahu loads its one or two tons of cargo: salt, bicycles, clay jars, textiles, sugar, sewing machines, matches . . . and sets sail back to Maluku where the goods will be bartered for another cargo of copra. The captains say that they now make little profit on the sale of copra but are able to place a mark-up of about 300 percent on the consumer goods. Because it is not the copra but the consumer goods trade which is the basis of their prosperity and they expect the demand for consumer goods in Maluku to increase, the captains see good prospects for the future and are not concerned about competition from *Nusantara* shipping which is hampered by high trans-shipment and distribution costs from Ambon to the multitude of islands and *kampong*.

Finally, traders have to factor in the advantages of extending or requesting credit and the disadvantages of nonrepayment, slow repayment, and debt dependency. There are various ways in which credit may be given, though bank credit is unknown. It may be given by a trader to a producer or another trader in expectation of delivery. Thus, a clove producer may sell his harvest in advance to a trader at a fixed price. The risk to the trader may be that the harvest is not as good as anticipated in the price paid up front or that the price will not ensure an acceptable markup when the trader comes to sell on the yield. For the producer, underproduction will risk further indebtedness and overproduction a potential loss. Another form of credit extension is that which some Geser traders extend to their suppliers working the New Guinea coast. Not many Geser traders deal in New Guinea products these days, but those who do will often not only agree to a buying price in advance but also provide the supplier with cash to make the purchases. The incentive for the supplier in this instance is to make purchases at a rate below that underpinning the calculations of the Geser trader, thus increasing his own profit margin. Then there is kredit toko, where an individual purchases goods and pays for them later in produce. Thus, fishermen in Geser mainly bring sea produce to traders to pay for goods that they have already obtained on credit. Ongoing relations of this kind between anak dagang, traders, and producers provide all three with a degree of security and short-term flexibility in the context of enduring conditions of trust grounded in common membership of a local community. A variation on the same theme is part payment in cash (for example, when buying a pok-pok or jonson), with the remainder to follow later as installments in kind. Most debts of this type take over a year to clear, with the debtor often paying off two-thirds or three-quarters of that owed and then trying to avoid the rest. In this way, middlemen are tied to other villagers through social obligations, and credit ties fishermen to certain middlemen. It is hard work for the creditor to press for repayment of debt, and bad debtors are seldom taken to court. So the sanction is the refusal to give further credit until a debt is cleared and the possibility of acquiring the reputation as a bad debtor. When debtors are kin, as they sometimes may be, things become more complex, and not surprisingly it is difficult to refuse credit to kin. Therefore, where kin are concerned it may make sense to represent what is in effect credit as a gift, with only a generalized expectation of return.

In the kinds of credit considered so far there is no explicit notion of interest involved, at any stage. Where a trader is prepared to extend credit but fears there might be a higher risk of nonrepayment than is normally acceptable, the parties may agree to use the ijon system. Ijon derives from "hijau" (green), referring to the principle that a harvest that is still green is used as a guarantee of eventual payment. With this arrangement a loan of 3,000 rupiah in the form of an advance on payment for cloves will allow the trader to take a further 5,000 rupiah. Put differently, for every 8,000 rupiah received by the lender the borrower receives just 3,000 rupiah. If the harvest turns out to be poor, payment can be made up in nutmeg (or some other agreed commodity) or paid later a little at a time. Mortgages of this kind are used to finance weddings, circumcisions, boat construction, and the building of both houses and mosques. The high rate of interest payable on such loans, it is widely believed by ordinary people, is one of the reasons why Chinese traders (who are those largely responsible for extending ijon credit) are so prosperous. Less than 10 percent of the population of Kataloka claimed to use ijon in 1981.

8.5. Determining Prices

Except where the norms and expectations of fixed-value barter make it unnecessary, prices are determined through a combination of estimated costs (of production, purchase, transport, storage) together with a calculation of what in addition the market will bear. Of course, it is sometimes the case that the market will bear less than the costs, in which case a trader will incur a loss. This may be thought to be fairly standard, but the interactional process by which a price is agreed between vendor and purchaser differs markedly from what is the norm in Western markets. Thus, contractual relations begin by being very open-ended. Initially there is no discussion of price, which would incur malu hati (embarrassment). Contracts begin instead with the parties making all kinds of overoptimistic promises as to what can be done, and how, and in what time. This has the advantage of establishing friendly relations and indicating a willingness to be generous and considerate. But when it comes to determining the price—closing in on the deal—hard bargaining takes over: producers deliberately suggest a price that, in the light of market information, is overoptimistic, the potential purchaser affects anger ("telingan panas, pusing kepala" [hot ears, dizzy head]), until, after many offers and counteroffers as the respective bids come closer together, there is final agreement. In the West, although such haggling is well known, it has become conventional for the opposite to be seen as the ideal rational model: for purchasers to locate a vendor based on an advertised price and conditions, for the price to be accepted beforehand, and for the parties to complain after the event if the product is found to be substandard or the work to be inferior. In the first a convenient fiction is accepted on the basis of status, the friendliness, and the good standing of the parties involved; in the latter case a convenient fiction is established on the basis of the trustworthiness of the contract. In both cases, the parties have to accept the existence of ideal values: the morality of status on the one hand and that of a contract on the other.[4]

The degree to which price fluctuates depends on the commodity, place, and season (Statistik Tahunan Kecamatan: Seram Timur, 1980). Some indicative price ranges for particular commodities have already been presented in chapter 7, and so I focus here largely on process. The price of sago, for example, is the least resistant to fluctuation and prices change only slowly. On the whole, it is not subject to seasonal variation, though where maritime transport is required this may have some influence. Sago also stores well, especially as lemping. Price is determined locally and is not, therefore, subject, like cloves or nutmeg, to regional and national, even international, factors. Moreover, the fact that much sago changes hands through fixed-rate barter has a stabilizing influence on the money price. There is, however, some variation. For example, in April 1986 Abdul Hasim Rumain from Aruan was able to sell one *ikat* of sagu lemping for 4,000 rupiah in Geser, although later the same month he could only command 3,000 rupiah per *ikat* and had twenty-five *ikat* to sell. He regarded this low price to be due to there being too much sago currently available. One of the advantages of barter, and one reason why it is still attractive to many, is that this kind of price oscillation is avoided. Even though the income to the vendor through barter may work out less if translated into current cash prices, cash does not have to be acquired in the first place, an important consideration for subsistence producers in remote areas with relatively few cash-generating opportunities.

For obvious reasons there is much more fluctuation in the fresh food market. The problems this can entail, and the strategies taken to avoid them, have already been discussed in the context of the julung example. Of the fresh fruits, durian is probably the most price sensitive. In Ambon in mid-January 1981 it was retailing at 1,000 rupiah, but by February it had fallen to 500 rupiah; in Geser at the same time durian fruits were available at 100 rupiah each and in Kataloka 25 rupiah each or even given away. As we move from one to the other, the size of the market is getting smaller and the supply larger compared with demand. Similar rules, of course, apply to all products, and producers seeking to sell commodities may preferentially take their stock to Geser, or even Ambon or Surabaya, where there is much more competition between traders, forcing prices up or down depending on the state of the market in a particular commodity. But even when the price fluctuates, the relative price of one commodity against another may be more stable, and this may be taken into account when determining what might be an acceptable payment. A trader in Kataloka will know that the price of long nutmeg will generally be 75 percent of the price of round nutmeg, and long nutmeg mace 80–90 percent of the price of round nutmeg mace; similarly the profit margin that a trader might expect to make in 1986 was 300 rupiah on long nutmeg (9 percent), 11 percent on round nutmeg, 4 percent on long nutmeg mace, and 3 percent on round nutmeg mace, though the price per kilogram was higher. These ratios were said to remain fairly constant.

Price is also affected by the degree to which a natural product has been processed, the resources a trader has for storage, and the degree to which a commodity can be safely stored. Nutmeg may be bought from producers dried or undried. Undried nutmeg (pala manta), with the mace still attached, is cheaper than dried nutmeg, even though the mace has been removed and can be sold separately. Thus, Wilhelmus Sauhupalla (Case 5 in chapter 9) bought one hundred undried nutmeg for 2,000 rupiah in May 1986, when the guide price per kilogram of pala manta was 300 rupiah. In Dulak he might pay 2,000 rupiah for 1 kilogram of shelled nutmeg. In this case his calculations as to the "right" price required that he convert between two forms of measurement, number of fruit and weight, and between two stages of preparation of the commodity, in addition to general matters of quality. If we now turn to the question of storage, copra, for example, is often kept until there is enough for one person to charter a boat. It may be stored in a shop or in the back of a house, if a trader has the space, or in a government godown for which rental is paid. If a producer or trader can afford to store a product he may benefit from cheaper transport costs attached to bulk goods, and he may be able to wait until prices rise. Selling prices fluctuate every day in Surabaya, particularly for cloves. In the past information concerning the market for any commodity in Surabaya was less reliable than it is now with telephone and other electronic forms of communication, and this may encourage storage rather than seeking risk-reduction strategies that have traditionally accompanied sale immediately after a harvest. If a trader has little capital and liquidity, he may seek a compromise solution by selling small quantities at a time to reduce risk. For all of these reasons figures in official statistics do not necessary reflect monthly production, but rather amounts reaching the official market when producers and traders decide to sell.

Finally, a note on the form of cash payment. With little cash in circulation in the smaller settlements and with cash payment opportunities restricted to trivial household necessities, there is little demand for high-denomination notes and, indeed, a positive reluctance to accept them. Thus, at those times when relatively large quantities of commodities are being sold to traders vendors will insist on being paid in small-denomination notes or coins (kepeng or pitis). On one occasion when a Chinese trader from Geser was buying trepang on Garogos the total purchase was sixteen sacks each containing 70 kilograms. The price negotiated was 400 rupiah a kilogram (this being mainly *kebi sisir* and *kebi metan*), coming to a total of 448,000 rupiah. But because the vendors insisted on being paid in 500-rupiah notes, the trader had to find 896 notes of that denomination. There are no banks anywhere in Southeast Seram.

8.6. The Regulatory Framework: Custom, Rulers, and Bureaucrats

Those stable social conditions and consistency in the application of rules and standards necessary for the effective conduct of trade can never be completely provided by traders themselves or their own institutions. Traders have always been beholden, not only to the tolerance of the political authorities with power in the territories in which they operated, but have also often relied on their direct intervention or at least the deliberate provision of an appropriate social regime that stimulated trade. This was often mutually convenient, and in this respect it makes no difference whether we are speaking of precolonial political regimes, the VOC period, the Netherlands East Indies, or the modern Indonesian state.

In the Conradian context of Southeast Seram there has been, over the course of five hundred years, no single overarching political authority that could provide that confidence, and traders have had to pay what was due to several Caesars to secure the proper conditions for commerce. Thus, before the arrival of Europeans, the appropriate political authority was effectively locally distributed: traders in Tidore were subject to edicts from the sultan, traders in Banda to the dispersed authority of the various orang kayas or their collective decisions; and in Southeast Seram to the *matlaen* of local domains and the alliances that they entered into. In some cases the presence of intermediary institutions, such as the syahbandar, assisted in this process, as discussed in chapter 4. By the mid-seventeenth century, in the area where it had influence, the VOC provided a framework for market trade, even though in the Moluccas it was from 1621 onward in theory implementing a command monopoly economy. With the demise of the VOC and with the creation of the Netherlands East Indies, the colonial economy was much more specifically concerned with regulating local markets, though in places like Geser and Gorom its control was never complete. Certainly, local traders found it convenient to seek the protection of the Dutch flag, but where authority had been devolved (as to the sultan of Tidore) and where that authority had little impact on the ground, traders were in the hands of local rulers.

At the local level ritual alliances, such as *pela* in Ambon-Lease and West Seram (chapter 1; and Bartels 1977) or *seri-tahun* and the various *tutu* in Southeast Seram (chapter 2.4), provided a framework for bilateral (in the case of *pela*) or multilateral security for exchange. Within the domain rulers could arbitrate in disputes, such as those concerning reef tenure, important in the harvesting of commercially important marine produce. But in return, as it were, for administrative services rendered rulers could claim tribute from traders or outsiders operating within their domain. Traders could advance credit, obtain desired goods, and provide other services for rulers, and rulers would provide privileged access to particular traders or groups of traders and guarantee necessary infrastructure and security.

In this latter respect little has changed. During the 1980s local rulers and custom were still a significant factor facilitating trade. For example, the raja of Kataloka could influence the marketing of sea produce and derive personal income from it, especially in the *Trochus* harvesting season. Thus, on Garogos, for any purchase over 100 kilograms a buyer had to pay 10 percent to a kepala soa "for the village" (*ngase*). Half of this stayed on Garogos itself and half went to the raja, "for the domain." All outside traders complied with this arrangement. Because of the levy the purchasing trader might attempt to lower the price. There was, therefore, an incentive for a producer to take large quantities of produce (illegally) to Geser where this levy was not deducted and where they would get the full price (Soselisa 1995:201). Not only was he entitled to a share of the harvest, but the raja could recommend particular traders, who would hold a near monopoly position and by virtue of this become indebted to him. The raja was also in a position to negotiate a fee from incoming commercial fishermen (who in some circumstances acted against the interests of ordinary fishermen by virtue of their technological advantages). In Ondor the prevalence of Bugis traders is not unconnected to the Bugis connections of the raja. By contrast, in Kataloka there are no Bugis traders, because, it is said, the late Raja Wattimena was influenced by their reputation for getting involved in knife fights. Between 1927 and 1972 there were no permanent Chinese traders in Kataloka either. This had been the express policy of successive rajas. All traders operated itinerantly. However, trade flourished in the neighboring domain of Ondor, which at that time had two or three shops, and in

Amarsekaru on nearby Manawoka, which had five or six. In 1972, at the suggestion of Sumarko, then port administrator in Amboina, Raja Wattimena of Kataloka embarked on the building of a pier and godown, and for the first time permitted traders to settle in his domain. The pier and godown, which were treated as his personal property and for which he received a small rent, were opened in 1973. Since then many more traders have settled in Kataloka (at least six families moved from Amarsekaru), resulting in an air of increased prosperity. Despite this, all traders operated under the express personal patronage of the raja. The newly achieved domination of commerce by Kataloka has hit Ondor badly; it has no pier of its own and its subjects have been frustrated by what they regard as the obstructive tactics employed by Wattimena. By the time of my departure from Gorom in May 1986, a trader had managed to extract from the provincial government the formal permission to build a separate pier in Ondor that would be capable of taking PELNI vessels. In doing this he not only circumnavigated the influence of Wattimena but also avoided the necessity of being dependent on his patronage.

Religion also affects the free flow of trade. Low productivity during the fasting month of Ramadan has some impact on trade. The month begins with a lull, but as cash runs out producers harvest and sell to traders; then there is another lull, and so on. The fasting month is therefore characterized by an overall low level of activity interrupted by episodic, irregular upswings. The effect on trade is somewhat reduced because produce acquired before Ramadan may be traded during the fast, or after, depending on prices. I noted feverish activity in Kwaos immediately before Ramadan in 1986. Where there are both Christians and Muslims the different patterns of religious festivals may give producers and traders of one confessional allegiance an advantage over the other. For example, during Ramadan, when prices rise, Christian traders may be able to benefit if they are selling or lose out if they are buying. In some areas advantages that might otherwise, and sometimes do, lead to conflict are evened out by employing the institution of *sasi* to limit harvesting of all of an important cash crop for the duration of an observance. Beliefs about inauspicious calendrical units may also affect trading: thus Tuesday and Saturday are regarded as bad days for a long voyage and for trade.

The most visible way in which the contemporary government, as with the preceding colonial government, interferes in the institutional infrastructure of trade is in the regulation of different physical outlets. Older traders insist that there is currently greater governmental control than during Dutch times. The conduct of all kinds of trading activity is bound by the requirement to obtain the correct permits and to pay taxes. Thus, even small vendors (harian) who operate from a patch of ground along the outer edge of Geser market pay 25 rupiah a day, though those farther away (outside the market area in the strict sense) pay nothing. Nan Kelian, who has a dry-food kiosk in the same market, pays a rent of 5,000 rupiah a month. To open a shop (toko) a trader needs to obtain a surat dagang from the Department Perdagangan in Ambon and to register at the office of the local camat; but if you wish to open a kiosk you only need to register at the camat's office. To open a warehouse a surat gudang is required, and so on. Thus, all resident traders in designated trading places, except the very smallest, require permission to operate, and the system inevitably works to the benefit of those who are better connected within the bureaucracy and who are sufficiently educated to negotiate the paperwork.

Trade is also affected by the taxes exacted by the Indonesian state. In a sense these are no different in their effects than the tribute or payments expected by local rajas and other customary payments or even the 10 percent tribute paid to *sengajis* or *kimalaha* or the 10 percent paid by the VOC to the sultans of Tidore or Ternate during the seventeenth century (Van Fraassen 1987). However, modern state taxes differ, at least from the contemporary customary payments, in the extent to which traders are successful in avoiding them. For example, in 1986 taxes had to be paid on all wholesale produce sold onward by traders, varying between 5 and 10 percent of the value of the goods, and it was expected that all produce exported from the subdistrict passed through Geser. In 1986 the avoidance of this tax had reached a critical level, and in May the camat went with a deputation to Ambon to complain in particular that there was too much direct trade between Kataloka (Gorom) and Surabaya that avoided paying daerah taxes, which are required to be paid on all goods passing through Geser and Ambon. There was a political dimension to this issue, given the long-standing tension between the independent-minded raja of Kataloka (with good direct access to government officials in Ambon) and the camat, trying to work through official channels. But apart from this, the ports of the Gorom, Watubela, and Teor groups are too distant from Geser for the smuggling of goods to be effectively curtailed, and some cargo-laden perahus escape without any official knowledge. This is so despite the presence of customs (Bea dan Cukai) officials, who, supposedly, like Somerset Maugham's tide-waiters, exercise a great deal of power by virtue of often being the only presence of government in a remote location other than teachers. Indeed, the customs official in Kataloka received a higher government salary than teachers and carried higher status, often being requested to deliver an oration at weddings. Another tax is IPEDA (Iuran Pembangunan Daerah), a development tax paid to the Kabupaten on land used for cash crops by registered producers; the amount paid depends on the area of land and kind of crop. It is paid annually after visits made by government assessors. Specific amounts of land are allocated for this purpose.

The classification of traders outlined in section 8.3 is far more inclusive than that reflected in official statistics, which tend to be confusing anyhow. It is only categories 4 and 5 that are recognized by the Indonesian and Provincial government as pedagang, and large numbers, especially in category 4, go unreported. Classification by official permit distinguishes between pedagang besar nasional (trader of national significance), pedagang perantara nasional (intermediary trader), pedagang pertokoan nasional (PN, shopkeeper), and pedagang eceran kecil (PK, small retailer) and indicates in each case whether a trader is Pribumi (an Indonesian citizen) or non-Pribumi (a foreign resident). Such a classification also serves as a controlling instrument. Thus, for the East Seram subdistrict as a whole, there had been, in 1973, 35 PN who were Indonesian nationals and 17 who were not, and 15 who were PK and Indonesian nationals and 20 who were not. By 1977 63 PN were reported and 27 PK (Statistik Tahunan Kecamatan: Seram Timur 1977–1978). By 1980 there were 288 registered traders overall. By 1981 this had risen to 318, and in 1982 to 352. During those years between 64 and 71 percent were PN and 29 percent PK: large-scale property-owning shopkeepers versus small, low-capital retailers. There is a gradual increase of PN during this period though government statistics are inconsistent. Of the PN, the overwhelming majority (93–94 percent) were classified as nonnative. Most of these were Chinese, but with some Arabs. Of the PK, nonnatives were only between 58 and 63 percent, and we must assume that most of these were Chinese though with some Arabs. Of the entire population of the East Seram subdistrict in 1979–1980, 297 are registered foreigners (WNA [warga negara asing]), 0.5–0.62 percent of the population. Of the total population of Geser, registered foreigners constituted 120 out of a population of 2,216 (between 5 and 6 percent). Registered foreigners are also present in Amaisekaru, Kataloka, Ondor, Dai, Mida, Amarwatu, Kotasiri, Utta, and Tamher Timur, but outside of Geser only in Kataloka and Amarwatu do they rise above 1 percent of the population (Statistik Tahunan Kecamatan: Seram Timur 1982:12, 37). In the next chapter the implications of recognizing traders (officially or unofficially) on the basis of ethnic origin are explored further.

9
Traders, Migration, and Ethnicity

> Appropriately enough, it is Hermes—the god of the boundary-stone—
> who becomes the Greek god of trade, embodying the suspicions and
> apprehensions towards strangers common to a household economy.
> He shares with Proteus the image of duplicity, if not of multiplicity.
> He is known as both trickster and thief, the two being difficult to
> distinguish . . . in a setting where no juridical concept of private
> property or contractual alienation exists. He is a messenger-god,
> a marginal figure known for his "skill at the oath," his deceptive
> manipulation of the literalism of the kinship or familial bond.
>
> J.-C. AGNEW (FOLLOWING N. O. BROWN)

9.1. Traders

In the preceding chapter I outlined the organizational context in which
traders operate and said something of the way in which trading works as a
process. However, it is also necessary to show how abstract rules and proce-
dures articulate with the lives of individual traders, how those traders perform within the context outlined to modify it, and specifically how the
lives of individual traders relate to processes of group creation, dissolution,
and maintenance. We have already seen that there is a rather loose fit
between the pragmatic functional typology of traders and official governmental categories. I wish now to take this further and show how traders,
within a lifespan, can move between different kinds and scales of trading
activity, how the same applies at a generational level, and how, within a
genealogically and ethnically defined set of relationships, trading operations of different types, scales, and official designations may inhere to create a dynamically responsive network.

   In chapter 8.3 I identified five kinds of traders operating in the Moluccan region:

1. Those who only occasionally trade the produce of the domestic
   unit, usually locally;
2. Those who regularly trade their own produce, usually locally, but
   sometimes taking the produce to more distant market centers;

3. Those who regularly trade their own produce and engage in some middleman activities;

4. Petty merchants relying on small capital, usually owning small shops (pondok, kios, toko), and where trade may occasionally be supplemented by some production where this is possible;

5. Major merchants relying on considerable capital, usually owning one or more shops (toko) and often with capital invested in transport and sometimes land. They may also sometimes have a stake in productive enterprises.

Categories 1 to 3 all apply to producers, and those traders who fit these descriptions largely identify themselves as ethnic Serammers, Goromese, and so on. There are some exceptions: Butonese and Bugis land settlers and those of Hadhrami Arab descent who have married into the settlement of Kwamar. The abbreviated case histories that follow are for traders who are best placed in categories 4 and 5, though the variation in scale of trading operation is very wide. This partly reflects different phases in a life cycle but also, to a considerable extent, ability to secure capital over the long term. Traders also vary in the extent to which they specialize, though all traders begin with the assumption that they will trade in almost anything as a strategy for risk reduction in a peripheral area with low levels of overall production. Specialization is generally a consequence of avoiding high-risk transactions and of avoiding commodities where (a) infrequent opportunities to trade are reflected in lack of confidence that traders have acquired the appropriate knowledge to judge the quality of the product and the market conditions, and (b) personal networks are insufficiently robust.

There follow eleven short case histories of various lengths obtained from individual traders in 1981 and 1986. I have deliberately not grouped them by ethnic labels. This is partly because I hope that this will allow for better understanding of the similarities in the operation of all traders, and partly because it is sometimes empirically difficult. Immigrant traders for various demographic and strategic reasons are more likely to seek partners from other ethnic groups than do local people who already have rights in land and resources and who perceive themselves as indigenous.

CASE 1: UMAR AL BAYIRI

In 1981 Umar Al Bayiri owned the Warung Gaya Baru near the harbor at Tual (in the Kei Islands), a coffee shop but with a takeout cake trade. His father had arrived in Indonesia from the Hadhramaut in 1888 and almost immediately settled in Tual. There he acquired a coconut plantation still retained by his children. He lived in Banda for some time, where he died. The income of his son depends mainly on the warung and on selling copra, which is sent to

Surabaya by perahu or motorboat. At the Surabaya end his business is handled by a brother, who in return sends retail goods to Tual in anticipation or on receipt of instructions from Umar. Some retail goods, such as palm sugar, he purchases in Ambon. Umar also trades in pearls from Dobo, which he sells mainly to visitors from Ambon, as a sideline. He does not deal in other sea produce. Umar has a brother in Tual and two children: a sixteen-year-old son currently resident in Jakarta and a daughter aged thirteen who assists in the warung. His nephew attended the SMA (secondary school) in Ambon and returned to Tual to set up as a small building contractor, relying mainly on government contracts for houses and offices; he has been married for eleven years to a Chinese woman who runs a small pondok and by whom he has six children. Umar also has family connections with two families of Arab descent in Geser. He describes himself as peranakan and basteran (mixed blood).

CASE 2: ACHMAD ZUBEIDA

Achmad Zubeida, an associate of Umar Al Bayiri, comes from a third-generation Arab family, and both his father and grandfather were born in the Hadhramaut. His grandfather established himself as a trader in bird of paradise feathers, trepang, and other high-value goods along the New Guinea coast, having first bought a perahu; his purchases were sold in Kaimana to the Nederlandsche Handel Maatschappij. Achmad claims that his grandfather was the first to convert Papuans to Islam and tells the story of a man who was about to throw his dead child into the sea and who was persuaded by Zubeida's grandfather (who was himself later to die at sea) to give him a proper burial. Achmad himself was born in Tual and is now 73. He spent a long time in Geser, where he married a woman of Arab descent. He is now a building contractor but also owns a warung.

CASE 3: MOHAMMED ACHMAD BAADILLA

Baadilla was born in Banda in 1927, and in May 1981 had lived in Geser for ten years. He still regards Banda as his home and Geser as his place of work. He comes from eleven generations of Bandanese Arabs and has Dutch perkenier (settler) blood in him. He is related to Des Alwi and Hal Putih is his brother-in-law, two individuals prominent in the small Bandanese elite. His wife is also a Bandanese Arab and his sister keeps a restaurant in Banda Neira. He owns the Kios Banda and a clothes kiosk on the Kilwaru side of the small market building on the Geser harbor front. He is the only Arab dealing in clothes (this is usually a Bugis speciality). He specializes in buying clothes from Jakarta, traveling there between one and (occasionally) four times a year to make his purchases. He has many "relatives" in Jakarta. He buys from market retailers, usually in Glodok, though also elsewhere (including Blok M). He does not buy directly from manufacturers, because they would want to sell by the bale. He sometimes flies to Jakarta, but always comes back to Geser by sea to accompany his cargo. His wife always remains in Geser to look after the kiosks.

CASE 4: YUSUF MUTAHU AL HAMID

Yusuf Mutahu Al Hamid was born in Hatumeten, Werinama subdistrict (on Seram). He was brought to Geser by his parents when young. He has nine children by his first wife, five of which survive; seven by his second wife (from Kei Besar), six of which survive. He has fourteen grandchildren, five male and nine female. When he first came to Geser he was a trader, but entirely through his wife's connections. He owned as many as nine perahu, including ones of 9, 15, and 30 tons. He traded in sagu laka or lemping (sago biscuits), sagu tumang (damp sago flour), and coffee, which he would take to Ambon. He would never go as far as Surabaya; that was left to Butonese. The items of trade have not changed much; only cloves have become more important. His boats were crewed by men from Geser, not necessarily kinsmen.

CASE 5: WILHELMUS SAUHUPALLA

Will or Welly (Figure 9.1), born in Banda Neira in 1946, comes from a first-generation Chinese family on his mother's side and nonfarming Ambonese stock on his father's side; his paternal grandfather was a teacher in Siresore Kristen on Saparua, and his father, who had himself been born in Banda, was an employee of a Dutch-owned oil firm and then of an electricity utility in Sorong. His father recently died and is buried in Banda. His mother is one of four sisters who accompanied their parents from Hokkien, settling in Banda Neira. On marriage, two sisters moved to Gorom and two (including his mother) to Sorong. It was in Sorong that Will attended a Dutch language school and where his mother was later to die. On Gorom, with the opening up of Kataloka to permanent Chinese traders, one of his mother's sisters acquired a shop in Kataloka with her husband and the second a shop in Dulak, in the domain of Ondor several hours' walk south along the west coast. Will moved to Ondor in 1967, where he married an ethnic Chinese woman from Makassar, Teh Peng Eng. Will too set up shop in Dulak (Toko Bunga Kencana) and in 1986 when I visited him was also renting a house in Amar-

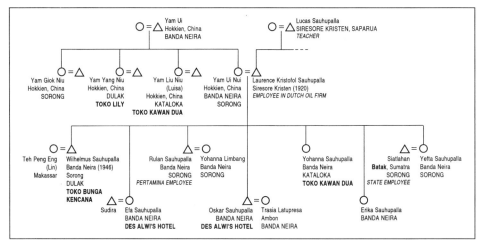

Figure 9.1. Genealogical fragment for a mixed Chinese-Ambonese family (Sauhu-palla), illustrating migration within three generations from southeastern China, via Banda, to Southeast Seram. Recorded 1986, Kataloka.

watu for the duration of the nutmeg season that served as a base for purchasing the crop from local producers. From there he also sells a selection of goods brought from Dulak in his jonson *Ocean Star*. He mainly concentrates on hasil darat—nutmeg, cloves, and copra— which he sells in Surabaya, transporting produce by ship, motor laut, and perahu, depending on the season and the relative costs. He moves between Gorom and Banda Neira, where he stays in the house of his elder sister. Before moving to Dulak, Will used to trade frequently with his father in New Guinea, especially in the larger places (such as Fak-fak) when they had the status of international ports through which you could export directly. This changed in the 1960s. On one occasion Will had taken some copra to Fak-fak, but discovered when he got there that he was unable to pay the exorbi-tantly high duty demanded by officials. Because he had already sold the copra, he made a quick getaway by jonson back to Gorom. He used a pocket compass and it took him twelve hours. In the 1970s he also traveled along the New Guinea coast buying lola and other products. Will claims that being a trader on Gorom requires patience; you have to be prepared to wait around for people and for them to do things in their own time.

CASE 6: ABDURAHMIN WARNANGAN

Abdurahmin (Figure 9.2) was born in Namlea, Buru, of a first-gener-ation Chinese father and a local woman. He moved to Ambon in

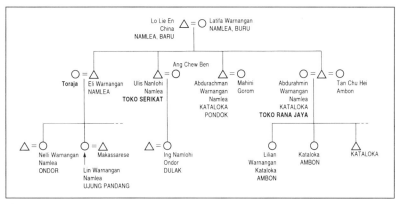

Figure 9.2. Partial genealogy for mixed Ambonese-Chinese trading family (Warnangan). Recorded 1986, Kataloka.

1961, where he married Tan Chu Hei and set up a textile shop in the market. Though his father is dead, his mother still lives in Namlea. He moved to Kataloka in 1975, finding Ambon "unhealthy" and "ramai terlalu" (too bustling), and where he now runs the Toko Rana Jaya, which he rents from the raja. He has four children, the youngest of which is Lilian born in 1980. He has no land and engages in no cultivation or fishing. When I first met Abdurahmin in 1981 he was concentrating on trade in the islands to the south of Gorom (Watubela, Teor, Kesui, and as far as Kur in the Kei Islands) as well as along the New Guinea coast. Abdurahmin is one of the few traders in Kataloka to visit New Guinea frequently. He goes with a juru batu (pilot and boatswain) mainly to Kaimana, Karas, and Adi where there are no settlements with permanent traders. He begins trading along the New Guinea coast in March, when the weather permits safe travel. There he stays with acquaintances for about a week, using Indonesian, not Goromese, as a medium of communication. The villages are mostly native Papuan, but with some admixture of people tracing descent from locations on Gorom and Seram. The incentives for trading in New Guinea are largely that buying prices are lower, though this has to be offset by the transport costs. Thus, 1 kilogram of *Trochus* in Karas in 1986 cost 1,250 rupiah, compared with 1,500 rupiah on Gorom. On one trip to Kaimana he obtained about three tons. On another he attempted to set up a joint venture with a Taiwanese businessman selling fish from Karas, but, he says, the potential partner vanished. From Kesui, Abdurahmin collects copra, usually traveling by his own jonson, securing a purchase and then arranging for its onward transport by motor laut, jonson, or perahu. More widely he trades in nutmeg (including pala onin from New Guinea) and cloves. Of the various hasil laut, he

fetches lola and batu laga from Kaimana, Adi, and Karas, and on
Teor focuses mainly on lola, though not trepang, which is relatively
unimportant in the islands south of Gorom. He buys sagu tumang
from Air Kasar on the Seram mainland but also from other villages;
and sagu kaspi on Pulau Panjang and from people who bring it to
Kataloka. In complete contrast, he also deals in "antiques." These he
collects from Kesui and Kaimana: one celadon kendi sold in 1986 for
500,000 rupiah, and others for 150,000 rupiah. The nutmeg is sent
to Surabaya as freight on larger vessels rather than by perahu, where
it is sold by a contact there who sends in return rice, sugar, and salt.
Cloves are disposed of in Ambon or Surabaya depending on opportunities and the price. The hasil laut he sells in Ambon to the Firma
Benteng Mas. On the whole he prefers to buy rice in Ambon when
the price is right, where he also buys textiles and sundries (kelon-
tong) for onward sale.

CASE 7: HENKE BULA

In February 1981 Henke Bula was proprietor of the Toko Sinar Baru
in Geser, where most of his close affinal relatives lived and where he
worked as a general trader between Geser and New Guinea. He has
few living consanguines. His father (who owned a tailor shop) is
dead, and his mother lives in Bula on the northeast coast of Seram.
His wife's father, now dead, was a Chinese who married a local
Moluccan woman born in Geser; her mother lives with them. Born
of Chinese parentage, Henke moved to Bula with his parents in
about 1939 and moved again to Geser, leaving his parents in Bula
when he was ten to attend the Chinese school that existed then.
However, he stayed at school for only one year or so. He married
locally and changed his name officially from Chin. Like most major
merchants, Henke has his own motor jonson: in his case one *bodi*
and three motors. He has coconut plantations that he pays someone else to tend and harvest. The most important commodities in
which Henke deals are nutmeg and copra, followed by cloves. He
also trades in a little damar, though did so much more during the
lifetime of his wife's father, who owned a perahu and went himself
to New Guinea to collect it. He is also involved in a little local trade
in fresh coconut and sago. Henke still has a Papuan trading partner
who also owns a perahu. Henke supplies manufactured retail goods
for sale in New Guinea, and his partner supplies agar-agar, lola, turtle shell, shark fins, and so on, which he obtains from Misool and
other islands in the Raja Ampat or Onin area (Papalab, Karas,
Waigama). In the past Henke has also traded in salt fish, but considers it much hard work for too little return. The turtle shell he may

sometimes take to Makassar, from where it is exported to Japan. Other produce is exported to Hong Kong and Singapore. The sea produce is taken to Ambon or Makassar when there is sufficient to fill a lambo or motorboat. Henke sometimes hires two or three perahu to buy stock in Surabaya. In Surabaya he buys manufactured goods for his shop, but tends to purchase cigarettes and some other items in Ambon. He employs Butonese in Banda to take any produce available to Surabaya during the musim timur and who return with stock for the shop. If he does not go himself, some other relative will.

CASE 8: JOHANNES RUMOLI

Johannes Rumoli was born in Geser in 1953, is married to an ethnic Chinese woman, Oe Hua Eng, and owns the Toko Sumber Tanya. The most important commodity that he handles is cloves, followed by nutmeg. He also handles some hasil laut. The cloves and nutmeg are taken to Surabaya, where the cloves are sold to those agents of the various kretek cigarette firms that make the highest bid and the nutmeg usually to the Toko Sumbar Mas. Hasil laut is sold in Ambon to Bendera Mas, C. V. Setudjuh, and Survei Angin Timur, though Rumoli sometimes sends trepang to Makassar, from where it is exported to Hong Kong and Japan. Dry food goods (sugar, flour, beans, and rice) to stock the shop are also bought in Ambon; all other things are brought directly from Surabaya by motor laut or perahu. Neither Rumoli nor any close kin associated with the Toko Sumber Tanya have a jonson, nor sufficient capital to purchase one. Rumoli takes the view that there are too many shops and traders in Geser (1986) to support the trade available.

CASE 9: FREDDY RUMAU

Freddy Rumau (Tong Yau) (Figure 9.3) was born in Wonomolio on Buton Island in Southeast Sulawesi in 1954 of ethnic Chinese parentage. His parents moved to Amarsekaru while Freddy was still young, where he married Agnes Tesman, of Indo-European extraction. His parents lived with his youngest sister in 1986 in Surabaya. Freddy and his wife moved with his two other sisters from Amarsekaru to Kataloka in 1976, at a time when the latter domain was replacing the former as the most important central trading place in the Gorom archipelago. The first family shop in Kataloka, Toko Udi, had been opened in 1971. In 1986 Freddy operated from the Toko Kembang Baru; the eldest sister was married to Joni Rumoi who owned the Toko Baru.

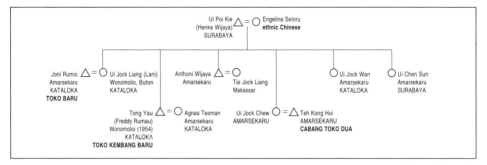

Figure 9.3. Genealogical fragment of predominantly Chinese trading family (Wijaya), illustrating migration from Java in the senior generation to Amarsekaru and then movement to Kataloka as new opportunities opened up there. Recorded 1986, Kataloka.

CASE 10: LIE PING GIE

Lie Ping Gie was born near Sorong, the son of a first-generation immigrant from China. When he was four years old his parents moved to Ambon. He was a teacher until 1965, when the school closed because of anti-Chinese sentiment. He worked in a shop in Ambon, where he was able to accumulate sufficient capital to buy a shop in Geser (1974). In 1981, when I interviewed him, he had no other business concerns except for the shop, from which he sold dry foods and tinned and bottled produce. Almost all of his stock had been bought from larger enterprises in Ambon; he cut the cost by making joint purchases with a similarly placed small trader in Wahai. He traded in a small amount of local produce, such as honey bought for 2,000 rupiah a bottle and sold at 2,500.

CASE 11: TITI TENG

Teng Ming That (Titi) (Figure 9.4) was born in Banda of a second-generation ethnic Chinese mother. His paternal grandfather had also been born in China, but had married a local Bandanese woman. Like many Chinese traders who had initially settled in Banda, the decline in Banda as a trading center throughout the twentieth century forced the couple to reemigrate, this time to Geser, where all of Titi's siblings were born. The eldest brother established the Toko Subur Jaya. In April 1986 Titi was living in Suru on the East Seram mainland with his new wife, Tan Ai In, whom he had recently married in Dobo. At that time he had been based for six years in Suru, traveling from village to village depending on the season, buying up harvests of nutmeg, cloves, and copra. The trade pickings are thought to be slender on this stretch of the Seram coast.

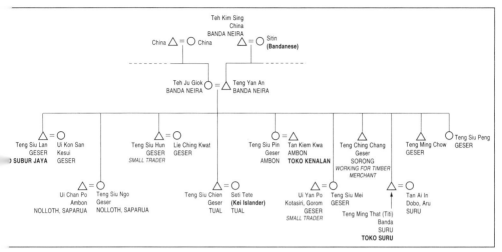

Figure 9.4. Genealogical fragment for a predominantly Chinese trading family (Teng), illustrating migration within three generations from South China, via Banda, to Southeast Seram. Recorded 1986, Geser.

9.2. Kinship, Ethnogenesis, and Identity

Migration and trade in the Moluccas have always been closely connected. What they have in common, of course, is the movement of people. In confining ourselves to the Banda zone, we can identify three kinds of semipermanent mobility that we might define as migration: (A) local migration within the area, which in the Moluccas generally is often complex and with a long history, as witnessed by the native Bandanese migration to Southeast Seram and Kei after 1621 (see also Lucardie 1980); (B) in-migration of traders and settlers from the western part of the archipelago; and (C) out-migration of Banda zone traders and settlers to the eastern periphery, including New Guinea.

At one end, local movement in category A currently entails temporary shifts, kinship and affinal visiting, and movement associated with spatially distributed marriage patterns. Here, a corresponding flow of goods and commodities is likely to be associated with the fulfillment of exchange obligations linked to close genealogical ties—the strongest of which are "hubungan darah" (blood ties)—where people can trace a common grandparent. Relations between more distant kin become increasingly ambiguous in their moral implications, not involving expectation of direct periodic exchanges yet providing opportunities and constraints when it comes to trade. Local migration of individuals up to and including the movement of entire villages is rather different. These latter migrations (in the East Seram subdistrict, of Kei Islanders and Timorese) are often government-assisted and not the outcome of spontaneous economic enterprise. Nevertheless, where local migration has occurred, especially where this has resulted in intermarriage, there is a high correlation with trading activity. Thus, in Warus-warus a Kei islander from Kur married to a local woman from Kilbat born in Banda of Bugis parentage had in 1981 been engaged in general trade for thirty-five years, though without a boat or shop. There were another six traders and several carpenters from Kur living in Kilbat and Tarui at the time. At this range of social distance, although kinship obligations might not be assumed to have the moral force to limit the accumulation of economic surpluses, the distribution of genealogical relationships means that trading networks are often insufficiently elaborated to permit effective participation in higher-order regional and long-distance trade. It is not, therefore, surprising that such traders are more likely to be in category 4 than 5.

We can now turn to category B movements. Oral and documentary traditions, such as the *Hikayat Tanah Hitu* (Manusama 1977), suggest that the formation of centralized polities in the central Moluccas was in part due to in-migration from Java. Certainly, by the beginning of the sixteenth century there were resident populations of Javanese, Arabs, Malays, Chinese, and others. The 1621 massacre of native Bandanese by the Dutch gave rise to an almost entirely immigrant population in the Banda Islands of Papuans, Ambonese, and Dutch plus a potpourri of other minorities (Hanna 1978:62–63), with the later addition of many Javanese coolies; in Ambon-Lease intermarriage with Europeans and other immigrants formed the basis of a distinctive creole culture. From before the arrival of Europeans until the late nineteenth century, and probably later, Papuan slaves were being brought to Gorom, Geser, and the east coast of Seram. Likewise (category C), Tidorese, Serammers, and Goromese were settling along the coasts of Onin and the Bird's Head in New Guinea (chapter 5 and section 9.7). The seventeenth century saw the rise of Bugis and Makassan trade and migration, though by 1980 the trading niche once occupied by these peoples had become dominated by Butonese, a pattern particularly well illustrated in the case of Banda.

Incoming populations have been progressively assimilated, and in many cases the outward signs of immigrant origin are a few traditions and perhaps the use of Malay rather than a local language. We can take a few illustrations from Southeast Seram. Air Kasar, for example, is a village of Bugis origin, founded about seventy years ago; Kilbat is of Timorese origin, founded before 1880 and now with few native-language speakers; there are two settlements of Kei islanders in the domain of Kilmuri; and Kilmoi is of Butonese origin, founded four hundred years ago. Recent immigrants, however, maintain links with their home villages and culturally are much more visible. This is particularly so for the Butonese, who constitute the largest single visible group of immigrants in Southeast Seram. In some places, immigrants outnumber the indigenous population. Ambon Island, for example, has many Butonese villages, some of which are extremely large and important in trade (e.g., Momokeng). Although there is the usual centripetal movement from periphery to center, this is compensated to some extent by the local migration of people from high population centers to the periphery. Thus, the Hoamoal Peninsula of West Seram, virtually depopulated by the Dutch in the seventeenth century, was during the 1970s and 1980s being rapidly repopulated by Butonese and local Moluccans from Ambon-Lease, Kei, and elsewhere. The present-day village of Loki, for example, is only one hundred years old, and most are more recent still. Although there has been an official ban on further spontaneous migration from Sulawesi, it still continues, with overpopulation in certain migrant areas. Only the civil unrest since 1998 has led to a partial reversal of this trend. By the late 1980s a process of local redistribution of Butonese migrants was evident. For example, with the decline of the sailing trade, land shortage, and the lack of alternative employment in the Banda Archipelago, many Butonese were moving to the Tehoru area of South Seram where land was available for establishing clove groves.

In some cases ethnic groups emerge or have their boundaries reinforced through functional specialization: Minangkabau run eating houses, Bugis trade in textiles, Butonese provide perahu transportation, Arabs deal in pearls, and so on. There is—at least in the perception of local people and in the expectation of some migrants—a normative ethnic division of labor, or what Gregory (1997:209, following Dewey 1962b:182 and Alexander 1987) called "mercantile stratification." In most cases this is context-dependent, and in Southeast Seram patterns of activity, specialist commodities, and levels of wealth within the Chinese community are varied and the functional overlaps with the Arab trading community extensive. A rather special case of the same phenomenon is that of the Sama-Bajau, who carry with them a generic ethnicity over a wide area, linked to aquatic mobility and fishing specialization both as primary collectors and as traders (Sopher 1965:112). These groups appear to have been important in some local Moluccan economies during the first half of the nineteenth century, but by 1872 their identity was already becoming lost. We know also that some accompanied Makassan trepang boats on their annual voyages to New Guinea (ibid., 156), but in the Moluccas generally Sama-Bajau have not been conspicuous in the modern period.[1]

I want to suggest here that the sociology of trade—the use of family linkages and general mode of operation—is in almost every case the same, irrespective of ethnic origin, that the social organization and culture of trade in archipelagic Southeast Seram is a hybrid of all this in-migration, and that it is this that gives it its special features. On the whole, although individual traders may exhibit preferences in terms of those commodities in which they deal, there is a tendency for general merchandising as opposed to functional specialisms linked to particular ethnic groups, in contrast with, say, India (Gregory 1997). Any specialization that exists is much more in terms of the scale of the operation or of the labor function within the market. Producers tend to specialize much more, but most traders find this too risky if they are to maintain viable levels of profit. However, I also suggest that ethnically identifiable groups can still be placed on a continuum based on approximate degree of cultural similarity. The extent to which ethnicity as such becomes important in trade is partly also a matter of demography, conventions as to specialization, and government expediency. Where large numbers of persons of a particular origin are involved in the same trade it is usual to find domination by the well-known "trading diasporas" (cf. Curtin 1975; Eades 1993; Lovejoy 1980). In Southeast Seram currently this means for the most part Chinese, Hadhrami Arabs, and the South Sulawesi 'seafaring trade diasporas" (Curtin 1984:160 n. 2), mainly "Bugis" and "Butonese." The small numbers of ethnic Javanese in trade are usually female jamu (folk medicine) sellers. For the purposes of this account I have elected to focus on four major bounded groups (Bugis, Butonese, Arabs, and Chinese) and to ignore smaller groups (Javanese, Minangkabau), but as I shall argue, although questions of ethnic identity and boundedness are never far away, in terms of the practicalities of trade and social life it is the heterogeneity and intermarriage in trading families that is really significant in the area under analysis.

9.3. Bugis

We know from the historical material reviewed in chapters 3 and 4 and from artifacts such as the Bugis grave in Ondor that traders of South Sulawesi origin have been involved in trade in archipelagic Southeast Seram at least since the first decade of the seventeenth century. But as Andaya (1991:73) noted, outside of Sulawesi the distinctions between Bugis, Makassans, and Mandarese were often conflated, such that the term "Bugis" was generally used loosely to refer to all of them. Households described as Bugis currently are found in Kilwaru, Air Kasar, and Ondor. Bugis in Kilwaru are of two types: asli, by which is meant in this context relatively recent immigrants with identifiable Bugis proper names (such as Haji Abdul Fatah Dain Perani, Lagusii, and Permana), and those belonging to the soa Bugis (e.g., Mohammed Kasim Bugis), who are presumably the much-intermarried descendants of a much earlier settlement. Indeed, it is said that there were many Bugis in Kilwaru formerly, which is consistent with historical data suggesting Kilwaru as the foremost trading post before Geser to host Sulawesi traders. The Air Kasar settlement falls into the asli category, being founded in 1916 by migrants voyaging in one *pelari* headed by Dain Perani. The rulers of Kilbat and Warus-warus argued for many years over who controlled Air Kasar, and in the end the Dutch arbitrated from Waru and made it an independent *negori* (desa), though with a sea front of only 270 meters and a territory extending no more than 1 kilometer inland. Air Kasar has been an independent desa ever since; colonial administrative fiat yet again enhanced ethnic difference. A branch of the Air Kasar Bugis has more

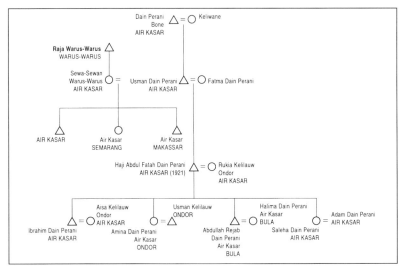

Figure 9.5. The genealogy of Haji Abdul Fatah Dain Perani, born in Air Kasar in 1921. The genealogy also illustrates the intermarriage between the Bugis lineage of Air Kasar (Dain Perani) and the ruling indigenous lineages of Warus-warus and Ondor. Recorded 1986, Geser.

recently (between 1980 and 1987) moved to Ondor, though there has been a continuous presence of Bugis in Ondor since the first decade of the twentieth century and perhaps longer. There are also Bugis families in Kataloka and Geser, as well as in Tual, Fak-fak, and Dobo, places technically outside the administrative subdistrict of East Seram but within the traditional Southeast Seram trading area. Since 1916 there has been extensive Dain Perani endogamy, though some strategic exogamic marriages, such as to the raja of Warus-warus (Figure 9.5). Elsewhere Bugis have married into the Kastella lineage of Kiltai and the lineage of the raja of Kelu. Most people of Bugis origin are now settled in agriculture or fishing. The few involved in trade are from neither Kilwaru nor Air Kasar. For example, all the kiosks in Geser market are run by Bugis, mostly specializing in cloth; and there are eleven Bugis kiosk-level establishments in Ondor, again mainly selling cloth. Bugis tend not to be involved in the hasil (natural product) trade, presumably because of the larger amounts of capital required, and deal in retail goods bought mainly from other traders.

9.4. **Butonese**

Traders from Southeast Sulawesi (including those originating from the islands of Buton, Muna, Kabaena and Tukang Besi and who I here collectively describe [following Moluccan practice] as Butonese) have been operating in the waters of archipelagic Southeast Seram for almost as long as

Bugis. Butonese lambos (chapter 6.3) and villages are generally known by place of origin. Thus, we have Buton Tira, Buton Wanci, Buton Tomia, and Buton Bau-bau. By the mid-nineteenth century Butonese were sufficiently in evidence for Wallace (1896:128) to mention them as a significant group of traders, and it is likely that the settlement at Arbi on Seram Laut dates from that period. However, with the possible additional exception of Kilmoi on mainland Seram, settled by Bau-bau people in perhaps the eighteenth century or earlier, present-day Butonese settlements are all very recent. The land for those now living on Seram Laut (Figure 2.9) was gifted by the domains of Kelu, Kiltai, and Kilwaru, to whom they are in some important respects still subject. These settlements are no older than three generations, and in 1986 most of those persons with birth dates before 1916 were born in Southeast Sulawesi or Banda. Some of those born since 1946 were also born in Sulawesi, but since then most are native to the Seram Laut hamlets of Arkel (Kelu), Arbi (Kiltai), and Talang Baru, Bokan, Wawasa, Karang, and Tengah (all Kilwaru). There was relatively little in-migration of Butonese during the last two decades of the twentieth century, partly due to official government restrictions. In addition to Seram Laut and Kilmoi, there are Butonese settlements on Kesui and some households on Gorom. The principal and oldest settlements in the Banda zone are in the Banda Islands themselves, where in 1981 they constituted 40 percent of the total population of 13,530, largely located on Run and Gunung Api.

Traditionally, Butonese are mainly sailors, boatbuilders, and small merchants, combining their role as traders with that of boat owners and bulk transporters of goods. However, currently few of those settled on Seram Laut actually own a lambo and trade with it. All boats once owned by Butonese are now beyond repair, and there are no plans to build anew. It is the Banda population that is much more oriented to this older way of life, as described by Southon (1995). Evers (1988:94–95) provided us with some insightful evidence on Butonese traders from the Sulawesi end, working with people of the Tukang Besi Islands. He recorded 169 lambos for Wangi-wangi in the early 1980s, compared with the 48 I noted as registered with Butonese names in Banda for 1978 (chapter 6.3; Table 6.2). Merchandise was bought mainly in Gresik or Makassar and then peddled around eastern Indonesia. Sea captains and their crew members tended to know village headmen in the villages where they traded, who would be responsible for placing orders for the next voyage. On this basis, long-term relationships often developed and a "secret language of contacts" (*rahasia juragan*) accumulated (Southon 1995:32). Sometimes traders rented or even bought land in the villages of trading partners, starting coconut or clove plantations of their own. Others moved into already established Butonese villages.

By contrast, most Butonese on Seram Laut are farmers, and some in coastal settlements are also fishermen. All rely heavily on petty trade in fresh foodstuffs, especially vegetables. People may paddle over the narrow strait to Geser three or four times in a single day, even paddling back late at

Table 9.1. Registered sailing boats entering and departing from selected
Moluccan harbors, 1980–1985

Boat Type	Ambon 1980	Banda 1984	Geser 1985	Kataloka 1985
Perahu layar	283	47	77	47
Perahu layar with registered Butonese owner	164	35	40	no data
Percentage	60	74	52	
Total number of records	1,526	106	192	1,005
Percentage of Butonese	11	33	21	no data

Source: Kantor Syahbandar registers for Ambon (1980), Banda (1984), Geser (1985),
and Kataloka (1985).

night after watching a video. Most vendors in Geser market are Butonese
women, though none rents a permanent stall. There is relatively little land
on Seram Laut, but Butonese cultivate what they have in a fairly intensive
way, planting coconut for Kelu, Kiltai, and Kilwaru landowners, the permission of whom they require when harvesting and who are entitled to
take 50 percent of copra profits. There is some intermarriage (e.g., Figure
9.8), but Butonese are predominantly endogamous.

Despite the fact that resident Butonese in archipelagic Southeast Seram
are no longer active as boat owners, sailors, and long-distance traders, in
Geser at any one time you are likely to find two or three Butonese lambos,
mostly owned by Butonese residents in Banda or other Bandanese, or by
Butonese from places such as Wangi-wangi in Southeast Sulawesi. Owners
of these lambos, such as La Donggala, owner of *Pasir Kai*, moored off
Gunung Api in March 1981, undertake on average two voyages a year to
Surabaya or Gresik, where they stay for about twenty days to a month.
Geser traders easily can obtain a Butonese perahu by using the government
radiotelephone to Banda, and most of them know many perahu owners
personally and vice versa. In 1981, 58 percent of all lambos registered as
arriving or departing Ambon were Butonese owned, 52 percent for Geser in
1985, and 74 percent for Banda in 1984. The Butonese share of the trade is
also holding up in terms of percentage of overall registered movements
(Table 9.1).

9.5. Hadhrami Arabs

There is a long history of Arab contact with the Moluccas. We know that
Arab merchants were present on Neira in the Banda group when the Dutch
first arrived in 1599, and after the massacre of the indigenous Bandanese in
1621 the Dutch depended heavily on Arabs for their trade. However, at that
stage there can have been few permanent Arab residents. Wurffbain's

account (Van den Berg 1872), written in 1638, provided some population information for different ethnic groups, but figures for Arabs (as such) are not included among them. With the establishment of a Dutch settler colony of perkeniers, Arab traders on Banda served as middlemen and moneylenders. By the late eighteenth and early nineteenth centuries Arab "country traders" based on the Coromandel coast of India were visiting Banda regularly (Hanna 1978).

The most important change in the position of Arab traders on Banda, and one with permanent consequences, came with the second British occupation of 1810–1817, after the annexation of the Netherlands to the Napoleonic empire. This resulted in "the permanent settlement... of new and more numerous Chinese and Arab merchants from Surabaya and Batavia, Bombay and Calcutta, Bencoolen and Penang" (ibid., 98). These traders opened small shops that soon monopolized local retail trade and eventually replaced the perkeniers in the trade with other islands. Population figures provided by Bleeker (1856:111) for 1854 do not separately list Arabs, though they are probably included in the category of "native Muslims": 841 of a total population of 6,333. However, the same authority noted that in Ambon in 1833 there were in the region of 400 Arabs and "andere vreemde oosterlingen" (other foreign Asians) compared with 200 Chinese, and 283 Arabs and others compared with 246 Chinese by 1855 (ibid., 11, 80). Clarence-Smith (1998:34) provided us with more specific figures for Ambonese Arabs culled from various archival sources: 1859 (53), 1870 (170), 1885 (444), 1905 (875). Such figures need to be interpreted with circumspection, but they do suggest a greater proportion of Arabs to Chinese in the eastern archipelago in the early part of the nineteenth century than was the case later or indeed is the case currently.

Whatever the precise demographic picture, by the late nineteenth century Arabs appear to have briefly achieved some degree of commercial supremacy over both Chinese and Europeans (ibid.; cf. Van den Berg 1886: 134). Travelers' descriptions begin to indicate vividly the role of Arab traders. In April 1882, for example, on Neira, Anna and Henry Forbes viewed Bin Saleh's bird of paradise and other New Guinea bird skins, which were being dispatched to the Paris markets (H. O. Forbes 1885:286); he appeared also to run a religious school (A. Forbes 1887:59–60). From that period onward Arabs and families of mixed Arab descent became prominent in the non-European Bandanese elite. For example, Seyid Abdullah Baadilla had acquired great wealth in the schooner trade and as a dealer in Aru pearls, as well as owning nutmeg estates (Broersma 1934:325). By the time of my own fieldwork in the 1980s, the population of Banda was around 14,275 (2,830 households) (Statistik Tahunan Kecamatan: Banda 1977), of which between ten and twenty families on Neira were of acknowledged "Arab descent," depending on the criteria used to determine what this might mean, all of them in trade. Most of them were descended from individuals who had migrated from the Hadhramaut around 1900.

There is little direct evidence of Arab traders operating east of Banda before the late nineteenth century, though it is quite plausible that they did so, and there is one reference for 1824. Anna Forbes (1887:131) reported Arab merchants on Dobo in the Aru Islands in 1882. Many of these individuals, such as Baadilla, were attracted there because of the lucrative market in pearls. It was this that also drew them to Tual on Kei Kecil (approximately midway between Banda and Aru) and where there is still a small but prominent Arab community involved in the pearl trade and in shopkeeping. Consider, for example, Cases 1 and 2 in section 9.1. The establishment of Geser as a stapling and administrative center in the 1880s marked a major change in the organization of local trade and was followed by the arrival of more Hadhrami Arab migrants. Families of Arab descent in the Geser-Gorom Archipelago currently are mainly a result of migration from the Hadhramaut at that time or shortly afterward. Of this cohort, which included Al Bayiri's father in Case 1, none appears to have returned to their homeland, though it is said that some who settled in Ambon have done so.

We can identify several patterns of Hadhrami settlement and assimilation. First, there are those families in the larger trading centers (such as Geser) who support themselves entirely through trade. Second, and outside the main trading centers, individual Arab males have married local women. In this way Arab families have become integrated into particular polities and have begun to take on the characteristics of indigenous descent groups, or *etar*. Thus, on mainland Seram we find in Kwaos the *etar* Iskandar, in Belis Bin Hatim, and in Warus-warus Bin Tahir (one of eight *etar*); and on Gorom, in Dinama, Musad and Zubeida. The fact that most *etar* (non-Arab as well as Arab) are represented as incomers of some kind in historical and mythic narratives in a sense serves to legitimate their status. Third, there is the rather exceptional case of one locality (Kwamar Kecil) in which a significant proportion of the population claims Arabic descent, but where participation in subsistence and primary production for exchange has replaced intermediary trading. However, let us first return to the main trading community.

In 1986 of a total of forty-nine shops in Geser (both toko and kios), five (10 percent) were Arab owned: Toko Danny, Toko Solo, Toko Surabaya, Kios Banda, and C. V. Seram Timur.[2] Elsewhere in the Geser-Gorom area Arab-owned shops are rare. Of the fourteen shops in Kataloka in 1986, only one was Arab owned, that of Alik Alkatiry. In Guli-guli there is one Arab shop established in 1981 by a migrant from Banda, one Machsin Kilualaga, and a second Bandanese Arab shop in Kwaos. The dominant Arab family in Geser in the late 1980s was Alkatiry. As can be seen from Figure 9.6, this is a three-generation family with roots in the Hadhrami village of Biherik. Although there has been some intermarriage with other Arabs from Banda and Geser and a couple of unions with non-Arabs, there is a high rate of Alkatiry endogamy. All Arab-owned shops are run by members of the family (Figure 9.7). There are a few Arabs on Geser who are not part of this network and

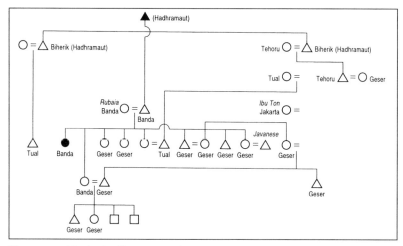

Figure 9.6. The basic Alkatiry genealogy for Geser (1986) with places of birth where known. All persons shown are part of the Alkatiry descent group unless otherwise indicated (in *italics*).

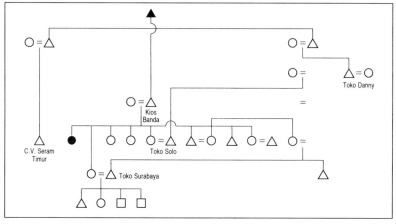

Figure 9.7. Kinship connections linking Arab-owned shops in Geser, 1986.

who operate smaller enterprises. Two such are Mohammed Achmad Baadilla and Yusuf Mutahu Al Hamid, Cases 3 and 4 in section 9.1.

Up until the 1970s most of these businesses dealt in maritime produce, in particular agar-agar. This is no longer the case. Most activity now involves the collection of terrestrial produce (hasil darat) such as coffee and its onward sale to bigger Chinese merchants in Ambon or Surabaya. Whether coffee is sold in Surabaya or Ambon or stored depends wholly on the market price in those two places, though there is a limit to how long traders are able to store produce until the price rises sufficiently for them to make an acceptable profit.

Compared with Geser, the situation in Kwamar is very different. Kwa-mar, situated within the desa of Urung, is located on a sandbank within the mangrove area that covers much of the easternmost tip of mainland Seram (Figure 2.4). Here, the economy revolves mainly around fishing and the cut-ting of mangrove wood, which is exported to Geser and other timber-depleted islands as fuel. Copra was important until 1982. Urung as a whole has no registered foreigners, but a relatively large number of households claim to be of Arab descent. Most of these live in the settlement of Kwamar and, within that, in Kwamar Kecil rather than in Kwamar Besar. Kwamar Kecil is, in fact, predominantly Arab in composition and economically bet-ter off than Kwamar Besar (the older part of the settlement), a fact reflected in its possession of two mosques. The two main Arab (sayid) families are Al Hamid (Case 4 in section 9.1) and Al Modali (Ellen 1996:246). Most Kwamar Arabs are married to others claiming Arab descent, although some of these are of mixed parentage (peranakan). Only one of the six marriages indicated in Figure 9.6 is with a non-Arab. Indeed, there are only two indigenous fam-ilies: Mokan and Mohu. The imam (Sayid Hasan Al Modali), khatib (Sayid Salim Al Modali), and the kepala kampung (Sayid Hussein Al Hamid) are all of Arabic descent.

9.6. Chinese

Traders of Chinese descent or extraction have been present in archipelagic Southeast Seram, in some form or another, for almost as long as records are available. As early as the late seventeenth century they are reported as far east as the Onin coast, though there is little evidence that they settled (Andaya 1991:76). As with the Arabs, and especially after the massacre of indigenous Bandanese in 1621, the Dutch came to depend on Chinese, who with the establishment of a colony of perkeniers served as middlemen and moneylenders. However, the Chinese soon became a threat to VOC trading interests and by 1712 had been prohibited from navigating east of Makassar, and non-resident Chinese were thereafter threatened with deportation. Although the VOC had some effect in controlling Chinese activity, it continued on a decreasing scale, picking up again in the late eighteenth century as the Dutch became less and less able to enforce the policy and as traders were more brazenly courted by Moluccan local rulers (ibid., 78–79). As was the case with Hadhrami Arabs, the second British occupation of 1810–1817 resulted in the arrival of migrants from Surabaya, Batavia, and beyond. It is interesting that we have a report of a visit by the Kapitan Cina (see section 9.9) of Ambon to Geser shortly after that period to supervise an increase in the Chinese population (Bik 1928 [1824]:8).

As we have seen in chapter 4.6, the establishment of Geser as a Dutch stapling and administrative center in the 1880s marked a major change in the organization of local trade and was followed by the serious expansion of Chinese migration into archipelagic Southeast Seram and thereafter New

Guinea. Most of the immigrants came via Surabaya, Makassar, and Banda and then from Geser to the surrounding islands or to New Guinea. This pattern is well illustrated genealogically in Figures 9.1 and 9.8 or more locally between Amarsekaru and Kataloka (Figure 9.3) and between Banda, Werinama, Kataloka and Miran, Teor, and Ambon. There have been, therefore, resident Chinese traders in Geser for at least one hundred years, and this is attested in the existence of a large Chinese graveyard, with some particularly old individual graves, and a temple. In Dutch times there was also a community association: Ciong Hu Gong Hoi. The oldest Chinese trader in Geser in 1986 was Ho Gah, then eighty-five years old, who had been born in China and who first arrived on Geser in 1920. The majority of Chinese are Hokkien, followed by Cantonese. Currently, most are at least nominally Christian (both Protestant and Catholic), though many still adhere to Chinese religious practices, as evidenced by the upkeep of house shrines, temples, and ancestral halls in Poka (Ambon) and Banda, as well as in Geser.

There were in 1986 more "Chinese" of all descriptions (both ethnic Chinese and peranakan) in the East Seram subdistrict than before World War II, though precise numbers are difficult to ascertain. We do know that in 1976 there were 139 Chinese residents who had not become Indonesian nationals compared with a total population of 14,138 for all ethnic groups. In 1981 the local camat reckoned that about 50 percent of the ethnic Chinese population had not yet taken up citizenship, which would put the total adult ethnic Chinese population at something in excess of 278 and the overall broadly defined Chinese community at over 1,000. The number of Chinese who remain "orang luar negeri" (noncitizens) is what differentiates them in the perceptions of many people from other groups of traders. For although some Arabs retain this status, other factors (most markedly religious orientation and skin color) tend to compensate. On taking Indonesian citizenship, Chinese are required to change their name. Considerable ingenuity may be shown in devising a name that is appropriate. Thus, the name Rumoi adopted by a second-generation peranakan family in Amarsekaru (Figure 9.3) is said to derive from "Rum" (SSL *rumara*, the syllable of which is a common prefix in *etar* names) and "oi" (from Ui, the Chinese family name). In such contexts the usual patronymic rule may break down, as where a mother has an Indonesian family name that her children adopt. This is the case with Warnangan in Figure 9.2 (Case 6). Although the proportion of the Chinese community that has not taken up citizenship is diminishing all the time, many Chinese are prevented from becoming nationals because of the costs involved. Others, usually of the older generation, still harbor some desire to return to China or are loathe to break a legal status that might provide them with an exit when times get rough. In grappling with the official and folk representations of Chinese internal differences, it is worth noting that in a Moluccan context "Baba" refers to persons born in Indonesia of Chinese parentage, and "peranakan" are the progeny of mixed marriages. It is often said that the most effective

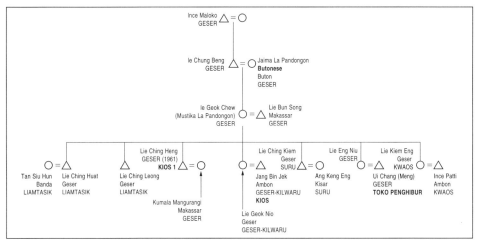

Figure 9.8. Geser (Chinese-Butonese) peranakan genealogy showing distribution of siblings in settlements surrounding Geser. Recorded 1986, Geser.

traders throughout Indonesia have been peranakan (those with mixed backgrounds) and local wives of foreign merchants have often proved crucial in obtaining desired goods (Andaya 1991:77). However, with the growth of the immigrant Chinese community, intermarriage with recent arrivals, such as that between Lie En Chow, born in Makassar in 1916, and Oe Eck Pahng, born in China in 1906, has also had the effect of reinforcing an eroding identity. Similarly, even where there has been intermarriage in an earlier generation, as between Ie Chung Beng and the Butonese woman Jaima La Pandongon, intermarriage with Chinese in the second-generation descendant has restored a firm Chinese identity (Figure 9.8)

One of the main differences between the Chinese community in the broadest sense and other ethnically focused trading groups is its size, dispersal, and internal economic differentiation. These characteristics have made it more effective in terms of networking and its capacity to pool capital and buffer risk. In 1986, twenty to thirty families (however "families" might be calibrated) owned thirty-two of the forty shops and eight kiosks in Geser. A few were traders without shops. In Kataloka and Samboru all the shops were owned by ethnic Chinese or peranakan, though in 1981 they owned only eight of the then nine shops. Elsewhere where shops existed, these were also mainly run by Chinese. There were, for example, three Chinese shops in Arou on Gorom island; and where there were no shops there were temporary trading premises, agents, or relations with itinerant traders. In terms of the total volume of trade in and out of the Southeast Seram area in the hands of independent traders, rather than being handled directly by producers themselves, most passes through Chinese business concerns, the controlling families of which reach out into the periphery either through ownership of village shops, visiting production areas in season, or buying from producers who bring their products to Geser or Kataloka. Indeed, Chinese traders are to be found wherever there is produce to buy and sell, a flexibility in trading operation that distinguishes them from most other persons involved in trade.

But this degree of adaptability, range of enterprise scale, type of activity, and geographical dispersal is only really viable through the utilization of genealogical and affinal relations that connect in various ways different places, stages, and functions involved in trade. It is true that in the larger centers (such as Ambon), population size and economic differentiation permit a degree of internal stratification and centralized economic elite formation, but in archipelagic Southeast Seram there are advantages in linking through kinship persons of different levels of wealth and over a wide geographic area. The kinship links between the different shops in Geser and their effectiveness are very clear. Thus, although Lie En Chow and Oe Eck Pahng had only daughters, all of them have nevertheless married into other Geser Chinese families, each owning a different shop, making affinal alliances between the Toko Olympic, Toko Sumber Jaya, Toko Sumber Tanya, and Toko Sumber Mas. In the latter three cases the segmentary linkage is even reflected in the names of the shops. In the case of the children of Asunato Toh and Tina Tan, a combination of in-law and sibling links connect the Toko Harapan Baru, Toko Bentoel, Toko Dua, and Toko Tanjung Harapan.

Similar links join trading operations on the periphery with those at the center, temporary and younger outlets often feeding longer-established enterprises. Thus Teng Ming That (Titi) runs a shop in Suru on the Seram mainland, the principal purpose of which is to feed the Toko Subur Jaya in Geser, owned by his eldest brother (Case 11, Figure 9.4). Kinship may thus link siblings operating on different scales and at different stages in a developmental cycle, in the context of Geser itself connecting, say, owners of kiosks with owners of shops (Figure 9.8). The same kind of functional interface is repeated between businesses in Geser and in larger centers, such as Ambon. Thus, the genealogy in Figure 9.4 also demonstrates linkage between the Toko Subur Jaya in Geser and the Toko Kenalan in Ambon, this time through sibling affinity. The relationships are not always genetically legitimated, and adoptive siblingship may serve the same purpose, as in the case of Efa, who owns the Toko Gaya Baru in Geser, and Ici, his adopted brother in Ambon, who owns the Toko Mascot in Jalan Patty. Comparable kinship links can be shown repeatedly for places of increasing distance from Geser and incorporation into the global marketplace: especially for Banda, Makassar, and Surabaya.

Long-distance trade direct to Java is almost entirely in the hands of Chinese, despite the role of the Butonese peddling trade discussed in section 9.4. Upwardly mobile traders characteristically move back through those links from the periphery to the center (say, Geser to Ambon or Banda to

Makassar to Surabaya) that first brought their elder siblings, parents, or grandparents in the opposite direction and where they can find larger businesses in which to invest their capital. Success in terms of long-distance trade, therefore, is again partly a matter of access to capital and partly of networks. Of course, in such trade control of the means of transport becomes crucial. Chinese use a variety of vessels that ply between Ambon and Geser, and between Southeast Seram generally and Banda, Makassar, and Java, many of which they own. This pattern is hardly new and goes back at least one hundred years; Beccari (1924:233), for example, reported Chinese ownership of Bugis vessels in the Aru-Kei area. Chinese own most of the motor craft and motorized perahu and even some of the sailing perahu; but although they own and commission the building of boats, they are almost always constructed, maintained, and operated by Butonese. Indeed, most of the sailing vessels used in this trade, as in the short-haul trade within the Moluccas, are hired from Butonese, and it has been historically difficult for Chinese and others to break Butonese domination (Dick 1975, 1:73).

If size and dispersal of genealogically linked persons make for effective networking, then the extended morality of kinship ensures the trust needed for the pooling of capital and workable credit extension. Chinese traders trust each other partly because of a common history of migration but also because of their experience that debts will be repaid, and debts are repaid largely because the cycle of trust upon which business depends will break down if they are not, and as immigrants they have nothing else to fall back on. By contrast, local small-time traders, or traders from other incoming groups such as Butonese and Bugis, often have a subsistence base to fall back on and therefore lack the same incentive to maintain the cycle of trust. A consequence is greater difficulty in gaining credit and establishing long-term business contacts. Thus, the measure of success in trade has little to do with essentialist ethnically bound values, and the differences between rich and poor traders are largely about access to credit, not marketing skills (cf. Alexander 1987:3). This is true within the Chinese community as well as outside it.

9.7. Settlement and Trading Culture along the Papuan Coast

The migration pattern of traders to the Papuan coast and its consequences for ethnicity have been very different from migration into Southeast Seram from outside the Banda zone. One of the main reasons for this is the way in which the *sosolot* system privileged Serammers and Goromese over other outsiders for so long. We have seen that speakers of SSL have been settling and intermarrying along the southern shore of Teluk Berau and on the Onin and Kowiai coasts for more than five hundred years. The main locations have, significantly, been small islands, such as Arguni, Kokas, and

Karas. Only in the last one hundred years have traders from farther afield formed a significant permanent presence, encouraged by the Pax Neerlandica. But whereas it is reasonable to describe the in-migration of Bandanese, Bugis, Arabs, even Chinese to the Southeast Seram area in terms of various degrees of accommodation to the host society, along the Papuan coast the process has been much more of the assimilation of local people into the intrusive SSL cultural sphere (chapter 5). There has been little published research on these communities, but we do have the account of Roland Walker (1982) for Namatote that provides what must be fairly typical of a more general process.

The physical features and languages of Namatote people bear witness to the heritage of cultural mixing and interethnic marriages between archipelagic Southeast Seram and Papuans (ibid., 80). Thus, the native language of Koiwai is 55 percent cognate with contemporary Goromese, three people speak Goromese as their mother tongue, and members of their families speak it a little. It is not uncommon for Goromese to be spoken daily in at least one home, usually sandwiched between the use of Malay and Koiwai. All contacts with outsiders are nowadays conducted in Malay. Apart from completely foreign households, eight households contain a spouse who has come to Namatote from outside: three from Gorom, two from Kokas, one from Kei, one from Babar, and one from Makassar. One-third of households have members who are nonnative and speak Koiwai as a second language. Some have married into influential families; thus the raja's grandmother is from Gorom, and the village headman's wife is from Kei. All Namatotens are Muslim.

Many boats stop at Namatote because it provides a safe anchorage in all seasons. Usually government representatives from Kaimana stop there on their way to villages east of Namatote; people from Koiwai villages on Aiduma and Kayu Merah Islands stop on their way to Kaimana. Inhabitants of Mairasi villages located on Teluk Triton commonly stop there as well. Even traders and fishermen from Tanimbar and Butonese occasionally call. Intermarriage with Mairasi continues today, resulting in a social relationship that depends upon Malay for communication (ibid., 81). The most important relationship that requires use of Malay is the economic tie with the Chinese merchants in Kaimana. Some of the men of Namatote also act as middlemen in trade between the Chinese and men of other villages (e.g., Mairasi on Teluk Triton). They make arrangements to buy the forest products these men have gathered and in the course of their dealings use Malay (ibid., 83).

9.8. Trade and Cultural Liminality

That there should be an ethnic dimension to trade at all, anywhere, arises from the juxtaposition of social and cultural differences that the spatial movement of people brings about. As Agnew (1979:101, following Brown 1947) asserted, trade is about crossing boundaries and strangers who operate in a liminal zone where uncertainty prevails; about those who operate through the idiom of kinship and yet appear to defy basic axioms of altruism embedded in the logic of kinship and of community. Of course, traders themselves, pragmatically and in a taken-for-granted kind of way distinguish between values of the marketplace ("mercantile kinship") and the values of blood kinship and commensality—eating, drinking, and praying together (Gregory 1997:208, following Shakespeare in *The Merchant of Venice*). In Southeast Seram, this is made explicit in terms of the contrast between urusan keluarga and perjalanan dagang (chapter 8.1). But it is this apparent duplicity in moral behavior that differentiates traders from ordinary producers and consumers. No wonder also that the labor of trade, no less than that of any other economic specialism, should so often be divided along ethnic lines, given that ethnicity is the aggregate outcome of so many ties of kinship, both in terms of empirical networks and metaphorically.

Traders in archipelagic Southeast Seram not only occupy a marginal and ambiguous social position and moral universe but are also less likely to inhabit a social space that has clear local physical correlates than almost any other group. Theirs is a social world that is essentially regional or at least supralocal, in which the intimacies of kinship compress the extricacies of spatial distance. Moreover, there is a widespread tendency in the Moluccas to manage a discourse of unbounded spaces in terms of specific central places. In the model of the world of those living in particular places the periphery is divided into dominant secondary centers. Thus, traders in Ambon or Banda usually speak of Tual, Geser, Dobo when referring not to particular places but to entire zones on a periphery, because such places are the main channels through which all commodities and information are channeled. Relocation of production on the periphery is not directly visible because it takes place within regions with their own centers that are themselves constant. Therefore, "going to Tual" may mean virtually anywhere in the Kei Islands for a merchant in Amboina. Timber is still reckoned to come from Geser, even though Geser itself is an atoll with no timber of its own and regardless of whether it has been imported to Geser from Warus-warus on the east coast of Seram or from Sorong in New Guinea. A similar widespread usage in Ambonese Malay and Geser-Gorom that evokes much the same spatial compression of distance is "belakang," as in "belakang Geser, belakang Dobo . . . " (lit., behind Geser, behind Dobo . . .). This refers to, in the case of Geser, the whole of mainland Southeast Seram, and in the case of Dobo, to the hinterland of the Aru Islands (Spyer 2000: 5). It sometimes occurs in the nominal form as "dibelakang," (lit., out the back), a convention that in some respects is similar to Australian English "outback" or "the back end." I was often amused by people who told me that so-and-so was "out the back" (ada dibelakang), when it transpired that they were in fact 30 kilometers away in the mountains and would not be back until the following day. Although "belakang Geser" may be the scrub, coconut groves, and mangroves on the southwest side of the lagoon on the island of that name, farthest from the old settlement around the mouth, from the point of view of Ambon, Aru (1,000 kilometers to the southeast) is also "belakang (beyond) Geser." Such forms of talking about space, and the means by which they reflect a world of trade, connect in important ways with the discussion of orientation and geographic deixis in chapter 6.

Although I do not wish to underestimate the conflict that historically has accompanied competition between traders of different ethnicities (chapters 4 and 5), I wish to suggest here that in some ways the picture of ethnic separation, with its individual accounts of Bugis, Butonese, Arab, and Chinese traders, is in its modern understanding relatively recent, a product of the colonial period. This appears to be so, both in the passive sense that the VOC and the Netherlands East Indies provided a context in which large numbers of outside traders could operate, and in the active sense that the needs of colonial (and then postcolonial) administration actively fostered ethnic difference. To operate as a trader, whatever the linguistic and geographical origins, requires assimilating a commonly held culture. This is so both in the sense that good business dealing requires a shared set of understandings and practices that cut across local differences, and in the sense that effective trade encourages those values and norms that best facilitate certain kinds of exchange and capital accumulation. This kind of culture existed in Banda before the arrival of Europeans and allowed them to manage the specialized risks of an entrepôt and cash-cropping economy. It also existed among those Southeast Seram traders who operated along the New Guinea seaboard. One of the institutional factors that needs to be satisfied if trade is to be successful in such "frontier" areas is the development of close links with producers and trading partners through marriage or other fictive kinship links; and we have seen that where outside traders are demographically weak local intermarriage, anyway, became imperative. In such circumstances, trading communities rapidly become very ethnically mixed, and this is what we find in Southeast Seram and to a lesser extent in other trading frontiers in the Moluccas. As groups of traders with a common cultural origin grow, the institutional imperative to intermarry declines and the dynamic of social interaction reinforces difference. We have even seen that in some circumstances, a second- or third-generation marriage between a peranakan and a "pure blood" may serve to reassert difference.

Thus, there are families that become wholly absorbed into their host societies, and others (such as migrant Bandanese in Southeast Seram) that maintain a historical memory of distinct trading identity. In other cases the intermixing is so complex that attaching particular conventional cultural labels becomes hazardous. In some contexts in which the term "Bandanese" is used it is certainly not referring to any remnant of the indigenous pre-1621 Bandanese genome but rather to representatives of the hybrid culture that superseded it and that involved intermarriage between locals, Ambonese, Papuans, Javanese, peoples of South Sulawesi origin, as well as Arabs and Chinese. Moreover, is is likely that the Bandanese population before 1621 was already more mixed than most other populations in the Moluccas. A similar process of cultural creolization took place in Ambon during the colonial period. Two trading families in the Southeast Seram area where this heterogeneity is well developed are illustrated through genealogies in Figures 9.1 and 9.2: the first the Sauhupalla family (an Ambonese name) with intermarriage with second-generation Hokkien Chinese and in the third and fourth generations with Ambonese, Bandanese, Batak, and Makassar Chinese; and the second the Warnangan family, the result of a marriage between a first-generation Chinese male and a woman from Buru (whose name he adopted) and involving intermarriage with other ethnic Chinese, Toraja, Buruese, Goromese, and Makassans in the following two generations. The one superficial difference between the two families is that the first remained predominantly Christian and the second predominantly Muslim. In circumstances where multiplex ethnic labels become ambiguous means of organizing group differences, more simplistic markers such as religious affiliation may come to occupy this role. And this again we see in the civil unrest in the Moluccas from 1998 onward.

9.9. The Cultural Economy of Arab and Chinese Ethnicity

Looked at broadly, it is evident that certain essentializing ethnic labels (Ambonese, Bandanese, Butonese, Bugis) map only crudely onto the present-day genealogies of trading families in Southeast Seram through assimilation and movement into other occupations, usually farming. In a modern context what these groups have in common is that they are unambiguously Indonesian and usually Muslim. Muslim traders, as I shall argue for the Moluccan context, almost always carry the burden of being coreligionists with most of their poorer customers and the shared values of Islam rest uneasily with the moral economy required to be individually successful in trade. We can examine the plausibility of this contention by comparing Arab and Chinese traders who both have access to capital and credit (though to different degrees) but who differ in terms of focal religious and cultural sentiment.

If traders of Arab descent in the Banda zone once had an obviously different niche in the market or an immediately distinctive mode of operation, this is no longer the case. Currently they operate using social networks that are largely indistinguishable from those used by the most important other local reference group, the Chinese, and deal in much the same range of commodities. If any differences remain, these are largely in terms of the scale of business that they can manage given their demographic profile and access to capital. In the Geser-Gorom area they have,

on the whole, become general storekeepers with some dealing in agricultural cash crops. Apart from the residual traditional Arab dealing in pearls,
they no longer feature in the trade in marine produce. As a group, they are
economically less powerful than the Chinese and tend to focus on smaller
enterprises. This, perhaps, has made them vulnerable, and more likely to
move out of trade in part or altogether when opportunities arise.

It is, however, unusual for Indonesian Arabs to move out of intermediary trading in the way they appear to have done in Kwamar (see section
9.5), but a possible explanation for it can be found in the economic and
cultural strategies open to Chinese immigrants. The Chinese have historically been dominant in interisland trade in terms of the volume of goods
shifted, the capital they have at their command, and often demographically as well. But, to put it crudely, whereas Chinese must at all times rely
on economic position for their advancement, Arabs are in addition able to
fall back on cultural strategies. This has not, however, always been the case.

During the colonial period the communal participation of Arabs was
constrained in ways that were relaxed after Indonesian independence.
Arabs, in theory anyway, were, as "foreign orientals," subject to different
judicial rules from local Muslims (Ter Haar 1948:11, 36, 41), were subject
until 1919 to a regime of required residence (De Jonge 1993:77–78), and were
treated as a collectivity for certain administrative purposes. It was the policy of the Dutch to administer nonnative Asiatic or trading minorities by
appointing a leader with whom they could deal (Ellen 1986b:56–57), and
this official recognition placed legal boundaries around particular ethnic
groupings, making them more visible through the legal implications of
being grouped with one rather than the other. Thus, in the Geser-Gorom
area there was a Kapitan Bugis in Air Kasar and a Kapitan Cina in Geser.
There was a kapitan for the Arab community in Banda for the period
1850–1888 (Hanna 1978:125; see also Van den Berg 1886:118–122), and in
1936 we know that the same status was accorded to Seyid Abdullah
Baadilla. Because the Arab community in such trading posts was usually
small, the official representative was often a lieutenant (see, e.g., Dermoût
1955:56, on the "Luitenant der Arabieren" in her fictive Ambon), though
in 1936 this function in Geser was performed by a "Wijkmeester."[3] By the
end of the Dutch period the Geser Arab community was evidently considered large and important enough to warrant a "kapitein." The last Kapitan
Arab in Geser was Habib Al Hamid, whose descendants today live in Kwamar.

The special status accorded Arabs was abandoned with the postindependence era, and most Arabs have in addition taken on Indonesian citizenship. Moreover, the period between 1900 and World War II in the Pacific
had already seen significant changes in Arab social consciousness in the
context of the Netherlands East Indies. The old closed and hierarchical
Hadhrami social order that had typified many immigrant communities
during the nineteenth century was replaced by a more open organization in

which orientation tended to be much more to the Indies than to the Hadhramaut (de Jonge 1993:89). What has always made this process of reorientation easier and has in general facilitated cultural integration has been adherence to Islam and in particular to the Shafi'i rite of Sunni Islam. Commonality of religion among natives and "foreign orientals" was underplayed by the Dutch (possibly quite deliberately), who preferred to use non-religious ethnic categories (Ellen 1983:51–52). Nevertheless, one of the enduring cultural consequences of the presence of the Arab migrant community in the Geser-Gorom area has been in the area of religious practices.

As in other parts of Southeast Asia, it is difficult to separate Muslim tradition from Arabic cultural practice, and often things Arabic introduced to indigenous Muslims were acceptable and encouraged because they were thought to be more authentically Islamic (Ibid., 55). Persons of Arabic ethnicity (particularly if they have the title sayid, indicating them to be descendants of the Prophet) are often perceived as more religious and more fit for religious office (de Jonge 1993:78). So in the Geser-Gorom area we find that families of Arab descent often provide the imam, even if the majority of the population is not ethnically Arab. We have already noted the situation in Kwamar where Arab families are dominant. However, in Geser also the imam is of Arabic descent (Al Hamid), and formerly this family also provided an alim ulama.

Religious position therefore brings status and power. The same cultural privilege extends to particular kinds of ritual practice, and throughout this area we find local evidence of Shia customs, presumably a consequence of Arabic influence. Thus, the debus knife dance performed for seven days after death, which is led by a religious leader dressed in Arabic clothes and which was supposedly introduced by Sheikh Abdul Khadir Jailani, is found not only in Kwamar but in other places (such as Kataloka, Warus-warus, and Maar on Seram Laut) with no or a negligible resident Arab population. Similarly, other dances of Arabic origin, such as the *hadarat* (Warus-warus), *dunedin,* or *sambera* (Warus-warus) are performed at weddings.

For these and other reasons of perceived ethnic similarity, Arabs, unlike Chinese, have had no particular difficulty in obtaining Indonesian citizenship, although they encounter the same bureaucratic obstacles and requirements for payment in the police and subdistrict offices. Intermarriage has been relatively easy, and anyway as a smaller group than the Chinese they were forced to marry into the local community to survive. Such advantages have provided Arabs with a security net that they can fall back on, and because, on the whole, Arab traders have less capital than the Chinese this has often been important. Apart from cash and stored goods, Arab capital generally takes the form of the shop itself and transport facilities. Different Arab families vary in the amount of capital they have. Beda bin Ahmad Alkatiry, who owns Toko Danny on Geser, is in a position to purchase relatively large quantities of goods and owns a dugout canoe (*bodi*) with an outboard motor (jonson). Abdurachman, by comparison, has a jonson, but no *bodi*, which he has to rent as he needs it. Similarly, opening shops and warehouses, other than the smallest, also requires government permission (chapter 8.6). The costs involved are much easier to mobilize in the larger Chinese community than among Arabs.

Economically, therefore, Arabs are more vulnerable to economic decline in the intermediary trading niche. Their numbers are small and their ethnic-based networking consequently more precarious, with fewer opportunities to raise capital and ride out troughs in the business cycle. In a paradoxical way, their capacity to be absorbed into local indigenous populations has not provided them with the incentives to maintain the kinds of linkages and infrastructures required for a wholly trading way of life. Indeed, a common religion and associated cultural capital have bound them into a moral economy where individual advancement becomes more difficult, where obligations to extend credit and remain part of a community conflict with the usual entrepreneurial imperative: what Hans-Dieter Evers and Heiko Schrader (1994) called the "trader's dilemma." In other words, opportunities to deploy cultural risk-reducing strategies have lessened the likelihood of their engaging in intermediary trading activities as a sole means of livelihood.

10
Conclusion

In this monograph I have sought to examine some aspects of the spatial economy and time-geography[1] of archipelagic Southeast Seram in the light of a critical literature that repeatedly asserts that anthropologists often fail to situate the ethnographic data upon which they focus in regional and historical contexts; that they place them, somehow, "out of time" (Thomas 1990:9) and out of place. More specifically, I have attempted to demonstrate how trade has been socially and spatially organized in the Geser-Gorom zone over a period of some five hundred years and how that organization can be understood in terms of a combination of local ecology and its articulation with regional and ultimately global trading patterns. Almost incidentally I have been able to show why the conventional division of academic labor between Melanesianists and Indonesianists — the one facing eastward toward the Pacific, the other facing westward toward mainland Asia (or "back-to-back," as one might say)—is seriously unhelpful and how it has prevented the making of connections crucial to the understanding of real-world global history: that despite the ecological and cultural transitional discontinuities detectable in that region that naturalists describe as Wallacea, Melanesia is socially and economically an extension of island Southeast Asia (Healey 1998:337; Spriggs 1998b; Urry 1981).

10.1. The Anthropological Study of Trade as a Spatially Distributed Process

The writings of professional ethnographers on the Moluccas have hitherto made little contribution to the study of trade. This is odd given that the region is one that has been ethnologically articulated through trade, whose history can ultimately only be explained in terms of the maritime factor. Rather, professional ethnography has concerned itself hitherto primarily with the description of isolated or reconstructed tribal societies, with periphery rather than center. Such an approach reflects in part the specific influence of Dutch structuralism and in part a continuing pervasive anthropological cult of the autonomous and distant "other." There can be no doubt though that things are changing, and fast. There is now a preparedness, for example, to show the "complex entanglements" between traders and producers (Spyer 1997:519), and this is also what I have tried to do here, though in a situation where the roles of producer and trader have been historically more fluid, diverse, and conceptual, rather than indicating merely two quite separate persons in an exchange relationship.

Moreover, neither anthropologists nor historians have paid much attention to short-distance trade in the eastern archipelago, meaning here that within island groups or between coasts and interiors. This is so even when such trade, almost more than anything else, was least influenced by VOC and Dutch activities (Knaap 1989:16),[2] an observation that must be linked to the equally notable absence of major anthropological studies of Indonesian societies based on maritime activities (MacKnight 1980:120; but see, e.g., Ammarell 1999, Barnes 1996, Sather 1997, Southon 1995). The explanation for this may be that where boats are involved, easy movement by sea and the mobility of artifacts obscures any tight patterns of spatial or social differentiation. Discrete geographic boundaries appear to encourage the discovery of social cohesion. Nevertheless, there is reason to believe that short-distance trade has been just as important as long-distance trade in shaping major economic patterns and in the creation of those preconditions necessary for the development and maintenance of formative states (Slamet-Velsink 1995:224). As has been demonstrated throughout this study, local networks were the essential underpinning of long-distance global trade and also subject to the vicissitudes of such trade.

The foregoing analysis provides, therefore, an addition to the small number of ethnographic studies of Indonesian local trade, though it admittedly does not begin to compare in terms of detail at the level of individual transactional behavior. Although marketplace studies have become relatively commonplace, there have been relatively few full-scale studies for Indonesia (Alexander 1987, Dewey 1962a, Geertz 1963, Mai and Buchholt 1987). Moreover, although trade is palpably an activity that goes on in specific places (and it is this that gives it its ethnographic visibility), it is also something that connects distant points; and that relationship too involves a social dimension amenable to anthropological study. So, although it may be true (Renfrew 1975) that archaeologists have rarely studied "trade" (meaning a socially constructed activity) but only the material flows of limited objects, so anthropologists have generally studied the dynamics of local exchange but rarely long-distance trade as a spatially distributed social behavior. The reason is obvious: it is physically difficult and amenable to conventional ethnographic approaches only with modification. Thus, in that most classic subject for anthropological studies of trade, the Massim *kula* ring, we find tantalizing analyses of its parts from the viewpoint of particular participating groups (Leach and Leach 1983; Macintyre 1983; Malinowski 1922; and especially Leach 1983) but seldom the *kula* in its entirety. Given the formidable logistical and technical problems such a study would entail, one can see why the anthropological study of trade has concentrated on marketplaces and exchange fragmenta.

The study of trade as a process requires fieldwork techniques other than those traditionally the métier of a social anthropologist. Trade, in terms of the usual typologies, is precisely that kind of exchange that cuts across conventional social relationships and connects different kinds of groups. If we take our cue from Melanesianist studies, trade networks might be better viewed as several patterns of trade imposed on a landscape (or seascape) over time (Goodman 1998:440). In the case of trade between Southeast Seram and New Guinea, what we are presented with is the interface between apparently different forms of exchange, where goods are valued differently between vendor and buyer. In trade generally this is, of course, very common, but in the case examined here it is presented starkly. Moreover, the social world of a sailor or that of an interisland trader goes far beyond his or her own neighborhood. In terms of "small world" modeling (Watts 1999), traders are typically more likely than other people to be connected to all others in the universe designated and to be so through the smallest number of links; and where there is a high concentration of trading activity compared with the overall size of the population, it can be said that such populations are better connected than many others. In any ethnographic study we must best examine the trader in a variety of widely spaced geographical contexts, though it is true that such persons are enclosed at all times in a semipermeable cultural capsule that accompanies them irrespective of the specific geographic coordinates they might occupy at any one moment. In studying the social organization of trade it would be thoroughly misleading and diversionary to study just one (say, ethnic) group in one place. Even if the studies were to be repeated in many societies, this would in sum still not constitute a study of trade. Moreover, as an aspect of distribution, trade has uncomfortably wide spatial ramifications. It is for these reasons that this study has employed a combination of contrasting cross-disciplinary methodologies, such as network theory and life histories, and drawn on the insights of both geographers and historians.

If methodological difficulties have in the past handicapped the analysis of local trade, then they are surely compounded in the study of long-distance trade, which must take on board macrotheory as well as a sensitive appreciation of the articulation of different social systems. And because long-distance trade has been shaped by documentable historical process, its anthropological study is necessarily historical. This is well exemplified in the case of the Asian spice trade, to which this book is a long footnote. As such it demonstrates, I believe, the necessity of taking a "production-end view" and looking closely at the context in which producers articulate their own local system and the wider world system. Far from being "the passive objects of their own history," Serammers, no less than other producers and traders, have been active contributing authors, "shaping the material circumstances laid on them according to their own conceptions" (Sahlins 1988:2–3) and considerably more than the "victims and silent witnesses" of their own subjugation (Wolf 1982:x). In the case of archipelagic Southeast Seram we have a double misconception of center over periphery: the European misconception of the Moluccan world, and the Tidore misconception of their role in relation to parts of the Moluccas (especially Geser-Gorom) and the Papuan coast. The Serammers were, it seems, prepared to conform passively to neither political model, and neither were the Papuans acquiescent in Tidorese political hegemony, even if both were periodically subjected to physical battering. And as we have seen, on the best evidence available the accommodation between Serammers and Papuans was not based on this kind of illusion.

10.2. System Resilience and Innovation

Changes in demand in international trade may, of course, lead to the modification of local networks. Such changes may be met up to a point by home production but on any scale will require expansion at the periphery. If the changes in demand are qualitative, this may result in a gradual shift in the sites of production and the kind of production on the periphery. However, in the history of central Moluccan trade since the fifteenth century, the primary centers have remained remarkably constant. This reflects patterns of trade and, latterly, the Dutch monopoly. There have been population movements and changes in the ethnic composition of those groups controlling and facilitating trade, but much of this has simply been ethnic replacement within the same niche. The trade in certain high-value commodities, such as bird of paradise feathers and massoi bark, remained surprisingly stable over many centuries. Centers such as Banda could, therefore, fall back on the entrepôt trade if spice harvests failed or if demand slackened. Moreover, from the seventeenth century onward, the Dutch themselves required supplies (such as slaves and food) from the periphery to support their own settlements and to subsidize trading activities. The foreground temporal trend in all of this has been, therefore, the expansion, control, decline, and then reexpansion of clove production and the growth and then steady decline of nutmeg production. Within this period we have also seen the eighteenth-century growth in trade in agar-agar, pearls, trepang, and other maritime products, largely in response to demand of the Chinese market.

The only major systematic innovation from well before 1500 to the present was the creation of the Amboina network. Before the sixteenth century, Ambon and the Lease Islands were relatively unimportant as trading or political centers or in production for exchange, although they had been in contact with Javanese, Malay, and more distant Asiatic traders (Abdurachman 1981:2). The area now incorporated into this system was probably previously integrated through more local coastal networks with linkages to Ternate and Tidore; the interiors of the large islands of Seram and Buru must have been relatively unintegrated through trade. Hitu on Ambon and Luhu on the Hoamoal Peninsula of West Seram, used as watering and victualing points for passing traders and with connections with Java, provided incipient centers.[3] With the increase in trade, Hitu became important. During the sixteenth century clove cultivation expanded, first on the Hoamoal Peninsula and later on Hitu, where by 1570 they grew in abundance (ibid., 12). The Portuguese and then the Dutch tried to centralize their activities on Amboina, and this led increasingly to its development. The Portuguese fort and its associated township fed on each other symbiotically and gave rise to a new kind of human settlement hitherto unknown in the Moluccas, resembling much more towns like Malacca (ibid., 15). It was then almost entirely a creature of European interests. As Amboina developed it began to dominate and bring within its sphere of influence other (older) traditional systems in the Moluccas, in particular the Banda and Ternate-Tidore systems. As Ambon eclipsed Banda as an administrative and economic center in the nineteenth century, and as the Dutch became less preoccupied with illegal smuggling and the breaking of their monopoly, so Serammers, Goromese, and Aruese sold their massoi, pearls, trepang, gum, bird of paradise feathers, agar-agar, and so on directly in Ambon, thus subsuming Banda in the wider Ambonese system (Bleeker 1856:129). In this the Amboina and Banda systems contrasted with other trading centers in the region, which despite the monopoly managed to sustain a surprisingly free trade in commodities other than nutmeg and cloves, sustaining the "Conradian" model elaborated in chapter 4.

10.3. Environmental and Political Instability at the Center

In chapter 2 I illustrated the remarkable environmental precariousness of those trading settlements at the very heart of the Banda-Onin corridor in Southeast Seram and their inability to sustain human habitation without economic subsidies from outside. This account was augmented in chapter 4 by demonstrating how, over a period of several hundred years, shifting sandbanks, destruction of mangroves, and storm damage have affected the microgeography of Southeast Seram, and how human populations and political centers have shifted to accommodate this. Indeed, the demographic and subsistence insecurity of the area is difficult to exaggerate. The Seram Laut Archipelago even had a long-standing reputation for endemic smallpox, which in 1859 had more or less decimated the population (Van der Crab 1862:63–64, 69). The picture painted for the Seram Laut Archipelago is a familiar one in the history of Moluccan trading systems. Banda, Ternate, Tidore, and many other places, all major primary centers, were at the same time minuscule and vulnerable to periodic environmental degradation. And Dobo, the historic primary center for the Aru group, was no more than an anchorage and sandy spit of land about 420 meters east of the small island of Wamar (Bik 1928 [1824]:41). Many of these same places were also subject to periodic volcanism and seismic activity of other kinds.

To the environmental threats we must add the political. Although we have little knowledge of Moluccan political history before the arrival of the Portuguese, pre-European Banda was most unlikely to have been the congeries of Arcadian republics or Athenian democracies suggested by Villiers (1981b). From oral tradition there is evidence of interdomain conflict. There was warfare with Ternate. Likewise, Ternate and Tidore were never at peace for long, and their political relations with the periphery that they controlled was partly in terms of the provision of warriors and war canoes (*kora-kora*). But whatever the situation before European intervention, the arrival of the Dutch led to a period of immense political turmoil, culminating in 1621 with the massacre of the indigenous inhabitants of Banda and attempts thereafter to protect the spice monopoly through raiding and extirpation. In 1624 Van Speult attacked villages in Southeast Seram and Gorom to which the Bandanese had fled (Tiele and Heeres 1886:ix; cf. Valentijn 1724-1726, 2:54). In 1633 the first Ambonese hongi took place to Seram Laut (*Daghregister* 1631-1634:196; Rumphius 1910 [1687], 1:93–95; Wurffbain 1931: 85, 90). During the seventeenth and eighteenth centuries there were periodic Dutch raids on Gorom and other places, as well as raids from Papuan "pirates."[4]

During the nineteenth century there was endemic rivalry and feuding in Southeast Seram (Kniphorst 1883:311; Kolff 1927 [1840]:287–288) and in Dobo. There were, for example, disputes between Kelu and other rulers arising from the war between Kwaai and Kilberau on Seram Rei (Bik 1928 [1824]:16). Bik (ibid., 48) reported on a war between Wamar and Wadheir, in which the latter replaced the former as the power more influential with the Alifuru (native population) of the east coast of Aru, the source of trepang and birds' nests. There was migration within and between island groups as a result of endemic local warfare, and Bik (ibid., 11) also tells us of a headman from Teor living on Seram Laut on account of intervillage warfare on his own island. There are constant references in the Mail Reports to the liveliness (levendig) of trade, but often these are accompanied by or juxtaposed to accounts of unrest and fighting between intrusive traders (vreemde) and natives, often resulting in the death of Chinese and Makassans and the plundering of villages by traders. Many of these reports come from Ternate and Dobo in the last quarter of the nineteenth century.[5] And with the final arrival of secure Dutch administration the records are full of litigation between intrusive traders and local rulers and between the local inhabitants over rights in extraction and ownership of particular commercially valuable resources (Holleman 1925:134–147). However, open conflict between rulers of local polities often deescalated into cases brought before colonial magistrates (raad) (Adatrechtbundels 1925:177–208).

None of this should be surprising, for at the end of the day we would expect centers to be politically turbulent compared with their peripheries, partly because they *are* centers.

10.4. **Why Central Places Remain Central**

So why do people persist in locating the centers of networks in such places? Indeed, why do they not only remain but also expand areas of cultivation into environmentally more precarious zones and intensify population levels? Part of the answer must be that the dynamics of the system require it; that given the prior existence of the system, there is a built-in conservative force in people's perception, scheduling, and habitual decision making that is geared to preserving the existing systemic order. This involves weighing the costs of periodic natural disasters against long-term economic security. For, when all is said and done, although these islands are by comparative standards highly active seismically, in the experience of individuals and families crippling eruptions or earthquakes or tsunamis occur only infrequently and also irregularly. In an average lifetime crippling earthquakes are not automatically expected. Such irregular periodicity does not encourage major capital investment in either relocating sites or developing strategies to alleviate or prevent disasters. At the same time, the effects of disasters (though feared) are measurable and predictable. They destroy only easily renewable resources and result in very little loss of life. All this may explain why people currently seem so unprepared for such events and fail to respond to them with specially elaborated cultural mechanisms.

This tolerance of imminent physical disaster is reinforced by the security of well-worn short-term material advantages: the constancy of trade in certain high-value goods; investment in the primary production of nutmeg, cloves, and later in the extraction of maritime products; and development of a geographic division of labor involving centers of specialist production. This latter has been explored for the late twentieth century in chapter 7, but it is worth summarizing a few historical instances here. For example, in the early nineteenth century, Gorom and other places in Southeast Seram, including Kilmuri and Kilwaru (Bik 1928 [1824]:16) were centers of a weaving industry exporting to other parts of the archipelago. This export trade had probably been in existence since at least the seventeenth century, as indicated by a reference in Valentijn (Niggermeyer 1952:3883, 3892). Kilwaru, Seram Laut, and Gorom monopolized the trade in massoi from very early on. In the 1680s there was a division of labor in the massoi and slaving trade between two villages of the Seram Laut group, most likely Kilwaru and Kiltai, though there is no indication how long this might have lasted. The Seram Laut group also provided ironsmiths, goldsmiths, silversmiths, carpenters, potters, and boatbuilders (De Hollander 1895:501; Riedel 1886:169). Gorom was a center for the manufacture of lola (*Trochus*) shell armbands (Ellen 1984:185) and boxes made from sago leaf stalk. In western New Guinea Goromese are still renowned as smiths. In the late nineteenth century carpenters and bricklayers from Geser found work in West New Guinea and the Raja Ampat Islands (Bruijnis 1933:96). Before 1621 Banda was an important center of pottery production.

All this was in turn facilitated by underlying environmental factors.

Wind systems and currents restricted those areas in which central places could be effectively located.[6] In those areas that were accessible given the exigencies of navigation and seamanship, further considerations came into play, such as the availability of harbors that might be used by incoming traders and refugees as safe havens in otherwise hostile territory. But more than this, the networks themselves had a cushioning effect and possessed a flexibility that enabled change through internal modification and replacement. This in part stemmed from the conservative system-maintaining behavior and views of the inhabitants. This was done partly through the replacement of commodities decreasing in demand with those growing in demand and may point to a previously unelaborated characteristic of pre-capitalist mercantile systems, namely that commodities underwrite trading relationships, which endure independently of individual commodities themselves. In capitalism, the social relations of trade are entirely subservient to the needs of obtaining not only particular commodities, but particular commodities at the cheapest market price.

Moreover, centers can rearrange their activities to cope with damage to their parts, because "centers" themselves are spaces rather than points. There can be a temporary move to the periphery, or the locus of trade and political power may shift within the center. The effects of Dutch and native raids during the seventeenth century were lessened by the ease with which the inhabitants could escape to other islands or remove settlements farther inland. As we saw in chapter 2, at low tide one can walk across from Seram Laut to Kiltai and from Kwaos to Seram Rei (Bik 1928 [1824]:16; Rosenburg 1867:132). Keffing (on Seram Rei) to Kilwaru is no more than a half hour away with a good wind and no more than an hour under most conditions; Kilwaru to Geser is only 15 minutes in a favorable wind. Geser and Kilmuri are less suitably placed for rapid evacuation, and this journey may take eleven hours by sail (Table 7.4). In traditional Banda, the polities of Neira were no more important than those of Lonthor, Run, and others with which they were in alliance. In the North Moluccas, Ternate and Tidore, though often politically hostile and with distinct social and trading connections, can be seen in wider geographic and economic terms as a single system.

As discussed in chapters 3 and 4, we now know that within the Southeast Seram Archipelago political and trading power shifted between the islands of Seram Rei (Keffing), Geser, Kiltai, and Seram Laut and more widely still to include places on the mainland of Seram and the polities of Gorom. There have been important trading centers in Southeast Seram since before the Portuguese arrived, and we may reasonably infer that they go back much further into the prehistoric period. "Serdenha" is mentioned in de Brito's manuscript of 1582–1590, but in a sense its precise location is beside the point. It could have been Seram Rei, Seram Laut, and Gorom individually, but all are historically related by language, culture, and politics and are part of a 25-square-kilometer area—what I have called the Geser (or Banda-Onin) corridor—in which the center of the historical moment shifted from place to place.

In what is perhaps the earliest map of locations in Southeast Seram and its adjacent archipelago, that drawn by Rodrigues in about 1513 and discussed in chapter 3, Guli-guli is marked. On later maps, different islands and polities are mentioned and not others, and although presences and omissions on early maps must be interpreted with circumspection, the evidence is sufficient to infer the changing significance of places in the perception of those who provided mapmakers with their original data. In fact, the Seram Laut and Gorom Archipelagos were a network of fluctuating political alliances, reinforced by marriage: integrated social formations covering several islands, with a flexible organization. Northward on the east coast of Seram there were autonomous orang kayas in Dinama, Kilmoi, and Kilbat, and westward the orang kaya of Urung and the rajas of Kilmuri, Tobo, and Hatumeten; on the islands of Geser, Kiltai, and Serum Laut the rajas of Kilwaru and Kelu, the mayor of Keffing, and on Gorom the rajas of Amar, Kataloka, and Ondor. These polities were connected through various alliances that may have shifted over time. For example, the *seri-tahun* alliance covered the area between Kwaos, Urung, and Keffing, and possibly other places; the *tutu tolu* (three) alliance encompassed Dinama, Kilmoi, Kilbat, Gah, Warus-warus, Kiltai, and Kilwaru; the *tutu hitu* (seven) alliance connected Kelu and Amar; and the Raja Empat alliance connected Kilmuri, Tobo, Sepa, Mengeli, and Werinama. There were others as well, but in all this, as we have seen in chapter 4, Tidore, which claimed authority over the area, had little influence. The Seram Laut Archipelago currently consists of five desa units: Kiltai, being half of Kiltai Island and part of Seram Laut; Kilwaru, being the other half of Kiltai and part of Seram Laut; Kelu, being half of Keffing Island and the remaining part of Seram Laut; Keffing, being the remaining part of Keffing Island; and Geser. Geser, so important at the end of the nineteenth century when its status as a central place was bolstered by its becoming an administrative center and coaling depot, had been empty not so many years previously. Thus, within the "center" the importance of particular places shifted from time to time, as did the settlements themselves.

It appears that the preconditions necessary for permanently abandoning central places are demanding and complex, although the Dutch seem to have come perilously close to abandoning Banda in the nineteenth century (Ellen 1987:49). What seems to be crucial in the long run is not the finer points of geography nor the crude tabulation of hazards but the extent to which there is an overarching social system that can cushion a precarious center (cf. Alkire 1965:2). Such social systemic properties not only account for the persistence of centers, but explain short-term political shifts as well. Consequently, in the real world the conventional wisdom of central place theory has relatively little to offer. Geography (coastline patterns, wind systems, currents, and navigational and sailing factors), given a particular level of technology, tends to funnel networks into corridors and warp ideal Christaller-Lösch landscapes. Here "strategically placed communities may then become nodes through which many strands are drawn, and may be able to establish an oligopolistic control over traffic" (Brookfield with Hart 1971:317). Fixed boundaries are inclined to interfere with classical properties, and insular systems are bad exemplars of central place theory anyway. The reasons are topographic: the high proportion of uninhabitable space (in this case sea), approximately 85 percent in the Moluccas,[7] and the lack of uniformity in the distribution of the land areas. This affects virtually every aspect of the classic Christaller-Lösch predictions: with respect to the spacing of settlements, the shape of trading area (that is, degree of "hexagonality"), threshold sizes (the lower limit on number on consumers required before a given type of function, such as commodity specialization, can come into existence), trip (though in this context we should perhaps use the term voyage) frequency (the farther the distance, the fewer the voyages), and hierarchy and rank size rules. On this latter, Geser, which is highly connected, should have grown substantially in size. Instead it has remained a small town. Riedel (1886:148) gave a figure of 306 persons for the beginning of the period when it became a Dutch administrative center; in 1978 the population was only 2,200. Of the other alternative "centers within the center" Riedel gave 527 for Seram Rei Island (Keffing), 568 for Kilwaru, and 448 for Seram Laut. In fact, the percentage of the population located at the center in such systems may be very low indeed. The evidence therefore conforms to the general criticisms of the usefulness of central place theory made by Walter Isard (Smith 1976:24), on the grounds that it uses untenable assumptions of an isotropic landscape, perfect competition among suppliers, threshold governance of supplier location, single suppliers of each good at each center, and single-purpose trips by consumers.

10.5. Moluccan Trading Networks and the Problem of State Formation

If their geographical position or monopoly power had been different, the islands of Southeast Seram might have rivaled Ternate and Tidore and Banda as political forces to be reckoned with during the period immediately preceding and following European first intrusion. But the question, let alone the answer, is more difficult than this. Ternate and Tidore achieved hierarchical centralization, economic dominance, and political influence over a wide area; the Banda Islands achieved a kind of economic dominance until 1621 but without either political centralization or an extensive sphere of influence. By comparison, archipelagic Southeast Seram was in the middle: no political centralization integrating large areas but rather a dispersed group of small local domains in various conditions of alliance and enmity, limited economic power, and political influence (to begin with mainly by virtue of its privileged access to the New Guinea coast, and during the seventeenth century as a challenge to Dutch monopoly power). The domains of Southeast Seram are hardly agrarian kingdoms, with few opportunities of acquiring and mobilizing surpluses on staple crops: sago and fish have never presented such opportunities. In some ways, Ternate and Tidore lie intermediate to the rice-based states of, say, Java, and Banda. At least here, though dependent on imported starch staples (sago from Halmahera and rice from the West), the wealth of the sultan was related to his powers in controlling exchange in cloves, produced through an economically significant if not territorially extensive base, against incoming valuables. We thus have a graded spectrum of political centralization for the precolonial period: the agrarian-based states of precolonial Java; the maritime clove-producing sultanates of the North Moluccas with degrees of control over surrounding territories, which themselves contained centers of lesser political centralization; the precolonial nutmeg-producing and noncentralized polities of Banda; and the dispersed polities of Southeast Seram that depended largely on trade rather than production.

If we are looking for comparative models for the process of political development in Southeast Seram, Kiefer's (1971, 1972) study of the Jolo sultanate combined with Warren's (1981) history of the wider Sulu zone is instructive. During the nineteenth century the Sulu Archipelago bridged two worlds and lay at a strategic point for maritime trade, conducted on a scale much larger than was ever found in the Geser-Gorom corridor. Sulu consisted of a loosely integrated political system embracing both island and coastal populations, nomadic seaborne fishermen as well as swidden cultivators. Surrounding the center was a distant assemblage of islands constituting a hinterland (Spoehr 1960). There were no clear or fixed territorial boundaries; the state, like many other traditional states, was defined by various relationships to the center. The core social organization at the center operated through bilateral kinship with no fully corporate groups, alliances through aggregations of persons tied to a common leader, and three ranked estates (aristocrats, commoners, and slaves—regular slaves and debt slaves). The emergence of the Sulu state depended on the growth of trade in trepang, bird's nests, wax, and camphor for Chinese consumption during the nineteenth century, and by the beginning of the nineteenth century slavery and slave raiding had become fundamental to its dynamic. Raiding enabled the sultanate to incorporate vast numbers of people and reached its peak around 1800–1848. The demands of trade kept forcing the sultanate to incorporate more people, rewarding those "datus" who provided most wealth (Warren 1979:223, 227–228).[8]

All the conditions that it is argued were present in the Sulu zone and that led to spiraling centralization there in the nineteenth century had been met on a lesser scale in Southeast Seram centuries earlier. First of all, the islands were located on key trade routes and provided centers of exchange between local and incoming traders. In their account of the characteristics of the "inchoate" early state, Claessen and Skalnik (1978:644) did not attribute a formative role to trade, but in parts of archipelagic Southeast

Asia it was clearly crucial (Slamet-Velsink 1995:230; cf. Claessen and Van der Velde 1987). Second, there was an underpinning multiniche ecological division of labor that has been suggested elsewhere as a powerful precondition for the existence and growth of centers of exchange (Flannery 1972) and therefore of political domination. Third, although incipient stratification and forms of bondage may at first have been marginal factors in state development, involvement in raiding and slavery has widely been accepted as a necessary condition for hierarchicalization (Slamet-Velsink 1995:245, 250), and as we see from the Sulu example, it can become part of a powerful amplifying loop contributing to state growth. In Southeast Seram slave trading and acquisition was important from the earliest times, and all component polities had three-tier stratification.

These combined factors, however, have resulted in limited political centralization in archipelagic Southeast Seram: evident only at the domain level, with aggregations of clans into three strata, slavery, some functional division of administrative labor in the service of a symbolically legitimated ruler, but incorporating no more than several thousand individuals. The basic fish-for-sago barter that underpinned these subsistence economies brought no special privileges that we know of to rulers or ruling clans. Instead, incipient economic inequalities between rulers and ruled arose through the trade in luxury goods over long distances (for example, nontimber forest products and slaves in exchange for prestige goods) and to a lesser extent control of nutmeg and other estates where topography permitted and (probably at a later date) reefs yielding sea produce. This pattern is by no means unique to Southeast Seram, but it is insufficiently unusual in the literature on state formation for it to be much remarked upon (Claessen and Van der Velde 1991:15). Eventually, dependency on certain prestige goods promoted further long-distance trade: cannons required for bride-wealth, textiles, gongs, and porcelain all became necessary for social reproduction, both of basic social units, clan, and house rituals but also sustained the ritual means of reproducing inequalities between ruler and ruled. This was all in addition to those valuables that formed part of the onward trade to mainland Seram and New Guinea.

Whether or not what is described here constitute "complex chiefdoms" or "small-scale states," to use the typological language of political anthropology, is really rather unimportant, and indeed there remains a conspicuous lack of clarity in the comparative literature as to how we might deal with such "transitional" political forms.[9] What I wish to suggest here is that in Southeast Seram a particular set of circumstances conspired to prevent further political centralization,[10] state formation above the local domain level, and significant domination of any one domain over another for any length of time. These were partly to do with the sociology and ecology of the area itself and partly to do with a regional dynamic emerging well before 1500. We can, however, exclude from these any superficial differences in the social infrastructure. I do not think these would have had much effect either way. It could be argued that the *etar* and *rumara* represent more promising organizational units in terms of achieving overarching centralization (cf. Winzeler 1976; Wolters 1982) than the absence of kinship-based corporations in Sulu. On the other hand it has been argued that those societies with more "flexible" kinship systems are those most likely to respond to new contacts and opportunities leading to state formation. But as in the debate concerning whether descent group flexibility or inflexibility in highland New Guinea is a function of population pressure (Kelly 1968), I think both could be true.

One ingredient that was certainly relevant and that we have already examined at some length is the physical fragility and shifting of settlements in central places. Second, there is the existence of a network of fluctuating alliances reinforced by dynastic marriages, where polities at the center could never rely entirely on their own production, the difficulty faced by any individual ruler in controlling dispersed economic activity, and the individualistic trading ethic at the heart of the *sosolot* system. All these worked against the consolidation of centralized power and arrested further state development. No single domain in archipelagic Southeast Seram could alone cope with the demands of stable food production, had the ability to effect rapid demographic adjustments, possessed a well-developed network of traditional internal exchange, or—apart from the shifts in domain geography referred to in chapter 4—could sustain a reliable mechanism for integrating outside polities (Slamet-Velsink 1995:242). Neither were individual domains able to monopolize trade, partly because of the *sosolot* system, partly because there was no significant home production of a cash crop, and partly because of the economic domination of Banda. Tidore, despite its periodic political incursions and the establishment of emissaries in the form of *sengaji*, never posed an economic threat to Southeast Seram. Such factors recall other explanations for the difficulty of establishing stable relations of subordination in tribal society due to reliance on conspicuous and generous redistribution (Webster 1976).

What distinguishes both Banda and the Southeast Seram polities is the greater freedom they permitted individual traders. In this respect the system was different from that of Tidore and Ternate and certainly from the agrarian states of Java. To the extent that the polities of the Banda zone, and of the Geser-Gorom area within it, provided a relatively neutral space for both local and incoming traders to operate, free from the intrusions of other states, and a set of supporting institutional practices, they conform to the "port of trade" model (Leeds 1961; Polanyi, Arensberg, and Pearson 1957; see also Dalton 1968 and Chaudhuri 1985:223–224). The wealth that supported the domains of Southeast Seram came from taxing incoming traders, a certain amount of exchange of goods produced by themselves, but, most important, from the middleman role in the *sosolot*s. In the sixteenth century the *sosolot* system was dominant; the arrival of the VOC affected some of this trade—mainly the trade in long nutmeg and local production of nutmeg—but it stimulated the entrepôt trade in the Banda-Onin corridor by making it a safe haven for those wishing to avoid the monopoly, including Bandanese fleeing their own homeland after 1621. Moreover, VOC successes in restricting the direct trading activities of the courts of Ternate and Tidore had the effect of pushing trade to the periphery. With the arrival of Sulawesi traders and the rise in the China trade, the entrepôt role became more important, and this in turn stimulated home production through increased extraction of maritime produce. By the late nineteenth century the domains of Southeast Seram had become weak, to some extent because they were not given the recognition and support that the European powers had given Ternate and Tidore and also because of the growing domination of incoming traders from the western archipelago. Indeed, the political support given Tidore by the Dutch and the British actively undermined the *sosolot* system. Under the Pax Neerlandica (and for a short period the Pax Britannica), more and more outside traders could trade directly with New Guinea, and the *sosolot* system was eventually undermined.

Although the *sosolot* system was much more egalitarian than the means of political control exercised by Tidore along the New Guinea coast, *matlaen* had advantages over commoners in mounting expeditions. Once there, they could exercise more effective power by virtue of their access to resources, but also by recognizing—like all Serammers working their *sosolots*—the reality of trade in New Guinea: that the local people had a political culture that made conventional forms of symbolic and physical domination inappropriate. It was this style of participation in, and control of, much of the New Guinea trade that reinforced the position of *matlaen* at home. They could deal directly with outside traders from the West. With the rise of the China trade they could exploit the assertion that the "raja" owned the reefs on behalf of the people. With incoming traders they could extract anchorage fees, and when the successors of those same traders set up first temporary and then semipermanent residence, they could claim rent. As more traders from the West traded for themselves on the New Guinea coast, independently of the *sosolot* system, rajas could substitute their own activities with those of the Bugis and Chinese traders—granting them privileges to trade in areas along the New Guinea coast where they had trading rights and receiving tribute as a share of the profit. In this way rajas accrued more wealth and power to themselves while undermining the very thing that provided them with an advantage outside their domains: the ability to trade along the New Guinea coast.

10.6. History, Anthropology, and Systems

This study of trade in a small area of eastern Indonesia demonstrates the plausibility of an exercise of linked historical and anthropological study. Though it may be conjectural and hybrid, the history contained within it does not simply provide background; neither is it an "anthropology of history." That it is conjectural (not speculative) I accept, but conjecture subject to refutation. I hope we have outgrown Radcliffe-Brown's admonition about conjectural history (which was anyway directed at an altogether different specter and situated in a wholly different discourse). Instead I am here suggesting that there are some distinct methodological advantages in recognizing that systems do not simply exist in space but also over time, and that by carefully using evidence drawn from different temporal horizons we can provide insights into the natural history of local systems over the longer term. This does not mean that we should abandon periodization, deny that change takes place, or shed high standards of scholarship or respect for the construction of facts, only that we should also argue on the basis of reasonable probabilities, just as we do when monographing a single well-documented and temporally tightly defined period. In terms of system dynamics and the comparative method there should, in theory, be little difference between generalizing arguments incorporating spatial variation and those incorporating temporal variation: it is all social, cultural, and ecological difference perceived in relation to aggregated regularities ("periods," "areas," or "societies"). Moreover, there is a point in historical analysis when it must grapple with the empty spaces in chronological knowledge and make sense of that shadowy point where history meets prehistory. Conventionally, we are required to choose between a synchronic ethnographic analysis and a diachronic historical one, each with its own methodological and disciplinary markers and each of which tends to accentuate the difference between one and the other. Yet in real life, cause-and-effect loops in systems of human activities cut right across such a distinction. We have yet to find an approach that encompasses both, though we can see ways forward in Giddens' (1981) concept of structuration and in the time-space trajectories discerned by the likes of Carlstein and Hägerstrand.[11] It is this kind of long-term, theoretically informed modeling based on documented empirical realities drawn from different time horizons that is precisely what historical anthropology should be about. Though it is not only what it should be about.

There exists, therefore, a level of analysis where history and anthropology have common theory and aims. All understandings of social systems that ignore historical process are inevitably theoretically weak and prone to substantive error (Thomas 1990:9), temporality being "constitutive of, rather than marginal to, social and cultural systems" (ibid., 5). Moreover, "the structural practices of social systems 'bind' the temporality of the durée of the day-to-day life-world to the longue durée of institutions, interpolated in the finite span of existence of the individual human being" (Giddens 1981:28). This is not to say that empirical history is the same as ethnography. The relationship between subject and object in each case is profoundly different, and those who glibly talk of archives as the historian's "field" are indulging in gross oversimplification. The process of knowledge production is quite different. Historical data are in the first instance limited by decisions made by accountants, rulers, bureaucrats, clerks, scribes, and archivists as what to place on record. Ethnographic data, by contrast, are actively solicited and produced for the purpose of analysis. Writing ethnography is a theoretically informed undertaking based on direct observation of group behavior and individual interaction; empirical history is the inference of group behavior or that of individuals from a preselected sample of "facts." The nature of "the fact" in history and ethnography is quite differently constructed. Thus, to distinguish the production of empirical historical data on which such analyses are based from historical anthropology more conventionally understood we should perhaps speak of "historical ethnography."

There are a number of clear areas in which historical ethnography can bring together historical and ethnographic evidence: through clarification of terms and institutions referred to in the documents (for example, in the context of this study, the concept of *sosolot*), corroboration, analogy, supplementation, and, of course, contextualization. Ethnography can provide entirely new kinds of historical evidence, no less historical because it is not located in old documents and, like documents, subject to the same processes of inference and interpretation. We might include here oral history, comparative linguistics, toponyms and other linguistic evidence, cultural survivals, mythology, tradition and ethnohistory, material culture, site surveys and excavation of historically important sites, settlement patterns, physical geography, and processes of social change. Historical ethnography, therefore, is the matching of two different kinds of data to elucidate the other.

The historical dimension of this project has raised a large number of issues that can be tackled only through detailed ethnographic research. Fieldwork alone can provide essential information on basic technical questions relating to the organization of production for exchange and trade at the local level, on the character or significance of current environmental constraints, on the ecology of systems composed of different (but complementary) subsistence strategies, on technology and equipment, on the types of trading centers in the network, and on traditional types of trading mechanisms. And the Moluccas possibly still offers a unique theatre for linked ethnographic and historical research. The documentary material is relatively abundant because of early European interest in these islands, and some of the local underlying conditions of trade have not altered since the seventeenth century, partly due to the demise of the Indonesian spice trade and the relegation of the islands to a peripheral position in colonial and postcolonial economies. Few other traditional systems of local maritime trade in Southeast Asia are so accessible to study, so historically important, and yet so little understood. Its further investigation should contribute significantly to our understanding of the functioning of regional systems and the organization of trade over large areas under preindustrial and precolonial conditions. However, we should always be mindful of Bowen's

(1991:30) cautionary advice concerning the problems of projecting field-work findings backward into time, what he describes as "a retroactive form of the fallacy of the ethnographic present." "The trick," he said, "is to use ethnography to make sense of history and yet recognise that ethnography does not replace historical reconstruction."

Appendixes

Appendix 1. Administrative units (desa), their constituent hamlets (kampung), and populations in the subdistrict of East Seram, 1983.

Island	Desa	Kampung	Population	Notes
Geser	Geser	**Geser**	2,216	Formerly under Kilwaru (De Hollander 1895:501). In 1862 divided between Kelu and Kilwaru (Van der Crab 1862:60–61)
Seram Laut	Kiltai	**Kiltai** Arbi	402	
Kidang	Kiltai	Kidang Mata Uli		
Seram Laut	Kilwaru	Kilwaru	1,189	Formerly included northern part of Seram Laut (De Hollander 1895:5) (Kilwaru, Geser, Kiltai, Maar, Namalas, Namalomin, Kilberau). Bosscher (1855) listed Maar as a separate domain, including Maar, Enemelan, Kilhuran, together with all small islands to Garogos under Kilwaru
		Talang Baru Namalomin Karang Namalas Maar Wawasa Also includes Maar Laut and Kifar		
Seram Rei	Kelu	**Kelu** Kilberau	894	Van der Crab (1862) included Kilberau, Kotabaru, Pagar, Kotabanda, and Kwaai
		Kwaai		Formerly independent
Seram Laut	Kelu	Arkel Kilfura		
Seram Rei	Keffing	**Keffing**	485	Van der Crab (1862) included Keffing, Rumonin, Rumanama, Kasongat, and Rumakat. Riedel (1886:47) included Kwaai, Kelu, Pagar, Kotabanda, Kotawau, and Kilberau

continued on next page

Island	Desa	Kampung	Population	Notes
South Coast of Seram	Urung	**Urung**	2,719	
		Dawang		
		Nekan		
		Afang		
		Kumelang		
		Taa		
		Woluk		
		Undur		
		Kamar		
		Gunak		
		Batu Manggar		
		Bitorik		
		Sumbawa		
		Akat Padedo		
		Mogosinis		
		Ainena		
		Guli-guli		
		Kwamar Besar		
		Kwamar Kecil		
	Kilmuri	**Kilmuri**	2,920	
		Mising		
		Selor		
		Tala		
		Kilboo		
East Coast of Seram	Kwaos	**Kwaos**	1,976	
		Air Nanang		
		Suru		
		Liangtasik		
		Keta		
	Kianlaut	**Kianlaut**	1,597	
		Rumadan		
		Nama		
		Selagur		
		Aruas		
		Gauer		
	Kiandarat	**Kiandarat**	3,582	
		Artafela		
		Anger		
		Kilgah		
		Kilaba		
		Kilwou(awo)		
		Watabau		
		Rumfakar		
		Usung		
		Kilsauer		
		Rumoga		
		Rumbow		
		Kelusi		Mountain Bati

Island	Desa	Kampung	Population	Notes
	Dinama	Walang Tengah	1,193	
		Dinama		
		Tarui		
		Loto		
		Erlang		
	Kilmoi	**Kilmoi**	489	
		Saiye		Mountain Bati
		Aruewe		Mountain Bati
	Kilbat	**Kilbat**	756	
	Sesar	**Sesar Pantai**	168	
		Sesar Gunung		
	Warus-warus	**Warus-warus**	582	
		Anglu		
		Mateu		
	Air Kasar	**Air Kasar**	145	Shares kepala soa with Sesar
	Gah	**Gah**	870	
		Kufar		
		Garikit		
Pulau Panjang	Pulau Panjang	**Wisalen**	870	
		Rukruk		Orang kaya under Amar (Bosscher 1855)
		Lalanwou		
		Argam		
		Lalasa		
		Magat		
		Basarangi		
Manawoka	Amarsekaru	**Amarsekaru**	1,362	All except Sera under Amar (Bosscher 1855)
		Derak		
		Kilurat		
		Pancalang		
		Loko		
		Inlomin		
		Wawasa		
		Matleu		
		Arwou		
		Siksir		
		Sera		
		Also includes Pulau Kun		
Gorom	Kataloka	**Kataloka**	3,930	
		Samboru		
		Dadaa		
		Rumeon		
		Aroa		Formerly under Ainikke
		Sikaru		
		Namalen		
		Kinali		
		Kulgoa		
		Usung		Contains *etar* (formerly domain) of Ainikke

continued on next page

Island	Desa	Kampung	Population	Notes
		Buan Rumanama		
		Adar-Kataloka		Formerly under Ainikke
		Also includes Garogos, Nukus, Kidang, Makoka, Neding, and Masangerat		
	Ondor	**Ondor**	1,013	Includes Kilsodi, Kilsuangi, Kilgoa, Ulong, and Kataower
		Dulak		
	Dai	**Dai**	1,270	Formerly part of Amarsekaru
		Kelibingan		
		Kelaler		
	Mida	**Mida**	406	
		Arewan		
		Kelili		
	Amarwatu	**Amarwatu**		
		Amar Laut	1,333	
		Sagei		
		Tunastolu		
		Udur		
		Ilur		
	Kilkoda	Kilkoda	1,061	
		Gota		Formerly under Ainikke (Bosscher 1855)
		Arang		Formerly under Kailakat
		Bas		Formerly under Kailakat
	Kotasiri	**Kotasiri**	705	
		Kiltufa		
	Miran	**Miran**	925	Formerly under Ainikke
		Kinarin		
	Rarat	**Rarat**	585	Formerly under Ainikke
		Usung		
Watubela	Ilili	**Ilili**	320	Formerly under Kesui
		Ahema		Formerly under Amar
		Effa	269	
		Lahema	455	
Kesui	Uta	**Uta**	500	
	Amarlaut	**Amarlaut**	666	
	Tamher	**Warat**		
	Tamher Timor	**Kota**	517	
Teor	Rumoi	**Rumoi**	1,331	
Total population			13,165	

Note: The locations list the central archipelagic districts around Geser first, then the mainland, then southwestward toward Kei. Places in **boldface** indicate current centers of desa administration. Only selected hamlets are listed, usually those mentioned most frequently in the text.

Appendix 2. Estimated levels of boat ownership in selected Southeast Seram settlements, 1981–1986.

Location	Ang guik	Ang kalulis	Angbot	Jonson
Geser				
Geser-Keffing	6			
Geser			1	4
Seram Laut				
Kiltai			1	1
Kidang		1	3	
Kilwaru		1		0
Karang			8	
Seram Rei				
Kelu	3	1		
Kelu (Keffing)	9		2	2
Kilfura		1	1	1
Keffing	6+			
South coast of Seram				
Urung (aggregate figure for desa)				23
Afang				2
Woluk				2
Undur				4
Guli-guli				11
Kwamar	2			6
Kilmuri				1
Selor				2
East coast of Seram				
Kwaos	3+			4
Kilgah			1	1
Kilaba				2
Dinama		1		1–2
Tarui	2			1–2
Kilmoi	6		2	2 (3)
Kilbat			3	1 (2)
Sesar		0		0
Warus-warus			3	1 (3)
Anglu				0
Air Kasar		3		2 (3)
Gah				1
Kufar				0

continued on next page

Location	ang guik	ang kalulis	angbot	jonson
Manawoka				
Derak			2	
Matleu			4	
Arwou			2	
Gorom				
Kataloka			1	3+
Samboru			2	
Aroa	2			
Sikaru	3			
Namalen	2			
Garogos	0	3	2	2 (12 pok-pok in 1994)
Kelaler	1+			

Note: Figures refer to bodies (numbers of engines are shown in parentheses). The figures are estimates of operational vessels based on information provided by selected informants in the localities listed. However, boats are mobile property and move along kinship and affinal lines, as well as between different locations in the course of their working lives. Therefore, vessels in any one place at a particular time may not be regarded as "belonging" there.

Appendix 3. Base list of places used as vectors in network analysis

	Map Reference in Figure 2.2	Place	Domain	Domain Population	Distance Centrality Shortest Distance	Rank	Distance Centrality Hugging Distance	Rank
1.	1	Geser	Geser	2,216	1,096	5	1,288	4
2.	2	Kiltai	Kiltai	402	1,095	3	1,307	6
3.	6	Kilwaru	Kilwaru	1,189	1,095	3	1,307	6
4.	13	Kelu	Kelu	894	1,063	1	1,271	2
5.	18	Keffing	Keffing	485	1,063	1	1,271	2
6.	19	Urung	Urung	2,719	1,482	24	1,778	21
7.	38	Kilmuri	Kilmuri	2,920	2,239	27	2,657	27
8.	43	Kwaos	Kwaos	1,976	1,148	6	1,288	1
9.	48	Kianlaut	Kianlaut	1,597	1,225	8	1,271	5
10.	56	Kiandarat	Kiandarat	3,582	1,207	7	2,153	25
11.	69	Dinama	Dinama	1,193	1,258	10	1,613	9
12.	74	Kilmoi	Kilmoi	489	—	—		
13.	77	Kilbat	Kilbat	756	1,307	14	1,665	10
14.	78	Sesar Pantai	Sesar	168	1,326	15	1,665	10
15.	80	Warus-warus	Warus-warus	582	1,329	17	1,691	12
16.	83	Air Kasar	Air Kasar	145	1,326	15	1,702	13
17.	84	Gah	Gah	870	1,410	19	1,743	16
18.	87	Argam	Panjang	870	1,247	9	2,289	26
19.	94	Pancalang	Amarsekaru	1,362	1,262	11	1,502	8
20.	105	Kataloka	Kataloka	3,930	1,281	12	1,747	18
21.	110	Ondor	Ondor	1,013	1,282	13	1,770	20
22.	112	Dai	Dai	1,270	1,468	22	1,704	14
23.	115	Mida	Mida	406	1,382	18	1,761	19
24.	118	Amarwatu	Amarwatu	1,333	1,481	23	1,727	15
25.	123	Kilkoda	Kilkoda	1,061	1,491	25	1,785	22
26.	127	Kotasiri	Kotasiri	705	1,505	26	1,744	17
27.	29	Miran	Miran	925	1,436	20	1,843	23
28.	135	Rarat	Rarat	585	1,436	20	1,862	24

Appendix 4. Distance centrality and connectivity judgments for the Seram Laut area

Locality	Guli-guli	Kwamar	Seram Rei	Kwaos	Geser	Kiltai-Kilwaru	Kilfura	Maar	Namalomin	Namalas
Guli-guli		4 (1)	12 (1)	23 (2)	14 (1)	16 (2)	17 (2)	22 (2)	23 (4)	19 (3)
Kwamar	4 (1)		6 (1)	18 (1)	10 (1)	12 (2)	13 (2)	17 (3)	17 (4)	15 (3)
Seram Rei	12 (1)	6 (1)		12 (1)	3 (1)	4 (1)	5 (1)	10 (2)	11 (3)	7 (2)
Kwaos	23 (2)	18 (1)	12 (1)		12 (1)	13 (1)	15 (2)	15 (2)	17 (3)	17 (4)
Geser	14 (1)	10 (1)	3 (1)	12 (1)		1 (1)	4 (1)	6 (1)	8 (2)	6 (2)
Kiltai-Kilwaru	16 (2)	12 (2)	4 (1)	13 (1)	1 (1)		3 (1)	5 (1)	9 (2)	7 (2)
Kilfura	17 (2)	13 (2)	5 (1)	15 (2)	4 (1)	3 (1)		11 (2)	6 (2)	3 (1)
Maar	22 (2)	17 (3)	10 (2)	15 (2)	6 (1)	5 (1)	11 (2)		3 (1)	7 (2)
Namalomin	23 (4)	17 (4)	11 (3)	17 (3)	8 (2)	9 (2)	6 (2)	3 (1)		4 (1)
Namalas	19 (3)	15 (3)	7 (2)	17 (4)	6 (2)	7 (2)	3 (1)	7 (2)	4 (1)	
Index	150 (18)	112 (18)	70 (14)	142 (17)	64 (11)	64 (11)	77 (14)	96 (16)	98 (22)	85 (20)
Rank	10 (7)	8 (7)	2 (3)	9 (6)	1 (1)	2 (2)	4 (3)	6 (5)	7 (10)	5 (9)

Appendix 5. Distance centrality and connectivity judgments for the Gorom Archipelago

Locality	Wisalen	Kataloka-Ondor	Amarsekaru	Mida	Dai	Rarat-Miran	Amarwatu
Wisalen		19 (1)	9 (1)	19 (1)	20 (1)	33 (1)	29 (1)
Kataloka-Ondor	19 (1)		14 (1)	4 (1)	7 (2)	21 (1)	19 (3)
Amarsekaru	9 (1)	14 (1)		12 (1)	12 (1)	31 (2)	18 (1)
Mida	19 (1)	4 (1)	12 (1)		4 (1)	26 (2)	14 (2)
Dai	20 (1)	7 (2)	12 (1)	4 (1)		22 (2)	10 (1)
Rarat-Miran	33 (1)	21 (1)	31 (2)	26 (2)	22 (3)		10 (1)
Amarwatu	29 (2)	19 (3)	18 (1)	14 (2)	10 (1)	10 (1)	
Index	129 (7)	84 (9)	96 (7)	79 (8)	75 (9)	143 (9)	100 (9)
Rank	6 (1)	3 (5)	4 (1)	2 (3)	1 (5)	7 (5)	5 (5)

Notes

Chapter 1. Introduction

1. For further elaboration of these points see Reid and Marr (1979:391–419), Wang (1958:90), and Wertheim (1954:167–173).

2. One of the criticisms of this claim has been that some centers (most notably Ambon-Lease) were not as dependent on imported sago as I suggested. This may well be so, though since 1979 new evidence has come to light that lends further support to the importance of the flow of sago from Seram to Ambon-Lease. For example, we now know more concerning the *babulu* and *papalele* (*lelang*) institutions and other arrangements for trading, collecting, and securing sago from Seram, especially before the clove season, Ramadan, and other important festivals, institutions that were still operating in places such as Oma (on Haruku), Saparua, and Nusalaut in 1981 (Ellen, field notes 3-21, 3-14).

   In addition we now have historical evidence for concessions made by the VOC in the nineteenth century to maintain the supply of sago from Seram to Ambon and the role of barter, share harvesting, and *pela* (Brouwer 1998:346, 355 nn. 13, 14; 359–360; Heeres 1908:343; MINKOL 1817, 2954 [2.10.01]). Existing *pela* ties (ties of blood brotherhood between villages) were utilized to gain access to sago on Seram, and new *pela* were commonly created specifically for this purpose (Bartels 1977:142; Van Hoevell 1875:159): *pela-bonang* (commodity *pela*) or *pela perut* (stomach *pela*). One specific case is an application to establish a *pela* relationship with the negeri Hatusoa (Seram) dated 15 March 1820, from the orang kaya and oldest member of the *negori* Tengah-Tengah (Ambon) to the governor of the Moluccas, Tilenius Kruytoff A. N. The shortage of food in Tengah-Tengah is given as the reason for the application. By establishing the *pela* food would have been more easily obtained and cheaper, if not actually free (Manusama 1977:44–45). Since 1900 *pela* based on economic considerations has become legitimate and has superseded *pela-bonang* (Bartels 1977:147).

   Sago shortfalls in Ambon, certainly since the nineteenth century, and probably earlier, led to groups of individuals, sometimes entire villages, going to Seram to obtain sago, often staying several months to extract enough for one year (ibid., 141. The price paid to the owners depended on the size of the tree, but often trees were obtained through the *sagu ma-anu* relationship, in which those extracting sago gave one-third of the yield to the owners (Van Hoevell 1875:54–55). In the nineteenth century, in times of low clove prices and inability to acquire cash to buy sago, we find an increase in *sagu ma-anu* pacts and barter. In the long term, as Jouke S. Wigboldus (personal communication, 1987) has suggested, the Moluccas may have moved from an agricultural economy to being increasingly sago-dependent, directly as a result of the growth of the spice trade.

Chapter 2. Archipelgic Southeast Seram

1. Belis also speaks SSL (see Figure 3.3). Along the north coast, west of Bula there are a number of SSL-speaking villages interspersed with villages of Seti and Masiwang speakers (J. Collins 1984:119). In view of this, it is worth noting that during the Dutch period the subdistrict (that is, the onderafdeeling) of East Seram included both Bula on the north coast and Werinama along the south.

2. There are dialectal differences between different parts of the area, most markedly between the Gorom and Seram Laut Archipelagoes, and between the Bati area of the east coast and the rest. To simplify matters in this account, where differences occur in broad transcription, and unless otherwise clearly stated, I use the Seram Laut variant.

3. Rijksarchief VOC 3966-23, 26 September 1792.

4. Notes accompanying map 9, Netherlands Forces Intelligence Service, no. 216a, updated 1943, 17.

5. Rijksarchief VOC 3966-22, 23. Bataviase secrete inkomende brieven overgekomen in 1793 (intelligence report). Book 22, part 1.

6. Decree enacted by Resident Lans on 19 January 1840 relating to a disagreement between Keffing and Kelu over rights to authorize *sasi* (in this case regarding sea produce) on the fringing reefs of Seram Laut. Romanized Malay; original in the possession of the raja of Kelu.

7. The matter was first drawn to the attention of Resident Lans in Banda on 14 August 1838, but the issues were still a subject of contention on 31 March 1911 and not completely settled until 23 February 1920. As with the document concerning the Keffing-Kelu dispute, a copy of the original "Pembritamuwan" (this time typed, and in Jawi) still exists, now in the hands of the raja of Kilwaru. The dispute is also published as a report of the Court of Heads of Geser and summarized by Holleman (1925: 145–146).

8. The literature on *sasi* is now extensive, having become emblematic of traditional mechanisms for regulating natural resources. For some recent general accounts see F. von Benda-Beckmann, K. von Benda-Beckmann, and Brouwer (1995) and Zerner (1994). Soselisa (1995:82–90) described *sasi* for Kataloka. For an early account of *sasi* in this area see Riedel (1886:166–170), who discusses *sasi* trepang (and *sasi* agar-agar).

Chapter 3. A Conjectured History: The Origins of a Trading Zone

1. Of a total of 297 marriages appearing in genealogies collected from twenty locations in 1986, eighty-eight (30 percent) were to persons with the same *etar* name. In some places it was much higher. The sample included people of Arabic, Bugis, and Butonese origin. For example, in a Kidang genealogy, one Mohammed Amin Rumakat married late after living for eleven years trading in Sorong on the Bird's Head (Kepala Burung) of New Guinea. He then sequentially married and divorced four women, all from Rumakat, before marrying a fifth who bore him children. What is of additional interest is that each Rumakat woman came from a different place: Kilura (Amarsekaru), Laha-Kristen (Tehoru), Hara (Sorong), Artafela (Kiandarat), and Kidang itself.

2. Kepeng is a common Moluccan Malay word for money, usually small change. Historically it referred to coins with square holes worth an eighth of a Netherlands Indies cent during the colonial period. It is not a word of obvious Portuguese etymology, though that Keffing is derived from a word for wealth is not implausible.

See, for example, the discussion of pala in chapter 1.2 and the ideas of Chlenov (1980). The term "mayor" probably derives from Dutch "majoor" (major) (J. H. F. Sollewijn Gelpke, personal communication), contra Ellen (1986b).

3. Surat Pengasihan from Namasawar village in Banda to the raja of Kelu confirming the Urlima link between the two places. Typed copy belonging to the raja of Kelu in 1986, itself a copy of the original written in 1890.

4. And in the remaining years of the seventeenth century an equally dramatic transformation took place in Ambon and West Seram: villages were moved, plantations extirpated, clove harvests confiscated, and political organization was radically altered, resulting in a social formation that was almost entirely the product of colonial administration, but that would nevertheless be seen as "traditional" by the nineteenth century (Manusama 1977).

Chapter 4. The Political Economy of a Conradian Space

1. I have mentioned constituent settlements that can be identified from contemporary toponyms; others either no longer exist, were erroneously recorded at the time, or cannot be identified ethnographically.

2. ARA Mail Reports: Sterker, 1881:310.

3. Wichmann 1909:188, fig. 29: [Gilles)] Robert de Vaugondy. Theil von Australasien 1756. Joh. Chr. Adelung. *Vollständige Geschichte der Schiffarthen nach den noch grösten-theils unbekannten Südländen aus em Französischen Herrn Präsidenten de Brosse[s].* Halle 1767, Taf. IV, auch Ch. de Brosses. *Histoire des navigations aux Terres Australes.* II Paris, 1756, pl. V.

4. ARA VEL 1345. Caarte van Groot Ceram, midsgaders alle d'Eylanden van Amboina en Banda 1651. Behoort bij het rapport van Arnoldus de Vlamingh van Outshoorn.

5. See, for example, map ARA KOLA 40 De Molukken 1847. Door P. Baron Melville de Carnbee Gegraveerd door D. Heijse te Den Haag. Lithografie door Ch. van Lier te Den Haag.

6. ARA VEL 475. Kaart van het Eiland Ceram, Bouro, Amboina en bijgelegen Eilanden; ARA VEL 485 Kaart van het Eiland Ceram, Bouro, een gedeelte van de Westkust van Nova Guinea, de Arouw Eilanden, Timor-laut, het Oostelijkste gedeelte van Tymor en de daar tusschen gelegen Eilanden.

7. ARA VOC 11245. Rumphius, *Landbeschrijving.*

8. ARA VOC 1855–1856, 3561. Brief van gemelde Bandas gouverneur Pelters aen generael en raden van 14 December 1780 over de Cerammers enz. (see also De Hollander 1895:50).

9. ARA MINKOL 1824, 2766. Reglement op het Binnenlandsch Bestuur en dat der Financiën op Amboina en Onderhoorigheden. Ambon, 15 April 1824.

10. ARA MIKO III-973. Geteekende kaart van het eiland Ceram (1835).

11. ARA MIKO III-207. Geteekende kaart van het eiland Groot Seram (1835).

12. ARA MIKO III-1082. Figuratieve schets van het eiland Ceram, residentie Amboina (1872).

13. Part of Schetskaart van Oost-en Midden Seran door C. W. W. C. Baron van Hoëvell. (scale 1:250,000.) 1894. The main feature of note in this map is the island labeled "Kwamur" in relation to the mainland and Keffing. See also ARA MIKO III-1875, Schetskaart van het eiland Ceram (1909).

14. ARA VOC 3966-21, 22, 23, 25. Bataviase secrete inkomende brieven overgekomen in 1793. Twee en Twintigste Boek Eerste Deel. Copie aparte brieven en bijlagen van Ambon voor Nederland in 1792.

15. Here I suggest the following approximate equivalences: 1 pikul = 60.4 kilograms; 1 kati = 600 grams; 1 koyong = 1,812 kilograms (or 30 pikuls). However, the values of such weights and measures varied notoriously from place to place and from time to time (Ellen 1979:72 n. 3; Meilink-Roelofsz 1962).

16. A padewakang (or paduwakang) was a large but light trading vessel with a square poop, double rudders, a large rectangular sail and a smaller fore-and-aft sail on a tripod mast, two jibs on the bowsprit, and a smaller rectangular sail on a second tripod toward the stern (MacKnight 1976:26).

17. ARA Mail Reports. Verslag van de reis van een kontroleur te Oost-Ceram, 1881, 1–791.

18. *Encyclopaedie van Nederlandsch-Indië*, 2d ed., s.v. "Ceram-Laoet."

19. Ibid., s.v. "Geser" and "Goram-eilanden."

20. VOC currency unit, equivalent, at the time, to 3 shillings and 8 pence in British coinage.

21. ARA VOC 3561 (Eerste Afdeeling). Brieven en papieren van Batavia overgekomen in 1781. Vijfde boek, vijde deel, pp. 1855 to 1856. Brief van gemelde Bandas gouverneur Pelters aen generael en raden van 14 December 1780 over de Cerammers enz.

22. ARA, MINKOL, 1814–1849, 3089.

23. ARA Mail Reports 2766. Reglement op het Binnenlandsch Bestuur en dat der Financien op Amboina en Onderhoorigheden, Ambon, 15 April 1824. Also in *Bronnen betreffende de Midden Molukken 1900–1942*, IV, 1–38.

24. ARA Comite Oost-Indische Handel en Bezittingen 1791–1800, Banda (Tweede Afdeeling), p. 84; ARA Mail Reports 1872, 6368-725, 764; 1876, 6372; 6470-773; 1889.

25. ARA, MINKOL (Tweede Afdeeling), 2766-7. Register der handelingen en besluiten van de Gouverneur-Generaal, tijdens zijn reis naar de Molukken en Celebes 1824 (Maart–April). [Report of March–April 1824 to G. G. van de Capellen.]

26. ARA Mail Reports 1872, 6368-725, 764.

27. ARA VOC 1784, 3677. Copie secrete resolutie van 10 Juli 1784 inhoudende's gouverneurs voornemen tot sluiting van verdere te samenrottinen door het stabiliseren van een fortje op Po. Gisser; Plan van een fortres hetwelk de gouverneur geïntentioneerd was om op Po. Grisser [*sic*] op te rigten; ARA, MINKOL, 1814–1849, 3089; ARA Mail Reports 1874, 196, 6363-354; 1876, 6373, 47, 194, 381, 654.

28. ARA Mail Reports 1876, 6373, 519-722, 649.

Chapter 5. Southeast Seram and the Papuas

1. For a critical disussion of the term "Papua" see Sollewijn Gelpke 1993.

2. "Lantaka" is apparently a Tagalog term for bronze cannon used by pre-Spanish Filipino and present-day Moro (Malay = rentaka). In Malay "lantaka" is sometimes used for a cannon of a particular type, generically called *lilla* or *lela*, possibly a corruption of the name for pieces of Egyptian origin (laylah) used in Gujerat in the sixteenth century. The term "mariam" is also used in Malay, from the Arabic proper name Miriam, originating in Muslim India. We know also that by the beginning of the sixteenth century pieces of brass Chinese ordnance were reaching the Moluccas (Manguin 1976:238, 245).

3. A similar arrangement appears to have been in place along the northeastern coast of Seram, whereby inland Alifuru established a ritualized relationship with a person (*kamal*) in a coastal village, usually someone from outside who had married into the village, who would be provided sago in exchange for fixed quantities of trade goods (Leirissa 1994:103).

4. I use the term "slave" here in the broad sense of a bonded person. Within the archipelago, between the sixteenth and twentieth centuries, various forms of bondage and proprietorial relationship are evident. There were differences in the scale of bondage, the proportion of slaves to free persons, in terms of degree of control, the role of bondage, and rights to land and bonded labor, perhaps most obviously between the slave-master relationship established between Europeans and Asians on Banda and the more diffuse relationship known from Seram Laut and Gorom (Slamet-Velsink 1995: 99, 162–165; cf. Watson 1980).

5. ARA Mail Reports 1876–1878: 6373-654; 1877: 6380-509, on the slave trade along the Papuan coast; ARA Mail Reports 1887:6380 mentions children as young as six being exchanged for ironmongery and linen, and sometimes "stolen" and sent to Ternate; the raja of Salawati was implicated.

6. ARA Mail Reports 1886:6470-864, on the murder of three bird hunters.

Chapter 6. Boats and Boat Handling

1. Local terminology for basically the same kind of vessel varies geographically. I include here some of the more general terms current in various local languages (in *italics*), as well as standard Indonesian (in roman text).

Chapter 7. The Structure of Contemporary Trading Networks

1. Kantor Wilayah Perdagangan Maluku, 1981; Statistik Tahunan Kecamatan Seram Timur 1977–1978. See also Figure 7.4.

2. Dafter Perahu, Kecamatan Banda, 16 November 1978. I am grateful to Ny. H. Montolalu and L. Tariola for this information.

3. Direktorat Jenderal Bea dan Cukai, Kataloka 1981.

Chapter 8. The Social Instruments of Trade in Late Twentieth-Century Seram

1. Soselisa (1995:177) reported that on Garogos *waya* are made from the coconut leaf midrib (*gulma*) or pandanus root.

2. Tobacco was still important in the Papuan trade during the first decade of the twentieth century (Haga 1911:342). On the moneylike role of tobacco and sago see also chapter 5.4. It is also worth noting that earlier in the nineteenth century Bik had reported the use of silver coins on Aru (chapter 4.2).

3. Pondok, literally a hut or shed, is used widely in the Moluccas to refer to a small stall or domestic retail outlet. The term "warung" used elsewhere for much the same thing usually refers here to a small fast-food stall (see, e.g., Alexander 1987:42–45).

4. This is not the place to discuss the dynamics of bargaining in detail or the merits of alternative theoretical models. I have no reason to conclude that the situation in Geser during the late 1980s was substantially any different in terms of the range of possible strategies from that reviewed by Alexander for Java (1987:189–201).

Chapter 9. Traders, Migration, and Ethnicity

1. The predictability of the market with China from A.D. 220 onward, arising from an established "rhythm" in demand for particular maritime goods (Wolters 1970: 39–48), helped sustain the lifestyle and economic importance of aquatic populations. Their viability as a group depended in the early nineteenth century on the demand for trepang and turtle shell, and this influenced their distribution, most considering themselves subjects of the Bugis sultanate of Bone. Some groups of

these boat-dwelling nomads, fishermen, strand collectors, and traders impinged on Moluccan trading networks, through migration into the Sula and Obi Straits and along the shores of the Bacan area (Andaya 1980:1; Sather 1985:166–167). Lacking internal political integration, they formed marginal subject populations in regional trading states dominated by other ethnic groups, for example Ternate. Indeed, even in the Southeast Sulawesi area, and as early as 1683, some Bajau acknowledged the overlordship of Ternate (Andaya 1980:18). But in the Moluccas, where we have already noted their involvement in late slaving (chapter 5.7), they also encountered other groups, such as the traders and maritime producers of the Southeast Seram Archipelago, who, although not nomadic sea people, tended to occupy a similar economic niche. This may have halted Bajau eastward expansion. There appears to have been some direct contact between Bajau and the Serammers: Andaya (1980:7), for example, reported that there was a Bajau settlement at Palette, under the influence of Bone, in the late seventeenth century, where Serammers came to trade.

2. We can compare this situation with that in Ambon, where of a total of 519 registered shop owners in the central market in 1982, 43 (8 percent) were persons with recognizably Arabic names. Most los (stall) places were rented by Butonese. (Source: Nama penyewa ruangan toko dan perusahaanya dalam kompleks pasar Gotong Royong Kodya Ambon, 1982 [unpublished municipal document]).

3. Uittreksel uit het Register der Besluiten van den Resident van Zuid-Molukken dd. 30 Augustus 1947 No. 269. Original document in possession of Hi. I. Wairooy, Raja Kelu.

Chapter 10. Conclusion

1. I use here the expression "time-geography" to register the relevance of Hägerstrandian models of space-time regions. These envisage that "as time flows, organisms and objects of different life-spans describe paths which together form a large and complex web..., (emergent paths)...combining all the time into different constellations depending on diversity and mobility constraints" (Carlstein 1982:40). It would be highly instructive, for example, to examine the characteristic time-space trajectories for Southeast Seram traders over the course of one year and how these form patterns that reflect both the constraints of topography, resource distribution, and the temporal rhythms of seasonality; and to compare hypothetical graphs for different historical epochs.

2. When export of nutmeg and the entrepôt trade was disrupted, as under the Japanese occupation, the Bandanese fell back on a subsistence economy and imported sago from Ambon (Hanna 1978:131).

3. Some evidence to support the assertion that, prehistorically, Ambon-Lease was relatively unimportant in east-west archipelagic or extraarchipelagic trade is to be found in the distribution of artifacts of Javanese or western Indonesian origin. Bronzes and Hindu-Buddhist monuments are found in Banda, Gorom, Kei, and even New Guinea, but not Ambon-Lease (Van Heekeren 1958: fig. 1; Ellen, field notes, 1981). On the fragmentary literary evidence pointing in the same direction, see Van Fraassen (1976).

4. Rumphius, Landbeschrijving. ARA VOC 1124, 120–126.

5. ARA Mail Reports 1871, 6353-503: Onrust onder de bevolking en aanvallen op handelaren; 1872, 6355-609: Handel op Dobo/Aroe-eilanden is levendig, Toestand op de Aroe-eilanden/res. is rustig; 1892, 6498-1191, 1201: Bestrijding van onlusten op de Aroe-eilanden door SS. Java.

6. With the demise of sailing vessels as the most important conveyors of goods, such factors became irrelevant, but by that time the social and economic dynamics of the systems themselves had become sufficient to maintain certain locational patterns.

7. To be exact, 85 percent of the rectangle bounded by 3° North to 9° South and 125° East to 134.5° East; this includes the large landmasses of the Kepala Burung (Vogelkop) of New Guinea, as well as part of East Timor.

8. There is an interesting connection for this period between Sulu and Southeast Seram: so-called "pirates" from the Sulu zone are reported as ranging eastward as far as Tobelo, after which they voyaged south to the north coast of Buru, Seram, and Gorom (Gorong) and then southwestward to Buton, Salayar, Flores, and Bali (Lombard 1979:235).

9. *Encyclopedia of social and cultural anthropology,* 1st ed., s.v. "State."

10. Some scholars have argued recently that centralization was not necessarily achieved in the earliest states reported for the Indonesian region (Boechari 1979:477; Bronson 1979).

11. See note 1.

Works Cited

Archival Source Materials

Full references to archival sources appear as notes.

DUTCH GOVERNMENT DOCUMENTS

ARA	Algemeen Rijksarchief, The Hague, Netherlands
VOC	Archief van de Vereenigde Oost-Indische Compagnie
	(Dutch East India Company Archive)
OBP	Overgekomen Brieven en Papieren
	Rumphius, *De generale Landbeschrijving van het Ambonsche*
	Gouvernement. ARA VOC 1124, 120–126.
OIC	Oost-Indisch Comité, 1793 onward
MINKOL	Ministerie van Koloniën
	Mailrapporten (Mail Reports)

Map Archives

VEL	Verzameling Eerste Leupe
MIKO	Ministerie von Koloniën
KOLA	Koloniale Aanwinsten

INDONESIAN GOVERNMENT DOCUMENTS

Subdistrict (Kecamatan) reports
        Statistik Tahunan Kecamatan Seram Timur 1977, 1978, 1980, 1982
        Statistik Tahunan Kecamatan Banda 1977, 1978
Harbormaster (Syahbandar) reports
        Ambon 1980
        Banda 1978, 1980, 1984
        Geser 1980, 1985
        Kataloka 1985
        Dafter Perahu, Dewan Pimpinan Cabang PELRA, Kecamatan Banda
        Port Information Ambon, 1980
Departemen Perhubungan, *Badan Meteorologi dan Geofisika Balai Wilayah IV*
Stasiun Meteorologi, Geser. Data Klimatologi, 1985
Direktorat Jenderal Bea dan Cukai [Customs], Kataloka 1981
Kantor Wilayah Perdagangan Maluku, Daerah Tingkat (Dati) II, Maluku Tengah,
        1981

Published Sources and Unpublished Academic Papers and Reports

Abdurachman, P. R. 1981. New winds, new faces, new forces. Paper presented at the
conference on "Southeast Asian responses to European intrusions." British
Institute in Southeast Asia, Singapore.

Adatrechtbundels. 1925. Uitspraken van Gecommitteerde Ambtenaren voor Ceram, Ceramlaut, Goram, Aroe- en Kei-eilanden (1853–1857), *Adatrechtbundels* (24:177–208)

Agnew, J.-C. 1979. The threshold of exchange: Speculations on the market. *Radical History Review* 21:99–118.

Alatas, Syed Hussein. 1977. *The myth of the lazy native.* London: Cass.

Alexander, J. 1987. *Trade, traders and trading in rural Java.* Oxford: ASAA Southeast Asia Publication Series No. 15.

Alkire, W. H. 1965. *Lamotrek atoll and inter-island socioeconomic ties.* Urbana: University of Illinois Press.

Allen, G. C., and A. Donnithorne. 1954. *Western enterprise in Indonesia and Malaya.* London: Allen and Unwin.

Allen, J. 1977a. Fishing for wallabies: Trade as a mechanism for social interaction, integration and elaboration on the central Papuan coast. In *The evolution of social systems*, ed. J. Friedman and M. J. Rowlands, 419–455. London: Duckworth.

———. 1977b. Sea traffic, trade and expanding horizons. In *Sunda and Sahul: Prehistoric studies in Southeast Asia, Melanesia and Australia*, ed. J. Allen, J. Golson, and R. Jones, 387–417. London: Academic Press.

Ammarell, G. 1999. *Bugis navigation.* New Haven, Conn.: Yale University Southeast Asian Studies, Monograph 48.

Andaya, L. Y. 1980. Historical links between the aquatic population and the coastal peoples of the Malay world and Celebes. Paper presented at Eighth Conference, International Association of Historians of Asia, Kuala Lumpur, Malaysia, 25–29 August.

———. 1991. Local trade networks in Maluku in the sixteenth, seventeenth and eighteenth centuries. *Cakalele: Maluku Research Journal* 2 (2): 71–96.

———. 1993. *The world of Maluku: Eastern Indonesia in the early modern period.* Honolulu: University of Hawai'i Press.

Anonymous. 1882. Zeevisscherij langs de kusten der eilanden van Nederlandsch-Indië. *Tijdschrift van Nijverheid en Landbouw in Nederlandsch-Indië* 26:73–145, 157–201, 257–302, 313–370.

Appadurai, A. 1986. Introduction: Commodities and the politics of value. In *The social life of things: Commodities in cultural perspective*, ed. A. Appadurai, 3–63. Cambridge: Cambridge University Press.

Barnes, R. H. 1988. Moving and staying space in the Malay Archipelago. In *Time past, time present, time future: Essays in honour of P. E. de Josselin de Jong*, ed. D. S. Moyer and H. J. M. Claessen, 110–116. Dordrecht: Foris.

———. 1996. *Sea hunters of Indonesia: Fishers and weavers of Lamalera.* Oxford: Clarendon Press.

Barraud, C. 1985. The sailing boat: Circulation and values in the Kei Islands, Indonesia. In *Contexts and levels: Anthropological essays on hierarchy*, ed. R. H. Barnes, D. de Coppet, and R. J. Parkin, 117–130. Journal of the Anthropological Society of Oxford Occasional Paper 4.

Bartels, D. 1977. *Guarding the invisible mountain: Intervillage alliances, religious syncretism and ethnic identity among Ambonese Christians and Moslems in the Moluccas.* Ph.D. diss., Cornell University, Ithaca, N.Y.

Beccari, O. 1924. *Nuova Guinea, Selebes e Molucche: Diarii di viaggio ordinati dal figlio prof. dott. Nello Beccari.* Florence: La Voce.

Bellwood, P. 1985. *Prehistory of the Indo-Malaysian Archipelago*. New York: Academic Press.

Benda-Beckmann, F. von, K. von Benda-Beckmann, and A. Brouwer. 1995. Changing "indigenous environmental law" in the central Moluccas: Communal regulation and privatisation of sasi. *Ekonesia* 2:1–38.

Berg, L. W. C. van den. 1886. *La Hadhramout et les colonies arabes dans l'archipel indeien*. Batavia: Imprimerie du Gouvernement.

Berg, N. P. van den. 1872. Fijf jaren op Banda (1633–1638). *Tijdschrift voor Indische Taal-, Land- en Volkenkunde* 18:332–366.

Beversluis, A. J., and A. H. C. Gieben. 1929. *Het Gouvernement der Molukken*. Weltevreden: Landsdrukkerij.

Bik, A. J. 1928 (1824). *Dagverhael eener reis, gedaan in het jaar 1824 tot nadere verkenning der eilanden Kefing, Goram, Groot- Klein Kei en de Aroe-eilanen*. Leiden: A. W. Sijthofff.

Bleeker, P. 1856. *Reis door Minahassa en den Molukken Archipel gedaan in de maanden september en oktober 1855 in het gevolg van Gouverneur Generaal Mr. A. J. Duymaer van Twist*. Vol. 2. Batavia: Lange.

Blust, R. A. 1979. Proto-Western Malayo-Polynesian vocatives. *Bijdragen tot de Taal-, Land- en Volkenkunde* 135:205–251.

Boechari. 1979. Some considerations on the problem of the shift of Mataram's centre of government from central to east Java in the 10th century. In *Early South east Asia: Essays in archaeology, history and historical geography*, ed. R. B. Smith and W. Watson, 473–491. Oxford: Oxford University Press.

Bokemeyer, H. 1888. *Die Molukken. Geschichte und quellenmässige Darstellung der Eroberung und Verwaltung der Ostindischen Gewürzinseln durch die Niederländer*. Leipzig: F. A. Brockhaus.

Bosscher, C. 1853. Staat aantoonende der voornaamste eilanden der Aroe-groep, benevens de voornaamste negorijen en het aantal van hare bewoners en huizen, in 1850. *Tijdschrift Bataviaasch Genootschap* 1:323–326.

———. 1855. Bijdrage tot de kennis van het Oostelijke gedeelte van Ceram en omliggende eilanden. *Tijdschrift voor Indische Taal-, Land- en Volkenkunde* 4:34–42.

Bowen, J. R. 1991. *Sumatran politics and poetics: Gayo history, 1900–1989*. New Haven, Conn.: Yale University Press.

Boxer, C. R. 1969. *The Portuguese seaborne empire 1415–1825*. London: Hutchinson of London.

Boxer, C. R., and P.-Y. Manguin. 1979. Miguel Roxo de Brito's narrative of his voyage to the Raja Empat, May 1581–November 1582. *Archipel* 18:175–194.

Braudel, F. 1949. *La Méditerranée et le Monde Méditerranéen a l'Epoque do Philippe II*. Paris: Librarie Armand Colin.

Brauw, C. P. de. 1854. Reis naar Banda, de Ceram-laut-eilanden, het zuidwestelijk gedeelte van Nieuw-Guinea, de Aroe- en de Zuid-wester-eilanden. *Verhandelingen en Berichten betrekkelijk het Zeewezen* 14:199–235.

Broersma, R. 1934. Koopvaardij in de Molukken. *Koloniaal Tijdschrift* 23:129–147, 320–350.

Broeze, F. J. A. 1979. The merchant fleet of Java (1820–1850). *Archipel* 18:251–262.

Bronson, B. 1979. The archaeology of Sumatra and the problem of Srivijaya. In *Early South east Asia: Essays in archaeology, history and historical geography*, ed. R. B. Smith and W. Watson, 395–405. Oxford: Oxford University Press.

Brookfield, H. C., with D. Hart. 1971. *Melanesia: A geographical interpretation of an island world*. London: Methuen.

Brouwer, A. 1998. From abundance to scarcity: Sago, crippled modernization and curtailed coping in an Ambonese village. In *Old World places, New World problems: Exploring resource management issues in eastern Indonesia*, ed. S. Pannell and F. von Benda-Beckmann, 336–387. Australian National University: Centre for Resource and Environmental Studies.

Brown, N. O. 1947. *Hermes the thief: The evolution of a myth*. Madison: University of Wisconsin Press.

Bruijnis, N. W. van. 1933. Ethnologische economie en de studie van het economisch leven der inheemsche bevolking in het oosten van de Indischen Archipel en Nederlandsch Nieuw-Guinee. Thesis, Rijksuniversiteit te Utrecht Arnhem: Paap.

Bruin Kops, G. F. de 1854. Iets over de zeevaart in den Indischen archipel.*Tijdschrift van Nijverheid in Nederlandsch-Indie* 121–69; 97–135.

Brumund, J. F. G. 1845. Aanteekeningen gehouden op eene reis on het oostelijke gedeelte van de Indischen Archipel. *Tijdschrift voor Nederlandsch-Indië* 7:39–89, 251–299.

Bruyn, J. V. 1962. New bronze finds at Kwadeware, Lake Sentani. *Nieuw Guinea Studiën* 6:61–62.

Buddingh, S. A. 1860. *Neêrlands-Oost-Indië: Reizen 1852–1857*. 3 vols. Rotterdam: M. Wijt en Zonen.

Cannon, L. R. G., and H. Silver. 1987. *Sea cucumbers of northern Australia*. South Brisbane, Queensland: Queensland Museum.

Capellen, G. A. G. Ph. van der. 1855. Het Journaal van den baron van der Capellen op zijn reis door de Molukkos. *Tijdschrift voor Nederlandsch-Indië* 17 (2): 281–315, 357–395.

Carlstein, T. 1982. *Time resources, society and ecology: On the capacity for human interaction in space and time*. Vol. 1. *Preindustrial societies*. London: George Allen and Unwin.

Chaudhuri, K. N. 1985. *Trade and civilisation in the Indian Ocean: An economic history from the rise of Islam to 1750*. Cambridge: Cambridge University Press.

Chijs, J. A. van der. 1885–1900. *Nederlandsch-Indisch Plakaatboek, 1602–1811*. 17 vols. Batavia.

Chlenov, M. A. 1980. Cultural vocabulary as an indicator of interethnic relations: Eastern Indonesian evidence. *Bijdragen tot de Taal-, Land- en Volkenkunde* 136: 426–439.

Claessen, H. J. M., and P. Skalnik, eds. 1978. *The early state*. The Hague: Mouton.

Claessen, H. J. M., and P. van der Velde. 1987. Introduction. In *Early state dynamics*, ed. H. J. M. Claessen and P. van der Velde, 1–23. Leiden: E. J. Brill.

———. 1991. Introduction. In *Early state economics,* ed. H. J. M. Claessen and P. van der Velde, 1–29. Political and Legal Anthropology 8. New Brunswick: Transaction.

Clarence-Smith, W. G. 1998. The economic role of the Arab community in Maluku, 1816 to 1940. *Indonesia and the Malay World* 26 (74): 32–49.

Coedes, G. 1944. The empire of the south seas. *Journal of the Thailand Research Society* 35 (1): 1–15.

Cohen, A. 1971. Cultural strategies in the organization of trading diasporas. In *The development of indigenous trade and markets in West Africa*, ed. Claude Meillassoux, 266–281. International African Institute. London: Oxford University Press.

Collins, G. E. P. 1937. *Makassar sailing.* London: Jonathan Cape.

———. 1940. *East monsoon.* London: Jonathan Cape.

Collins, J. T. 1980. The historical relationship of the languages of central Maluku, Indonesia. Ph.D. diss., University of Chicago.

———. 1983. Syntactic change in Ambonese Malay: The possessive construction. *NUSA* 17. Badan Penyelenngara Seri NUSA.

———. 1984. Linguistic research in Maluku: A report on recent fieldwork. *Oceanic Linguistics* 21 (1–2):73–146.

———. 1986. Eastern Seram: A subgrouping argument. In *FOCAL II: Papers from the Fourth International Conference on Austronesan Linguistics,* ed. P. Geraghty, L. Carrington, and S. A. Wurm, 123–146. Special Issue, *Pacific Linguistics.*

Collins, J. T., and T. Kaartinen. 1998. Preliminary notes on Bandanese: Language maintenance and change in Kei. *Bijdragen tot de Taal-, Land- en Volkenkunde* 154 (4): 521–559.

Conrad, J. 1896. *An outcast of the islands.* London: Fisher Unwin.

Cooley, F. 1962. Ambonese kin groups. *Ethnology* 1:102–112.

Coolhaas, C. P., ed. 1960–1979. *Generale missiven van Gouverneurs-Generaal en Raden aan Heren XVII der Vereenigde Oost-Indische Compagnie (1610–1725).* 7 vols. Rijks-geschiedkundige Publicatiën, Grote Serie, nos. 104, 112, 125, 134, 150, 159, 164. The Hague: Nijhoff.

Cortesão, A., ed. 1944. *The Suma Oriental of Tomé Pires . . . and The Book of Francisco Rodrigues.* Vol. 1. London: Hakluyt Society.

Crab, P. van der. 1862. *De Moluksche eilanden: Reis van Z. E. Den Gouverneur Generaal C. P. Pahud.* Batavia: Lange.

———. 1864. Reis naar de zuidwestkust van Nieuw-Guinea, de Goram- en Ceram-Laut eilanden en Oostelijk Ceram. *Tijdschrift voor Indische Taal-, Land- en Volkenkunde* 13:531–556.

Curtin, P. D. 1975. *Economic change in precolonial Africa: Senegambia in the era of the slave trade.* 2 vols. Madison: University of Wisconsin Press.

———. 1984. *Cross-cultural trade in world history.* Cambridge: Cambridge University Press.

Daghregister. 1624–1682. *Daghregister gehouden in't casteel Batavia,* in 31 parts (1887–1931), ed. J. A. van der Chijs, H. T. Colenbrander, W. Fruin-Mees, F. de Haan, J. E. Heeres, and J. de Hullu. The Hague.

Dalton, G., ed. 1968. *Primitive, archaic and modern economies: Essays of Karl Polanyi.* Boston: Beacon Press.

Davis, J. 1992. *Exchange.* Buckingham: Open University Press.

Dermoût, M. 1955. *De Tien-duizend Dingen.* Amsterdam: N. V. Em. Querido's Uitgeversmij.

Dewey, A. G. 1962a. *Peasant marketing in Java.* New York: The Free Press of Glencoe.

———. 1962b. Trade and social control in Java. *Journal of the Royal Anthropological Institute* 92:177–190.

Dick, H. W. 1975. Prahu shipping in eastern Indonesia. Parts 1 and 2. *Bulletin of Indonesian Economic Studies* 11 (2): 69–107; (3): 81–103.

Dissel, J. S. A. van. 1904. Reis van Atiati-Onin over Patipi en Degen naar Kajoni (1902). *Tijdschrift van het Nederlandsch Aardrijkskundig Genootschap* (Series 2) 21:617–650.

———. 1907. Reis van Goras langs de Bedidi naar Ginaroe. *Tijdschrift van het Neder-landsch Aardrijkskundig Genootschap* (Series 2) 24:992–1030.

Doren, J. B. J. van. 1857. *Herinneringen en schetsen van Nederlands Oost-Indië: Vervolg op de fragmenten uit reizen in die gewesten.* Vol. 1. Amsterdam: J. D. Sybrandi.

Eades, J. S. 1993. *Strangers and traders: Yoruba migrants, markets and the state in northern Ghana.* International African Library, 11. Edinburgh: Edinburgh University Press, for the International African Institute.

Earl, G. W. 1853. *The native races of the Indian archipelago: Papuans.* London: Bailliere.

Echols, J. M., and H. Shadily. 1989. *An Indonesian-English dictionary.* 3d ed., rev. and ed. J. U. Wolff and J. T. Collins, with H. Shadily. Ithaca, N.Y.: Cornell University Press.

Eerde, J. C. van. 1911. De Madjapahitsche onderhoorigheden Goeroen en Seran. *Tijdschrift van het Koninklijk Nederlansch Aardrijkskundig Genootschap te Amsterdam* 28:219–233.

Ekholm, K., and J. Friedman. 1993. "Capital," imperialism and exploitation in ancient world systems. In *The world system: Five hundred years or five thousand?* ed. A. G. Frank and B. K. Gills, 59–80. London: Routledge.

Ellen, R. F. 1978. *Nuaulu settlement and Ecology: An approach to the environmental relations of an eastern Indonesian community.* Verhandelingen van het Koninklijk Instituut voor Taal-, Land- en Volkenkunde 83. The Hague: Martinus Nijhoff.

———. 1979. Sago subsistence and the trade in spices: A provisional model of ecological succession and imbalance in Moluccan history. In *Social and ecological systems,* ed. P. C. Burnham and R. F. Ellen, 43–74. Association of Social Anthropologists Monographs in Social Anthropology 18. London: Academic Press.

———. 1983. Social theory, ethnography and the understanding of practical Islam in South-East Asia. In *Islam in South-East Asia,* ed. M. B. Hooker, 50–91. Leiden: E. J. Brill.

———. 1984. Trade, environment and the reproduction of local systems in the Moluccas. In *The ecosystem concept in anthropology,* ed. E. F. Moran, 163–204. AAAS Selected Symposium 92. Boulder, Colo.: American Association for the Advancement of Science.

———. 1986a. Change and the social organisation of regional trading networks in the Moluccas: An ethnographic study. University of Kent at Canterbury. Final Report, presented to Lembaga Ilmu Pengetahuan Indonesia.

———. 1986b. Conundrums about panjandrums: On the use of titles in the relations of political subordination in the Moluccas and along the Papuan coast. *Indonesia* 41:47–62.

———. 1987. Environmental perturbation, inter-island trade and the re-location of production along the Banda arc; or, why central places remain central. In *Human ecology of health and survival in Asia and the South Pacific,* ed. Tsuguyoshi Suzuki and Ryutaro Ohtsuka, 35–61. Tokyo: University of Tokyo Press.

———. 1988. Fetishism (The Curl Lecture). *Man (n.s.)* 23 (2): 213–235.

———. 1990. Nuaulu sacred shields: The reproduction of things or the reproduction of images? *Etnofoor* 3 (1): 5–25.

———. 1992. A vertical wedge press from the Banda Islands. *Technology and Culture* 33 (1): 122–131.

———. 1993. Faded images of old Tidore in contemporary southeast Seram: A view from the periphery. *Cakalele, Maluku Research Journal* 4:23–37.

———. 1996. Arab traders and land settlers in the Geser-Gorom Archipelago. *Indonesia Circle* 70:238–252.

———. 1997. On the contemporary uses of colonial history and the legitimation of political status in archipelagic Southeast Seram. *Journal of Southeast Asian Studies* 28 (1): 78–102.

Ellen, R. F., and I. C. Glover. 1979. A further note on flaked stone material from Seram, eastern Indonesia. *Asian Perspectives* 20 (2): 236–240.

Ellen, R. F., and N. J. Goward. 1981. Change and the social organisation of regional trading networks in the Moluccas: A preliminary report on a pilot ethnographic study. Centre for Southeast Asian Studies, University of Kent at Canterbury.

Elmberg, J. E. 1968. *Balance and circulation: Aspects of tradition and change among the Mejprat of Irian Barat*. Ethnographical Museum Monograph Series No. 12. Stockholm.

Emmerson, D. K. 1980. The case for a maritime perspective on Southeast Asia. *Journal of Southeast Asian Studies* 11(1): 139–145.

Errington, S. 1990. Recasting sex, gender, and power: A theoretical and regional overview. In *Power and difference: Gender in island Southeast Asia*, ed. J. M. Atkinson and S. Errington, 1–58. Stanford, Calif.: Stanford University Press.

Evers, H.-D. 1988. Traditional trading networks of Southeast Asia. *Archipel* 35:89–100.

Evers, H.-D., and H. Schrader, eds. 1994. *The moral economy of trade: Ethnicity and developing markets*. London: Routledge.

Fallers, L. A., ed. 1967. *Immigrants and associations*. The Hague: Mouton.

Flach, M., and M. Tjeenk Willink. 1999. *Myristica fragrans* Houtt. In *Plant resources of South-east Asia*. Vol. 13. *Spices*, ed. C. C. de Guzman and J. S. Siemonsma, 143–148. Leiden: Backhuys.

Flannery, K. 1972. The cultural evolution of civilizations. *Annual Review of Ecology and Systematics* 3:399–426.

Forbes, A. 1887. *Insulinde: Experiences of a naturalist's wife in the Eastern Archipelago*. London: Blackwood.

Forbes, H. O. 1885. *A Naturalist's wanderings in the Eastern Archipelago, a narrative of travel and exploration from 1878 to 1883*. London: Sampson, Low.

Forrest, T. 1969 (1779). *A voyage to New Guinea and the Moluccas, 1774–1776*, ed., with an introduction by D. K. Bassett. Kuala Lumpur: Oxford University Press.

Fraassen, C. F. van. 1976. Drie plaatsnamen uit Oost-Indonesië in de Nagara-Kertagama: Galiyao, Muar en Wwanin en de vroege handelsgeschiedenis van Ambonse eilanden. *Bijdragen tot de Taal-, Land- en Volkenkunde* 132 (2–3): 293–305.

———. 1987. Ternate, de Molukken en de Indonesische Archipel: Van Soa-organisatie en vierdeling: Een studie van traditionele samenleving en cultuur in Indonesia. Ph.D. diss., Leiden University. 2 vols.

Friedberg, C. 1977. The development of traditional agricultural practices in western Timor: From ritual control of consumer goods to the political control of prestige goods. In *The evolution of social systems*, ed. J. Friedman and M. J. Rowlands. London: Duckworth.

Galis, K. W. 1953. Geschiedenis. In *Nieuw-Guinea 1*, ed. W. C. Klein, 1–65. The Hague.

Galis, K. W., and F. C. Kamma. 1958. Het fort te Jêmbekaki. *Nieuw-Guinea Studiën*
2:206–223.

Geertz, C. 1963. *Peddlers and princes: Social change and development in two Indonesian
towns*. Chicago: University of Chicago Press.

Giddens, A. 1981. *A contemporary critique of historical materialism*. London:
Macmillan.

———. 1986. *The constitution of society: Outline of the theory of structuration*. London:
Polity.

Gijsels, A. 1855 (1634). De beschrijvinge van de Molucse eijlanden. *Bidragen tot de
Taal-, Land- en Volkenkunde* 3:85–105.

Gills, B. K., and A. G. Frank. 1993. The 5,000-year world system: An interdiscipli-
nary introduction. In *The world system: Five hundred years or five thousand?*, ed.
A. G. Frank and B. K. Gills, 3–58. London: Routledge.

Gladwin, T. 1970. *East is a big bird: Navigation and logic on Pulawat Atoll*. Cambridge,
Mass.: Harvard University Press.

Glamann, K. 1958. *Dutch-Asiatic trade, 1620-1740*. Copenhagen: Danish Science
Press.

Glover, I. C. 1979. The late prehistoric period in Indonesia. In *Early South east Asia:
Essays in archaeology, history and historical geography*, ed. R. B. Smith and W.
Watson, 167–184. Oxford: Oxford University Press.

———. 1989. *Early trade between India and Southeast Asia: A link in the development of a
world trading system*. Occasional Paper 16. United Kindgom: University of Hull,
Centre for South-East Asian Studies.

Goodman, T. 1998. The sosolot exchange network of eastern Indonesia during the
seventeenth and eighteenth centuries. In *Perspectives on the Bird's Head of Irian
Jaya, Indonesia*, ed. J. Miedema, C. Odé, and Rien A. C. Dam, 421–454. Proceedings of a conference in Leiden, 13–17 October 1997. Amsterdam: Rodopi B.V.

Graaff, H. J. van de, and G. J. Meijlan. 1856. De Moluksche eilanden. *Tijdschrift voor
Nederlandsch-Indië* 18 (1): 73–137, 167–196, 231–265, 315–360.

Gregory, C. A. 1982. *Gifts and commodities*. London: Academic Press.

———. 1997. *Savage money: The anthropology and politics of commodity exchange*.
Amsterdam: Harwood.

Grimes, B. D. 1993. The pursuit of prosperity and blessing: Social life and symbolic
action on Buru Island, eastern Indonesia. Ph.D. thesis, Australian National
University, Canberra.

Groenevelt, W. P. 1960 (1880). Historical notes on Indonesia and Malaya compiled
from Chinese sources. *Djakarta* 10. Reprinted from *Verhandelingen van het
Bataviaasch Genootschap van Kunsten en Wetenschappen* 39.

Grzimek, B. 1991. Social change on Seram: A study of ideologies of development in
eastern Indonesia. Ph.D. thesis, London School of Economics and Political
Science, University of London, London.

Gudeman, S. 1986. *Economics as culture: Models and metaphors of livelihood*. London:
Routledge and Kegan Paul.

Haar, B. ter. 1948. *Adat law in Indonesia*. New York: Institute of Pacific Relations.

Haddon, A. C. 1920. The outriggers of Indonesian canoes. *Journal of the Royal
Anthropological Institute*. 50:69–134.

Haga, A. 1884. *Nederlandsch-Nieuw-Guinea en de Papoesche Eilanden: Historische
Bijdrage, 1500-1883*. 2 vols. Batavia: Bruining.

———. 1911. De handel in de zoogenaamde "Groote Oost." *Tijdschrift voor Ekonomische Geographie* 2:342.

Hage, P. 1977. Centrality in the kula ring. *Journal of the Polynesian Society* 86:27–36.

Hage, P., and F. Harary. 1991. *Exchange in Oceania: A graph theoretic analysis.* Oxford Studies in Social and Cultural Anthropology. Oxford: Clarendon Press.

Hagen, J. 1999. The good behind the gift: Morality and exchange among the Maneo of eastern Indonesia. *Journal of the Royal Anthropological Institute* 5 (30): 361–375.

Haggett, P., and R. J. Chorley. 1969. *Network analysis in geography.* London: Edward Arnold.

Hall, K. R. 1981. Trade and statecraft in the western archipelago at the dawn of the European age. Paper presented at the conference on "Southeast Asian responses to European intrusions." British Institute in Southeast Asia, Singapore.

———. 1985. *Maritime trade and state development.* Honolulu: University of Hawai'i Press.

Hanna, W. 1978. *Indonesian Banda: Colonialism and its aftermath in the nutmeg islands.* Philadelphia: Institute for the Study of Human Issues.

Harding, T. G. 1967. *Voyagers of the Vitiaz Strait: A study of a New Guinea trade system.* Seattle: University of Washington Press.

Harris, D. R. 1979. Foragers and farmers in the western Torres Strait Islands: An historical analysis of economic, demographic, and spatial differentiation. In *Social and ecological systems*, ed. P. C. Burnham and R. F. Ellen, 75–109. Association of Social Anthropologists Monographs in Social Anthropology, 18. London: Academic Press.

Healey, C. J. 1998. Political economy in the Kepala Burung region of old western New Guinea. In *Perspectives on the Bird's Head of Irian Jaya, Indonesia*, ed. J. Miedema, C. Odé, and Rien A. C. Dam, 337–350. Proceedings of a conference in Leiden, 13–17 October 1997. Amsterdam: Rodopi B.V.

Heekeren, H. R. van. 1958. *The bronze-iron age of Indonesia.* Verhandelingen van het Koninklijk Instituut voor Land-, Taal- en Volkenkunde 22. The Hague: Martinus Nijhoff.

Heeres, J. E., ed. 1908. Een Engelsche Lezing omtrent de Verovering van Banda en Ambon in 1796 en omtrent den Toestand dier eilandengroepen op het eind der achttiende eeuwe. [Journal of an expedition to the Molucca Islands under the command of Admiral Rainer, by Caulfield Lennon.] *Bijdragen tot de Taal-, Land- en Volkenkunde* 60:249–368.

Heeres, J. E., and F. W. Stapel, eds. 1907, 1931, 1934, 1935, 1938, 1955. *Corpus Diplomaticum Neerlando-Indicum: Verzameling van politieke contracten en verdere verdragen door de Nederlanders in het Oosten gesloten.* 6 vols. The Hague. (Vols. 1–5 published in *Bijdragen tot de Taal-, Land- en Volkenkunde* 57, 87, 91, 93, and 96.)

Hicks, D. 1990. *Kinship and religion in eastern Indonesia.* Gothenburg Studies in Social Anthropology 12. Gothenburg: Acta Universitatis Gothoburgensis.

Hille, J. W. van. 1905, 1906, 1907. Reizen in West-Nieuw-Guinea. *Tijdschrift van het Koninklijk Nederlandsch Aardrijkskundig Genootschap* 22:233–330; 23:451–541; 24:547–635.

Hoevell, G. W. W. C. van. 1875. Ambon en meer bepaaldelijk de Oeliasers, geographisch, ethnographisch, politisch en historisch geschetst. Dordrecht: Blussé en Van Braam.

Hollander, J. J. de. 1895. *Handleiding bij de beoefening der land- en volkenkunde van Nederlandsch Oost-Indië.* Vol. 2. Breda: Broese.

Holleman, F. D., ed. 1925. Jurisprudentie van de inheemsche rechtspraak op Boeroe, Ceram, Aroe en Tenimbar (1883–1923). *Adatrechtbundels* 24:131–148.

Horridge, A. H. 1978. *The design of plank boats of the Moluccas*. Maritime Monographs and Reports 38. London: National Maritime Museum.

———. 1979. *The lambo or prahu bot: A Western ship in an Eastern setting*. National Maritime Museum Monograph 39. London: National Maritime Museum.

———. 1986. A summary of Indonesian canoe and prahu ceremonies. *Indonesia Circle* 39:3–17.

———. 1995. The Austronesian conquest of the sea—upwind. In *The Austronesians: historical and comparative perspectives*, ed. P. Bellwood, J. J. Fox, and D. Tryon, 134–151. Canberra: Australian National University.

Humphrey, C., and S. Hugh-Jones. 1992. Introduction: Barter, exchange and value. In *Barter, exchange and value: An anthropological approach*, ed. C. Humphrey and S. Hugh-Jones, 1–20. Cambridge: Cambridge University Press.

Irwin, G. J. 1974. The emergence of central places in coastal Papuan prehistory: A theoretical approach. *Mankind* 9 (4): 268–272.

———. 1978a. The development of Mailu as a specialised trading and manufacturing centre in Papuan prehistory: The causes and the implications. *Mankind* 11 (3): 406–415.

———. 1978b. Pots and entrepots: A study of settlement, trade and development of economic specialisation in Papuan prehistory. *World Archaeology* 9 (3): 299–319.

———. 1983. Chieftainship, kula and trade in Massim prehistory. In *The Kula: New perspectives on Massim exchange,* ed. J. W. Leach and E. Leach, 29–72. Cambridge: Cambridge University Press.

Jansen, H. J. 1928. Gegevens over Geser, Boela en de Gorong- of Goram-eilanden. *Adatrechtbundels* 36:490–494.

———. 1977 (1933). Indigenous classification systems in the Ambonese Moluccas. In *Structural anthropology in the Netherlands*, ed. P. E. de Josselin de Jong, 101–115. The Hague: Martinus Nijhoff.

Jonge, H. de. 1993. Discord and solidarity among Arabs in the Netherlands East Indies, 1900–1942. *Indonesia* 55:73–90.

Kamma, F. C. 1948. De verhouding tussen Tidore en de Papoese eilanden in legende en historie. *Indonesië* 2:177–188.

———. 1972. *Koreri: Messianic movements in the Biak-Numfor culture area*. Koninklijk Instituut voor Taal-, Land- en Volkenkunde, Translation Series 15. The Hague: Martinus Nijhoff.

Kamma, F. C., and S. Kooijman. 1973. *Romawa forja: Child of the fire*. Mededelingen van het Rijksmuseum voor Volkenkunde, Leiden, No. 18. Leiden: E. J. Brill.

Kelly, R. C. 1968. Demographic pressure and descent-group structure in the New Guinea highlands. *Oceania* 39:36–63.

Kemp, P. H. van der. 1911. Het Herstel van het Nederlandsch Gezag in de Molukken in 1817. *Bijdragen tot de Taal-, Land- en Volkenkunde* 65:337–736.

Kennedy, J. 1981. Ahus of another colour? A comparison of two potting centres in the Admiralty Islands. *Australian Archaeology* 12:45–60.

Kiefer, T. M. 1971. The sultanate of Sulu: Problems in the analysis of a segmentary state. *Borneo Research Bulletin* 3(2): 46–51.

———. 1972. The Tausug polity and the sultanate of Sulu: A segmentary state in the southern Philippines. *Sulu Studies* 1:19–64.

Klerk, Reiner de. 1894 (1756). *Belangrijk verslag over de staat van Banda en omliggende eilanden aan zijne excellentie de Gouverneur-Generaal . . . met eene korte beschrijving van Banda . . . door C. A. M. van Vliet.* The Hague: W. P. van Stockum.

Knaap, G. J. 1985. Kruidnagelen en Christenen: De Vereenigde Oost-Indische Compagnie en de bevolking van Ambon 1656–1696. Ph.D. Diss., University of Utrecht, Utrecht.

———. 1989. *Transport 1819–1940.* Vol. 9 in Changing economy in Indonesia: A selection of statistical source material from the early 19th century to 1940. Amsterdam: Royal Tropical Institute.

Kniphorst, J. H. P. E. 1883. Een korte terugblik op de Molukken en Noordwestelijk Nieuw-Guinea. *De Indische Gids* 5 (2): 293–345, 465–526.

Kolff, D. H. 1927 (1840). *Voyages of the Dutch brig of war Dourga through the southern and little known parts of the Moluccan archipelago and along the previously unknown southern coast of New Guinea, 1825–1826,* trans. G. W. Earl. London: Madden.

Koningsberger, J. C. 1904. *Tripang en tripangvisscherij in Nederlandsch-Indië.* Mededeelingen uit 's Lands Plantentuin 71. Batavia: G. Kolff and Co.

Kostermans, A. J. G. H. 1950. Notes on New Guinea plants I–III. *Bulletin of the Botanic Gardens, Buitenzorg,* Series III 18:435–448.

———. 1955. *New and critical Malaysian plants III.* Djawatan Kehutanan Indonesia Bagain Planologi Kehutanan. Surabaya: H. van Ingen.

Krause-Katola, H.-J. 1988. Die Gewürznelken produktion auf den Molukken: Soziale Auswirkungen langfristiger Weltmarktintegration. Ph.D. diss., University of Bielefeld.

Lape, P. V. 2000. Political dynamics and religious change in the late pre-colonial Banda Islands, eastern Indonesia. *World Archaeology* 32 (1): 138–155.

Lapian, A. 1981. The contest for the high seas (with special reference to the Celebes Sea during the sixteenth and seventeenth centuries). Paper presented at the conference on "Southeast Asian responses to European intrusions." British Institute in Southeast Asia, Singapore.

Lauer, P. K. 1970. Amphlett Islands pottery trade and the Kula. *Mankind* 7 (3): 165–176.

Leach, E. 1983. The kula: An alternative view. In *The Kula: New perspectives on Massim exchange,* ed. J. W. Leach and E. Leach, 529–538. Cambridge: Cambridge University Press.

Leach, J. W., and E. Leach, eds. 1983. *The Kula: New perspectives on Massim exchange.* Cambridge: Cambridge University Press.

Leeden, A. C. van der. 1983. Gale Maya: Phonology of a tone language of the Raja Ampat Islands. In *Halmahera dan Raja Ampat sebagai kesatuan majemuk: Studi-studi terhadap suatu daerah transisi,* ed. E. K. M. Masinambow, 77–146. Bulletin LEKNAS 2 (2), Special Publication. Jakarta: Lembaga Ekonomi dan Kemasyarakatan Nasional Lembaga Ilmu Pengetahuan Indonesia.

Leeds, A. 1961. The port of trade as an ecological and evolutionary type. *Proceedings of the 1961 Annual Meeting of the American Ethnological Society.* Seattle: American Ethnological Society.

Leirissa, R. Z. 1981. Notes on central Maluku in the nineteenth century. *Prisma: The Indonesian Indicator* (22 September): 53–66

———. 1994. Changing maritime trade patterns in the Seram Sea. In *State and state-craft in the Indonesian archipelago,* G. J. Schutte, 99–114. Koninklijk Instituut voor Taal-, Land- en Volkenkunde Working Papers 13. Leiden: KITLV Press.

————. 2000. The Bugis-Makassarese in the port-towns Ambon and Ternate through the nineteenth century. *Bijdragen tot de Taal-, Land- en Volkenkunde* 156 (3): 619–255.

Leirissa, R. Z., Z. J. Manusama, A. B. Lapian, and P. R. Abdurachman, eds. 1982. *Maluku Tengah di Masa Lampau: Gambaran Sekilas Lewat Arsip Abad Sembilan Belas*. Penerbitan Sumber Sumber Sejarah No. 13. Jakarta: Arsip Nasional Republik Indonesia.

Leur, J. C. van. 1955. *Indonesian trade and society*. The Hague: W. van Hoeve.

Linden, H. O. van der. 1873. *Banda en zijne bewoners*. Dordrecht: Blussé en van Braam.

Linschoten, J. H. van. 1955 (1596). *Itinerario, voyage ofte shipvaert van Jan Huygen van Linschoten naer Oost ofte Portuguels Indien, 1579–1592*, ed. Prof. Dr. H. Kern. 2d ed., rev. Dr. H. Terpstra. The Hague: Works of the Linschoten-Vereniging, nos. 57, 58, 60.

Lombard, D. 1979. Regard nouveau sur les "Pirates Malais": 1ère moitié du XIXe siècle. *Archipel* 18:231–50.

Loski, R. A., and G. M. Loski. 1989. The languages indigenous to eastern Seram and adjacent islands. In *Workpapers in Indonesian languages and cultures*, ed. W. D. Laidig, 103–136. Ambon, Indonesia: Pattimura University and the Summer Institute of Linguistics.

Loth, V. C. 1998. Fragrant gold and food provision: Resource management and agriculture in seventeenth century Banda. In *Old World places, New World problems: Exploring resource management issues in eastern Indonesia*, ed. S. Pannell and F. von Benda-Beckmann, 66–93. Canberra: Australian National University, Centre for Resource and Environmental Studies.

Lovejoy, P. 1980. *Caravans of kola: The Hausa kola trade, 1700–1900*. Zaria: Ahmadu Bello University Press.

Lucardie, G. R. E. 1980. The Makianese: Preliminary remarks on the anthropological study of a migration-oriented people in the Moluccas. In *Halmahera dan Raja Ampat: Strategi penelitian*, ed. E.K.M. Masinambow, 347–373. Jakarta: Lembaga Ekonomi dan Kemasyarakatan Nasional.

Macintyre, M. 1983. *The kula: A bibliography*. Cambridge: Cambridge University Press.

MacKnight, C. C. 1976. *The voyage to Marege: Macassan trepangers in northern Australia*. Melbourne: Melbourne University Press.

————. 1980. The study of praus in the Indonesian archipelago. *The Great Circle* 2(2): 117–128.

MacKnight, C. C., and Mukhlis. 1979. A Bugis manuscript about praus. *Archipel* 18:271–282.

Mai, U., and H. Buchholt. 1987. *Peasant pedlars and professional traders: Subsistence trade in rural markets of Minahasa, Indonesia*. Singapore: Institute of Southeast Asian Studies.

Malinowski, B. 1922. *Argonauts of the western Pacific*. London: Routledge and Kegan Paul.

Manguin, P. Y. 1976. L'artillerie légère nou-santarienne. *Arts Asiatiques* 32:233–268.

Mansoben, J. R. 1995. *Sistem politik tradisional di Irian Jaya*. Jakarta and Leiden: Lembaga Ilmu Pengetahuanm Indonesia and Leiden University.

Manusama, Z. J. 1977. Hikayat Tanah Hitu: Historie en sociale structuur van de Ambonse eilanden in het algemeen en Uli Hitu in het bijzonder tot het midden der zeventiende eeuw. Ph.D. diss., University of Leiden.

Meilink-Roelofsz, M. A. P. 1962. *Asian trade and European influence in the Indonesian archipelago between 1500 and about 1630.* The Hague: Martinus Nijhoff.

Merton, H. 1910. *Forschungsreise in den Südöstlichen Molukken (Aru und Kei- Inseln).* Frankfurt am Main: Im Selbstverlage der Senckenbergischen Naturforschenden Gesellschaft.

Miedema, J. 1984. *De Kebar, 1855–1980: Social structuur en religie in de Vogelkop van West-Nieuw-Guinea.* Dordrecht: ICG Printing B.V.

———. 1986. *Pre-capitalism and cosmology: Description and analysis of the Meybrat fishery and kain timur-complex.* Verhandelingen van het Koninklijk Instituut voor Taal-, Land- en Volkenkunde 120. Dordrecht-Holland-Riverton: Foris

Miklouho-Maclay, N. 1982. *Travels in New Guinea: Diaries, letters, documents.* Moscow: Progress Publishers.

Miller, J. I. 1969 *The spice trade of the Roman Empire, 29 B.C. to A.D. 641.* Oxford: Clarendon Press.

Miller, W. G. 1980. An account of trade patterns in the Banda Sea in 1797, from an unpublished manuscript in the India Office library. *Indonesia Circle* 23, 41–57

Mills, J. V. G., ed. 1970. Ying-yai sheng-lan: "The overall survey of the Ocean's shores," 1433 by Ma Huan, translated from the Chinese text edited by Feng Ch'eng-Chün. Cambridge: Cambridge University Press.

Monk, K. A., Y. de Fretes, and G. Reksodiharjo-Lilley. 1997. *The ecology of Nusa Tenggara and Maluku.* The Ecology of Indonesia 5 Hong Kong: Periplus.

Moreland, W. H. 1920. The Shahbandar in the eastern seas. *Journal of the Royal Asiatic Society* 28:517–33.

Müller, S. 1857. *Reizen en onderzoekingen in den Indischen Archipel, gedaan op last der Nederlandische Indische regering, tusschen de jaren 1828 en 1836.* Amsterdam: Frederik Muller.

Needham, R. 1983. *Sumba and the slave trade.* Centre of Southeast Asian Studies, Working Paper No. 31. Melbourne: Monash University.

Niggermeyer, H. 1952. Ceramische Baumwoll- und Fasergewebe. *Ciba-Rundschau* 106:3881–3893.

Northrup, D. 1978. *Trade without rulers: Pre-colonial economic development in southeastern Nigeria.* Oxford: Clarendon Press.

Ossewijer, M. 2000. "We wander in our ancestors' yard": Sea cucumber gathering in Aru, eastern Indonesia. In *Indigenous environmental knowledge and its transformations: Critical anthropological approaches,* ed. R. Ellen, P. Parkes, and A. Bicker, 55–78. Studies in Environmental Anthropology, 5. Amsterdam: Harwood.

Platenkamp, J. D. M. 1993. Tobelo, Moro, Ternate: The cosmological valorization of historical events. *Cakalele, Maluku Research Journal* 4:61–89.

Polanyi, K. 1975. Traders and trade. In *Ancient civilisation and trade,* ed. J. A. Sabloff and C. C. Lamberg-Karlovsky, 133–154. Albuquerque: University of New Mexico Press.

Polanyi, K., C. M. Arensberg, and H. W. Pearson. 1957. *Trade and markets in the early empires.* Glencoe: The Free Press.

Polo, Marco. 1958. *The travels of Marco Polo.* Trans., with an introduction by Ronald Latham. Harmondsworth: Penguin.

Pouwer, J. 1955. *Enkele aspecten van de Mimika-cultuur.* The Hague: Staatsdrukkerij.

———. 1957. Het vraagstuk van de kain timoer in het Mejprat-gebied (Ajamaroemeren). *Nieuw-Guinea Studiën* 1.

Purnadi Purbatjaraka. 1961. Shahbandars in the archipelago. *Journal of Southeast Asian History* 2 (2): 1–9.

Quarles van Ufford, H. 1856. *Aanteekeningen betreffende eene reis door de Molukken van zijne excellentie den Gouverneur-Generaal Mr. A. J. Duymaer van Twist, in de maanden september en oktober 1855*. The Hague: Nijhoff.

Quiason, S. D. 1981. The Tiangui: A preliminary view of an indigenous rural marketing system in Spanish-Philippines. Paper presented at the conference on "Southeast Asian responses to European intrusions." British Institute in Southeast Asia, Singapore.

Reid, A. 1983. *Slavery, bondage and dependency in Southeast Asia*. New York: University of Queensland Press.

———. 1993. *Southeast Asia in the age of commerce, 1450–1680*. Vol. 2. New Haven, Conn: Yale University Press.

Reid, A., and D. Marr, eds. 1979. *Perceptions of the past in Southeast Asia*. Asian Studies Association of Australia Southeast Asia Publications Series, 4. Singapore: Heineman Educational Books (Asia).

Renfrew, C. 1975. Trade as action at a distance. In *Ancient civilisation and trade*, ed. J. A. Sabloff and C. C. Lamberg-Karlovsky, 3–59. Albuquerque: University of New Mexico Press.

Resink, G. J. 1968. *Indonesia's history between the myths: Essays in legal history and historical theory*. Selected Studies on Indonesia, 7. The Hague: W. van Hoeve.

Ribbe, C. 1892. Ein Aufenhalt auf Gross-Seram. *Jahresbericht des Vereins für Erdkunde zu Dresden* 22:129–217.

Riedel, J. G. F. 1886. *De sluik- en kroesharige rassen tusschen Selebes en Papua*. The Hague: Martinus Nijhoff.

Robidé van der Aa, P. J. B. C. 1879. *Reizen naar Nieuw-Guinea ondernomen op last der regeering van Nederlansch-Indië in de jaren 1871, 1872, 1875–1876 door de heeren P. van der Crab en J. E. Teysmann, J. G. Coornengel, A. J. Langeveldt van Hemert en P. Swaan*. Koninklijk Instituut voor Taal-, Land- en Volkenkunde. The Hague: Martinus Nijhoff.

Rockhill, W. W. 1913–1915. Notes on the relations and trade of China with the Eastern archipelago and the coast of the Indian Ocean during the fourteenth century. *T'oung Pao* 14:473–476; 15:419–447; 16:61–159, 234–271, 374–392, 435–467, 604–626.

Rosenberg, C. H. B. von. 1867. Beschrijving van eenige gedeelten van Ceram. *Tijdschrift voor Indische Taal-, Land- en Volkenkunde* 16:97–182.

———. 1875. *Reistochten naar de Geelvinkbaai op Nieuw-Guinea in de jaren 1869 en 1870*. Koninklijk Instituut voor Taal-, Land- en Volkenkunde. The Hague: Martinus Nijhoff.

Rouffaer, G. P. 1905. Tochten (oudste ontdekkings-) tot 1497. In *Encyclopaedie van Nederlandsch Indië*, 363–95. Vol. 4.

———. 1908. De Javaansche naam "Seran" van Z. W. Nieuw Guinea vóór 1545; en een rapport van Rumphius over die kust van 1684. *Tijdschrift van het Nederlandsch Aardrijkskundig Genootschap* (Series 2) 25:308–347.

———. 1915. Oudjavaansche eilandnamen in de Grote Oost: Sergili, Seran, Boeroe (Hoetan Kadali). *Tijdschrift van het Nederlandsch Aardrijkskundig Genootschap* (Series 2) 32:642–649.

Rumphius, G. E. 1741–1755. *Herbarium Amboinense—Het Amboinsche Kruid-boek*. Amsterdam: First impression.

———. 1856. Antwoord en rapport op eenige pointen uit name van zeker heer in t' Vaderland, voorgesteld door den edelen Heer Anthony Hurt, Directeur-Generaal over Nederlandsch-Indië en Beantwoord door Georgius Everardus

Rumphius, oud-koopman en Raadpersoon in Amboina. *Tijdschrift Staathuishoudk Statistiek* 13:125–141.

———. 1910 (1687). De Ambonsche Historie. *Bijdragen tot de Taal-, Land- en Volkenkunde* 64. Two parts in one volume.

Sahlins, M. 1972. *Stone age economics.* London: Aldine.

———. 1981. The stranger-king; or, Dumézil among the Fijians. *Journal of Pacific History* 16:107–132.

———. 1988 Cosmologies of capitalism: the trans-Pacific sector of "The world system." *Proceedings of the British Academy* 74:1–51.

Sande, G. A. J. van der. 1907. Ethnography and anthropology of New Guinea. *Nova Guinea* 3. Leiden: E. J. Brill.

Sather, C. 1985. Boat crew and fishing fleets: The social organization of maritime labour among the Bajau Laut of southeastern Sabah. *Contributions to Southeast Asian Ethnography* 4:165–214.

———. 1997. *The Bajau Laut: Adaptation, history, and fate in a maritme fishing society of south-eastern Sabah.* Kuala Lumpur: Oxford University Press.

Schrieke, B. 1955. *Indonesian sociological studies.* The Hague: Van Hoeve.

Schwartz, T. 1963. Systems of areal integration: Some considerations based on the Admiralty Islands of northern Melanesia. *Anthropological Forum* 1:56–97.

Sen, S. P. 1962. Indian textiles in south-east Asian trade in the seventeenth century. *Journal of Southeast Asian History* 3 (2): 92–110.

Slamet-Velsink, I. E. 1995. *Emerging hierarchies: Processes of transformation and early state formation in the Indonesian Archipelago: Prehistory and the ethnographic present.* Verhandelingen 166. Leiden: KITLV Press.

Smail, J. R. W. 1961. On the possibility of an autonomous history of modern Southeast Asia. *Journal of Southeast Asian History* 2 (2): 72–102.

Smith, C. A. 1976. *Regional analysis.* Vol. 1. *Economic systems.* London: Academic Press.

Soedjatmoko, Mohammed Ali, G. J. Resink, and G. McT. Kahin, eds. 1965. *An introduction to Indonesian historiography.* Ithaca, N. Y.: Cornell University Press.

Sollewijn Gelpke, J. H. F. 1992. The Majapahit dependency Udama Katraya. *Bijdragen tot de Taal-, Land- en Volkenkunde* 148 (2): 240–246.

———. 1993. On the origin of the name Papua. *Bijdragen tot de Taal-, Land- en Volkenkunde* 149 (2): 318–322.

———. 1994. The report of Miguel Roxo de Brito of his voyage in 1581–1582 to the Raja Ampat, the MacCluer Gulf and Seram. *Bijdragen tot de Taal-, Land- en Volkenkunde* 150 (1): 123–145.

———. 1995. Alfonso de Albuquerque's pre-Portuguese "Javanese" map, partially reconstructed from Francisco Rodrigues' book. *Bijdragen tot de Taal-, Land- en Volkenkunde* 151 (1): 76–99.

Sopher, D. E. 1965. *The sea nomads: A study based on the literature of the maritime boat people of Southeast Asia.* Memoirs of the National Museum, 5. Singapore.

Soselisa, H. L. 1995. A place of fish: Subsistence and production for the market in Garogos Island, Maluku, Indonesia. M. A. thesis, Northern Territory University. Darwin.

———. 1996. Development and sea rights in Garogos, East Seram. In *Remaking Maluku: Social transformation in eastern Indonesia*, ed. D. Mearns and C. Healey, 27–38. Special Monograph No. 1. Darwin: Centre for Southeast Asian Studies, Northern Territory University.

Southon, M. 1995. *The navel of the prahu: Meaning and values in the maritime trading economy of a Butonese village.* Canberra: Australian National University.

Spoehr, A. 1960. Port town and hinterlands in the Pacific islands. *American Anthropologist* 62:568–592.

Spriggs, M. 1998a. Research questions in Maluku archaeology. *Cakalele: Maluku Research Journal* 9 (1–2): 51–64.

———. 1998b. The archaeology of the Bird's Head in its Pacific and Southeast Asian context. In *Perspectives on the Bird's Head of Irian Jaya, Indonesia*, ed. J. Miedema, C. Odé, and Rien A. C. Dam, 931–939. Proceedings of a conference in Leiden, 13–17 October 1997. Amsterdam: Rodopi B.V.

Spyer, P. 1997. The eroticism of debt: Pearldivers, traders, and sea wives in the Aru Islands, eastern Indonesia. *American Ethnologist* 24 (3): 515–538.

———. 2000. *The memory of trade: Modernity's entanglements on an eastern Indonesian island.* Durham, N.C.: Duke University Press.

Suárez, T. 1999. *Early mapping of Southeast Asia.* Singapore: Periplus.

Sutherland, H. 1989. Eastern emporium and company town: trade and society in eighteenth century Makassar. In *Brides of the sea: Port cities of Asia from the sixteenth to the twentieth centuries*, ed. Frank Broeze, 97–128. Kensington, New South Wales: New South Wales University Press.

———. 2000. Tripang and wangkang: The China trade of eighteenth century Makassar, c. 1720s–1840s. *Bijdragen tot de Taal-, Land- en Volkenkunde* 156 (6): 451–472.

Sutherland, H., and D. S. Brée. 1987. *Quantitative and qualitative approaches to the study of Indonesian trade: The case of Makassar.* Rotterdam School of Management Management Report Series, No. 17. Rotterdam.

Swadling, P. 1996. *Plumes from paradise: Trade cycles in outer Southeast Asia and their impact on New Guinea and nearby islands until 1920.* Boroko: Papua New Guinea National Museum, Robert Brown and Associates.

Tan, S. K. 1981. The Filipino Muslim naval response to Spanish colonial challenges. Paper presented at the conference on "Southeast Asian responses to European intrusions." British Institute in Southeast Asia, Singapore.

Taylor, P. M. 1984. Tobelorese deixis. *Anthropological Linguistics* 26 (1): 102–122.

Thomas, N. 1990. *Out of time: History and evolution in anthropological discourse.* Cambridge Studies in Social and Cultural Anthropology, 67. Cambridge: Cambridge University Press.

Tiele, P.A. 1877–1887.De Europeërs in den Maleischen Archipel 1509–1623. *Bijdragen tot de Taal-, Land- en Volkenkunde* 25 (1877): 321–420; 27 (1879): 1–69; 28 (1880): part 4, 260–340, 395–482; 29 (1881): 153–214, 332; 30 (1882): 141–242; 32 (1884): 49–118; 35 (1886): 257–355; 36 (1887): 199–307.

Tiele, P. A., and J. E. Heeres. 1886, 1890, 1895. *Bouwstoffen voor de geschiedenis der Nederlanders in den Maleischen archipel.* 3 vols. The Hague.

Tonkin, E. 1992. *Narrating our pasts: The social construction of oral history.* Cambridge: Cambridge University Press.

Urry, J. 1980. Goods for the oriental emporium: The expansion of trade in the Indonesian archipelago and its impact on the outer periphery. Department of Prehistory and Anthropology, Australian National University, Canberra. Unpublished manuscript.

———. 1981. A view from the West: Inland, lowland and islands in Indonesian prehistory. Paper presented at 51st Australian and New Zealand Association for the Advancement of Science Congress, Brisbane, May.

Utami, N. W., and M. Brink. 1999. *Myristica* Gronov. In *Plant resources of South-east Asia* Vol. 13: *Spices*, ed. C. C. de Guzman and J. S. Siemonsma, 139–143. Leiden: Backhuys.

Valentijn, F. 1724–1726. *Oud en Nieuw Oost-Indiën*. 8 vols. Amsterdam: Dordrecht. (Re-edition of the parts relating to Indonesia in 3 vols. by S. Keyzer, 1856–1858.)

Valeri, V. 1975–1976. Alliances et échanges matrimoniaux a Seram central (Moluques). *L'Homme* 15 (3–4): 83–107; 16 (1): 125–149.

———. 1989. Reciprocal centers: The Siwa-Lima system in the central Moluccas. In *The attraction of opposites*, ed. D. Maybury-Lewis and U. Almagor, 117–141. Ann Arbor: University of Michigan Press.

Vansina, J. 1985. *Oral tradition as history*. London: J. Currey.

Villiers, J. 1981a. Makassar and the Portuguese connection, 1540–1670. Paper presented at the conference on "Southeast Asain responses to European intrusions." British Institiute in southeast Asia, Singapore.

———. 1981b. Trade and society in the Banda Islands in the sixteenth century. *Modern Asian Studies* 15 (4): 723–750.

———. 1983. Review of "R. Z. Leirissa and others, Maluku Tengah di masa lampau." *Indonesia Circle* 32:51–54.

———. 1990. The cash crop economy and state formation in the spice islands in the fifteenth and sixteenth centuries. In *The southeast Asian port and polity: Rise and demise*, ed. J. Kathiramby-Wells and J. Villiers, 83–105. Singapore: Singapore University Press.

Walker, R. 1982. Language use at Namatota: A sociolinguistic profile. In *Papers from the Third International Conference on Austronesian Linguistics,* ed. A. Halim, L. Carrington, and J. A. Wurm, 79–94. Special Issue, *Pacific Linguistics*.

Wall, V. I. van de. 1928. *De Nederlandsche Oudheden in de Molukken*. The Hague: Martinus Nijhoff.

Wallace, A. R. 1962 (1869). *The Malay Archipelago*. London: Dover.

———. 1896. On the trade of the eastern archipelago with New Guinea and its islands. *Journal of the Royal Geographical Society* 32:127–137.

Wallerstein, I. 1979. *The capitalist world economy*. Cambridge: Cambridge University Press.

Wang Gungwu. 1958. The Nanhai trade. *Journal of the Malay Branch of the Royal Asiatic Society* 31 (2): 1–132.

Warburg, O. 1893. Vegetationsschilderungen aus Südost-Asien. *Botanische Jahrbuch* 17:169–176.

———. 1897. *Die Muskatnuss, ihre Geschichte, Botanik, Kultur, Handel und Verwerthung, sowie ihre Verfolschungen und Surrogate, zugleich ein Beitrag zur Kulturgeschichte der Banda-Inseln*. Leipzig: Wilhelm Engelmann.

Warren, J. F. 1977. Joseph Conrad's fiction as Southeast Asian history: Trade and politics in East Borneo in the late nineteenth century. *The Brunei Museum Journal* 4 (1): 21–34.

———. 1979. The Sulu zone: Commerce and the evolution of a multi-ethnic polity, 1768–1898. *Archipel* 18:223–229.

———. 1981. *The Sulu zone, 1768–1898*. Singapore: Singapore University Press.

———. 1998. The Sulu zone: The world capitalist economy and the historical imagination. *Comparative Asian Studies* 20:1–71.

Waterson, R. H. 1986. The ideology and terminology of kinship among the Sa'adan Toraja. *Bÿdragen tot de Taal-, Land- en Volkenkunde* 142 (1): 87–112.

Watson, J. L. 1980. Slavery as an institution, open and closed systems. In *Asian and African systems of slavery*, ed. J. L. Watson, 1–15. Oxford: Blackwell.

Watts, D. 1999. *Small worlds: The dynamics of networks between order and randomness.* Princeton, N. J.: Princeton University Press.

Webster, D. L. 1976. On theocracies. *American Anthropologist* 78:812–828.

Wertheim, W. F. 1954. Early Asian trade: An appreciation of J. C. van Leur. *Far Eastern Quarterly* 13 (1): 167–173.

Wheatley, P. 1959. Geographical notes on some commodities involved in Sung maritime trade. *Journal of the Malay Branch of the Royal Asiatic Society* 32 (2): 5–140.

Wichmann, A. 1909. *Nova Guinea, Résultats de l'expédition Scientifique Néerlandaise à la Nouvelle-Guinée en 1903 sous les auspices de Arthur Wichmann. I Entdeckungsgeschichte von Neu-Guinea (bis 1828).* Leiden: E. J. Brill.

Wilde, W. J. J. O. de. 1990. Conspectus of Myristica (Myristicaceae) indigenous in the Moluccas. *Blumea* 35 (1): 233–260.

Winzeler, R. L. 1976. Ecology, culture, social organisation, and state formation in Southeast Asia. *Current Anthropology* 17:623–640.

Wolf, E. R. 1982. *Europe and the people without history.* Berkeley: University of California Press.

Wolters, O. W. 1970. *The fall of Srivijaya in Malay history.* Ithaca, N.Y.: Cornell University Press.

———. 1982. *History, culture, and region in Southeast Asian perspectives.* Singapore: Institute of Southeast Asian Studies.

Wood, D. 1992. *The power of maps.* New York: The Guilford Press.

Wouden, F. A. E. van. 1968 (1935). *Types of social structure in Eastern Indonesia,* trans. R. Needham. The Hague: Nijhoff.

Wurffbain, J. S. 1931. *Reise nach den Molukken 1632–1646.* Vol. 1. 2d ed. The Hague: Nijhoff.

Yambert, K. A. 1981. Alien traders and ruling elites: The overseas Chinese in Southeast Asia and the Indians in East Africa. *Ethnic Groups* 3:173–198.

Yoshida, S. 1980. Folk orientation in Halmahera with special reference to insular southeast Asia. In *The Galela of Halmahera: A preliminary survey*, ed. Naomichi Ishige, 19–88. Senri Ethnological Studies No. 7. Osaka: National Museum of Ethnology.

Zerner, C. 1994. Through a green lens: The construction of customary environmental law and community in Indonesia's Maluku islands. In *Community and identity in sociolegal struggles*, ed. E. Mertz, 1079–1122. Special issue of *Law and Society Review* 28 (5).

Index

Conrad, J., 90
Conradian model, 91, 231, 271
Coolhaas, C. P., 81–82, 86–89
Coral, 24, 27–28, 29 fig. 2.7, 30, 71, 113, 117, 128
Cortesão, A., 5, 58, 65, 68
Crab, P. van der, 22, 34, 88, 92, 94, 100, 102, 105–107, 114–116, 124, 127, 131, 140, 206, 271, 285
Credit, 212, 219, 225, 228
Cross–cultural brokers, 7
Cryptocarya massoy. See Massoi
Currents, 168–169, 170 fig. 6.8, 274–275
Curtin, P. D., 7, 248

Dai, 31, 41, 92, 181 fig. 7.2, 194, 196, 206, 235, 288, 291, 293
Dalton, G., 279
Davis, J., 212
Dermoût, M., 264
Descent groups: 31, 36–46; names of immigrant, 38 table 2.2. See also *Etar,* Soa
Dewey, A. G., 247, 268
Dick, H. W., 150–151, 160, 175, 190, 192, 209, 227, 259
Diesel ferries, 187
Dinama, 35, 73 table 3.1, 204, 206, 253, 275, 287, 289, 291
Disputes, 296n.7
Dissel, J. S. A. van, 133–135
Distance centrality, 176–181, 292–293
Distribution, concept of, 212–215
Division of labor: ecological, 194, 207–208; ethnic, 247; geographic, 51, 207–208;
Dobo, 14, 16, 57, 72, 90, 105–106, 146, 152 fig. 6.1, 166, 186 fig. 7.3, 189, 210, 238, 244, 249, 253, 261, 271–272, 300n.5
Domains, 31, 33 fig. 2.9
Doren, J. B. J. van, 30, 83, 86
Dual economy, 114
Dugongs, 46, 204
Dutch administration, 113–118
Dutch East India Company (Vereenigde Oost-Indische Compagnie, VOC), 1–3, 12, 19, 58, 81, 83, 85, 87–89, 95, 97–103, 107–108, 113–114, 123, 126, 134, 137–138, 141–144, 182, 231–232, 234, 255, 262, 268, 279–280, 295n.2, 296n.3

Eades, J. S., 248
Earl, G. W., 122, 128–129, 134
Earthquakes, 272–273
Economy: embeddedness of, 6; moral, 214, 263; specialization of, 225, 237, 247
Ekholm, K., 6 fig. 1.1, 6–7, 15

Elat, 14, 61, 152 fig. 6.1, 198 fig. 7.6, 206, 210
Ellen, R. F., 3, 4, 11 fig. 1.2, 15, 20, 32, 34, 43, 57–58, 75 table 3.3, 76, 84, 88, 92, 99, 107, 115, 130, 134, 144, 148, 162, 166, 182, 196, 208, 226, 255, 264–265, 273, 275, 295n.2, 297n.2, 298n.15, 300n.3, 75
Elmberg, J. E., 125, 127, 131, 133–134, 144, 182, 189
Emmerson, D. K., 1
Endogamy, 40, 44
English East India Company. See British
Enneka. *See* Ainikke
Environment and trade, 54–59
Errington, S., 75
Etar (lineages), 36, 37 table 2.1, 38–40, 42, 51, 73 table 3.1, 74 table 3.2, 77, 83, 253, 278, 287, 296n.1. *See also* Descent groups
Ethnicity, of traders, 236–266
Ethnogenesis, 245–248
Evers, H.-D., 14–15, 192–193, 210, 250, 266
Exchange: concept of, 213–215; medium of, 216; diagonal nexus of, 211 fig. 7.7
Extirpation, 87, 100, 134

Farquhar, R. T., 103
Firewood, 182, 199, 207, 217
Fish (and fishing): 46–50, 48 fig. 2.12, 181, 190, 198–199, 207, 210, 211 fig. 7.7, 218 table 8.1, 219, 224, 226, 255, 277; distribution of, 213; dried, 14, 78, 214, 225; nets, 47; trade in, 197; traps, 43, 48–49, 71–84
Fish-for-sago exchange, 193–197, 215–229, 278; fish-sago-export product nexus, 14, 210
Flags, role of, 90, 91 fig. 4.1, 113–114, 125–126, 138
Flannery, K., 278
Floods and flooding, 22–23, 58
Folk etymologies, 73 table 3.1; histories, 76–77, 79, 84
Forbes, A., 252–253
Forbes, H. O., 119, 136, 252
Forrest, T., 119, 128
Fraassen, C. F. van, 31, 34, 64–65, 79, 234, 300n.3
Frank, A. G., 5, 8
Friedman, J., 6 fig. 1.1, 6–7, 15
Fuel, 200, 255

Gah, 35, 194–196, 206, 287, 289, 291
Game–theory rationality, 18
Garogos, 17, 40, 44–45, 46 fig. 2.11, 49, 51, 92, 110 table 4.1, 156, 158, 163, 165, 167 fig. 6.7, 170 fig. 6.9, 173, 180, 182, 184 table 7.2, 193, 195–197, 199–204, 207, 210, 213, 216–217, 218

About the Author

Roy Ellen is professor of anthropology and human ecology at the University of Kent at Canterbury, where he has taught since 1973. He was trained at the London School of Economics under Raymond Firth and has conducted fieldwork in the Moluccas over a period of thirty years. Although he is best known for his work on people-environment relations and ethnobiological knowledge, his published output has been varied. His six single-authored and seven edited works include *Environment, Subsistence and System* (1982, recently reissued), *The Cultural Relations of Classification* (1993), *Understanding Witchcraft and Sorcery in Southeast Asia* (1995, coedited with C. W. Watson), *Redefining Nature* (1996, with Katsuyoshi Fukui), and *Indigenous Environmental Knowledge and Its Transformations* (2000, with Peter Parkes and Alan Bicker). He was the Curl Lecturer for the Royal Anthropological Institute in 1987, delivered the Munro Lecture at the University of Edinburgh in 1994, was a Fellow at the Netherlands Institute for Advanced Study in 1984, and was elected to a Fellowship of the Linnean Society in 2001.

Production Notes for Ellen/*On the Edge of the Banda Zone*

Jacket design by Santos Barbasa Jr.

Text design and composition by Kaelin Chappell in QuarkXPress using ITC Stone Sans and ITC Stone Serif

Printing and binding by The Maple-Vail Book Manufacturing Group

Printed on 60 lb. Text White Opaque, 426 ppi.